RIVERS OF AMERICA

THE SUSQUEHANNA

CARL CARMER

Illustrated by Stow Wengenroth and J. Craig Thorpe
With a new foreword by Alfred Runte

LYONS
PRESS

Guilford, Connecticut

LYONS
PRESS

An imprint of The Rowman & Littlefield Publishing Group, Inc.
4501 Forbes Blvd., Ste. 200
Lanham, MD 20706
www.rowman.com

Distributed by NATIONAL BOOK NETWORK

First published in 1955 by Rinehart & Company

Foreword copyright © 2021 by Alfred Runte

British Library Cataloguing in Publication Information available

Library of Congress Cataloging-in-Publication Data available

ISBN 978-1-4930-5936-2 (paper)
ISBN 978-1-4930-6183-9 (electronic)

to Elsie Murray
uncompromising scholar, generous friend

Contents

Contents

Acknowledgments

Much water has flowed under the bridges of the Susque-hanna since the late Hervey Allen, my friend and former colleague in editing the Rivers of America Series, somehow persuaded me into undertaking the writing of a book about this long and winding stream. I might still have avoided the project had I not fallen in love with the river when another friend, Conrad Richter, gave me my first long ride along its banks. These two accomplished novelists, then, .should be first in my listing of those to whom I am grateful.

I should add at once the names of certain historians who have sacrificed generous amounts of their time to help a writer bewildered by vaster masses of material than he had ever before been called upon to evaluate. I have ded-icated this book to Elsie Murray of the Cornell University faculty in Ithaca, New York, and Curator of the Tioga Point Museum at Athens, Pennsylvania. Her encouragement and her patient, though spirited, correcting of my errors of fact or interpretation, have done much to bring me to this book's completion. I think I should add that the dedication to her implies my gratitude as well, to all her colleagues in the field of state and local history who have untiringly and without stint, given of their abilities to strengthen my faltering labors. Some of them will be adversely critical, I am sure, of my choice of subjects, since I have been obliged by limitations in length, to omit or to pass over lightly important matters to which they have given their most strenuous efforts. I can only plead here that my judgment in these respects may be faulty, but depending on any other would have created quite as great a disagreement.

My heartiest thanks then to Louis C. Jones and James Taylor Dunn of Cooperstown, Gerald Houk of Owego, all of New York State; to Charles L. Lucy of Athens, L. E. Wilt of Towanda, Frances Dorrance of Dallas, Lewis Edwin Theiss of Lewisburg, Gilbert S. McClintock of WilkesBarre, S. K. Stevens and J. Herbert Walker of Harrisburg, T. Kenneth Wood and Marshall R. Anspach of Williamsport, Charles F. Snyder of Sunbury, all these of Pennsylvania.

Of less formal but no less valuable aid were many friends, old and new, whose experience has included pertinent matters of interest. Among those were Tom Cawley of Binghamton, New York, Professors Arthur Herman Wilson and William A. Russ, Jr. of Susquehanna University at Selinsgrove; Professor Gertrude Marvin Williams at Wilkes College, Miss Annette Evans and Mrs. Ernest G. Smith all of Wilkes-Barre; Mrs. Gladys De Puis of Athens, Mrs. Grace S. Parker of Arlington, Virginia; Kenneth W. Slifer of Woodbury, New Jersey; Joseph M. Stevens of New York City; William G. Ellis, James Truman, Frank Taylor, Dr. Tracy Gillette, and Mrs. Max Farnham Harris, of Owego; Nancy Van Auken of Elmira, New York; Mrs. Andrew B. Duvall, Jr. and Judge William Rosenfield of Towanda; Charles F. Welles of Terrytown, Pennsylvania; Miss Edith Malcolm White of Morristown, New Jersey.

The lively researchers, checkers and assistants who added to my knowledge and aided in preparing my manuscript are Mrs. Marcel Livaudais of New Orleans, Mrs. J. King Gordon

Acknowledgments

and Mrs. Stewart Graff of Irvingtonon-Hudson, Mrs. Violet Earle Baker of Hastings-onHudson and Miss Liesel Eisenheimer of New York. My debt to them is large and they have my deep gratitude.

Finally and in a very special group who adopted my project as if it were their own and worked on it far beyond the call of duty and friendship combined I would list, with a feeling of helplessness at my inability to express my thanks, Eve A. Thomas of the Old Ladies Home of Owego; Mrs. Charles Brayton of Elmira; my colleague the Associate Editor of the Rivers of America Series, Miss Jean Crawford; my wife, Elizabeth Black Carmer, and especially Louise and Paul Trescott of Berwick, Pennsylvania.

Carl Carmer

Foreword: The River of the Winding Shore
By Alfred Runte

A noted storyteller and historian, and among the original editors of the Rivers of America Series, Carl Carmer left off this narrative of the Susquehanna River in 1955. I first read the book as a history major at Harpur College, now Binghamton University, in upstate New York. I had attended a meeting of the Susquehanna Conservation Council and been invited to sit on the board. The Council, formed in 1964 to protect the local environment, wanted more young people on its staff. Where possible, I wrote college papers relevant to the interests of the Council, and so discovered Carl Carmer's books.

In public, we sought the attention of Binghamton's two newspapers, the *Sun-Bulletin* and *Evening Press*. David Bernstein, the owner and editor of the *Sun-Bulletin*, further disclosed a personal interest, announcing, in 1970, that he intended to run for Congress. How should the Susquehanna River be managed, he asked our board? Ensuring a full analysis, I wrote a position paper for his campaign. When he was not elected, he followed up with another proposal, suggesting that I write an article for the newspaper. Nor would length be a problem, he assured me. Published March 12, 1971, "The Susquehanna: Use with Care," began on the front page and covered two full inside pages. He further published my cover letter on the editorial page. In retrospect, it was David's way of

David Bernstein
Author's Collection

salvaging both our efforts, and a reminder to the community the river mattered.

To be sure, I believe David, not to mention Carl Carmer, would be troubled by the state of the river today. As am I, if focused on details Carmer was free to avoid as a matter of timing. Let us begin, then, with what remains immutable about the river, no matter the writer, place, or time. Rising at Cooperstown, New York, on the southern shore of Otsego Lake, the Susquehanna begins what will be a 444-mile journey through New York, Pennsylvania, and Maryland. At Northumberland, Pennsylvania, midway through the commonwealth, the West Branch adds 243 miles to its flow. Even now, the upper reaches of the West Branch are sparely populated, an Eastern wilderness, as it were. Above Harrisburg, Pennsylvania's capital, another major tributary, the Juniata, also merges from the west. Finally, on crossing into Maryland the Susquehanna merges into the expanse of Chesapeake Bay.

Of Native American etymology, the word Susquehanna is harder to pin down. The Delaware translation is "Oyster River"; however, that best applies south of Harrisburg. More broadly, romanticists a century ago called it "the river of the winding shore." That is certainly appropriate for the upper river, or main stem, also occasionally called the North Branch. Lower down, swelled by its tributaries, the river both widens and straightens considerably. If any characteristic describes the entire river, that, I would suggest, is beauty.

My favorite description is by Robert Louis Stevenson, and revealingly acknowledges the name itself. Heading west in August 1879, the young Scottish author of *Treasure Island*, while crossing Pennsylvania, found his train running parallel to a river lined with farms. Might a brakeman know the river's name, he asked? "Susquehanna," the brakeman replied. Rarely had four syllables, Stevenson later recalled, seemed more in harmony with "the beauty of the land." Indeed, Susquehanna "was the name, as no other could be, for that shining river and desirable valley."

And still there are varied translations, among them "Muddy River" and "Crooked River." Again, if principally for the upper river, "Crooked River" gets my vote. No sooner does the Susquehanna enter Pennsylvania than it seems to change its mind, making a broad swing, called Great Bend, back into New York. There it lingers awhile, ambling west, through what is known as the Southern Tier. Here it meets Binghamton, my hometown, and obviously the fount of my experience.

Rod Serling, the creator of television's *The Twilight Zone*, also graduated high school here, not my high school (we were cross-town rivals), and he was ahead of me by twenty years. Serling is somewhat off the subject, I know, but the city would never forgive me if I failed to mention him. He loved Binghamton, and long after making it big in Hollywood returned repeatedly to reconnect, dutifully seeking out his former drama teacher, Helen Foley, whom he immortalized in one of his scripts.

Susquehanna River at Azilum, Pennsylvania
Collection of Dr. A. Louis Steplock, Jr., permission of J. Craig Thorpe

Back to ours. Exiting the Southern Tier at Waverly, shortly to meet the Chemung River at Tioga Point, the Susquehanna slips back into Pennsylvania, where it just as abruptly heads southeast. It is here, snaking through what locals call the Endless Mountains, that the Susquehanna truly is the river of the winding shore. Broad valleys spread between the coils of the river, each a colorful mosaic of villages and farms. Beyond rise forested hillsides, cresting into distant ridges of purple and blue. The north bank, also noticeably rugged, is in places wooded to the water's edge. The principal highway, US Highway 6, was then laid out to follow the ridgelines, thereby shortcutting the river's path.

SUSQUEHANNA RIVER AT AZILUM, PENNSYLVANIA

The historical backdrop is no less compelling, highlighted by Azilum and Wyalusing Rocks. Each became an overlook beside the highway with room for a souvenir shop and parking. My college friends and I, drawn to nearby state parks, would hurry back to Azilum to catch the sunset. "Sky water," Henry David Thoreau aptly described what we felt in *Walden*. The river mirroring red, and the ridges darkening in the distance, we thrilled at what seemed in the twilight an untouched slice of the American wilderness.

Allegedly, Azilum proper, in the valley below, was to have been the refuge of Marie Antoinette. The historical markers refreshed our memories, of course, the deposed queen of

Louis XVI of France. We could just imagine her making good her escape! Alas, the French Revolution was not a daydream. First Madame La Guillotine claimed Louis's head—then hers. The deepening darkness made the tragedy personal; in life, what would prove beyond our reach? And on that thought we soberly yielded our hillside, equally uncertain of our return.

No less historic, Wyalusing Rocks, just downriver, rises even more dramatically above the water's edge. Part of the so-called Warriors Path leading south into the Carolinas, native traders valued it as a lookout. In the American Revolution it was then a milepost for one of the critical campaigns of the war. Carl Carmer will tell you that story. What he could not foresee, nor could anyone in the 1950s, was the fate of Wyalusing Rocks. In 1968, the Pennsylvania Department of Highways proposed to widen US Highway 6. The original highway, rising and falling with the topography, was deemed unsafe for heavy trucks. Although Azilum overlook was to be bypassed, incredibly, Wyalusing Rocks was to be blown up. Blow up Wyalusing Rocks? How could Pennsylvania even think of such a thing? The engineers relented, or so they called it, but not before slicing deeply into the original overlook.

The highway, widened into four lanes, finally encroached on the rocks themselves. Long standing vigil across the road, the small cafe and souvenir shop had also been forced to close. Motorists flying past on the highway finally had no incentive to stop for either. Those who did stop, remembering the incredible views, were as readily shocked to find the sliver of space left for parking practically on top of the rocks, and they, now fully exposed, covered with graffiti and litter.

Carl Carmer, I began to appreciate, had lived in a different time, better said, in a different country, and one still protective of its past. Small-town America, for lack of a better

Susquehanna River at Wyalusing Rocks, Pennsylvania

Susquehanna River at Wyalusing Rocks, Pennsylvania
Collection of Dr. A. Louis Steplock, Jr., permission of J. Craig Thorpe

term, had always cared for these special places. Binghamton, early nicknamed the Parlor City, no less celebrated its quality of life, including spacious parks (two with famous carousels) and miles of tree-lined streets. A Binghamton park, Rod Serling evoked in one episode of *The Twilight Zone*, was a magical place for any child. Helen Foley, further drawing on Serling's example, might inspire her students to reach for the stars.

Simply put, America was still a place of opportunity, and with opportunity came a respect for discipline. Our valley, both as a place to live and work, was in fact called the Valley of Opportunity. It began with Endicott-Johnson, a company making shoes. Early in the twentieth century, its workers, principally immigrants, were recruited from southern and eastern Europe. On clearing Ellis Island in New York Harbor they boarded a train straight for Binghamton. "Which way EJ?" they asked on arrival. As promised, it was all the English they needed to know. Two neighboring company towns, Endicott and Johnson City, were further established to absorb the tide. Still in the 1950s, the company's pungent, vibrating factories employed an average of 16,000 workers. Thousands more were employed in companies making furniture, film, and cameras. The flight simulator was also invented in Binghamton, by another native son, Edwin A. Link. The up-and-coming industry was International Business Machines (IBM), producing electric typewriters and later computers. Critically, the success of those companies then rippled throughout the community, further to support family restaurants, shops, and stores.

A commitment to the future, again, to discipline, blossomed on that prosperity. In landscape known as conservation, it foreshadowed the environmental movement of today. As early as 1885, atoning for decades of destructive logging,

New York State established the Catskill and Adirondack Mountain forest preserves. Pennsylvania soon followed suit with its own generous system of state parks, forests, and game lands. Cresting the mountains of the Susquehanna Basin, indeed, framing the river along much of its length lay these growing blocks of protected territory. The rugged geography of the West Branch proved especially supportive, but every logged-over district was a candidate.

Most of these lands had simply been abandoned. After all, there were no forests left to exploit. The point of state ownership was to allow their return as healthy second growth. Occasionally, irreplaceable remnants of old growth were purchased directly, although that called for paying market price. The cheaper method, and by far more common, was to confiscate cutover lands for unpaid taxes. The acquisitions were then consolidated, named, and developed for public access. In 1894, New York State further added conservation to its constitution, pledging that its public forests would remain "forever wild."

New York was equally fortunate to have three conservation-minded governors, Grover Cleveland, Theodore Roosevelt, and Franklin D. Roosevelt. Each, of course, and further worth noting, went on to serve as president of the United States. In Pennsylvania, the celebrated name is Gifford Pinchot. After a distinguished career as a professional forester, including adviser to President Theodore Roosevelt and first to head the US Forest Service (1905), Pinchot returned to Pennsylvania and eventually ran for governor. Following in his own footsteps, so to speak, he made forest conservation his priority.

It is the final principal in the story that may surprise some readers—railroads. Of course, Robert Louis Stevenson

Printed as a keepsake for passengers, this pocket-size picture book, *The "Switzerland of America"* (1897), featured postcard views of the mountain and river scenery accessible via the Lehigh Valley Railroad. *Project Gutenberg*

was not surprised—nor anyone in the nineteenth century. Trains are heavy, and perform best on gentle grades, which railroads early achieved by following rivers. Again, for me, that history came meaningfully into focus at Azilum and Wyalusing Rocks. Below, paralleling the north shore of the river ran the tracks of the historic Lehigh Valley Railroad, which, in the humble opinion of its passenger department, served as the gateway to the "Switzerland of America."

Granted, the Endless Mountains were hardly the Alps, but exactitude was never the point. The point, as it was for all

From *The "Switzerland of America,"* this idyllic view of the Susquehanna River east of Standing Stone, Pennsylvania, is a common example
of how early railroads sold their presence on the American landscape.

railroads, was to entice passengers by promising them a scenic
ride. There, moreover, it gets interesting. Obviously, the cred-
ibility of that assurance depended on far more than the railroad. Every landowner on either side of the tracks had the
power to sully the view. Ideally, they resisted because they
wanted to; more practically, they did so because it paid. Bridg-
ing the nineteenth and twentieth centuries, railroad America
was resort America. Before the invention of air conditioning,
city-dwellers with the means escaped the summer heat by
train. Every mountain district close to a major city supported
lakeside camps and hotels. Private cabins lined rivers and
streams. These properties, interspersed with state-purchased

forests and parks, critically influenced the broader landscape. America's railroads, it may be said, were the key to a business model encouraging rural landowners to think of beauty as something saleable.

Today we would call them partnerships. The point is that Carl Carmer need not dwell on any of it. Those relationships still survived. Early highways mirrored them, too. Roadside America sold an experience inviting travelers to stop and savor the landscape, again, Azilum and Wyalusing Rocks. As rapidly, by the 1960s, those innate restraints were breaking down. Everywhere, thanks to modern highways, railroad-influenced landscapes were becoming passé.

Finally, railroads could no longer afford to set the example, having lost the revenue to compete. In the Susquehanna Valley the crippling loss was coal. Anthracite coal, or hard coal, was mined almost exclusively in Pennsylvania, and that principally in the Wyoming Valley. Here the Susquehanna, entering between Scranton and Wilkes-Barre, briefly exchanges beauty for a depressing landscape. Although Carl Carmer squarely faced that history, again, the changes in the air were outside his grasp. Dramatically, by the end of the 1950s, anthracite coal had lost market share to oil and natural gas. The railroads of the region, with good reason known as anthracite railroads, were caught totally unprepared.

The roof fell in, literally and figuratively, in January 1959. Bent on maximizing their haul, miners illegally ran a shaft directly beneath the Susquehanna River, and, doubling down on their carelessness, got too close to the riverbed above. As the ceiling of the mine collapsed, an estimated 10 billion gallons of water rushed in. Twelve of the miners were immediately entombed. It took three days of dumping railroad cars into the hole before the mine was finally sealed. This, the infamous Knox Mine Disaster, virtually ended all coal mining in the region.

No less ominous, manufacturers throughout the Susquehanna Basin had begun to discover that everything could be made more cheaply in the South—or Asia. Certainly, our Valley of Opportunity began showing the strain. By the mid-1960s Endicott-Johnson was laying off workers—and ultimately laid off thousands. A touted savior—interstate highways—meant high-paying jobs for a period, yes, but after construction those jobs disappeared. Unlike railroads, few permanent workers were needed to operate the trains and maintain the tracks.

It was, I came to realize, a critical subtly behind the threat to Wyalusing Rocks. Simply, as the region's population stagnated—and in many cities actually dropped—feelings of desperation grew. If rebuilding US Highway 6 would help jumpstart the economy, people were willing to take the risk.

As were some people willing to take even bigger risks, among them Binghamton's congressman at the time. Think of it, he proposed. What if the Susquehanna River, starting below Cooperstown, were dammed all the way to the Wyoming Valley? Listing flood control as the project's mainstay, his study added water for cooling nuclear power plants. Tributary dams would further stabilize the river's depth. "Low-flow augmentation," the engineers called it. In all, about 75,000 acres of farms, fields, and forests would be inundated behind the dams. Admittedly, some favorite trout streams would be eliminated and canoeing drop in popularity. Still, those tradeoffs were worth it, government planners agreed, in that thousands of workers would get to build the dams.

It was my wake-up call, and that of other activists, who foresaw a river bereft of beauty. Where was the common sense in controlling floods by flooding 75,000 acres of pristine real

As founder and executive director of the Susquehanna Conservation Council (1964), Nancy Ayers spearheaded efforts to protect New York State's Southern Tier from pollution, pesticides, and dams. *Estate of Nancy Ayers*

estate? And who needed a string of nuclear power plants with industry leaving town?

Across the Southern Tier, the fight was led by Nancy Ayers, founder of the Susquehanna Conservation Council. Dressed head to foot in shades of lavender, and renowned as the "purple grackle," she had a knack for making politicians squirm. David Bernstein, as editor of the *Sun-Bulletin,* further editorialized against the plan.

A modicum of protection, the Wild and Scenic Rivers Act, passed Congress in 1968. However, the government could always change its mind, David cautioned, and the Susquehanna be removed from consideration. Certainly, planning for the dams proceeded apace. Nancy, meanwhile, kept up the pressure for no dams, substituting a proposal for a string of new regional parks.

Ultimately, the war in Vietnam constrained government investment and the dam builders began pulling back. Nancy, meanwhile, did get five new parks, forging an alliance with another hometown hero, Johnny Hart, creator of the *B.C.* comic strip. Others prominent voices for conservation included Tom Cawley and David Rossie, both columnists with the *Evening Press.*

No matter our industrial voice for conservation, Binghamton's railroads only continued losing ground. The city would lose a fabulous passenger train, the *Phoebe Snow,* in November 1966. With it went a colorful history, and critically, the city's last daylight connection to New York City. Binghamton's very last train—a night train—was then dropped just after New Year's Day 1970.

What of it, many shrugged? We have interstate highways and airlines now. True enough, but lost was a serviceable industry that had made the Susquehanna River its enduring centerpiece.

Absent that level of conscience, industry got back to questionable ideas, among them exploiting the Marcellus Shale. Hundreds of millions of years ago, billions of cubic feet of natural gas became locked in the formation, which, although tantalizingly rich, was believed impossible to exploit. After decades of experimentation petroleum engineers proved that assumption wrong. The shale could be punctured with wells and cracked open by injecting water, sand, and chemicals into the cracks. Called fracking, the process holds the shale open long enough for recoverable amounts of gas (or oil) to escape.

As of 2021, New York State refused to allow the practice, but Pennsylvania has gone all in. For the upper Susquehanna Basin this has meant an invasion of drilling rigs and fracking trucks. Thousands of rigs and wells are currently operating. The beneficiaries call it progress, as the beneficiaries always do. But again, what of the natural environment? Outside of the Wyoming Valley, the Susquehanna Basin never endured mining on such a massive scale.

Nor does it end with fracking. Pennsylvania bluestone, another prized commodity, is everywhere mined, as well. No less visibly, hundreds of quarries have been opened and the slag pushed down the hillsides. Fortunately, it is a temperate, humid environment, and vegetation begins creeping back. Eventually, led by grasses and weeds, a thin layer of topsoil begins supporting trees. Within a century, and hopefully sooner, old quarries and drilling pads should fade from view.

However, it honestly is no panacea; the damage beneath will remain. Recall the Knox Mine Disaster of 1959. Everything downstream was contaminated. Acid mine drainage, as the condition is known, was the effect of those 10 billion gallons of water mixing with raw seams of coal. Compromised waterways are forever a problem wherever there are abandoned mines.

Wind turbines are another questionable development, such as those expected to tower above the hillsides east of Binghamton. Normally, zoning restrictions would have prevented wind farms in any pastoral landscape. Now, politicians

and industry plead for allowing turbines, arguing the calami-
tous effects of climate change.

In reality, wind farms will no more reverse climate change
than dams proved the answer to flood control. Certainly,
dams would not have saved the Susquehanna Basin from Hurricane Agnes in 1972. Agnes slammed into the region in June.
As proposed, the dams would already have been filled with
spring runoff, again, to provide "low-flow augmentation" in
the summer months. No way could they have prevented the
flooding when, in fact, it actually occurred.

Old-school environmentalism taught humility. No
technology is ever foolproof; rather, humans need to respect
natural limits. In March 1979, the Susquehanna River dramatically restaged that advice, when, at Three-Mile Island,
Pennsylvania, the core of the island's nuclear power plant was
seriously compromised. The containment dome secured the
accident, but not before some radiation had escaped. Immediately upstream, government officials seriously considered
evacuating Harrisburg. Further consider that Washington,
DC, the nation's capital, was itself only 75 miles away.

Three-Mile Island was just the latest example to confirm
that even promising technologies have consequences. The
same applies to climate change. How is a wind turbine built?
Where does a solar panel come from? None of it is benign.
Much as some in my generation regret pushing for dams, what
consequences, fifty years from now, will your descendants
wish they had avoided?

Before business modeling infiltrated the environmental
movement, environmentalists themselves respected the need
for caution. The popular term was technology assessment and
its philosopher king the ecologist Aldo Leopold. "Examine
each question in terms of what is ethically and esthetically

right," he wrote, "as well as what is economically expedient. A thing is right when it tends to preserve the integrity, stability, and beauty of the biotic community. It is wrong when it tends otherwise."

From Leopold's *A Sand County Almanac*, these words were indeed the foundation of American environmentalism. The Rivers of America Series similarly took us back to the basics, reminding us, if we wish for a livable world, that exchanging beauty for ugliness is never salvation. Certainly, Carl Carmer intuitively echoed Leopold. Before every river in the country could be treated properly, beauty was the operable word.

Whatever possessed us to think we could hope to save the American Earth by removing beauty from the equation? Fortunately, my friends and I were heard, and our shining river for the moment spared. Now what? There the pain from the past persists. Never again will the Susquehanna be more beautiful than it was. My privilege, and Carl Carmer's, was to have known the last days of that river. What river is coming next? That question, and the unwritten chapter of every landscape, is entirely up to you.

THE SUSQUEHANNA

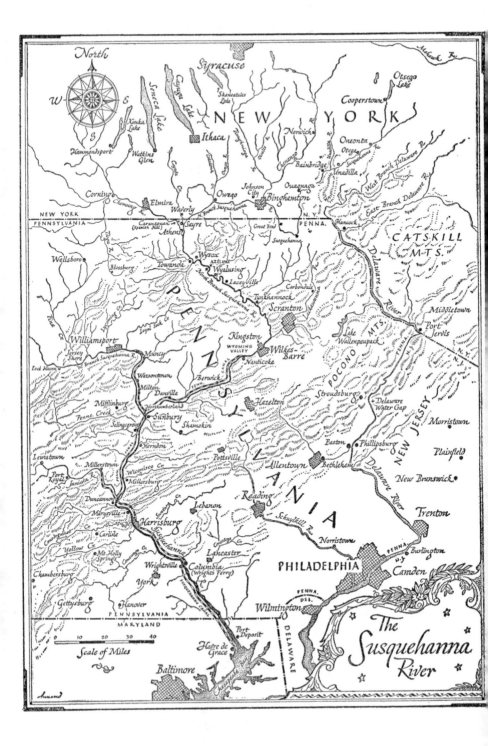

1

Great Waters and Barbarous Countries

> ❧ *History is the memory of time,*
> *the life of the dead,*
> *and the happiness of the living.*
>
> —CAPTAIN JOHN SMITH

In the hot summer of 1608 a small short-masted open barge "of neare three tuns burthen," flat-bottomed and cabinless, bobbed on the choppy upper reaches of a long bay which neighboring Indians called "Chesapeake" meaning "Great Water." Their square sail, riddled by the sudden squalls that plague these wide shallows, was a many-colored motley created by patches torn from the shirts of her crew. A few of the thirteen men aboard tugged at the oars to quicken progress as she slid awkwardly toward an open space where water entered the dune-lined coast.

Nine of the thirteen had been crowded together on this little vessel nearly every day of more than two months. On June second under command of Captain John Smith the expedition had embarked, seven "Gentlemen" and seven soldiers from the London Company's settlement, Jamestown, on the northward voyage. For seven weeks they had explored the inlets of the river-laced countryside bordering the bay. On July twenty-first they had inter-

rupted their voyaging by a three-day interim at Jamestown to secure proper treatment for a wrist wound of the
Captain—the poisonous stab of a stingray which had tried
to retaliate in kind when playfully nailed to the shallow
bottom with a sword. On the twenty-fourth they had set
out again, leaving five of their former crew behind and
adding four. The newcomers, being but recently arrived
at the settlement, now lay with an equal number of their
comrades weak and helpless amidships, suffering from
ship fever, a form of typhus which afflicted almost all of
the settlers.

The stocky, bearded twenty-eight-year-old leader and
his nine crew-men of most experience had endured together a difficult seasoning. "When we first set sayle,"
Smith later wrote, referring to himself, as was his habit,
in the third person, "some of our Gallants doubted nothing but that our Captaine would make too much hast
home," and he gave his opinions of those who so mis-
judged him with "nor had we a Mariner nor any had skill
to trim the sayles but two saylers and my selfe, the rest
being Gentlemen, or them were ignorant in such toyle and
labour."

A number of the crew had considerable reason for feeling distrust of their leader, for they had sailed with him
the year before in the little three-ship fleet of the London
Company sent out to settle the vast lands of South Virginia. When they made landfall on Nevis among the Summer Islands, these men heard the charges that Captain
Smith intended to usurp the government, murder all opponents, and make himself king. They could remember
the new-built gallows standing in pitiless sunlit clarity against the palm trees' green and the sky's blue,

4

though as matters turned out and were by the intended victim ironically reported, he "could not be persuaded to use them." The veterans had also watched the swaggerer brought ashore in irons at Jamestown and had witnessed in the first months of the colony's existence the bickering ("garboyle" Captain Wingfield, first president of the governing council, had called it) which had produced among other unpleasant results Captain Smith's second sentence to execution, this time for having, through foolhardy actions against hostile Indians, caused the death of two of his men. Only the arrival, at sunset on the eve of his hanging, of a vessel bringing new authorities from England had saved his life.

Smith's unpopularity among the expedition's leaders on the ocean voyage had stemmed from his assumption of authority over them which he demanded as one who had weathered greater trials than lay in their experience. As Captain of artillery in the Hungarian Army, he had rescued the occupants of the besieged town of Olumpagh by sending an escape plan which he signaled them with lights flashed at night from a nearby mountain. He had invented "fiery Dragons," incendiary bombs which streaked the sky with flame as they dropped into Stowlle-Wesenburg and contributed mightily to the capture of that city. As champion for a besieging army, he had met in public combat and beheaded three Turkish warriors in the Province of Transylvania, a feat which won him from the English College of Heralds a coat of arms depicting the three turbaned heads he had cut off, a motto "Vincere est Vivere" (to conquer is to live) and a crest (obviously intended as a whimsical comment on his lucky career)—an ostrich holding in its beak a horseshoe.

John Smith was the not infrequent type of raconteur whose virtuosity breeds suspicion of false report and whose hearers are sometimes amazed to find hard facts underlying elaborate veils of verbiage. He craved adventure and he had a passion for words. On the discovery barge on the Chesapeake he had a sure feeling that these moments were history and that he was not only their protagonist but their worthy recorder. In the months since he had been engaged on the Virginia colony project, his mind had bestirred itself over questionings and musings that he would eventually publish:

> What so truly suits with honor and honesty as the discovering things unknown? erecting towns, peopling countries, informing the ignorant, reforming things unjust, teaching virtue . . .

Whatever the magic that had kept him alive—destiny, or his admixture of strength, courage and cunning—he still had good reason for confidence in it. The two escapes from execution by his fellow colonists had been part of his constantly fortunate pattern. So had more recent incidents. Captured by Indians, he had saved his life by showing them the wonders of his ivory compass and lecturing them on "how the Sunne did chase the night around the world." When he was later brought before the great chief Powhatan, as many as could lay hands on him had forced his head down upon two great stones and were "ready with their clubs to beate out his braines." At that moment, according to Smith's account, twelve-year-old Pocahontas, "the King's dearest daughter, when no entreaty could prevail, got his head in her armes and laid her own upon his to save him death." (The truth of this story has often been attacked, but scholars with

6

knowledge of Indian customs and of the subsequent relationship of the Captain and his alleged rescuer make a logical defense of it.) Poisoned by the stingray's barb, his arm had swelled so dangerously that he had ordered his crew to say his funeral service and dig his grave, but a soothing oil had given such miraculous relief that he had been able to eat his assailant for supper. Returning to Jamestown where high officials had previously regarded him as worthy of hanging, he had found himself the chosen President of the Governing Council and had been able to turn that post over to a friend in order that he might continue his discoveries.

Soon after the barge had set out the crew had found an "abundance of fish, lying so thick with their heads above the water." They drove their craft among them, and later reported: "We attempted to catch them with a frying pan: but we found it a bad instrument to catch fish with." Since the men judged the Indians along the shores simple and credulous, the exploring party delighted in telling them fantastic lies, and they also amused themselves during sunny pleasant weather by naming bays, points and hills for each other. At one group of islands, however, they "discovered the winds and waters so much increased with thunder, lightning and raine" that their mast and sail blew overboard, and the waves breaking over the small barge kept them bailing frantically. For two days they "were inforced to inhabit these uninhabited Isles," then in humorous spite christened them Limbo. Their bread "spoyled with wet so much that it was rotten," but they were yet so in the mood for practical joking that when they sailed back down the bay for three days' respite at Jamestown they trimmed the barge with

7

painted streamers and other devices that would make her look like a hostile Spanish frigate and mightily frightened their friends on shore.

Now that the explorers were looking upon the funnel-like approach to the river's mouth—two receding lines of low sand dunes decorated at irregular intervals by the vertical grotesques of wind-bent cedars—the crew felt again the deep urges that had kept them persistently at their task of "passing along the coast, searching every inlet and Bay fit for harbours and habitations." Of the quality of the soil they had no doubts—"heaven and earth never agreed better to frame a place for man's habitation: were it fully manned and inhabited by industrious people."

Moreover this river whose upstream shores, coastal Indians said, were fortified by a powerful tribe called the Susquehannocks might lead them at some long-sought triumphant moment through a curving gap in the blue mountains edging the horizon to the South Sea. Before they found the short way to the riches of the East, however, they might come upon nearer treasures. Smith had already grown bitter over the ignorance and wishful thinking that had led the colonists to mistaking iron pyrites—fool's gold—for gold itself and to loading a shipment of it for transmission to the London Company. Though refiners with their glittering promises had already so hoodwinked the colonists that at Jamestown during a few gold-mad weeks there had been "no talke, no hope, no worke, but dig gold, wash gold, refine gold, loade gold," the hardheaded captain "was not inamoured with their durty skill and never any thing did more torment him than to see all necessary business neglected to fraught

8

such a drunken ship with so much guilded durt." The men of the Chesapeake expedition and their leader were aware, however, that the new world was capable of producing greater wonders than they had seen, and their hopeful hearts still skipped a beat whenever sunlight struck a yellow gleam from the river sands.

When the barge had come to the end of the bay where it was six or seven miles in breadth, Smith had seen that it divided itself into four branches. Of these the best seemed to come "northwest from among the mountains," and he therefore chose to ascend it. The little vessel stirred quiet ripples on the smooth surface as it slid against the current from the sand-lined mouth. She passed midstream a narrow wooded island and moved on between tree-covered banks a scant two miles to a spot where jagged brown boulders scattered over the river bed, made a bristling, irregular barrier beyond which they could not go. This they promptly designated "Smith's Fales," and into the foam-whitened water that beat upon the dark rocks they heaved their anchor while their eyes searched for a channel. There was none. The rushing water, they knew, had passed villages that were distant no more than two days' journey, and they scanned the green and tangled shore carefully. Below the line of stones the river of the mighty Susquehannocks was a lonely stream. When they tried to pull in their anchor, its flukes were so firmly locked among the boulders on the bottom that they could not raise it. Abandoning it, they drifted on the swift current toward the tossing bay. On another river they might find gold. Another valley might wind between the mountains toward the warm salt waves that pound the China coast. To them the short journey to

"Smith's Fales" had been a minor disappointment in a series of major frustrations. The river had allowed them less ingress than others they had explored.

Soon after their barge had entered the Chesapeake, more than a half-dozen war canoes darted toward it. At once the practiced eyes of the Captain recognized the paddlers as Massawomecs—the dreaded federation the French called *Iroquois* who were reported by nearby Indians to live far to the north. Since they seemed bent on attack, Smith had the eight sick hidden under a tarpaulin. Their hats he ordered put upon sticks by the barge's side, "And betwixt two hats a man with two peeces, to make us seem many." At once the canoes veered away and their occupants paddled frantically to the shore with Smith sailing boldly in their wake. After the barge had been anchored, the crew lured two timorous savages near enough for each to accept the gift of a bell, and the clappers had no sooner begun a clanging duet than envious visitors overwhelmed the white men with presents of "venison, beares flesh, fish, bowes, arrowes, clubs, targets and beare-skinnes." The members of the war party said they had already engaged their enemies, the Tockwoghs, on the shores of this very river "the which they confirmed by shewing their greene wounds," and as darkness came these friendly strangers left to make camp ashore with assurances that they would return to the barge in the morning. When daylight came they had disappeared.

As the barge moved up the Tockwogh River, it was suddenly surrounded by the canoes of the Tockwoghs. At once, with their customary humor and cunning, the white men showed the weapons given them by the Massawomecs and boasted that they had won them in fierce conflict. The Tockwoghs rejoiced at this and conducted Smith and his band to their "pallizadoed towne, mantled with the barkes of trees." They were welcomed by all inhabitants with fruits and furs, dances and songs "stretching their best abilities to express their loves."

Here for the first time the explorers heard of a river and a people that might fulfill the fantastic expectations that had been theirs when they had set out:

> Many hatchets, knives, pieces of iron and brasse, we saw amongst them which they reported to have from the Susquehanocks, a mightie people and mortall enemies with the Massawomeks. The Susquehanocks inhabit upon the chiefe Spring of these four branches of the Bayes head, two days higher than our barge could passe for rocks, yet we prevailed with the Interpreter to take with him another Interpreter to persuade the Susquehanocks to come visit us for their languages are different. Three or foure days we expected their returne, then sixty of these gyant-like people came downe, with presents of Venison, Tobacco-pipes three foot in length, Baskets, Targets, Bowes and Arrowes. Five of their chiefe Werowances came boldly aboard us to cross the Bay for Tockwogh, leaving their men and Canowes; the wind being so high they durst not passe.

Once more the imaginations of the white men, dormant through the dull preceding weeks, waked to anticipation of wonders. If human beings of such great size existed, other miracles might also be true—the vessels of gold, the short passage to the South Sea and Cathay.

"Such great and well proportioned men are seldom seene," Captain Smith wrote exultantly in his report, "for they seemed like Giants to the English. . . . Those are

11

the strangest people of all those Countries . . . for their
language it may well beseeme their proportions, sounding
from them, as a voice in a vault."

The five chiefs who made the voyage across the bay
were costumed as befitted their station. Some had:

> Cassacks made of Beares heads and skinnes, that a mans head
> goes through the skinnes neck, and the eares of the Beare fas-
> tened to his shoulders, the nose and teeth hanging downe his
> breast. . . . One had the head of a Wolfe hanging in a chaine
> for a Jewell, his Tobacco pipe three quarters of a yard long, pret-
> tily carved with a Bird, a Deere, or some such devise at the great
> end, sufficient to beat out ones braines.

The likeness of the largest of these big men Smith
thought worth immortalizing with a drawing on his map
of Virginia. It shows a magnificent Indian, well proportioned in all respects despite his incredible size. The calf
of his leg, Smith wrote, "was three quarters of a yard
about and all the rest of his limbes so answerable to that
proportion that he seemed the goodliest man we ever beheld." His hair on one side of his head was long and on
the other shorn close to form a ridge over his crown like a
cock's comb. His wolfskin quiver was filled with long arrows tipped with white crystallike heart-shaped stones.

After disembarking on the Tockwogh side of the bay,
Captain Smith, possibly to obtain a favorable attitude
from both God and his new acquaintances, ordered his
men to their daily prayers. The kneeling Christians intoned a psalm, "at which solemnity the poor Salvages
much wondered." As soon as the prayers were over, the
Susquehannocks held serious conference with each other,
obviously to determine, now that it was their turn, what

sort of ceremony they might perform in reply. Having decided:

". . . they began in a most passionate manner to holdup their hand to the Sunne, with a most fearefull song, then imbracing our Captaine, they began to adore him in like manner: though he rebuked them, yet they proceeded till their song was finished: which done with a most strange furious action, and a hellish voyce, began an Oration of their loves; that ended, with a great painted Beares skin they covered him: then one ready with a great chayne of white Beads, weighing at least six or seaven pound hung it about his necke, the others had 18 mantels made of divers sorts of skinnes sewed together; all these with many toyes they layd at his feet, stroking their ceremonious hands about his necke for his Creation to be their Governour and Protector, promising their aydes, victualls or what they had to be his, if he would stay with them to defend and revenge them of the Massawomecks. But we left them at Tockwogh, sorrowing for our departure yet we promised the next yeare again to visit them.

The white men knew the futility of their promise. Death was too close in this land for escape. A few days later Anas Todkill had the good sense to drop to the ground as a volley of arrows sang toward him. His friends thought him dead, but in a moment he rose and fought his way through his Indian assailants back to the barge, his face and clothes red with their blood. The explorers were not so lucky the next day when they came upon islands at a wide reach in the Rappahannock River. At this place "it pleased God to take one of our Company called Mr. *Featherstone,* that all the time he had beene in this country, had behaved himselfe honestly, valiantly and industriously." After they had buried him at this place they fired a volley above his grave and they named the waters there Featherstone's Bay. Of the living discoverers of the Susquehanna there were now only twelve. Besides Captain Smith, Anas Todkill, and the unfortunate Mr. Featherstone, the men who had gone to the rocky barrier and back and had talked to the Susquehannocks about their river were Nathaniel Powell, Thomas Monford, Michell Sicklemore, James Bourne, Anthony Bagnall (Doctor), Jonas Profit, Edward Pising, Richard Keale, James Watkins, William Ward. John Smith grew philosophic as the barge sailed toward Jamestown:

> *Thus have I walkt a wayless way, with uncouth pace*
> *Which yet no Christian man did ever trace*
> *But yet I know this not affects the mind*
> *Which eares doth heare as that which eyes doe find.*

Historically, the finding of the Susquehanna had had a curious significance which its discoverers would never suspect. In the six years from 1602 to 1608 the wayward and unpredictable Captain John Smith had linked in his own experience popular attitudes of four centuries. He who had in Hungary been a romantic champion in an environment of jousting tourneys, "Courts of Love" and flowering knighthood, had become in the late Elizabethan period the complete Elizabethan—poet, philosopher, man of action. Moreover, as Elsie Murray, perceptive Pennsylvania historian, has pointed out, Smith's account of the giant Susquehannocks whom he had met at the mouth of their river, had at least partially engendered the next century's delight in the idea of the "natural man" and the "Noble Savage." Smith's *General Historie of Virginia*, says Miss Murray, was a source book of inestimable riches to eighteenth century idealists. "The golden-agers, the back-to-naturists, and fanatics of equality—the Rousseaus,

Swifts, Defoes, Montesquieus of many generations must have dug pertinent facts from its pages. Even Milton's "Lady of the Masque" may derive, paradoxically, from the Indian princess, 'Powhatan's dearest daughter' whom 'darkest night could not affright, nor coming through the irksome wood.'"

In the flow of a river's story the mid-current incident, white man's discovery, had occurred. Ethnologists and archaeologists would find proof that men had lived beside this stream through more centuries before the event than after it. Geologists would surmise when the water began its flow. On scholars these activities would exert their magic. But to numberless people who trust for their knowledge of the past only written records of human experience, the narratives of Captain John Smith were the beginning of a river's history.

2

Carantouan

🌿 *No god from a vanished civilization*
is so dead that he does not
live in his ruined temple.

The currents that travel unrecognized channels from ancient generations to our own can be felt more strongly, I have come to believe, on the high mesa of Carantouan than elsewhere in America. Stand on a summer noon at the edge of its ten acres of thorn trees, scrub oak and pine and look down on the plain more than two hundred feet below, then up into the bowl of green hills at the center of which it is a lonely monument, and even though skeptic by nature you will begin to sense the deep past breathing here.

Carantouan is an American "Hill of Dreams" inducing a mystic mood as surely as ever fallen Roman walls black against an English upland sunset. "Spanish Hill" is the people's name for it and has been since before the Duc de la Rochefoucauld-Liancourt on a visit in 1795 came upon the joining of the Chemung River and the North Branch of the Susquehanna and in the triangle four or five miles to the north saw a mountain "in the shape of a sugar-loaf, upon which are seen the remains of some entrench-

16

ments." These, he wrote in his journal, the inhabitants call the "Spanish Ramparts."

There was a time when because of the surprising regularity of its contours the people living near it believed that all of Spanish Hill had been built by human hands. Now it is agreed that this was impossible, and geologists explain that it is a glacial drift mound, a "moraine of retrocession" so anchored by inner rock as to have withstood the erosion of the waters which poured about it while the ice sheet melted away. But it was inevitable that a natural phenomenon so striking as this isolated Pennsylvania tabletop should create among people living in its dark shadow a murky lore in whose depths history and legend are often indistinguishable. The swarthy gold-hunting Spaniard is a favorite folk fancy of Americans, but even the exacting scholar can find among old documents and relics bearing somehow on this place enough evidence of his past presence to initiate speculative revery.

In 1841 the American historian T. R. Brodhead found at The Hague a Dutch map made about 1614 and showing in the vicinity of Carantouan names of Spanish character, "Gachos" and "Capitanesses." And in the earth of this region men have found a medal whose Roman lettering indicates it was struck in 1558 to celebrate the accession to the throne of Germany and Hungary of Ferdinand, grandson of the Ferdinand and Isabella who aided Columbus. A crucifix, a sword, a casque, a black and waterlogged boat, each has its antiquarian champions who claim a Spanish origin for it.

Though oral tradition adds to the unreal quality which no doubt encourages the indefinable trancelike moments brought about by presence on Carantouan, what people have said about it must be given measured weight. Folk tales growing from the surmises of the irresponsible or the too imaginative have linked Carantouan with people of nations other than Spain. One of the tellers of these apocrypha, by the sort of clairvoyance the strange hill seems to inspire, believed the whole plateau had been piled up by prehistoric Mound Builders. Another suggested the ramparts lining the edges had been raised by French explorers. A third saw the fortifications as built for defenses against the Iroquois by the Susquehannocks under the direction of three soldiers from a Swedish settlement on the banks of the Delaware.

A mountain so mystic to the eye could not fail to fill settlers of the plain with a growing wonder of what lay inside. Tales of a cave and of buried treasure grew as naturally. The nineteenth century American poet and essayist, Nathaniel Parker Willis, after a visit to Carantouan, intimated that the manitou who haunted the summit was guarding a treasure with his thunder and added:

> An old lady who lives in the neighborhood (famous for killing two tories with a stone in her stocking) declares that the dread of this mountain is universal among the tribes, and that nothing would induce a red man to go on it and it is a modern fact that a man hired to plough the hillside suddenly left his employer and purchased a large farm, by nobody knows what windfall of fortune.

And some fanciful and unreliable folk used to say that Mormon Prophet Joseph Smith in his early days searched the windy summit of Carantouan for buried gold on a moony midnight, seerstone in hand, eager disciples behind him.

Nevertheless folksay of the past is overwhelmingly in

18

support of the theory of early Spanish occupation. In 1786, Alpheus Harris, one of a party of surveyors hired to define the New York-Pennsylvania boundary, helped build a crude observatory on the heights and there, with his comrades, taking observations from the star-crowded sky, made calculations. Twenty-four years later the spell of Carantouan was still so strong upon him that he bought four hundred acres at the foot of the mountain where, beneath its steep eastern wall, he made his home. His Indian neighbors often sat before his fire and talked of the wild plain above them. They called it "Espana" or "Hispan," and they said that an awesome spirit who lived there had once come upon a chief who had dared to climb the side, seized him by the hair and spirited him away forever. They said this spirit spoke with the voice of thunder and destroyed Indians by making holes through their bodies.

This, Alpheus Harris told a friend, might have some relation to the fact that Spanish buccaneers, driven from Florida in the late sixteenth century, had heard from the Indians near Chesapeake Bay of stream beds aglitter with shining metals and had journeyed up the Susquehanna in search of them. Above its confluence with the Chemung they had been attacked by a hostile tribe and had retreated to this impregnable hill and had constructed about its top the mile-long embankment where a trench gave all of the defenders the welcome protection of four to five feet of earth. Beset on all sides of their stronghold, the brave pirates had repelled many a charge, their guns speaking with the voice of thunder and making holes through the Indians. At length, still holding their fort, they had died of thirst and starvation.

This tale, at once accepted as gospel by many of the citizens of the vicinity, was soon romantically altered by a local author who stated that there had been among the Spaniards a beautiful girl who had offered herself as a bride to a stalwart Indian chieftain in return for sparing the lives of her companions. The folk then welcomed as authentic history their neighbor's conclusion that the girl's suggestion had been heartily approved and the couple had been happy ever after on the shores of a western river to which the fortunate husband had guided the whole party.

What truths we know of Carantouan are as appealing as the fictions built from community fancies. Eight years after the sixty tall Susquehannocks who had visited the thirteen Virginians of Captain John Smith's Chesapeake Bay expedition had returned to their upriver towns, another party of thirteen led by a white explorer appeared with two captives outside Carantouan, then a big Susquehannock town. Part of this at least was inclosed in a palisaded rectangle running north and south on a terrace below the heights. The strangers were joyously welcomed within the twelve-foot-high gate and there they told their story. They said that Sieur Samuel de Champlain, founder of Quebec and explorer of much of the north country, was planning with his Indian friends, the Hurons, to attack an Iroquois town south of Lake Ontario. His small force would need assistance, and he had sent them as messengers to Carantouan to ask for five hundred warriors who had previously been promised to him. Reluctantly Champlain had granted his best interpreter, young bold Etienne Brulé, the command of his embassy to the Susquehannocks "since he was drawn thereto of his own inclination, and by this means would see their country and observe the tribes that inhabit it."

Whatever the route taken by rough, tough Brulé and his Hurons to Carantouan, no one knows it now. When he finally returned three years later to the command he had left, he reported his adventures and Champlain recorded some of the things he said:

". . . they had to pass by the country and lands of their enemies: and to avoid evil designs they made their way through woods, forests and brush, heavy and difficult, marshy bogs and deserts very frightful and unfrequented. . . . And in spite of this great care Brulé and his savage companions, while crossing a plain, could not avoid encountering some hostile savages returning to their village: who were surprised and defeated by said party, some being killed on the field, and two taken prisoners whom Brulé and his companions took with them to Carantouan.

Champlain, to prepare Brulé for his job as interpreter, had sent him to live for considerable periods among the Hurons. There he had learned not only language but customs and had heard much of the Susquehannocks. He was therefore not surprised that his party was "received by the inhabitants with great affection and all gladness and good cheer, accompanied by dances and feasts, as they were accustomed to feast and honor strangers." But again and again as the stars came out over Carantouan, pulsing rhythms seized upon the town, deep voices rose as from the legendary caverns far beneath it to beat against the echoing log walls, and the long limbs of the tall people threshed about in wild dances. Under the curved roof-poles of the long lodges there was feasting on game killed down on the plain and dragged up to their cooking fires,

21

much talk and much smoking of tobacco in the long heavy pipes.

At a council meeting Brulé and the twelve Hurons had made their formal petition for military aid, and since it had been promised there could be only one answer. After the decision was official, war cries interrupted the beat of the battle dances. Still the chosen five hundred did not march from the hill-town. Brulé warned them that they would be late for their rendezvous with Champlain and his forces, but they went on dancing. Eventually they moved down the mountain and set out for the neighborhood of the Onondaga fort where they were to meet the French and Hurons. When they arrived they found on the trees messages that said Champlain's force had given up waiting for them and had left two days before. Philosophically the Susquehannocks went back home, taking with them their new friend, Etienne Brulé.

So it was that a young Frenchman was the first white man whose journeyings over a considerable length of the Susquehanna have been recorded (though three Dutchmen who later made a map of the region had been captured, brought to Carantouan and released a year before). Champlain wrote a brief summary of the explorer's oral report when, after three years of dangerous adventure, Brulé rejoined him. During his stay at Carantouan, which lasted through the fall and winter and ended in the spring of 1616, he set out with a few of his hosts to observe their river from Carantouan to its mouth. It is probable that he saw it in the spring of his departure since Champlain wrote that "he returned to Carantouan to seek an escort to return to us."

Brulé's canoe skimmed still waters beside treeless

grassy bottoms, slipped into half-light under boulder-strewn cliffs, traversed meanders so flawlessly curved they seemed drawn by a giant architect's compass. It passed through the brief shade of Standing Stone, rock pillar pitched by a glacier into the river where its roughly rounded upper end rises twenty-four feet above the surface like the marker of an enormous sundial. Forty miles below Carantouan the rock ledges of the Wyalusing lookout hung close to the blue and white cover of the sky. Two Susquehannock towns lesser than Carantouan lay along the banks and there, the travelers knew, waited the traditional effervescent hospitality of the giant tribe.

The bubbling of little streams swelled the waters. The river at its junction with the Lackawanna turns from its southeast course and rolls southwest in a wide gap which it has broken through the mountain range that once barred its passage. There the paddlers of the fragile craft, dwarfed by immensity, looked up to an ocean of blue hills tossing crooked crests against the sky. Soon they were running dark rapids streaked white by old brown rocks, drifting inches above mosaic bottoms where sunlight struck radiance from pebbles of jasper and chalcedony, rhyolite and serpentine, mica and iron pyrites (with its breathtaking though false promise of gold)—all rolled by the current into chancy kaleidoscopic designs. Augmented by the flood from the stream's twin, the West Branch, and by tributaries that would some day be called Juniata, Yellow Breeches Creek, and Conestoga, the river grew wider. The woods were dim under the crowding of heavy branches of giant trees—black walnut, white oak, maple, hickory, chestnut, and ash.

The canoe entered a region of alternate dappled shallows and green deeps which were invaded here and there by rocky promontories tall under scrambles of vines and hardy balsam. Brooks chattered down the ravines between them. Bald eagles circled slow above the islands. Farther on, Brulé's party came upon the jagged line of rocks that had barred the passage of Captain Smith's barge eight years before. They carried the canoe around "Smith's Fales" and launched it in swifter water. The hills sloped gently to flat levels. Whippoorwills in the tide-salted marshes called the nights through. Dawn lighted moveless herons like statues carved from blue stone. The banks receded on either side and they heard a sharp slapping against the sides of the canoe as it slid into the choppy glinting bay.

Champlain wrote:

". . . he employed himself in exploring the country visiting neighboring nations and lands and in passing the length of a river which discharges on the coast of Florida. The climate is very temperate and there are a great number of animals and game to be hunted. But to travel this country one must have great patience for difficulties are to be met in its wildernesses. And he continued as far as the sea along this river, past islands in it and lands that border it, which are inhabited by several nations and many savage peoples. And after he had traversed the country and discovered what was noticeable he returned to Carantouan.

Return against the current required "great patience" and more time, harder work at the paddles, more carries, but it gave the explorer a second and a longer look at every reach of the river before he passed the junction of the Chemung and saw again—rising from the triangular level between the two rivers—the brook-striped walls of ancient Carantouan and the town on the terrace below its summit. Before long Brulé, with five or six Susquehannock friends, would leave that town to rejoin his commander. Attacked by Iroquois the little party would be separated by flight. Capture awaited the Frenchman and, if his story is to be believed, an intervention by God himself who sent a thunderbolt to tell savage torturers that Etienne Brulé was not to be slain. Two more years among the Indians ended at Three Rivers in Canada in 1618 when he gave Champlain the geographical information which the commander somewhat inaccurately included in his maps.

The curious visitor of today will mark that the retreating glacier which created Carantouan left it in the shape of a comet with tail lying to the north. Its high plateau is lower than its edges, like the bottom of a saucer. After heavy rains have filled it up, the accumulated water overflows and, running down the sides, streaks them until the old hill looks like a scalloped cake tin turned upside down.

Elsie Murray has written, "The summit of Spanish Hill as well as the plain between hill and river is a palimpsest on which many races and cultures have left overlying traces." There are few evidences now, however, of the fortifications of Mound Builders, Spaniards, Swedes, Iroquois, or whatever. The great trees that once shaded the high plain are gone, too. Over the whole of it leafless and scrubby trunks, rotted stumps and dead weeds, waist-high, sleep in the sun. Breezes down by the rivers, whose placid waters are about to meet, become winds here, and while they blow they stir a constant crackling, the conversation that sun-dried limbs and stalks keep up with one another. The Scottish poet-ornithologist, Alexander Wilson, traveled the banks of the Susquehanna in 1804 and saw Carantouan much as it is now. In couplets from his verse narrative of his journey, *The Foresters,* are the lines:

> *Where, rising lone, old Spanish Hill appears*
> *The post of war in ancient unknown years*
> *Its steep and rounding sides with woods embrowned*
> *Its level top with old entrenchments crowned . . .*
> *Now overgrown with weeds alone it stands,*
> *And looks abroad o'er open fertile lands.*

3

Palmer's Isle

🌿 *When a great learned man,*
who is long in the making, dieth,
much learning dieth with him.

— EDWARD COKE (1628)

An island of nearly two hundred acres lies fair in the mouth of the Susquehanna River where hurrying waters swirl into Chesapeake Bay. It is an uninhabited, unobtrusive island, and its importance seems to the modern traveler to lie in its furnishing a base for the sturdy piers of two large steel bridges. Over one speed the trains of the Baltimore and Ohio Railroad, over the other the crowding motor traffic of a modern four-lane highway, U. S. 40. Since with modern bridgebuilding methods the piers might easily have been based in the bed of the stream itself, most users of either bridge are unaware when they have crossed over that midway they have visited an island.

John Smith and his twelve fellow discoverers passed the island in the summer of 1608 on their short and frustrated discovery voyage up the river to the point where "Smith's Fales" prohibited passage of their barge. The canoes of Etienne Brulé and his Susquehannock Indian companions raced by it eight years later borne by the

27

swift current into the bay. Both explorers being shrewd men must have realized that it divided the waters of the river's mouth and therefore dominated whatever commerce might make use of the broad stream as a highway.

The first three decades of the seventeenth century had passed, nevertheless, before two early observers, with curiously notable names, described the island. Then Cyprian Thorowgood, on a trading expedition to the Susquehannocks, stopped at Palmer's Isle, as it had been called since 1622 when included in a grant of lands to a member of the Virginia Company, one Edward Palmer. In his "relation of a voyage made by Mr. Cyprian Thorowgood to the head of the baye" the trader described the island as "some two miles about whereof the Southeast end is very good land, and at the Northwest end is a very high rocke. Towards the water is very steepe but on the other side it ascends by degrees." Fourteen years later Beauchamp Plantaganet in *A Description of the Province of New Albion* increased the general knowledge of Palmer's Isle by stating that it was "half meade, halfe wood" and added:

> On it is a rock forty foot high, like a Tower, fit to be built on for a trading house for all the Indians of the Chisapeak Gulf. The island lieth a mile from each shore in the Susquehanock's river mouth, and there four Sakers [an old type of short cannon] will command the river.

Edward Palmer, first owner of the isle, was a man of "plenteous estate" and of scholarly tastes. Since records of Oxford list him as a student at Magdalen College in 1572, he had passed middle age by 1622 when Palmer's Isle became his property. Its commercial advantages were so obvious that efforts to establish a trading center there were inevitable. But Edward Palmer, distinguished as a "curious and diligent antiquary," a collector of ancient coins and other rarities, rejoiced in his island investment not so much for its promise of profits in beaverskins as for its presenting a picturesque area for the campus of the first university in the Northern Hemisphere. A contemporary of the scholarly proprietor said that he spent thousands of pounds in the preparation of his educational project. We know that he also gave it much serious thought, and one of the requirements of his surprisingly modern curriculum was that students of the river-surrounded college should have the opportunity of taking courses in painting both with oils and water colors. When Edward Palmer, loyal alumnus, died three years after he acquired his island, his hopes for the establishment of Palmer's Isle as a seat of learning were so high that in his will he left his acres of mead and woods (providing that he and his brother had no sons) to Oxford University for the carrying out of his plans.

His desire to have painting taught has led some to believe that the elderly scholar had seen the beauty of the Susquehanna landscape and wished it to be recorded. This and the fact that when in 1627 his river property was appropriated as a trading post eager merchants found a number of learned books, pathetic evidences of his noble intentions, have led toward the conclusion that Palmer lived on the island himself for a while, supervising the landscaping of the institution he had contemplated. Despite his death and the dissolution of the London Company of Virginia, the island was to keep his name until his story had been almost forgotten many years later. His was the first of the series of high-minded and philanthropic daydreams which the Susquehanna has inspired, visions of a sort which both for their happy inceptions and their mournful deaths have long been associated with the stream. Though Palmer's Isle is now known as Garret's Island, having been renamed for a railroad president whose administration of the Baltimore and Ohio during Civil War days was once admired, and though the name of Edward Palmer is unremembered save by a few historians and educators, it was his ambitious and scholarly mind which first conceived a great university on the eastern coast of North America.

The friends of Captain John Smith were for the most part men of action like himself. He wrote a letter about his Virginia adventures to the English sea captain Henry Hudson, and just a year after Jamestown's discovery barge returned to her home port from her thwarted sail up the shallow Susquehanna, Hudson was sailing the deep river that bears his name.

William Claiborne, eight years younger than Smith, was another of the captain's favorites. On his New England voyage Smith even named a group of islands off Boston "Claiborne Isles." The younger man heard his friend's glowing accounts of the Chesapeake and its environs with such enthusiasm that in 1621 at the age of thirty-four he came to Jamestown as Royal Surveyor. He soon abandoned his duties with level and chain, however, to sail the long barge and "there to trade and truck with the Indians." As agent of a rich London merchant, William Cloberry, he made his headquarters on Kent Island on the eastern shore of the bay in what is now Maryland and began to trade with the Susquehannocks at the island in the mouth of their river soon after the death of Edward Palmer. Apparently the will of that learned gentleman with regard to the disposition of his precious isle had been received with indifference by both his kinsfolk and the university to which he had left a legacy of land and responsibility.

Claiborne went into the business of trade with the Indians with initiative, foresight, and dispatch. Having obtained a trading license from the colony, he made sure of his rights by obtaining another in 1631 from King Charles I. He sent employees, one a Negro, to live with the Susquehannocks to learn their language, tastes, and customs. He made it possible at the mouth of their own river for the big people to exchange their animal pelts for the blue beads, cloth, knives, axes, pipes, fishhooks, jew's-harps, bells, mirrors, which they prized, or for strings of their own shell currency of peak and roanoke, currency which John Smith said brought about "as much dissention among the Salvages as gold and silver among the Christians." The rich purple conch shells of peak were reckoned at about ten shillings an arm's length, while the same measure of roanoke's white cockles brought one or two shillings. Before his death these Indian monies must have delighted the heart of numismatist Edward Palmer. It may have amused this connoisseur of coinage also that the traded beaver pelts, which at their highest price on his island gave the Susquehannocks one arm's length of peak per pound, in turn became a kind of currency among the whites and many debts, fines, and salaries were paid in them.

As more and more heavy-laden canoes arrived from up the Susquehanna, knowledge of the giants of the mountain widened. They had begun to trade also with the Swedes along the Delaware, and Thomas Holn, describing them in the late 1630's wrote:

> They live on a high mountain, very steep and difficult to climb; there they have a fort or square building surrounded with palisades in which they reside. . . . They are strong and vigorous, both young and old; they are a tall people, and not frightful in appearance.

If there were further doubt of John Smith's seemingly fantastic report on them, it was dispelled some years later by George Alsop, a Maryland servingman who wrote down with more than a little skill the things he had seen. He reported the Susquehannocks:

> The most Noble and Heroick Nation of Indians . . . cast into the mould of a most large and Warlike deportment . . . their voice large and hollow, as ascending out of a Cave, their gate and behaviour strait, stately and mejectick, treading on the Earth with as much pride, contempt and disdain as can be imagined from a creature derived from the same mould and Earth.

When these impressive humans, great hunters as well as fighters, drew up their canoes on the shores of Palmer's Isle and offered heavy loads of peltry, Claiborne and his men sometimes found they had not enough trade materials to pay for them. His business continued generally profitable, however, and he was happy in it until an ominous incident occurred.

Sailing from his "intolerable plantation in Newfoundland," George Calvert, first Lord Baltimore, sought along the east coast warmer and more fertile lands. The Virginia Colony gave him reserved welcome, and he died before the property he chose could be made his by royal grant. This real estate, now Maryland, was given to George's son, Cecil Calvert, by Charles I through a charter dated June 20, 1632. It included Palmer's Isle and the trade headquarters on Kent Island—though His Majesty had in the preceding year allowed Claiborne his trading license covering the whole of Chesapeake Bay, and that merchant had established himself on Kent Island.

An expedition of the second Lord Baltimore had been settled at St. Mary's. Father White, Jesuit leader of its Catholic members, recommended that a trading post be set up at the mouth of the Susquehanna and urged Cyprian Thorowgood, who acted for the Jesuit priests of the colony in their profitmaking ventures, to journey there and begin trade.

Thorowgood set out for the head of the bay in his small pinnace manned by seven men, and when he arrived at Palmer's Island found a group of Claiborne's men already conducting their established business with a number of the Susquehannock Indians, "A very valorous and stout people." To the Virginians the Marylanders were invaders of their licensed rights. To the Marylanders this island was theirs, and the Virginians were pirates stealing profits where they had no rights. The two parties of white men looked across the piles of beaver pelts and hated each other. Thorowgood said later that the Virginians tried to enrage the Susquehannocks to the point of attacking the Marylanders and, having failed to do so, sailed away leaving him and his men to successful trading. Though the encounter was bloodless it led to a small, undeclared but savage war between the traders of the two colonies. Palmer's Isle, no longer a prospective campus half mead half woods, where scholars might wander in sun and shade and art students set up their easels, had become a prize worth fighting for. Human lives had no stated trade value, but they would be spent for coveted beaverskins.

Claiborne moved swiftly in the next few months. He had the qualities of magnetic and forceful leadership and he exerted them to the utmost to assure control of his trading stations. Palmer's Isle was a much more dangerous place than his Kent plantation, but courageous Englishmen willingly risked their lives there among the powerful and not always predictable Susquehannocks out of love for their chief. One of his admiring collaborators, George Scovell, said that if he and his companions had received what their services were worth it would have cost Claiborne "att least one thousand pounds sterling more than itt did." The Indians, frequently realizing that they were being bilked, revenged themselves by fits of outraged violence that often resulted in the deaths of traders. Nevertheless, they regarded Claiborne so highly that Thomas Hailes, eyewitness and trade participant, concluded that they loved him more than any other Englishman and that "noe English that traded with the Indians . . . gott soe much Beaver, with soe little Truche and soe little supplies."

Claiborne had sent his brother-in-law, John Butler, and his most valued aid, Captain Thomas Smith, to the island at the mouth of the Susquehanna with four or five men and the materials he thought necessary to the establishment of a fortified post—a chamber (small cannon), ten guns, a barrel of shot, a gourd of powder, bullet

molds and swords, pigs, cattle, garden and kitchen utensils, even "a pair of hinges & a latch and a house lock & a
key" for the yet unbuilt cabin where they would live.

So it was that when Sergeant Robert Vaughan arrived in
the summer of 1635 on a trading expedition similar to
Cyprian Thorowgood's of the previous year, he was
stunned with surprise when he and his men suddenly
found themselves captives under armed guard and their
"trucking commodities" confiscated. The Virginians took
the Maryland traders to Kent Island and there released
them, but the Maryland Assembly met in high dudgeon
"censuring Smith for Pyracie."

Captain Smith and his crew protested equal surprise
and more outrage when immediately thereafter Claiborne's new pinnace, the *Long Tayle*, while on a trading
expedition was seized by the Marylanders who set her
crew ashore to walk to St. Mary's. Smith and his interpreter, Henry Eubank, they allowed the dignity of passage on the *Long Tayle*. Arrived at St. Mary's, they were
informed that the pinnace had been confiscated and,
crowning humiliation, the Maryland governor forced them
to seek transport all of the "twenty leagers" back to Kent
Island in the canoes of Indians, because, he said, "hee
was sorrie hee had noe boate to send us home in, although having at that tyme three boates riding at his
dore."

This almost comic bickering continued and eventually
served to emphasize the tragedy that was rapidly developing. Supporters of Lord Calvert spread talk that Claiborne had told the Indians that the Marylanders were
Spaniards, bent on the destruction of all Indian tribes,

and Claiborne further incensed these gossips and gave credence to the rumor by shouting that "if my Lord's plantation should surprize or take any of his boates, he would be revenged though he joined the Indians in a canoe." The Marylanders were now convinced that Claiborne and his men were stirring up the Susquehannocks against them (as probably they were) through association with them at Palmer's Island. The Maryland Council was informed that the traders at this post might even furnish the Indians with guns. The bitterness between the two colonies suddenly flared into violence and bloodshed when Claiborne sent Lieutenant Radcliffe Warren and thirteen men in the shallop *Cockatrice* against two Maryland trading pinnaces in the Pocamoke River. Warren, two of his men, and one of their enemies were killed in this small naval engagement.

Though Claiborne had been obliged by his London employers to return there for conference in May, 1637, he sought to emphasize the logic of his position as proprietor of Palmer's Isle by consent of its original possessors by inviting the King of the Susquehannocks, his counselors and great men to meet at the post shortly after his departure to give formal approval of his ownership. The giant chieftains came swiftly down their river on the swollen waters of spring. They stepped from their canoes in the full regalia of tribal ritual. Their faces streaked with red and green and white and black, their arms and breasts vivid with painted pictures of bear, wolf and deer, and only partially hidden by their elaborate fur mantles, their breechclouts covering them, as George Alsop delicately put it, "where shame leads them by a natural instinct to be reservedly modest," they solemnly and pridefully

36

strode to their places beside the council fire. There in an elaborate and dignified ceremony the Indian king presented to Captain Thomas Smith, as representative of Captain William Claiborne, the whole of Palmer's Island, and, to brighten the chain of friendship between the Virginians and his subjects, he ordered a number of the latter to cut down the trees about them and to clear some of the ground in order that its owners might have a corn crop that year. In return for this handsome gift so eloquently and practically presented, Captain Smith assured the Susquehannock ruler that he and his absent employer would make the island safe from all enemies of the Susquehannocks and their friends the Virginians.

A traitor now entered the drama of Palmer's Isle and brought it swiftly to its denouement. Cloberry and Company had sent George Evelin from London to take Claiborne's place as their representative. The new agent had seemed at first as opposed to the Maryland claims as his predecessor. Apparently well acquainted with the Calvert family, he had intimated that the grandfather of Governor Leonard Calvert had been a simple farm peasant and said the "Governor of Maryland is such a Fellowe nowe, and that he was a very Dunce & blockhead when hee went to schoole." Not long thereafter, perhaps irked by Captain Thomas Smith's suspicions of his good faith, Evelin betrayed Claiborne by admitting he was an agent of the very governor he had attacked and by urging Calvert to seize by force the islands the Virginian claimed.

Leonard Calvert took George Evelin's advice and gave Sergeant Vaughan opportunity for a terrible revenge in return for his previous humiliation. A swift and secret raid captured all of Kent Island and brought Vaughan to the door of Smith's home there on Beaver Neck where he took the captain into custody. The governor who had himself sailed on the raid, flying the black-and-gold flag of Lord Baltimore on his pinnace, was delighted. Vaughan's taking of Palmer's Isle with the aid of two cannon was an easy matter. The post surrendered without offering opposition. At once the triumphant governor appeared in his pinnace ordering the destruction of all buildings and fortifications and the removal into Maryland of all men, cattle, and hogs, "together with all the goods & household stuffe."

On the afternoon of the fourteenth of March in 1638, Thomas Smith went on trial for his life before the Maryland Assembly. Sergeant Robert Vaughan and other Marylanders with whom he had fought for Claiborne's rights had sat on the grand jury that had indicted him for the crime of "Pyracie." Sergeant Robert Vaughan sat on the trial jury that found him guilty. Smith was allowed no attorney, no opportunity to challenge the jurisdiction of the court nor the fitness of the jurors. His sentence that he be hanged by the neck till dead and that all his lands, goods and chattels except his wife's dower "be forfeited to the Lord Proprietor" was confirmed by oral vote. He was executed immediately.

Palmer's Isle was to receive still another visit from Robert Vaughan. Apparently he had not completed the governor's previous orders in entirety, for Leonard Calvert sent him once more to the outpost to bring back five servants and certain goods and chattels belonging to Claiborne. The governor also ordered the building of a new defense appropriately named Fort Conquest so that Maryland might have absolute control of the mouth of the Susquehanna.

As the beaver trade gradually failed, the importance of the little island lessened, and it was no longer a priceless jewel on the lip of the river. Years later it was known as Watson's Island for a short period—then Garret's.

4

The Hawk of Roscommon

> 🌿 *It is a man of violent passions,*
> *bloodshot eyes and swollen veins that*
> *alone can grasp the knife of murder.*
>
> —PERCY BYSSHE SHELLEY

When George Talbot of Castle Rooney, Roscommon
County in the Kingdom of Ireland, received the thirty-
two thousand acres of Susquehanna Manor, settlers of the
river lands wondered why his cousin, Charles Calvert,
third Lord Baltimore, had given them to him. Some
thought Charles, first of the Calverts to govern the grant
which his grandfather had petitioned for and his father
had received, had more in mind than making the son
of his father's sister Grace Talbot a generous gift. On an
early spring day in March of 1680 Henry Johnson went
hunting "for Deare or Turkeys" with his friend John
Mould on Spesutie Island at the head of the Chesapeake
Bay. Whatever the difficulties that developed between the
two, they had hardly returned to the mainland before
Mould was reporting to John Waterton, "one of his Lordship's Justices for the County of Baltimore," significant
parts of the day's conversation:

40

. . . the said Johnson did enquire of me if I did heare of the Irish that was to come into this province, which I did reply I did not heare of any, then the said Henry Johnson replyed there is ffourty familys to come in under the pretence of seateing Susquehanna River, but that ffourty ffamilys will proove in the End to be ffourty thousand to cutt the Protestants throats for it is only a plot be betwixt my Lord and that Irish fellow Talbott and that we shall find, but I hope the Parliam of England will prevent their purposes or that they will sink by the way in comeing for I doe not desire their Company soe nigh me.

When Lord George Talbot and his wife and their retainers had completed the new manor house beside the river, however, the actions of Lord Baltimore proved to be based on land hunger rather than religious prejudice. William Penn had already claimed large areas which Baltimore regarded as part of Maryland, and in the ensuing controversy the latter's loyal and fiery cousin lost no time in making his stand very clear. Old-country names dropped upon the wild river country like bees on a tangle of honeysuckle and in such numbers that a Roscommon man might well feel at home there. Northern Maryland was New Ireland. Susquehanna Manor was New Connaught, the tract Talbot acquired for himself at Friendship (later Head of Elk and now Elkton) was Belleconnell, and through the valley of the river called the Northeast now rolled the waters of the Shannon. All these must be protected from hostile Indians if the lord of the manor was to keep his agreement with Lord Baltimore "to transport or cause to be transported into this province within twelve years of the date hereof [1680] 600 and 40 persons of British or Irish descent." So blockhouses sat in a frowning row across the manor and whenever a settler heard three quick shots from a

41

musket or the wild blowing of horns, or saw flames leap
from the top of a high hill, he gathered his family and
raced for the protecting walls while Talbot and his
mounted rangers galloped against the invaders. These
duties and others delegated to him by Lord Baltimore
gave Talbot little time for encouraging immigration from
his native soil. Only a few miles from his home, Penn's
followers were settling acres claimed as part of Maryland
and to the south the Virginians were showing resentment
of the Calvert grants.

Against the threat of William Penn and his colonists
Talbot acted with rash directness and unbridled temper.
The gracious and tolerant Quaker had been in America
only a few months before the Irish manor lord visited him
to protest the occupation by Pennsylvanians of lands along
the Delaware. With a boldness that obviously nettled
Penn, he announced that if he had been ordered to the
Delaware by Lord Baltimore to protest the settlement
of these lands he would have "stay'd there though I had
not above one man to keepe me Company," and that he
would hinder such settlement in the future. Proof that he
meant what he said peppers the minutes of meetings of
the Provincial Council of Pennsylvania held early in
1684: Colonel Talbot had visited the houses of the Widow
Ogle, Jonas Erskine and Andreis Tille and "tould them
that if they would not forthwith yield Obedience to ye
Lord Baltimore . . . and pay rent to him he would
Turne them out of their houses and take their Land
from them." Colonel Talbot would not suffer John White
to carry away the hay he had cut and told him that if he
and his companions cut any more his Marylanders would
throw it in the river. Colonel Talbot rode up to Joseph

Bowle's house and "was ready to ride over him," and cursed him and said, "you Brozen faced, Impudent, Confident Dogg, Ile Shartin Penn's Territories by & by."

George Talbot's gratitude to Charles Calvert, third Lord Baltimore, found only minor expression however in violent evictions of Pennsylvanians. It eventually led him to acts so strange and violent that the authorities of Virginia almost succeeded in their ambition to hang him.

The unhappy sequence began when honest, blunt Christopher Rousby, the King's Collector of Customs in Maryland, called upon Governor Calvert and in the presence of his lady accused him of obstructing the collection of export revenues. He called "his Lordship Traytor to his face" and added that he ought to be sent back to England in chains. At this insult Lady Baltimore "fell a crying," but Rousby, unmoved, shouted that he "had spoke noe more than what he could produce from under the King's hand and Seale."

Baltimore, realizing that King Charles was touchy where losses of royal income were concerned, immediately wrote an indignant letter to that monarch denouncing Rousby as "the most lewd, debaucht, swearing and most prophane Fellow in the whole government . . . as great a Traytor in his heart to his Sacred Majestie as is this day living." He added that Rousby's rude insolence and tyrannical manners had dissuaded many captains of commercial vessels from visiting Maryland ports "to the diminution of his Majesty's Revenue" and that Rousby had made malicious attacks on loyal officers of the Crown saying that they were "greater knaves and Turn Coates, and begin to pisse backwards."

This use of offense as defense worked rather well at

43

first. The king angrily directed Rousby to answer these accusations but the tax collector proved more than a match for his enemy. He became more specific in his charges and soon had convinced His Majesty that Lord Baltimore had withheld from the royal treasury lawful taxes to the amount of at least two thousand pounds. The King reprimanded Baltimore, fined him twenty-five hundred pounds and sternly ordered him to aid Rousby in the performance of his duties as collector.

When the temperamental Irish protegé of Charles Calvert heard this story, he stormed south through the falling leaves of a red-and-gold autumn to revenge the humiliation of his cousin.

Christopher Rousby was a Friday evening supper guest of Captain Thomas Allen of His Majesty's ketch, *Quaker*, then moored in the Patuxent River, when the Lord of Susquehanna Manor rushed aboard. The captain participated in the events that followed on that last night of October, 1684, and reported them as a not unprejudiced observer. Though he was considered by many Marylanders an arrogant and tyrranical officer who sometimes confiscated without warrant the livestock of honest settlers, his testimony was never substantially denied even by the man it was calculated to hang. It constitutes one of the strangest eyewitness narratives in the annals of American crime:

> Finding out that I was aboard, Talbot came running down to the cabin. Christopher Rousby, when he saw him, rose from his chair and asked him to sit down, for we were at supper. He declined to join us, saying that it was his fasting-day but I made him welcome, and when supper was ended he fell to kissing of me. I desired him to forbear for I was no woman, and then he hit

44

me a blow on the heart and a box on the ear. He did this again a quarter of an hour later, and I told him I would stand him no longer; and then he said he and I could not be friends till we had fought on shore, and I told him I would not refuse him. He then tried to kiss me again, but after a time he asked me to drink Lord Baltimore's health, and I said, with all my heart but Lord Effingham's [then Governor of Virginia] first, to which he objected, so I said that Lord Effingham's must come first or no health's at all.

Then Mr. Rousby came in and sat down on the opposite side of the table to Colonel Talbot, and presently he said he would sleep on board. Then Talbot went to Rousby and said, "Rousby, you son of a whore, you dog, give me your hand" but Rousby refused unless he gave him better words. And Talbot said again "Rousby, you dog, give me your hand. Don't you know that I am your Governor and can do you a kindness." Rousby answered, "I don't value anthing you can do to me." And with that Talbot started up and pulled Rousby's cravat to pieces. Rousby said nothing, but rose up to go, and Talbot started up and met him, and clapped him on the right shoulder with his left hand, saying "dear Rousby," with his dagger under his coat in his right hand, and then stabbed him in the right breast. My servant called out, "He has stabbed him," and my doctor, who was standing by, seized Talbot, and the men presently removed Talbot, while the doctor went to look after Rousby. But in half an hour Rousby was dead. I ordered the corporal to put Talbot in irons, but while this was doing, Talbot said that nothing troubled him so much as that he had not stabbed more, that he hoped to spill and drink a thousand of our bloods, &c.

Since Rousby's home was on the shore nearby, news of his death spread swiftly, and Maryland friends of the manacled prisoner immediately rallied to protect him. On Sunday morning Colonel Henry Darnell led a delegation of prominent citizens aboard the *Quaker* to demand custody of the accused. Captain Allen met them with icy hostility, denied their jurisdiction because the crime was committed aboard his vessel and stated that he would resist by force of arms any effort to take Talbot.

Before such an attempt could be launched, however, the *Quaker* was under sail for Virginia, and as soon as she had made port Lord Effingham, whose health her unwilling passenger had refused to drink, ordered the gentleman confined in the jail at Gloucester. There the murderous lord of New Ireland-on-the-Susquehanna languished for nearly three months before the next important event in his history.

Late in January of 1685, Roger Skreene, an experienced seafaring man widely known in the river country, set out in his shallop from a landing near the mouth of the Patuxent River with a surprising group of passengers—a young lady with a child of three, a sturdy man in the uniform of a cornet of Talbot's Rangers, four hands, one of whom had bright red hair, and a "servant wench."

As Skreene told the story later when hailed by John Rousby—brother of the slain tax collector—before a not very curious and singularly unhostile Maryland Council, he knew the lady to be "Madame Talbott" and her military companion to be Philim Murry, Lord Talbot's aide. He had set out on a Saturday and on the following Wednesday he had landed his passengers below the bluff at Wormeley's.

The Council knew well the lay of the land at Wormeley's, but it is possibly significant that they asked Skreene no questions about this phase of his journey. At the top of the bluff stood (and still stands) "Rosegill," one of the most elegant of Old Dominion plantation houses. Construction had begun on it a quarter century before when Ralph Wormeley, a distinguished and cultured planter,

46

had selected the spot—"a charming plateau above the Rappahannock" according to a contemporary seventeenth century observer, M. Durand—for his home.

Rosegill is a long, narrow house. Many tall windows look on its wide lawns from the brick first story which supports a second story of wood. In 1684 it held a chapel for religious worship and a library of many hundreds of volumes and an art gallery. It was moreover a byword for hospitality not merely among Virginians, but throughout the colonies and even in London. It contained twenty guest chambers, and in the attic above them was a dormitory holding fourteen beds for visiting bachelors. For fifteen years it had been the home of a royal governor, Sir Henry Chicheley, who had married the widow of Ralph Wormeley and had died two years before Skreene's shallop moored below it. Now Lady Chicheley, once more a widow, and her son Ralph Wormeley II, with wife and children, lived in Rosegill attended by many aids, servants and slaves who lived in a score of other houses on the estate.

Perhaps then, the Maryland Council was satisfied that Roger Skreene did not volunteer testimony as to why the expedition landed at Wormeley's. It might have been embarrassing if Governor Effingham had asked the family of a predecessor in his high office to explain why they had given aid and comfort to the wife and retainers of an imprisoned Marylander whose champions, it could logically be assumed, were up to no good in Virginia.

Whatever the underlying circumstances, all that Skreene told the Council was that Thursday morning Madam Talbot, Philim Murry, the servant wench and child rode with a servant of Wormeley's over to Gloucester County

47

where Talbot was in jail. Friday, Wormeley's man returned with the horses. Saturday, Madam Talbot and the rest came back to the shallop without the child whom, they reported, Colonel Talbot wished to keep with him. Noting the absence of the youngster, Skreene asked the red-haired man (according to his later testimony before the Council) if Madam Talbot intended to return to Maryland with him. The redhead replied that she did and would leave the child with the father until the next trip.

It seems likely that the baby was playing an important part in whatever plans were afoot. A prisoner playing with his own three-year-old might not be suspected of plotting immediate escape.

Skreene's narrative as he told it to the Council was artless and ingenuous. On Tuesday morning, Cornet Philim Murry, the redhead and one of the two new hands had gone ashore "to enquire (as they said) for a kinsman of the new hands." As a logical first step on this mission they told him they "would go to the ordinary and gett a bottle of Rum." Madam Talbot, saying "she had a mind to eate some Oysters out of a pitt there hard by which she had formerly tasted of," asked Skreene to put her ashore and he did so. She returned to the ship that night, but the three searchers for the kinsman did not.

About sunrise on Wednesday morning, Skreene said, he weighed anchor, to go to the other side to look for his company which he "thought (and so told Mad. Talbott) might be drunk at the Ordinary, staying soe long as they did," but "Just as the anchor was a peak" he saw a canoe with four men in it coming around the north point of the river's mouth. Puzzled, he called to Madam

48

Talbot in the cabin asking how the fourth man would be set ashore and she said, "What, is his cousin come then?"

Thereupon she came out of the cabin and "spoke Irish" to the new hand aboard and then said to Skreene, "It may be he (meaning the Stranger) will go for Maryland."

As soon as the four men made the canoe fast and came aboard, Skreene hoisted sail and at the order of Madam Talbot bore away for the Eastern Shore and stood along it until they came against Hooper's Island.

At this point Philim Murry thoughtfully suggested to Madam Talbot that the captain of the shallop had planned to obtain meat on the Eastern Shore before returning and the lady at once said, "Roger, since you have business here it will not be much hinderance to you but if your stay be anything long for want of a passage I will satisfy you for the time till you get over."

So all "went ashore to Mr. Hooper's where they got two pones of bread and went aboard again" leaving behind the unsuspecting seaman who later reported to the Council: "and immediately they went away with the shallop out of this Examinant's sight and he never saw them since."

After he had given his narrative this fairy-tale ending, the Maryland Council gravely summoned one Richard Keene to appear before them on February 27, 1685, to attest the truth of his testimony. Keene had a perfect memory of a conversation he had had with the frank and innocent witness the month before. He had met Skreene at Hungar River and asked him how he came there.

Reply: Was put ashore at Henry Hooper's.
Question: Where's Madam Talbot?
Reply: Gone up the Bay home to her own house.

49

Question: How will you get your pay?
Reply: Madam promised a hogshead of tobacco more than ordinary to put ashore at Hooper's Island. Expect pay from Colonel Darnall and Major Sewall as well.
Question: What news of Colonel Talbot?
Reply: Have not been within twenty miles of him, know nothing about him at this time.

If the members of the Council made query as to why part of the ingenuous seaman's wage was to come from two of the alleged murderer's most admiring friends, there is in the minutes of their meeting no record of it. Apparently, too, they callously failed to ask the question that would naturally come from anyone who had heard Roger Skreene's sketchy tale: "What became of the baby?" If they were doubtful as to the answer to a third and inevitable inquiry—"Who was the fourth man—the stranger?"—it was soon answered by a pathetic letter of the governor of Virginia.

> I am sorry to send you the News by these that Coll. Talbot hath escaped out of Prison. Ours are so weak here that I rather wonder he was kept so long, he had a guard of two men every night and one in the day, besides he was sufficiently ironed, but he corrupted his Guards and other persons in the house, and those that were assisting in his escape I had had under examination and found great suspicion tho' no positive proof against them but so much that I committed them to Prison from whence they are since likewise escaped.

This plaint was emphasized by an outraged statement from Tax Collector Blakiston, newly appointed to succeed the murdered Rousby:

> The most horrid murther of His M's Collector here hath been and is daily seconded with very apparent tokens of approvement

both from Talbot, the bloody Malefactor and all his adherents who are busy in extenuating his crime and have procured his Escape from Prison in Virginia and from thence transported him to Marry Land where he remains publickly known at his own House.

The Council had acted weeks before the "news" from Lord Effingham. About a week after their investigation of Skreene's actions they had sent out a Proclamation beginning with:

Whereas we are credibly informed that Coll. George Talbott, late an inhabitant of this Province who is charged with murder of Mr. Christopher Rousby, his Majties Collector is absconded and privately kept in the County of Cecill p t icularly at his own house and sometimes at the house of George Oldfield in Elk River and hath with him severall confederates and accomplices which doe hide guard and defend him from the hands of Justice and [and ending with the demand that sheriffs, military, and all good people use their] utmost endeavor, skill, cunning and power by all waies and means Imaginable to find him.

Spurred by constant urgings and complaints from Virginia and by fear of discipline from the crown, the Marylanders tried to prove they were sincerely trying to capture the fugitive by summoning the sheriff of Cecil County and rebuking him for not arresting Talbot. That officer, William Pierce, answered lamely that it was all the fault of Colonel Henry Coursey, commander in chief of all his Lordship's foot militia in Cecil and Kent counties. Coursey had advised him, he said, not to make the arrest until such time as Colonel Talbot's explanatory letter to the Council had been delivered. This seemed a little too much even for the prejudiced Council to condone, and they ordered the sheriff to start tending to his business. At about the same time Lord Baltimore tried to assuage

51

the growing resentment in Virginia by claiming that his cousin's escape was "occasioned by the corruption of the Guard and not procured by any Persons of Maryland" and added defensively that Talbot was never publicly seen at his own plantation but "always kept himself out in the mountains to the Norward."

In the meantime the object of the lethargic manhunt realized that he could no longer boldly reside at his manor house where a loyal officer of the crown might arrest him at any time. The story of his ensuing adventures is not documented except by prevalent and persistent folklore which, in this case, can well be believed. According to that he set out upstream in his boat and found on the east bank of the Susquehanna, just below the jagged rocks that had impeded Captain John Smith's passage, a large opening in Mount Ararat which towered above the river. This aperture, hardly a foot above the water and north of the little tributary, Herring River, led into a roomy cave, eighteen feet long, twelve feet wide, ten feet high, a natural chamber in the solid granite base of the mountain. In this he lived a Robinson Crusoe sort of life—sailing the river for pleasure, fishing for some of his food and sending aloft his Ireland-trained falcons to bring geese, ducks and pigeons down to his cooking fire. A criminal Elijah fed by birds as murderous as himself, he waited for the day to come when he might set his course downriver toward his manor home and his wife and children. He had good reason for such hopes. The death of Charles II had brought to the English throne James II, a monarch more friendly to Lord Baltimore, and the proprietor had already besought a royal pardon for his favorite and cousin.

Eventually, after more than a year as a fugitive, the Lord of Susquehanna Manor returned himself to the Maryland authorities and to documented history. Baltimore, who was by this time—the spring of 1685—quite sure of obtaining the royal clemency he had requested, immediately ordered him delivered to the governor of Virginia, and the Maryland Council in pursuance of the order commanded one Gilbert Clarke to transport the accused secretly to Jamestown—making it clear that Clarke should provide for the journey a "good and sufficient boate, Sloop or Shallop and four Rowers and . . . a guard of Six men well armed."

It was on the twentieth of April that George Talbot finally stood before a Virginia court to answer for his crime.

The men before whom he was tried—the Virginia Council and the jury—bore names long since famous in the history of Virginia. In the seats of the Council, Nathaniel Bacon presiding, were Colonels William Byrd, John Page, John Custis, John Lear, Phillip Ludwell, William Cole, Christopher Wormeley, and the Council Secretary, Nicholas Spencer. The foreman of the jury was Colonel William Kendall, and his fellows were Colonel Edward Hill and Messrs. William Randolph, Charles Goodrich, Thomas Hodge, Thomas Cock, Francis Epps, Joseph Mauldin, William Taylor, David Crafford, Thomas Toule and John Smith. Thomas Bullard and Arthur Spicer were "nominated and assigned" as Talbot's council—"to Argue all points of Law wherein he shall be concerned." The trial was short. George Talbot did not deny that he had killed the King's Tax Collector. In extenuation of the crime he claimed he had done so "without any manner of premeditated malice in the height of his passion for which he most heartily beg'd God and the King's pardon."

The jury were ready with their verdict the next day. It was long and formal but, stripped of its wordiness, it said that George Talbot "Not having the fear of God before his Eyes but being moved and seduced by the Instigation of the Divel" did with a "certaine dagger made of Iron and Steele of the Value of one shilling . . . stabb and thrust 'giveing' one deadly wound in & upon the right breast . . . of Chr Rousby . . . of wch sd Deadly wound the sd Chr Rousby then and there Instantly dyed."

The sentence approved by the court was death. News that the execution of Lord Baltimore's most arrogant and exasperating champion had been ordered was greeted by many Virginians with glee. But Maryland's governor had one more card to play in defense of his cousin. When the same court reconvened, the Lord of Susquehanna Manor made a last triumphant and hypocritical appearance before it "with all humility on his bended knees" and presented "his Majesty's most gracious Pardon for the felony by him committed on the Body of Christopher Rousby of Maryland, Esqr & humbly prayed that said pardon might be read in Court."

The Virginians could not convert the royal pardon, but had the last word after it had been read and recorded. Then His Excellency Nathaniel Bacon (who would yet be accused by a royal governor of crimes as heinous as Talbot's) gravely admonished the murderer to be moved "to a hearty and thorough Repentance of his great offence against God almighty & by a future peace-

able & quiet behaviour and demeanor to testify his true
and hearty sence of his Majestie's Grace & favour unto
him."

There is a record which proves that George Talbot was
soon back at his Susquehanna home. The motives that
sent him once more across the seas to his native Connaught and the valley of his beloved Shannon are not
known, but, as might have been expected, he was soon engaged in championing deposed King James against the
Protestant forces of William and Mary. After the disastrous defeat at Aughrim and the treaty of Limerick, he
was one of the officers allowed to take ship for France and
join the famous Irish regiment of the French army. He
was killed soon afterwards in battle.

Gradually then, the place names of Ireland's West
Country dropped out of use among the people who
lived at the mouth of the Susquehanna. The story of the
lone resident of Mount Ararat and his fierce hunting
birds, however, caught the folk fancy and even after quar-
rying had destroyed the granite cavern, when hawks and
sometimes eagles circled above the high peak, men said,
"George Talbot's falcons are flying."

5

The Sot-Weed Factor

❧ *The Vertues of Tobacco are these,*
it helps digestion, the Gout, the Tooth-ach,
prevents infection by scents it heats the cold,
and cools them that sweat,
feedeth the hungry, spent spirits restoreth,
purgeth the stomach, killeth nits and lice . . .

—JOHN JOSSELYN, GENT. (1663)

The planter was beginning to become more prosperous than the trader at the mouth of the Susquehanna as the second half of the seventeenth century began. Captain Claiborne, during the most prosperous period of the post at Palmer's Island, had given as high as ten shillings a pound for beaver. As a result he had done so much business that the beaver upriver were being wiped out. Traders went farther and farther inland to obtain the pelts, and the Susquehannocks were obliged to hunt at greater distances from their upriver forts. Gradually beaver were used less frequently as legal tender in business transactions, and tobacco became the medium of exchange.

As lands were cleared at the wide mouth of the river, long fields slanted away from the pebbly shores. Big houses rose on shaded lawns and the owners, now men of ample holdings, gave them names—Mount Ararat, The

Glasshouse, Larkin's Desire, Ryecroft's Choice, Anchor and Hope, Widdows Lott, Success, Heart's Delight.

To the midst of this new and impressive agricultural economy in the last quarter of the century came an English tobacco buyer, one Ebenezer Cook, who called himself The Sot-weed Factor and desired as much to learn of life in this new world as to make a satisfactory bargain with each "Oronokoe," popular nickname for a planter of river-valley tobacco.

Ebenezer Cook sat and smoked on the galleries of the tobacco plantation houses, talking business with the prosperous owners in their habitual blue-linen suits. He was a crotchety, whimsical fellow who knew well that men love to laugh at the exasperations and frustrations of their fellow humans, and as he went about his business he was aware that he had quite a funny story to tell. He told it in clever and often barbed couplets, which he published soon after his return to England in a volume entitled *The Sot-Weed Factor*.

> *Freighted with Fools, from Plymouth Sound*
> *To Mary-land our Ship was bound*
> *Where we arrived in dreadful Pain*
> *Shocked by the Terrours of the Main*
> *For full three Months, our wavering Boat*
> *Did thro' the surley Ocean float,*
> *And furious Storms and threshing Blasts*
> *Both tore our Souls and sprung our Masts.*

On his arrival he was intrigued by the lack of dress of the Indians:

> *His manly shoulders such as please*
> *Widowes and Wives, were bathed in grease,*
> *Of Cub and Beaver whose supple Oil*

> *Prepar'd his limbs 'gainst Heat or Toil.*
> *Thus naked Pict in Battel fought,*
> *Or undisguis'd his Mistress sought,*
> *And knowing well his Ware was good,*
> *Refused to screen it with a Hood.*

Cook thought the simple savage charm of a chieftain hardly made up, however, for the ridiculous lack of balance of his water transport:

> *The Indians call this Watry Waggon*
> *Canoo, a Vessel none can brag on*
> *Cut from a Popular Tree or Pine*
> *And fashioned like a Trough for Swine . . .*

One night of his journeying among the Maryland sot-weed growers, the factor was wakened from a sound sleep by a fox chasing ducks and geese through his bedroom.

> *Raging I jumped upon the Floar*
> *And like a Drunken Saylor Swore;*
> *With Sword I fiercely laid about*
> *And soon dispers'd the Feather'd Rout,*
> *The Poultry out of Window flew*
> *And Reynard cautiously withdrew.*

To avoid a similar disaster he decided to spend the next night stretched out in the planter's orchard. This was even worse.

> *. . . Fortune here, that saucy Whore*
> *Disturb'd me worse, and plagued me more*
> *Than she had done the night before.*

He complained that croaking of the frogs was so loud that it almost deafened him and added in a learned footnote, "Frogs are called Virginia Bells and make (both in that country and Maryland) during the night, a very hoarse ungrateful Noise."

As the "bells" ceased their chiming he went to sleep, only to be awakened by a rattlesnake's crawling near him. This led him to try to sleep in the limbs of a tree:

Not yet from Plagues exempted quite
The curst Muskitoes did me bite
Till rising Morn and blushing Day
Drove both my fears and ills away.

Occasionally the merchant turned from his own misfortunes to pillory those people he considered at least partially responsible for them. His adventure with one of William Penn's followers, not far from the Maryland Plantations on the Susquehanna, led to a bitterly satiric passage:

While riding near a Sandy Bay,
I met a Quaker, Yea and Nay;
A Pious Conscientious Rogue,
As e'er woar Bonnet or a Brogue,
Who neither Swore, nor kept his Word
But cheated in the Fear of God;
And when his Debts he would not pay,
By Light within he ran away.
With this fly zealot soon I struck
A Bargain for my English Truck
Agreeing for ten thousand weight
Of Sot-weed good and fit for freight.

The factor was a sincere lover of good food and drink and his efforts to express a dour antisocial bitterness were often interrupted by irrepressible outbursts of delight over the roasts and wines with which his genial hosts

59

regaled him as they offered to sell their finest and most fragrant leaf.

A particularly happy evening's debauch, he knew, would result in great physical unhappiness, but he had found a remedy.

> *Waking next day with aking Head*
> *And Thirst that made me quit my Bed;*
> *I rigg'd myself, and soon got up*
> *To cool my Liver with a Cup*
> *Of Succahana fresh and clear.*

Thus, as early as 1708 "Succahana" water was hailed as a remedy for the tortures of overindulgence in strong drink. Whether this discovery was disproved by later experimenters, or simply overlooked, the river's historians have not made clear.

As for the Sot-weed Factor, his business completed, he set out for England in a bitter mood, which probably inspired the last couplet of his verse-narrative:

> *May Wrath Divine then lay these Regions wast*
> *Where no Man's Faithful, nor a Woman Chast.*

Remembering whither he was bound, however, he added an asterisk after "Man's" and a footnote below: * "The author does not intend by this any of the *English* Gentlemen resident there."

6

Lord Baltimore's Rattlesnake Colonel

THE MARYLAND–PENNSYLVANIA WAR

🌿 *The frontiersman up
on his hind legs.*

—STEPHEN VINCENT BENÉT

Tom Cresap said he was a fifteen-year-old when he appeared at the mouth of the Susquehanna. Never sure of the year of his birth, he reckoned it around 1694 and said it was in Yorkshire, England. For nearly a score more years he seems to have been a not noteworthy character in a scattered wilderness community, for its records do not mention him. When he was thirty-four, however, he married a west-bank girl, Hannah Johnson, whose parents lived a few miles upriver from the mouth, where the village of Lapidum now stands. His mother-in-law, people said, had already outlived three husbands and at the time bid fair to outlast another, and it may have been that Tom, with a knowledge of himself better than that of his neighbors, considered Hannah of fitting stock to be the mate of a man of his nature.

The newlyweds went downriver to the mouth and set up a house on a section of the east bank, now part of the

61

town of Havre de Grace. While building and furnishing the new place the bridegroom purchased on credit materials valued at nine pounds by merchants who soon differed so emphatically with him as to when he should settle his account that he (temporarily) left Hannah to inspect a possible homesite in Virginia. Apparently his reputation had preceded him, for he had no sooner rented a farm from the Washington family and begun raising a cabin than a delegation of neighbors waited on him to say that his residence among them would be resented, and, if necessary, by force. In the engagement that followed Cresap, who had been hewing logs at the time of the visit, killed one of the group with a convenient ax. He then went back to Maryland with the avowed purpose of moving his wife to their new Virginia home. He found that in his absence Hannah had borne him a son, and perhaps the happy event helped her to persuade him not only to abandon his Virginia plans but to move the little family back upstream near her mother. Whatever his motivation he spent the next two years in the monotonous to-and-fro operation of a Susquehanna ferry, the western landing of which bordered Hannah's old home.

Then, dissatisfied, he applied to Lord Baltimore's government for a grant of land twenty-five miles upstream in the region where the Susquehanna flows between gently rising banks that form the Conojoharie valley. Baltimore granted five hundred acres with alacrity, since both he and William Penn claimed this land as part of their respective grants. At once Cresap gave his west-bank estate (now part of the town of Wrightsville) the idyllic title of "Pleasant Gardens," established a ferry and awaited developments which, since he was the northernmost Maryland settler of lands claimed by Pennsylvania, were likely to be interesting.

It was early spring in the Conojoharie valley when the Cresaps raised their cabin on the western shore of the Susquehanna. By midautumn the ferry was a proved success, and its owner and operator, busy on an October morning with the chores at Pleasant Gardens, heard from across the river the usual signal of westbound customers—three shots fired from the "blew rock." Sam Chance, who owed Tom money, was working with him to pay part of the debt and he helped shove the boat into the water. Then Sam poled Tom across the river. On the far bank they recognized Ed Beddock and Rice Morgan and a Negro man who belonged, Tom knew, to Ed Cartledge who lived in the Pennsylvania woods. Leaving the Negro, the two white men came aboard and when Tom with his back to them had poled them sixty or seventy yards into the stream he heard the voice of one of them say:

"Damn you, Cresap, turn to shore or you are a dead man."

According to his own later account, Tom looked around into the muzzles of two raised guns. Nevertheless he aimed a swipe at his passengers with the pole. Rice Morgan dodged and knocked Tom down with his gun while Ed Beddock threw Sam Chance overboard. Tom bounced up and again struck at Morgan with the pole, "but finding the same unhandy, quitted it and struling with the said Morgan threw him into the bottom of the boat." At this moment Ed Beddock got a hold on him and Morgan grabbed him by the feet and they heaved him "into the River out of his depth."

Like many another frontier boatman Tom could not

swim and therefore "kept hold of the boat for the Safety of his life" while one foe stomped on his hands and the other tried to shove him away with his gun.

"Do you mean to murder me?" said Tom and got an enthusiastic "Yes."

The current had moved the boat downstream, and Tom, thrashing wildly about, felt a rock just below the surface. He grabbed it and while he fought for a footing his assailants still striking viciously at him were swept onward. After the current had carried them around the next bend, he painfully waded "to an island opposite to the blew Rock where . . . he must have perished had not an Indian taken him thence an hour within night."

It took the outraged ferryman three weeks to get his boat back, "and then it was much Damnified" and repairs cost him ten shillings. He made formal complaint to a Pennsylvania court, and Judge Andrew Cornish, while granting a warrant for arrest of Beddock and Morgan, had the humor to ask Cresap where he lived. When Tom replied firmly that "he was an inhabitant of Maryland and Tenant of the Lord Baltimore," Cornish suggested that since Tom was living in Maryland he should apply to the courts of that province for justice. All of which the aggrieved Tom reported in a deposition against his attackers sworn "on the Holy Evangelists of Almighty God."

While Cresap continued his ferrying of travelers across the Susquehanna, Governor Sam Ogle of Maryland, after long delay, took up his supporter's cause with Governor James Gordon of Pennsylvania, gravely complaining of Judge Cornish's remark that a Marylander need not expect justice in his neighboring province. Gordon replied with crushing logic that Cresap, while admitting Cornish to be an officer of Pennsylvania, had built his own home five miles farther into Pennsylvania than that of the justice. Since Beddock and Morgan had been convicted and fined, he said, there was no need for further discussion.

Two uneasy years went by before the Pennsylvanians, irritated beyond endurance by Cresap's bold insistence that he was residing in Maryland and by his bland disregard of their laws, struck again. On the cold night of November 26, 1732, Tom was wakened by cries of "Murder" coming from the river side of his cabin. Jumping out of bed he ran to the door and saw a number of dark forms gathered on the thick ice that covered the Susquehanna. A "great noise and Hallowing" came from among them and he dashed out and found his friend and neighbor, John Lowe, lying on the ice and shouting for aid against a mob of Pennsylvanians bent on carrying him off. Cresap asked their leader James Pattison, "What is the matter?"

"Damn your blood, be easy or Quiet or I'll tell you what is the matter," said Pattison, and Cresap's answer, as he later told it, was:

"If any thing is a Miss, Go ashore for there is no occasion to Hall men away in the Night."

Pattison loudly denounced Lowe and Cresap for killing his farm animals, saying he would let them both know that they were in the province of Pennsylvania where such crimes would be avenged.

Cresap answered calmly and with infuriating assumption of innocence that if he and his neighbors on the

65

west side could not obtain protection from their ruler, Lord Baltimore, they would be obliged to appeal to the King.

"We have no business with the King nor the King with us," yelled Pattison, enraged at his failure to kidnap Lowe, "for Penn is our King."

In his deposition on this incident, Cresap wrote that he feared an invasion by residents of the east side of the river, who, he had heard, planned to burn his house. Since he was guilty, even by testimony of his own friends and servants, of killing those of James Pattison's horses and cows which had wandered the river flats and shallows into his land and since he had aggravated existing ill will by encouraging Marylanders to build on land claimed by Pennsylvania, his fears were justified. Peace would not last long beside the Susquehanna in the Conojoharie valley.

Three months after the incident on the river ice—on January 29, 1733, a mob of more than twenty Pennsylvanians moved silently through the woods at night against Cresap. Since four other Marylanders—William Boring, William Smith, John Lowe and his son—were with him in his cabin, it may be reasoned that the visit was not wholly unexpected. The raiders called upon Cresap to open the door and give himself up, and when he refused (as he told the story) they swore that "they would Oversitt the House" or they would "Burn it and the People in it." And they added the loud boast that they were fifty strong and if they were not enough to hang him they would enlist five hundred more. This, said Cresap, made him "Apprehensive that the said persons Intended to do him some Mischief" and he therefore "barred and

68

secured his doors in the best manner he could." His foes pried the door off its hinges, rushed in, and attacked him. Without describing in his later report what happened to them as a result of such foolhardy action, Cresap said that one of the band "had like to have killed a Young Child" of John Lowe's before they retreated across the river.

By this time the Maryland-Pennsylvania border was excited to fever pitch by the almost incredible successes of Tom Cresap in defending himself and his home against great odds. Marylanders sang his praises and told wild tales of his physical prowess. Pennsylvanians denounced him as a murderous outlaw frightening to all law-abiding people. The slight youth who had come to the mouth of the river had grown into a thickset muscular man whose physical strength was a byword for miles around. The commonplace and unsuccessful bridegroom who had fled Virginia had turned into a swaggering, swearing, overbearing bully-boy who had built his dwelling nearly twenty-five miles inside the borders claimed by Pennsylvania. This cabin, he asserted, was his Maryland home and he dared any and all to try to drive him from it. The motives that had changed him in his mid-thirties from an unremarkable, peaceful settler to an arrogant champion of Lord Baltimore, a subject of quarrelsome notes between governors, are yet to be discovered. His own narratives, mostly depositions virtuously complaining that Pennsylvanians had attacked him physically and had deprived him of his rights, were craftily worded to give the impression of an innocent, law-abiding householder assaulted by ruffians. Obviously by intention, they tell nothing of how he defended himself. Why did the mob leave John Lowe lying on the ice on the night it meant to kidnap him? How was the second mob driven from the cabin? Historical records give no direct answer, but it may be inferred that Pennsylvanians left him alone or wished that they had. Marylanders shouted he could lick any ten Pennsylvanians and no one denied it. He was the strongest, most ruthless, catch-as-catch-can, no-holds-barred scrapper on the whole frontier.

As if they intended to make a raid on Cresap an annual rite, the Pennsylvanians waited a year to the very day before resuming hostilities. On January 29, 1734, Cresap had furnished several men to help William Classpill build a cabin within a hundred yards of the home of John Hendrick, Pennsylvanian. Perhaps remembering the unpleasantness of the same day a year before, he had taken the precaution of sending his wife along to bring him news if a Pennsylvania party crossed the Susquehanna. Brave Hannah came full gallop home to tell him that the sheriff of Lancaster with a posse had surrounded his builders and carried eight of them off to the Lancaster jail. Surmising that the posse would not let matters rest there, her husband hastily prepared his home for siege and sent out a call for help to all Marylanders nearby. About ten responded. At "two hours within night" they heard horsemen approaching. As Cresap had suspected, while the sheriff was escorting his prisoners to Lancaster, a number of his posse had remained behind and decided to attack him. Came a knock on the door of the silent cabin and the voices of two men, William Linville and Knoles Daunt, asking for a night's lodging. "No," said Cresap, "and if you do not leave at once you will be fired upon."

70

"I warn you I have a warrant for your arrest," called Linville through a crack in the log wall of the cabin. "You will suffer no bodily harm if you give yourself up!"

The defenders could hear Knoles Daunt trying to force the door while Linville was talking, and one of them aimed his musket through the narrow opening below it and fired. Daunt cried out and fell, badly wounded in the leg.

"Look between the Logs and you can see eleven guns more," shouted Cresap. "You'll have the guts of it if you stay there!"

The posse's answer was to rush the door and force their way inside the cabin. Its defenders, unable to use their guns at such close quarters, grabbed up "Homany Pestles," however, and broke so many heads with them that the invaders ran out again "bruised & Bloody." After that there was silence—then a man's voice begging that Mrs. Cresap lend him a candle so that he might look over the wound in Knoles Daunt's leg.

"I had rather it had been his heart," said Hannah. "There'll be no candle."

Then the group standing to their guns at the walls heard the injured man telling his companions to leave him and go back to John Hendrick's, heard them tell him farewell and depart. Not long afterward Knoles Daunt died of his wound.

Now like members of a Greek chorus the two governors stiffly commented on the action and the protagonists of the drama. As raid followed raid and counterplot followed plot, the two executives wrote to each other from their respective capitals.

Protested Governor Gordon:

Cressap has been authorized, or at least is countenanced, to
Scatter & plant . . . Tenants, as they are called, where he and
they please.

And Governor Ogle replied:

When magistrates at the head of a Parcel of Desperate fellows,
come out of one Province, & attack in the [territory] of a magis-
trate in another, where blood is shed (and a great wonder it is
that there was no more); nobody can tell what dismal consequences may follow.

Said Gordon of Cresap:

From our Knowledge of him we have no reason to consider him
otherwise than an Incendiary, or publick Disturber of the Peace
of both Governments.

And Ogle answered:

By the best Information I can get from People of undoubted
Credit, he is a very sober and modest Person, and has been particularly careful, since I came into this Province to give No Offence to any Person under your Government; however, I hope,
he will always have Resolution enough to defend himself in Case
any unjust Attack should be made upon him, in which Case I
will be so free as to declare that I think myself obliged to countenance and support him to the utmost of my Power. . . .

The settlers of the disputed border lands were restless
and tortured. Cresap waxed more aggressive and quarrelsome. He led a vengeful expedition against the Pennsylvanians, captured a number of them and conveyed them
into Maryland prisons from which they were soon released. The Pennsylvania Council and Assembly accused
him ("a Person of mean Circumstances and Infamous
Character . . .") of persuading "some Innocent German
People lately come into Pensilvania who were Ignorant of
72

our Language and Constitution" to take up lands twenty miles inside their own province and yet acknowledge the jurisdiction of Lord Baltimore. The Maryland Assembly retorted that more than fifty families of these people "unquestionable Inhabitants and Tenants of this province" had been prevailed upon "through Unwariness and too much Credulity . . . to renounce their Submission to this Government & to declare their Resolution to transfer their Obedience to the Government of Pennsylvania."

Eventually, with the avowed purpose of establishing the truth of its claims and the exact line of the border, the Maryland government sent a surveying party into lands termed by Pennsylvanians, "the heart of Lancaster County," with a military guard of three hundred militia "with sound of Trumpet before." When some Pennsylvanians set out to cross the Susquehanna to investigate this party, Thomas Cresap, now made a captain as a reward for furthering the interests of Lord Baltimore, urged the troops to fire at their flatboat. The men objected and Cresap swore at them saying, "You're only afraid of your mother's calf skins." He aimed his own blunderbuss at the boat and the militia colonel curtly ordered him not to fire.

"You're a damned coward," said Cresap. "As soon as Lord Baltimore comes over to Maryland he will drive all Pennsylvanians to the Devil and the Court in Philadelphia will be called in his name."

Described as "Dangerous and barbarous" by the Pennsylvania Assembly, as a "Turbulent man" who "breathed Rage and fury, Threatned Distruction, Conserted with his People the Murther of some and burning the Houses of Others," Cresap was now too great a menace to be opposed by moderate measures. Accordingly, Samuel Smith, sheriff of Lancaster County, at the earnest appeal of his neighbors, organized an expedition for the purpose of ridding Pennsylvania of its incorrigible scourge.

In the darkness before sunrise on the Wednesday, November 24, 1736, the sheriff's party "armed with Guns, Pistols & Swords" stealthily surrounded the oft-besieged cabin at "Pleasant Gardens" for the final battle of the Conojacular War. Cresap, ever watchful, wakened "much surprised, I being then in Bed," and demanded that the Pennsylvanians state what they wanted. They replied that he was under arrest for the murder of Knoles Daunt and that he had better give himself up for they now had him in a cage and would not leave until they had taken him, dead or alive.

Cresap later set it down that he replied nobly, saying, "I will not surrender for I am in my own house which is my castle. Neither the laws of God or Man can compel me to surrender and if you attempt to break into my house you can depend on my shooting some of you or at least trying to do so."

The besiegers' memory of the wording of this speech was somewhat different. They said it went like this:

"You damn'd Scotch Irish sons of bitches and you damned Quaking dogs and rogues, why would you fight for a parcel of damned Quaking sons of bitches instead of for a gentleman as I do?"

When the Pennsylvanians tried to persuade him to surrender with alternate promises of decent treatment and threats of siege until thirst killed him or forced him to give himself up, the raging Marylander shouted, "You shall never have me till I am a Corpse." After the sheriff's courteous offer to let his wife and the children withdraw to safety had been contemptuously refused by Hannah who was just then about to add a new baby to the flock, Cresap filled a glass with rum and saying, "I drink damnation to myself and all that are with me if we ever surrender," drained it.

The wily sheriff's next move was to call upon Cresap's companions to desert him promising them protection and a reward, but Cresap's "I'll shoot the first man who tries it" ended consideration of the idea. Dan Sutherland, a Pennsylvanian held captive in the cabin, thought this an opportune moment for escape, however, and startled the besiegers by suddenly popping, like a released Jack-in-the-box, out of the top of the chimney whence, he slid down the roof, and jumped to the ground.

As the day wore on, the besiegers from time to time withdrew to a safe distance to load their guns and share the victuals and rum they had had the foresight to bring across the Susquehanna on Cresap's own flatboat. Whenever they returned within earshot Cresap assailed their ears with renewed oaths or (as he told it) read to them some laws "to make Appear to them the ill Consequences Attending Persons breaking in or Offering so to do or Destroy or Burn Houses. . . ." As sunset neared, the sheriff realized that further talk was useless and led a reckless dash to break down the cabin door. At once the men inside fired at the invaders, and two sudden bulletholes in John Allison's hat served to discourage further frontal attacks.

Disgusted with the poor marksmanship of his guests, their host uttered curses so much louder, deeper and more blasphemous that the sheriff, apparently a pious man, was shocked into the desperate measure of setting fire to a shed adjacent to the cabin. The cabin immediately caught fire and was soon blazing so fiercely that its occupants were faced with being burned alive or leaving. They chose the latter and, opening the door, walked into the open, the imperturbable Hannah, now suffering labor pains brought on by the intense excitement, in the lead.

Tom Cresap was the last to leave his cabin. As he did so there was a volley of shots and a bullet struck and fatally wounded Loughlan Malone, an Irish servant, who had just come to Maryland to establish himself as a free man and had defiantly told the Pennsylvanians he was "resolved rather to lose his Life than be false to his trust."

In his apparently casual account of the final sortie, Cresap wrote, "Several Guns were fired Several of which shots hit me, particularly one in my shoulder, three small shott on my middle finger, and one on my right Eye brow, upon which I made Directly to my Landing." He won the race to his boat, but the men who had last poled it over had tied it securely and while he wrestled desperately with the knot he was overwhelmed by the entire Pennsylvania posse. Riddled with shot, he stood them off there at the dock until they beat him down with guns and clubs and then, when he was helpless, leaped upon him, tied him securely, and set him on the flatboat to take him across the river. The cabin was glowing embers, and darkness had settled on the Susquehanna when they set out with their prisoner who was guarded by two of the posse's strongest men. As they approached midstream, the bound man threw himself against the nearest guard, an Irishman, and upset him into deep water. The rest of the posse, unable to see in the blackness, assumed that their prisoner had dived overboard and at once began beating the struggling man in the water with poles, oars and gun butts. Only sudden recognition that his cries for succor were couched in Irish brogue rather than Yorkshire dialect saved him from being drowned.

In order to make doubly sure that their captive would not elude them, the posse immediately marched him to Lancaster and there employed a Negro blacksmith to fit him with iron handcuffs "which was no sooner done," one of his biographers states, "than, raising both hands together, he gave the smith such a tremendous blow upon his black pate, that it brought him to the ground."

Word that the "Maryland Monster," as his enemies had begun to call him, had been captured spread through Pennsylvania with incredible speed. Some days before the long journey to prison in Philadelphia had ended, the big town's people had heard of his coming. He wore his heavy irons jauntily, striding in the midst of his captors. A vast and noisy crowd lined the city streets and jammed windows and doorways. As these people who thought him an ogre, an inhuman beast in the likeness of a man, shrank away in fear, Tom Cresap turned to George Acton, one of the Pennsylvania guards marching beside him and said, in a voice that all the multitude could hear, "Damn it, this Philadelphia is one of the prettiest towns in Maryland."

Now that Captain Thomas Cresap had been captured and lodged in a Philadelphia jail, the authorities of Maryland at once raised indignant howls of protest. The governor of that province appointed Edmund Jennings and Daniel Dulany to draw up a petition to the President and Council of the Province of Pennsylvania, and these smart lawyers responded with a masterpiece of righteous wrath.

77

They painted a vivid word picture of the burning cabin and "the unhappy Wretches who endeavored to make their Escape from the Flames & defend themselves from those Monsters of Men" (riposte to the Pennsylvania habit of calling Cresap "the Maryland Monster"), and they added that the crime needed "no Colours to heighten the Blackness of it, or words to raise that Horror & Indignation which every humane Breast must feel at the bear Relation."

Governor Sam Ogle and both upper and lower houses of the Maryland Assembly also hastened to send aggrieved representatives to King George II, complaining that Pennsylvania was claiming lands that rightfully belonged to the Calvert grants and deploring the attacks on Cresap who lived on them and had with prosperity defended his "Own House" and been imprisoned for it on charges that were "only groundless Slanders raised Against the poor unhappy man."

The Pennsylvania Council and Assembly had anticipated such action and sent to His Majesty their own arguments with regard to land boundaries, but felt obliged in their lame effort to justify the burning of the cabin to resort to belittling the value of that dwelling ("some round unhewen Timber Logs Piled one on another of not above the value of five pounds Sterling"), to claiming that the Marylanders had killed their own man, Loughlan Malone, and to emphasizing Cresap's utterance of "Horrid Oaths and Imprecations and the Utmost Scurrility of Language."

While the King was considering both communications, the Maryland Monster chose not to languish in his cell. His boasts and curses and animadversions on Pennsylvanians in general so disgusted his jailers that they offered him release, then begged him to go back home, but he would not leave until so ordered by the King. George II very sensibly put an end to the Conojacular War on August 18, 1737, by commanding the residents of both provinces to cease hostilities. Then Thomas Cresap returned to Pleasant Gardens to his wife and offspring (including the new child who was being born even as he was being overpowered and taken across the Susquehanna).

The rest of Thomas Cresap's story, though important to the history of the western frontier, little concerns the Susquehanna River. Disgruntled that the King's Proclamation prevented his further bedeviling the Pennsylvanians, against whom he held a lifelong prejudice, he moved westward, then bought land along the Potomac and from his holdings there conducted his real estate dealings in Ohio and other western regions. He was in his early forties when he left Pleasant Gardens. As a champion of British expansion, he took an active part in the French and Indian Wars, then turned against his former employers as colonial resentment of English rule led to revolution. Always arrogant, aggressive and quarrelsome, always delighting in disagreement and physical combat, he was hailed into court by his enemies many times and never failed to oppose them with unflinching courage and crafty skill. He was a famous Indian fighter, but at the same time a valued ally of those savages who were friendly to the white man and who, because of the generous helpings he dipped for them from his ever-simmering kettle, dubbed him "Big Spoon." The famous surveyors Mason and Dixon were undoubtedly glad in 1763 that his attention had been diverted from the fixing of the

Maryland-Pennsylvania border when they finally accomplished it.

When he was seventy-six Cresap made a sentimental journey to his native Yorkshire, but his renewed love of his birthplace had no effect on his growing resentment of English rule. When, twelve days after the battle of Bunker Hill, a captain's commission arrived for Michael Cresap, who was away from home, Thomas, then in his eighties, happily announced he would lead his son's company to join General Washington's army, but Michael returned before the march began. Because of his record as a fighter, his cunning, his everlasting cranky aggressiveness, he was frequently referred to as a "Rattlesnake Colonel," a somewhat derisive term indicating an assumed but unofficial rank. His deals in real estate were generally very successful, and his dwellings were ever set at strategic points in the western progress toward valuable lands. He journeyed by land and water to a small island near Nova Scotia when he was ninety and was so pleased with himself as an explorer that he proposed to undertake an expedition to the Pacific coast which he was probably still planning in 1790 when he died at the age of ninety-six. Obviously puzzled that Providence had awarded a man of his sort so long a life span, a Methodist preacher, John J. Jacob, who had married son Michael's widow, wrote of him, "Although we believe every man is under the protection of Providence, yet . . . it would seem to appear that this old gentleman was more specially and peculiarly preserved."

7

The Oneida at Shamokin

❧ *A man's soul there may dwell in the*
roof of his house, in a tree, by a spring
of water, or on some mountain scaur.

—REVEREND JAMES MACDONALD, QUOTED BY
SIR JAMES GEORGE FRAZER IN *The Golden Bough*

Sunbury was once Shamokin, and Shamokin was the center of a great star of Indian trails that crossed where the West and the North branches of the Susquehanna join. It was inevitable that there should be a village there, though surprising that it should be so small (less than ten Indian dwellings) at the beginning of the eighteenth century. Nevertheless it was important, more important than larger towns above and below it, for here dwelt Shikellamy, vice-regent appointed by the Iroquois Confederacy to supervise the Susquehanna valley tribes that it had conquered.

Many of his prominent contemporaries, white and red, knew Shikellamy well, and some appraised him in writings modern historians know. These records only accentuate the mistiness of the aura in which he walked. There can be no doubt that the aura existed, however, for all his associates displayed a reverent feeling for this massive,

81

quiet man whose life was governed by motives of peace and good will.

Shikellamy had at an early age been adopted into the Oneida tribe, but his friends contradicted each other as to his origins. The most important of Pennsylvania's ambassadors to the Indians, Conrad Weiser, who had lived among the Iroquois tribes for years in his childhood, thought him a Cayuga. John Bartram, self-educated Quaker botanist, had bitter prejudices against Indians which may have encouraged him to believe that the sachem was, as he wrote, "a Frenchman born at Mont-real, and adopted by the Oneidoes, after being taken prisoner." Later admirers point out that the Iroquois conquered the tall and noble Susquehannocks and argue, since it was an Oneida custom to adopt captives into the tribe, the Shamokin diplomat may have been one of these.

Whatever his antecedents, the chieftain had already merited his name (Shikellamy is Oneida for "He has lighted the sky for us") when in 1728 he took up his duties at the confluence of the two branches of the Susquehanna. Twice in that year he made the long journey to Philadelphia to confer with the Provincial Council on Indian problems. Two years later, he went north to Onondaga to invite the chiefs of the Six Nations to come to Philadelphia to "brighten the chain of friendship" existing between them and the English. When he returned in December of 1731, with the message that the chiefs, being old and unable to make so long a journey in the winter, would come when the sun was warmer and the days were longer, his words were interpreted to the white men by his friend Conrad Weiser. The sun apparently did not become hot enough until the following August. Then the aged chiefs were heartily received, and it was decided by agreement between them and the Council that Shikellamy and Weiser should be accepted as permanent liaison officers between the Iroquois and the British authorities.

In the years that followed, Shikellamy welcomed to his home at the meeting of the waters many white men. Down the steep trail that led from a high crest above the river to Shamokin came the hotheaded and argumentative Count Zinzendorf, leader of a band of Moravian missionaries. With Conrad Weiser as guide, four Moravians and two Indian converts (baptized David and Joshua) as companions, the young German nobleman traversed the wilderness and, in time, "struck the lovely Susquehanna." Soon thereafter, he reported, they reached "a precipitous hill such as I scarce ever saw." Anna Nitschmann, a twenty-seven-year-old Moravian, boldly led the descent. "I took the train of her riding-habit in my hand to steady me in the saddle," wrote Zinzendorf. "Conrad held to the skirt of my overcoat, and Boehler to Conrad's. In this way we mutually supported each other, and the Savior assisted us in descending the hill in safety."

The Indian they had come to see was a more mature and kindly philosopher than the opinionated and condescending young proselyte. The spiritual message that the visitors brought was welcome and acceptable to the Oneida who had, through the traditional beliefs of his race and through his own experience, arrived at a serene personal philosophy which held few denials of Christian teachings.

Shikellamy had been a deeply religious man long before the Moravians clambered down the hillside to convert him. In the winter of 1737 when he and his friend

Weiser had set out for Onandaga on a mission of peace, they painfully struggled along the icy walls of a valley "between two terrible mountains." There, as recorded in Weiser's journal, Shikellamy "caught hold of a flat stone sticking in the root of a fallen tree, which came loose, and his feet slipping out from under him, he fell at a place which was steeper than the roof of a house." Unable to stop himself, he hurtled down the slope and would have gone over a hundred-foot cliff to his death on jagged rocks below had not his pack "passed on one side of a sapling and he on the other so that he remained hanging on the strap." Terror-stricken, his companions inched their way to his side, and after he had been rescued they crept down the rest of the slope in silence. "When we reached the valley," wrote Weiser, "Shikelimo looked around at the height of the steep precipice on which he had fallen. We looked at him; he stood still in astonishment, and said: 'I thank the great Lord and Creator of the world that he had mercy on me, and wished me to continue to live longer.'"

Not long thereafter the noble chief saved the life of his white friend under circumstances that revealed the consistency of his philosophy and his superiority in character. Weiser, uncertain in his religious convictions and often led astray by emotional storms, told the story to Count Zinzendorf before the two of them reached Shamokin, and the Moravian saw fit to set it down in the teller's words:

> While on a journey to Onondaga, whither I had been sent to negotiate a peace between the Iroquois and the Cherokees, and while passing through a savage wilderness, I was one day so completely exhausted that I left my companions, and sat down by a

tree, resolved to die. Starvation stared me in the face, and death by freezing was preferable to death by hunger. They hallooed and shot signal guns, but I remained quiet.

Shikellamy was the first one to discover me. Coming before me, he stood on deep thought, and in silence, and after some time asked me why I was there. 'I am here to die,' I replied. 'Ah brother,' said he, 'only lately you entreated us not to despond, and will you now give way to despair?' Not in the least shaken in my resolution to this appeal, I replied by saying 'My good Shikellamy, as death is inevitable, I will die where I am, and nothing shall prevail upon me to leave this spot.' 'Ah, brother,' resumed the sachem, 'you told me that we were prone to forget God in bright days and to remember Him in dark days. These are dark days. Let us then not forget God; and who knows but what He is even now near, and about to come to our succor?' Rise, brother, and we will journey on.' I felt ashamed at this rebuke administered by a poor heathen, rose, and dragged myself away.

Zinzendorf persisted in regarding Shikellamy as a savage despite this story and incidents that proved the sincerity and mature dignity of the sachem: ". . . perceiving he had no shirt, I handed him one, begging him to accept it as a token of my childlike intercourse with him and not as a gift. 'I thank you,' he replied as he took it. . . .

"On Saturday, the 28th, we wished to pray the Litany but the merry-making of the Indians disconcerted us. I accordingly dispatched Conrad to Sachem Shikellimy to inform him that we were about to speak to our God. This had the desired effect . . . the beating of drums ceased and the voices of the Indians were hushed. . . ."

In the following decade, the town of Shamokin more than doubled in size. The builders of the new houses were not fit to associate with their distinguished neighbor. Shikellamy had his own house placed on high pillars to protect it from entry by roisterers. He made protest to the British governor against the sale of alcoholic liquors to Indians, and he continued to fight against drunkenness among his people to the end of his days. Though his wife on at least one occasion became drunk, he would not drink because, he said, he did not wish to become a fool.

Shikellamy performed his diplomatic duties conscientiously and successfully. He did much to keep the Iroquois loyal to the British when the French were trying their best to curry Indian favor. When disaffected tribesmen stated that they had heard from underground reports of British plots against them, he replied that the rumor had indeed come from underground, the ground under their own homes.

Other missionaries visited his home at Shamokin—Christian Frederick Post, David Brainerd, John Hagen, Bishop Joseph Spangenberg, Bishop J. C. F. Cammerhof, and John Martin Mack and his wife, an earnest couple who chose to live at Shamokin. All were cordially welcomed and fed by the old gentleman who in humility offered them the best of what he had.

As the town grew larger, life became hideous at Shamokin. The Indians danced and yelled and drank and sometimes threatened to kill the pious Moravians. Shikellamy walked in dignity among rioting and the dissolute. At night, he retired to his high house, shut and barred the door.

In October of 1747, Conrad Weiser wrote a letter to the governing Council in Philadelphia: "I was surprised to see Shickelmy in such a miserable Condition as ever my Eies beheld he was hardly to stretch forth his hand to bid me welcome." A fever had struck the vice-regent's entire family. Three had died and the others were deathly sick. At the end of his letter, Weiser said:

> I must. . . . Recommend Shickelmy as a proper object of Charity he is extremely poor in his Sickness the horses has eat all his Corn his clothes he gave to Indian Doctors to Cure him and his family. . . . he has no Body to hunt for him and I cannot see how the poor old man Can Live he has been a true Servant to the Government. . . .

A year later, the old chieftain left his home on the Susquehanna to visit the Moravian Mission at Bethlehem. He knew that his end was near and he wanted to find out more about the creed which gave solace and serenity to those who believed in it. He told the brothers of the faith there that when he was a young child he had been baptized by a Roman Catholic father in Canada, and the Moravians told him that there was no need for another such ceremony. They said, though, that the true Christian forswears the symbols of other faiths, and suggested that he take from his neck the little manitou that he wore there as a magic protection against disease. To prove his conversion to their beliefs, he threw this "graven image" away. On his way home, then, a sickness came upon him. Moravian David Zeisberger joined him and helped him totter back to the house standing on the pillars. Once there, he lay down to die. Death came slow, but when the cold time of the Wolf Moon drew near, Shikellamy weakened. On December 6, 1748, the sky darkened along the river, for he who lighted it had ceased to be.

Three days later, a procession wound through the town

87

to the Indian burying ground beside the running waters. Now the wild rioters lamented, loud in grief. The wooden coffin that sheltered the old body also held the provisions that the family thought Shikellamy might need on his long journey to the country beyond the Milky Way.

8

The King of the English Houses

❧ When I am alone, I am very little in myself.

—TEEDYUSCUNG

On the twelfth of March, 1750, a big swarthy middle-aged man in a spreading white robe knelt in the shadowy interior of the little Moravian chapel beside Mahanoy Creek at Huts of Grace (Gnadenhütten). Though the words of the ritual, intoned in the guttural language of the officiating missionaries, were unintelligible to him, the Indian Teedyuscung knew that when he rose after partaking of the sacrament he would be Gideon, a baptized Christian.

As he walked into the light outside where shadows of little turrets on the roof made patterns on the ground he saw a familiar landscape—the neat farmhouses and outbuildings of the German settlers, the sawmill, and, eastward across the creek the log houses of his own people lying in a dark half-moon arc against the new-greening orchards behind them, and he was greatly moved. He had longed for this moment. Born to Delaware parents a half century before, near Trenton, New Jersey, he had been smart and sensitive enough to know the contempt of white neighbors for his people and not wise enough to realize that being an Indian had its compensations. Unlike the great Shickellamy, whose courage, serene philosophy and pride of race had made him respected and obeyed along the Susquehanna, Teedyuscung admired the whites for their way of life and at the same time felt a jealous hatred of them. He had yearned all of his earlier years to "belong," to be a part of a civilization from which he was a lonely outcast, a poor man dependent on the pennies he received for weaving baskets. When, at fifty, he had watched the conscientious efforts of the Moravian men of God to bring an understanding of Christianity to the Indians, he was overcome with emotion. After seeing a baptism he reported to one of the missionaries, "I cannot describe it but I wept and trembled."

The Moravians were doubtful of the advisability of christening this "Gideon" even as they performed the ceremony. Though his desire to be one of their brotherhood was not to be questioned, they knew him to be a man of much wickedness, "unstable as water and like a reed shaken with the wind," a drinking man capable, some said, of putting away a gallon of rum a day without seeming to be drunk. "The chief among sinners," wrote the Moravian bishop that day into the record of his baptism.

The forebodings of the white Christians were soon justified. Among the peaceful dwellers in the Huts of Grace —German clergy, English converts, Pennsylvanian Delawares, Wampanoags from New England, and other Indians of that region—was a Mohican who had been baptized as Abraham. The first Moravian convert in America, he had belonged to a mission at Shecomeco in Connecticut in 1745 when racial feeling during King George's War grew so strong that even Christian Indians were no longer safe. Following an established policy of presenting homeless tribes with such lands as would make them buffer units capable of protecting their northern confederacy from white invasion, the Great Council of the Iroquois had granted the request of the German Moravians to permit the frightened Connecticut group to make a settlement on the grassy Wyoming meadows along the Susquehanna. This, despite their fright, the mission Indians firmly refused to do because, as they said virtuously, the proposed new site was in "a country abounding in savages where the women are so wanton as to seduce the men."

Whether this argument had proved more alluring than repelling to Teedyuscung is not known, but the Delaware, with Abraham as collaborator, was soon heading a considerable dissident group of Indians demanding that the Huts of Grace on the Mahanoy be abandoned for others on the Susquehanna. Ambition had led him to picture himself as an important chieftain controlling not through the matriarchal heritage-law of his tribe but through strength and courage the Indian population at the very important spot where white influence ended and Iroquois sovereignty began. And so in the months that followed Teedyuscung, unaware that both in character and mentality he was unsuited to face the multiple and complicated conflicts that would center about the river lands, was the most ardent advocate of removal northward to the Susquehanna flats.

By 1753 the Wyoming country, then occupied by an inconsiderable number of non-Christian Nanticokes, Mohicans, and Delawares, was highly prized by the French who were edging eastward from Ohio and by the people of Connecticut who, after years of disregarding the fact, were now emphatically proclaiming that King Charles II had granted their colony ownership of these lands some nineteen years before he had granted them to William Penn. Settlement of the strategic valley by a friendly population therefore seemed most desirable from the respective points of view of the Iroquois and of the Pennsylvanians. Teedyuscung realized that he could please the authorities in control by moving a number of Indians to Wyoming and by so doing become a leader whose power must be reckoned with. The motivation of his tragedy had been established.

There were many prayerful discussions in the Huts of Grace before action indicated that the curtain was rising on the drama to be played in the amphitheater of the Susquehanna bend at Wyoming. Though the majority of the Indians of the settlement bitterly opposed removal, the missionaries took the democratic stand expressed by Bishop Spangenburg in a letter to Conrad Weiser: "No one here is required to stay; whoever wants to go, we will not restrain him." Of the five hundred only seventy chose to leave their families and friends and go with Gideon and Abraham. They gathered to begin their journey to Wyoming late in the April of 1754. Many had premonitions that their faith would be put to severe test in the new land to the north where they would live among followers of the old "pagan" beliefs without the counsel of white teachers' creed of Christ, and they wept and renewed their vows of everlasting loyalty to Him. As they turned their tearful faces northward and set their feet on the Wyoming trail, neither they nor Teedyuscung realized how soon their trial would come.

Two months later Martin Mack, one of the missionaries

at Huts of Grace, visited the Wyoming Indians on a mission prompted by solicitude and found them confused and troubled. The Connecticut claimants were belligerently announcing that they would shoot the Indians' horses and cattle if they would not bargain for the acres on which they lived. The Pennsylvanians were demanding that they repel all Yankee efforts to settle near them. And a week after Mack's arrival Major George Washington surrendered Fort Necessity in Ohio, thereby strengthening immeasurably the prestige of its French conquerors. Teedyuscung, still aspiring to be ruler of the harassed Indians, faced a situation that would have confounded much abler brains than his. Though both Christians and pagans (members of the Nanticoke, Delaware, Shawnee, Mohican and other tribes) considered him their leader, he was troubled as he began to realize that he would soon be forced to ally himself and his people with one of the contending forces.

At Albany, in July of 1754, he was convinced that his future would be bright if he continued his loyalty to the English cause and the government of Pennsylvania. He was greatly disturbed to discover later, however, that unauthorized but prominent Iroquois chiefs had "sold" the Susquehanna lands to Connecticut. After a year of tortured indecision, the depredations of his old friends, the French-influenced Indians from Ohio—including the massacre of a number of white missionaries and Christian Indians at Huts of Grace—convinced him of an ultimate conquest of the Susquehanna lands from that direction, and he went on the warpath for the French. A few minor but successful winter raids on plantations near the Delaware River had the surprising result of making the English and the Iroquois, who had previously ignored him, recognize him as an important figure.

Suddenly the pendulum of success swung toward the English and, after a visit to Niagara where the French failed, despite bribes, to satisfy him that they would eventually win, Teedyuscung loftily offered to negotiate a peace with his former English friends in Easton at the forks of the Delaware. The Pennsylvanians were delighted to accept, and the big warrior began preparations for an event which would prove the happiest of his life.

He rode through Bethlehem, lately grown to a town of eight hundred, and he saw nearby at Huts of Grace the evidences of the massacre, the charred ashes of the chapel where he had been baptized, the lonely ruins of the homes of the murdered. He had left his former friends in the humble garb of a convert. He had worn the black hat over the long hair that distinguished the Christian Indian's head from the shaven poll of the wild warrior. His body had been covered with a drab costume (shirt and pants) like that worn by his companions of the little mission where all were taught to scorn personal vanity. These, like the vows of his baptism, he put aside for habiliments more suited to the person of the "King of Ten Nations" as he now called himself. On his great torso rippled the folds of a garment given him by the French, "a fine dark brown Cloth Coat very much laced with gold." Beneath it English pants of a checkered pattern were short enough to show stockings trimmed in scarlet that was sometimes mirrored in just-bought silver buckles affixed to his riding boots. He had traded a female English prisoner for his fine horse, and he sat on a new saddle of gleaming leather. Behind him in colorful parade moved his painted

94

warriors and their wives who wore shirts cut from bright tablecloths which, during raids, had been snatched from the tables of burning Dutch homes.

Though Easton was but a log-cabin Persepolis for this tawdry latter-day Tamerlane, it was still sweet to be a king and ride its streets. Teedyuscung's triumph there was heightened by the report that on his way from Bethlehem he had struck dead, possibly to avenge the massacre of his old friends, a Shawnee warrior who had been one of those participating in the French-Indian raid on Huts of Grace. By the time of the public dinner cunningly given in his honor by the governor of Pennsylvania, the King of Ten Nations was so overcome with the recognition of his rank and glory that, looking over the table where sat twenty-three of his retinue (seven of them sons, grandsons, or nephews) each flanked with distinguished white men, he burst into a flood of tears, told his white brothers he had been a bad King and made them all the promises they asked of him.

Even as he rode proudly back to his Susquehanna home, feeling that whether the English or the French were successful he would be safely in their favor, a magnificent idea was forming in his mind. He broached it a year later at another treaty-gathering at Easton. His people, he told the English, should live on the flats of Wyoming in houses of such European excellence as no Indians had inhabited before. Now that the danger of attack from the French was lessening, he would establish an English town with Indian residents on the Susquehanna meadows. The Quakers of the Pennsylvania Assembly were touched by this appeal. When they heard that the governor had promised to send white carpenters and laborers up the river to build such houses for the King and his people, they saw to it that five hundred pounds was appropriated from the Colony treasury "towards erecting Indian houses at Wyoming." The construction party which consisted of about one hundred and fifty whites guarded by a company of militia did not move its boats up the Susquehanna until the late fall of 1757, however, and Teedyuscung sent them back home and decided to lead his band to Bethlehem for the winter.

He led them back through the new leaves of mid-May, 1758. A Moravian missionary recorded the departure with some bitterness: "on the going out of these spirits 'The Crown' [a tavern] was swept and garnished and Ephraim Colver, the publican, had rest." The carpenters and builders had come back to Wyoming, and the houses were raised as the new corn lifted above the dark earth. For a while the King lived in the most elaborate of them, surrounded by his warriors whom he admonished to live in such polite and civilized ways as befitted their habitations. He had himself taken on what he believed to be the customs and social attitudes of a colonial governor. He strolled about in his English house clad in an elegant vested suit of tobacco-colored broadcloth and shalloon given him by the Quakers and adorned at his own order with buckram, mohair silk, linen, and forty-two shiny buttons. He dipped snuff, drank rum, played cards, refreshed himself with gingerbread made tastier with molasses, all in a manner he assumed to be that of a British gentleman. Only the problem of continuing such a happy situation troubled him. Though weakening, the French had not given up their ambitions to conquer the Susquehanna lands. The Iroquois, moreover, looked upon the English houses with distrust, wondering what bargain the self-titled King had struck with the white men to obtain them. They had heard a rumor that there would be an English fort at Wyoming. The lack of respect in which he was held by the Six Nations' chiefs made Teedyuscung morose and he continually found escape from melancholy in being drunk. One of his Quaker friends, surprisingly gay and brutally frank, told him in un-Quakerlike language:

> Teedyuscung You are a *damn'd* Fool. You shou'd go over to Your Brother, King George and shake hands with him and tell your own story and Then You would have justice done You; for many an one has made themselves clever Fellows who could not tell so strait a story as you can. But you would get so damned Drunk you would fall over Board and be drowned.

The King of Ten Nations answered such accusations with dignity and wit. "The Indians think it no harm to get drunk whenever they can," he would say. "But you white men say it is a sin and get drunk notwithstanding." Nevertheless criticism increased his deep feeling of inferiority. In a rare moment of honest self-appraisal he said, "When I am alone I am very little in my self."

The Iroquois in 1758 decided that they had had enough of the braggart King's boasting and posing and they so informed the English at Easton. "We do not know he is such a great Man. If he is such a great Man, we desire to know who has made him so?" As their attacks became more bitter Teedyuscung defended himself with the only weapons of diplomacy he knew—evasion and appeasement. He had come to the treaty meeting in a drunken state, mouthing blasphemous English oaths, threatening to cut English throats, calling the Six Nations fools, proclaiming that he was "King of All Nations and of

97

the World." A few days later, meek, miserable and sober, he addressed his "uncles," the Iroquois, begging them to give him permanent title to the Wyoming meadows.

"I sit there as a Bird on a Bow," he said pitifully. "I look about and do not know where to go; let me therefore come down upon the Ground, and make that my own by a good Deed, and I shall then have a Home forever."

Shrewdly the Iroquois encouraged him but evaded direct action. They still felt that the Delaware King's settlement on the Susquehanna fortified them against the whites of Pennsylvania, Connecticut, and France, any or all of whom might yet prove dangerous to their ascendancy. The Pennsylvania authorities did their best to inflame him against the growing threat of a Yankee invasion and, once more feeling important, King Teedyuscung went back to his English houses to work at further Anglicizing his willing but ever-backsliding subjects.

By 1760 the French power to the west had all but disappeared, and the Wyoming Indians could congratulate themselves that their chief had wisely guided them in the ways of the victorious British. His vanity was further fed when at his own suggestion he was sent by William Hamilton, new governor of Pennsylvania, with two white companions (one of whom was Christian Frederick Post, Moravian missionary whose wife was a Delaware Indian) to represent the colony at Fort Pitt where a great treaty-meeting of the Ohio tribes had been scheduled for July. The white men observed, as the expedition moved up the Susquehanna, that the Indian King on two successive days lectured the approximate dozen of his retinue on their table manners and their neglect of polite and ethical conduct. His audience, they noticed, was obviously bored.

When the party reached the upper Susquehanna, Tee-dyuscung was emphatically made aware of a new obstacle in the road which he still hoped to travel to popular eminence among both whites and Indians. For months the Munsee tribe and others had been increasingly disgusted with the hypocrisy and double-dealing of all whites. The contradictions between creed, as taught by the missionaries, and deed, as exemplified by avaricious land-grabbers, had fostered among them a desire to return to their native religious teachings and the customs of their fathers. In a town of forty well-built bark houses not far from Wyalusing they formed a community which, according to Christian Post's journal, was "strictly adhering to the Antient Customs and Manners of Their Forefathers, thinking it is pleasing to God That they strictly observe and keep the same." Though a kindly people, they were unalterably opposed to receiving any instruction from whites and particularly determined not to drink the rum which had debauched many of their race.

At Assinsink above Tioga the travelers found no prejudice against rum, but an enthusiastic revolt against all other white influences. There, after the May moon had waned and the slim arc of the first summer moon dropped its image in the river, the King of Ten Nations and his companions saw primeval rituals danced wildly in the meadows to the rhythms of water drums and high-pitched ululating song. In the straight black hair of the dancers were bright spring flowers. On their dark-skinned naked torsos they had painted in vivid colors birds which

101

their movements seemed to set flying, writhing snakes, and animals of the forest. In their hands were green wands waving in unison as they performed the dance figures. Between dances they enacted the ancient ceremonials of thanksgiving to the spirits of wild beasts—the bear sacrifice (in which a hog was substituted because no bear could be found), the clothing of the eldest man in the skin of the first deer killed that season. Eloquent orators described dream-visions they had beheld and interpreted them while their hearers shouted staccato cries of approval.

The white men were frightened as they saw the growing emotional intensity of the crowd. They were not comforted when they saw the King of Ten Nations, known along the Susquehanna as the man "who would make Indians into Englishmen," stop playing his English game of cards and race into the midst of the swaying dancers. Before the two departed from that place they were to face a mob of Indians drunk with rum who threatened to roast them in their fires and were dissuaded only by intervention of their Indian host.

While Teedyuscung was in Ohio, still another threat to his plans developed. The threatened invasion by Connecticut had begun with a settlement at Cushietunk (Coshecton) on the Delaware. On his return, however, he found that this had brought about an increase in his importance. While the Iroquois still would not grant him the land on which stood his precious English houses, they recognized the advantage of his living in them and willingness to protect them from Yankee encroachment. Basking once more in the favor of his "uncles" and claiming more than was his rightful share of the credit for the peaceful attitude of the Ohio tribes, the Delaware King, during the years of 1761 and 1762, lent his services to the Quakers who were deep in the complicated political intrigues of Pennsylvania and New York. He denounced rum, but he drank more of it than ever. He recommended Christian virtues and spoke wistfully of the days when he had known the peace of mind of a new convert, but his vanity and self-importance would not let him seek it again.

In the summer of 1762 he and his male subjects traveled importantly to Lancaster for the formal peace treaty with the Indians of the west. There to his happiness he witnessed the return of the Ohio tribes to the English sphere of influence. His joy was even greater when Tom King, chieftain representing the Six Nations, emphatically restated the Iroquois claim to Wyoming, ordered him to live there and protect it, and finally presented him with a belt of wampum as official seal of the command, saying, "By this Belt I make a Fire for Teedyuscung at Wyoming."

When he came back to his royal seat, however, he discovered to his horror that Tom King, preceding him up the Susquehanna to report the treaty to the Iroquois, had on September twenty-second come upon an armed expedition of 119 Yankees making themselves at home beside the stream. They had built huts for themselves, planted several acres of grain, cut fifteen tons of hay. More ominous still was the fact that they had cut from the Delaware to the Susquehanna a road which they said two hundred Connecticut families would soon travel to Wyoming. Tom had waited to tell Teedyuscung this. He said he had threatened the Yankees who had rather indifferently agreed to leave, having done most of the work they had planned. They started back to Connecticut boasting that they would return with an overwhelming number of companions in the coming spring and they would be protected by artillery.

Teedyuscung had been considering what steps he would take in such a case when he was amazed by the arrival early in October of a hundred and fifty New Englanders planning to build houses and settle on the riverbank a few miles to the north of the English houses. At the head of his Wyoming band the big chief ranted and scolded until the Yankees again left. "I threatened them hard," he reported to Governor William Hamilton in Philadelphia.

The invaders had no sooner gone than fourteen more of the same sort appeared announcing that they intended to build a sawmill only a mile above Teedyuscung's home. When he protested, he said they offered to employ him "to assist them in surveying the lands," an insult which brought from him such threats that they buried their tools and set out on their return journey, arrogantly announcing that, come spring, they would be back as part of an army of three thousand Connecticut men.

Less than a week after they had gone another small party of nine Yankees—eight whites and a mulatto—insolently signalized their arrival by stealing the King's horse. This so enraged Teedyuscung that by threatening to deliver them as prisoners to the Pennsylvania governor he compelled them to give him another mount and five pounds besides.

All that winter, after Teedyuscung's visit to Philadelphia where he received pledges of support, the big man, whom the Moravian Bishop Spangenburg had called "the

Apostate who had raised himself to a King," took council with his wisest subjects as to how they would meet the invasion of the persistent men of Connecticut. Some were for removing at once to Ohio, but the assurances of help from the Iroquois and colonial officials prevailed. In the meantime the Yankees were sending more and more bloodthirsty threats to Wyoming.

With the spring came suspense—weeks of quiet, uncertain waiting. No recent word had come from the East. Now that the Connecticut people felt the combined weight of their opposition perhaps they would give up their greedy scheme.

On the evening of April 19, 1763, as the Delaware King lay asleep, fire licked along the outside walls of the English house the white carpenters had built for him. Soon it was a roaring pyre within which lay the huge seared corpse of Teedyuscung. The homes of the Indians he had striven to make into Englishmen were blazing, too, and their occupants, terror-stricken, racing away to other communities for safety. In the morning the English houses were a pathetic row—each in its separate place a pile of ashes, broken melted glass, and those domestic articles that fire sometimes passes over—a pipe, a kettle, a child's toy.

The Yankees were quick to deny the murder of the man who had stood in their way. They said the Iroquois were guilty. But the Iroquois to the north and the Pennsylvanians to the south did not believe them. Teedyuscung had been a faithful protector of the land, they said, and even as they said it, a dozen New England families arrived in the forsaken valley, followed in mid-May by a hundred and fifty more, many of these the very ones whom the Delaware King had thundered at in October.

Their cows browsed in the grassy bottoms, their corn showed green above the dark loam of hundreds of level acres. Unopposed, the Yankees raised blockhouse forts. They said this was Connecticut land and they were here to stay. The tale of the big vain drunken King with his fancy clothes and his boasts of power, his troubled indecisive mind and his dream of ruling mannered, Anglicized Indians in a town of English houses beside the Susquehanna brought laughter to Yankee firesides at Wyoming.

9

Pennymites vs. Yankees

THE CONNECTICUT–PENNSYLVANIA WARS

Revenge for the burning of the King of the English Houses came soon. In mid-October Captain Bull, Teedyuscung's son, was emboldened by the western uprising of Pontiac to take the warpath. He led his band into Northampton County where they slew fifty-four whites (about half he killed with his own hands), then moved on to the place of his father's murder. There, they captured nearly all of a settlement of about forty Yankees. Two days afterward a military company, sent against the Indians by the Pennsylvania colony, found the scalped bodies of nine men and one woman. "The woman was roasted," wrote a soldier of the expedition, "and had two hinges in her hands—supposed to be put in red hot—and several of the men had awls thrust through their eyes." When Thomas Penn, then in England, heard this, he wrote, "I am concerned for the fate of those deluded Connecticut people, tho the consequence of their own folly."

Now there were no houses at Wyoming, no white settlers on the upper river. The Indians had saved the Pennsylvanians the trouble of driving the Yankees from the lands they claimed. But the Connecticut men would not

107

be deterred. Though their New England counties were not so crowded as to compel removal elsewhere, they were motivated, as Julian Parks Boyd, distinguished historian of their enterprises, has pointed out, both by land fever and by a "crowded state of mind." Many felt as did the sixty-eight comprising the population of Suffield, that their town had "Grown full of Inhabantants so that a Great many must unavoidably move to Sum other place." This and similar arguments brought about the founding of the Susquehanna Company in the summer of 1753 "To Spread Christianity as also to promote our own Temporal Interest." Other colonies felt that the Connecticut men had by specious rationalizations reversed in their own minds the order of importance of these motives. In the Hudson valley, through which the Yankees must pass to arrive at their Susquehanna claims, Lewis Morris, a respected man of property, wrote into his will that his son, Gouverneur, should never for his education be sent into "the Colony of Connecticut, lest he should imbibe in his youth that low craft and cunning so incident to the people of that country, which is so interwoven in their constitutions that all their art cannot disguise it from the world, though many of them under the sanctified garb of religion, have endeavored to impose themselves on the world as honest men."

Though the Susquehanna Company came into existence in the summer of 1753, the threat of a considerable armed invasion of Pennsylvania did not materialize until sixteen years later. Then, on May 12, 1769, a large body of armed Yankees, under the leadership of Major John Durkee, proved that they meant business. Within one week of their arrival at Wyoming, they erected twenty-five roomy cabins, and a week later they were briskly raising a tall stockade around them. Fort Durkee, as they called this settlement, was completed before, at the order of Governor John Penn, a Philadelphia company of Pennsylvania militia could be sent up the Susquehanna. On the twentieth of June, the Yankees behind the timbered walls saw this unit, under command of Colonel Turbut Francis, "in full military array with colors streaming and martial music" parade down the mountain plain. The fort, however, proved too formidable for direct attack and the colonel marched his smart command back downriver.

Siege was soon renewed with Captain Amos Ogden in command of Pennsylvania troops which were augmented by a large posse raised by the sheriff of Northampton County. Captain Durkee and several of his men were captured by surprise, and the fort was soon forced to surrender. So began the first of the three interregional conflicts known to the Yankees as the Pennymite Wars. Five times the New England settlers were driven from their homes in the two years that followed—but the dogged Yankees would not give up. Again and again, they were forced to leave the fertile valley and plod on rocky trails over precipitous cliffs, and through the junglelike woods, to return to their friends and families in Connecticut. Yet they would not be denied. They grew to fear the Pennymites, as they called the Pennsylvanians who opposed them, more than they did hostile Indians. They plowed and reaped the Susquehanna bottoms with anxious eyes on the hill slopes, rifles within easy reach. Some of them died as a result of the sufferings inflicted on them by hard and cruel men of their own race. All New England was horrified by the story of a young widow who roasted the body of her starved-to-death baby in order to feed the rest of her brood as they stumbled over the high passes of the Connecticut trail. Yankees caught in sudden raids by fellow-American settlers were beaten and chained, imprisoned and starved in the effort to make them promise to go back where they came from and not return.

The disturbances known as the Pennymite Wars are usually considered to be three. The first, between armed bands of settlers in the two English colonies of Connecticut and Pennsylvania, ended in 1771 with the Yankees definitely in the ascendancy. The second saw small armies of the disagreeing areas engaged in military combat during 1775 while the American Revolution was being desperately fought and while General Washington was in dire need of every available man for his dwindling forces. The third, 1783-84, involved an effort to establish a new state, populated by Yankees, within the boundaries of the State of Pennsylvania.

PENNYMITE WAR I

❦ CONNECTICUT INVADES PENNSYLVANIA

The first bloodshed in the struggle took place in 1769 after the Yankees had obtained unexpected help from a strong downriver ally. Six years before, despairing of adequate defense against Indians from colony authorities, John Elder, a Presbyterian dominie, had organized a band of mounted rangers from the men of his Scotch-Irish congregation living just south of Harris's Ferry (now Harrisburg) in a settlement known as Paxtang. The grim precepts of Calvinism were more consistent

110

with cruel fanaticism than with the gentle teachings of Moravian missionaries or the peaceful democratic creed of Quakers, and the "Paxtang Boys" were known throughout the region for their swift, merciless raids against the Indians. Soon this band of hard-riding, sure-shooting Presbyterians had struck fear into the hearts of the hostile tribes, and there is little doubt that their very existence prevented many a massacre of white settlers. To the Paxtang Calvinists, however, even an Indian convert to Christianity could never be of God's elect, nor could he be trusted not to return to his treacherous heathen ways. The only solution of the problem of frontier security, said the bold troopers of Paxtang, was the annihilation of the entire Indian race. News of the vengeful massacre of the Yankees at Wyoming by Captain Bull, Teedyuscung's son, had no sooner come down the Susquehanna than the riders planned a rendezvous. Since they did not know where they could find the offending savages, they decided to attack a peaceful Indian village of Christian Conestogas, near Lancaster. Among these, some Pennsylvania historians say, were the last remnants of the noble, deep-voiced, giant people whom Captain John Smith had admired—the Susquehannocks. Accepting as truth a malicious rumor that a few Conestogas had either been of Captain Bull's party or had furnished some of them secret refuge, the Paxtang Boys planned vengeance.

Vainly Dominie Elder ordered them to desist. The riders threatened to shoot the old man's horse, and he withdrew. Then, led by twenty-nine-year-old Lazarus Stewart, the Paxtang Boys rode for Lancaster. They later claimed that their intention was merely to force removal of the Conestogas, but when a few of the Indians, surprised on

111

October fourteenth by an early-morning attack, tried to defend themselves, the white men massacred by gunfire every Indian man, woman and child in the village. Then they rode back to Paxtang. On discovering later that a few of the Conestogas had been absent during the raid and that Lancaster folk, fearing further attacks, had given them protection in the workhouse, Lazarus Stewart and the Paxtang Boys rode again. Once more galloping wildly through the night, they arrived at Lancaster on Sunday, December twenty-seven, while most of the townsfolk were in church at Christmas services. The Indians, realizing that they were doomed as the relentless fanatics broke down the workhouse gate, gathered into family groups and knelt in prayer as the raiders shot them down.

Threatened by the bitter Pennymites with the loss of their homes, the Yankees welcomed heartily the services of so renowned a fighter as Lazarus Stewart. He hated Indians, he hated Quakers, he hated the governing authorities of Pennsylvania (who were offering a reward for his arrest), and he could present passionately religious arguments for all of his acts of violence. He and his troopers, the New England men realized, were insurance against all their enemies. It was not surprising, therefore, that soon after the alliance, in February of 1770, Lazarus Stewart and John Durkee led Yankees and Paxtangs against the Pennymites in an attack so violent that one man was killed and others were wounded. The disagreement between Pennsylvania and Connecticut had flared into a war.

Though the attack failed, the Paxtang-Yankee allies instituted a siege of the Pennymite leader, Captain Ogden, which forced his surrender and evacuation of the valley. With the arrival of Captain Zebulon Butler, an officer who had seen active service against the French and Indians, and the continuous drifting of more New England settlers into Wyoming, the re-enforced Yankees had a happy summer. The river bottoms grew a plentiful harvest, the water was full of fish. They cleared new lands and raised new farmhouses. Then, in September, without warning and very quietly, Ogden struck. With a command of a hundred and forty Pennymites, he swooped down on the peaceful fields and arrested many of the workers in them. Before the Connecticut men could organize for defense, their enemies swarmed into their fort. Captain Butler and his aides they sent to a Philadelphia jail, and many of their subordinates they set behind bars in Easton.

Secure in the belief that a minor rebellion had been ended, Ogden left a garrison of twenty inside the fort and retired. He had failed to realize the stubborn courage of his Scotch-Irish foes.

A week before Christmas, Lazarus Stewart and thirty of his men suddenly at night broke down the fort gate and, crying "Hurrah for King George," rushed the half-clad, sleep-drugged garrison out into the wintry dark. In the morning the Paxtang Boys proudly claimed the fort and the Wyoming lands for the state of Connecticut.

Ogden was back with a hundred men on the twentieth of January. Once more he attacked the Yankee fort, but this time his force was driven off, his brother Nathan was killed and many Pennymites were wounded. Stewart realized, however, that he could not hold out against so large a besieging party. He and more than a score of his men stealthily retired from the fort in the middle of the

113

night, and in the morning the remaining Yankees surrendered. This time Ogden, who had erected a bastion he called Fort Wyoming, elected to stay inside its walls and insure continued possession of the valley.

His occupation was short. On an April morning he and his men awakened to find themselves surrounded by a hundred and fifty men led by the persistent duo, Captain Zebulon Butler and Lazarus Stewart. Since his fort was cut off from food, wood and water, he knew that he must obtain aid or surrender. Having tied his clothes together with his hat on top, he waded naked into the Susquehanna, towing the whole parcel behind him at the end of a cord. When he reached deep water he floated himself in the starlit current and spent the next long moments praying that the aim of the Yankee sentinels firing at his hat would prove so accurate that no errant shot would touch him. After the firing at the floating bundle ceased, he swam ashore, pulled in his bullet-riddled garments and, not quite adequately covered, set out to obtain help from Philadelphia. Before long he was back in the valley with a pack train of supplies.

Butler and Stewart proved too clever for him, however. Informed of its arrival, they ambushed the relief party and captured the provisions, though Ogden and the rest of his party escaped into Fort Wyoming. Relentlessly, the Yankee-Paxtang force continued its siege, whittling down the garrison with deadly attacks in which many were slain and wounded. Throughout most of the summer of 1771 the Pennymites held out, but in mid-August they surrendered, pledging evacuation of the cherished river lands. Disconsolately they set out southward.

The first Pennymite war was over. The Yankees and

114

the Paxtang Boys had won; the tide of settlers from the east began to swell. Connecticut men, who had come to Wyoming to claim their land, went back to bring their wives and children to the wide fields beside the Susquehanna. Ardently rebellious against British rule, the Yankees regarded their settlement as a New England township and named it after two English champions of the colonial cause, Wilkes-Barre. In the years that led up to the Revolution, the Yankees came in increasing numbers into Wyoming valley. Against strong protest from Pennsylvania authorities, the Susquehanna Company started the new year of 1774 by declaring five thousand square miles of their claim to be a part of Litchfield County, Connecticut. The settlers adopted New England methods of government, elected selectmen, and held town meetings in established Connecticut style. For many miles along its curving course the Susquehanna was a Yankee river!

PENNYMITE WAR II

❧ PENNSYLVANIA ATTACKS THE
CONNECTICUT INVADERS DURING
THE AMERICAN REVOLUTION

Pennsylvania and New England troops
would as soon fight each other as the enemy.
—A NEW ENGLAND BRIGADIER GENERAL

The battles of Lexington, Concord, Bunker Hill, Ticonderoga had been fought before the Pennymites tried again to dislodge the Yankee settlers on the upper river. While Washington was striving desperately to maneuver his inexperienced army against trained British troops,

115

while Benedict Arnold was organizing his heroic but
doomed expedition against Quebec, William Plunkett of
Sunbury, an eccentric, loud-talking physician with military
ambitions, led an armed force in September of 1775
against Yankee settlers who had spilled out of Wyoming
to the West Branch of the Susquehanna. Plunkett was
said to have participated in a robbery in England and
escaped that country by hiding himself in a barrel which
was then placed aboard an American-bound ship. Though
a fugitive from the British law, he was a violently out-
spoken Tory and maintained his loyalty to the Crown
even after the Revolution had been won.

Since the sentiment of Pennsylvania was still in the
autumn of 1775 against separation from the mother country, the doctor easily attained command of the expedition
against Muncy and other West Branch settlements whose
inhabitants, being Yankees, were strong for independence. His military aspirations were encouraged when he
found no serious opposition and was able to capture
many of the New Englanders and to compel others to return to Wyoming. The next logical step, he felt, was a
powerful attack upon that center of Yankee arrogance and
rebellion, Wyoming. At the head of nearly seven hundred men, marching in cadence to martial airs provided
by fifes and drums, and with a supply fleet of boats carrying food, ammunition and a cannon, he set out up the
west side of the Susquehanna on an expedition which he
confidently expected would bring the Yankees to their
knees. To give this elaborate military enterprise a sem-
blance of legality in the eyes of the Continental Congress,
which was endeavoring to avoid at all costs such regional
differences (at least until the successful ending of the

116

Revolution against Britain), he chose to call his army a "posse" and took along with him as further proof of civil rather than military action one William Cook, the high sheriff of Northumberland County.

News of the upriver advance of this threatening invasion reached Wyoming a few days before Christmas. Though it caused consternation among them, the Yankees determined to meet force with force, and their oddly assorted leaders, Captain Zebulon Butler, experienced and conservative, Captain Lazarus Stewart, still fanatic and hotheaded, planned to meet the invaders before they reached the town. The rumble of the drums, the squealing of the fifes was suddenly turned back on itself as the Pennymites marched briskly into the ravine of Nanticoke Creek and echoes, with march rhythms, filled the deep narrow channel with shattering sound. The big force, with the military-minded doctor and the high sheriff at its head, stepped briskly along the river road. As they approached the foot of a high mountain, however, a perpendicular cliff blocked their path. At its foot there was no more than room between high rock and river for the long column to pass. At its brow which projected from the steep slant of the mountain, a fringe of musket barrels slanted toward them. The Connecticut men had made perfect use of a natural fortification, adding only where its irregularities made human supplement necessary, log barricades that also bristled with Yankee guns.

"My God!" exclaimed Colonel Plunkett, "what a breastwork!" At this moment the Yankees fired a warning round along the whole length of their position, and Plunkett's men, breaking ranks, jumped for shelter. They formed again out of range of the high bastion and waited

117

until darkness settled. Then Plunkett ordered a boat up from below and climbed into it. Soon, with a few of his men and a dog aboard, he directed its passage across the swirling Susquehanna. He had done exactly what the cunning Yankees had anticipated. On the opposite bank, concealed by rocks and bushes, lay ruthless Lazarus Stewart and a detachment of his riflemen. As the craft swung near the shore, fire stabbed the darkness and the sound of a ragged volley stuttered over the dark stream. The dog fell dead. A man near Plunkett cried out that he had been hit, and his frightened companions let the rushing current sweep the boat, bobbing dangerously, through the Nanticoke rapids which streaked the black river with white foam.

Soon after the dawn of Christmas Day, Plunkett tried to deceive the Yankees by pretending a frontal attack while he sent a detachment to outflank them, a maneuver also anticipated by the experienced Captain Butler. Once more an ambush waited, and this time several men of both forces were killed and more were wounded. On the next morning, the crestfallen Tory commander led the Pennymites on their dreary return march to Northumberland. So ended temporarily the intercolony war-within-a-war. While at Quebec, Arnold and Montgomery planned for their exhausted freezing army the disastrous attack which would result in the latter's dying for the cause of American freedom, troops from Pennsylvania and Connecticut had engaged in one more deadly conflict of a civil war which had cost the lives of many patriotic men.

10

The Battle at Wyoming

🌿 *Mourn Susquehanna! Mourn thy*
hapless sons, thy defenseless
farmers slaughtered on the shores.
— HECTOR ST. JOHN DE CREVECOEUR (1782)

The town had known for a year and more that the Tories
and the Indians were coming. In the spring of 1777 Nat
Landon had found a letter, written from Wyoming by
Nicholas Pickard to his cousin John Pickard down below,
and had turned it over to the Northumberland County
Committee of Safety. It said that as soon as the river was
clear of ice "we shall march from every part" and that it
would be better for John "to go out of the way." Summoned before the committee on April seventeen, John
said that he had gone with Nicholas about Christmastime
upriver about twenty miles to Tunkhannock to see some
friends and that there a Nicholas Phillips had said the
Indians had told him that come spring they would be
striking "upon the Mohawk river and the waters of the
Susquehannough." John then took an oath of allegiance
to the United States and put up bail for his good behavior.

Tory Nicholas Pickard, brought before the committee
on the same day, defiantly confessed that he had written

119

the letter "in a kind of mysterious manner by reversing the letters so that it might not be understood." He added that there were fifteen thousand British troops at Niagara and that four thousand would be coming down the North Branch and four thousand down the West Branch and the rest would march along the Mohawk. There would be Indians with them.

The committee decided Nicholas was an enemy to the states and ordered John Coates to take him to the Supreme Executive Council of Pennsylvania.

Spring came and went and there were no further reports of a great invasion from York State. Summer passed and the Yankees worked in their fields gathering their harvests. Occasional postriders brought news from the two hundred or more young men of Wyoming Valley who were enlisted in Washington's forces. As the winter began, Indian raids on frontier farms to the north increased. Men grown careless through months of safety raced for their muskets when they heard owl answering owl from the nearby thickets, or saw quick shadows flit from corncrib to barn. Too often swifter Indians, tomahawks upraised, split their skulls and left them lying grotesquely in pools of blood that had poured from the ragged holes where their scalps had been. Neighbors barred their doors, cowered in the dark and waited while frantic screams echoed between the river hills and the sky was streaked by the flames of burning cabins. When, banded together, the next day, they saw the desolate ashes, the twisted lifeless bodies lying beside them, they shuddered, talked of vengeance, resolved to move to the protection of the nearest fort just as soon as they finished their work in the sugarbush, or clearing the lower forty, and went

120

back to their daily routines. Stories of strange doings drifted down with the spies and traders and suspiciously friendly Indians as their canoes arrived from the river's upper reaches on the high water of early spring. Tales of captive widows too soon married to Indian warriors, who for all they knew were their husbands' murderers, tales of adopted white boys and girls who loved the wild life of their new Indian parents so well they hid from blood relatives trying to rescue them, made fascinating folklore by Wyoming firesides.

Elisha Harding was about fifteen then, and sixty years later he still remembered and wrote down the story folks told of Dan Walter. Dan was a large dark man and, after he was captured, the Indians were kind to him and wanted him to marry a squaw of noble blood. They dressed him in all the finery of a chief and prepared for the wedding ceremony, but Dan would not go through with it, so they stripped him and made him run the gantlet and whipped him cruelly. "I thought his Judgement was poor," wrote Elisha Harding, "for he after his return married a woman not as likely as a common squaw." Nevertheless, Elisha concluded that Dan had "acted the free man" in this respect and deserved no censure.

Elisha told of another incident that also made much talk along the river:

> The Torys took old man Fitchjerl [Richard Fitzgerald] and placed him on a flaxbrake and told him if he did not renounce his rebel principal and declare for the king they would kill him but the old Dutchman Evertime said he Could not live but a few years at the longest he being very old but had rather die now a good friend to his country than live a few years and die a damned tory.

121

Finally his captors let him go downriver. "A few such men will perform wonders," wrote Elisha, "and their memory ought not to be forgotten."

In May, 1778, the river settlers finally realized with sickening fear that all their lives were in danger. Now even large parties guarded by soldiers were being attacked and destroyed. A man made prisoner up above escaped and reported that the Indians said they would clear their enemies from both branches of the Susquehanna this moon. Two weeks later Colonel Samuel Hunter wrote from Buffalo valley:

> We are in melancholy condition. The back inhabitants have left their homes. All above Muncy are at Samuel Wallis's. The people of Muncy are at Captain Brady's. All above Lycoming are at Antes' mill and the mouth of the Bald Eagle. The people of Penn's valley are at one place in Potter township. The inhabitants of White Deer are assembled in three different places. The back settlers of Buffalo have come down to the river.

The frightened people signed and sent to the Congress a petition begging aid, but there was no answer. They sent messages to the two companies of valley soldiers in the army—but new disciplines had been instilled at Valley Forge and permissions to return home were hard to get. All desperate actions of the valley dwellers seemed to them the straining, helpless movements of a nightmare from which they could not waken.

Meanwhile, to the great triangle formed by the joining of the Chemung and the Susquehanna at Tioga, Colonel John Butler, Tory leader from the Mohawk valley, had led his green-and-buff uniformed Rangers and a detachment of Sir John Johnson's more brightly clad Royal Greens. From the woods beyond their campfires came the

122

tinkle of little bells on the dresses of Indian squaws and on tree-hung cradles, the liquid-hollow thudding of water drums, the smell of the roast as the warriors ate the slain white dogs whose meat would give them battle courage. For weeks hundreds of Senecas and Cayugas had been moving from the Niagara and the Genesee west and south until they might follow the clear waters of the Chemung to this place. Their canoes skittered on the river like water bugs. They had blacked their faces and striped them red, and they sang and stamped furiously through their nightly war dances. The moon of the conquest of the Susquehanna was in the sky.

The whole expedition—four hundred whites and about seven hundred Indians—set out from Tioga on the last day of June. The river current took them swiftly downstream to the mouth of Bowman's Creek, below which they landed. They marched thence into Exeter Township and encamped that night about three miles north of Fort Wintermoot. In the morning they found the doors of that fort open, as Colonel Butler had known they would. The Wintermoot family had turned Tory and they welcomed the invaders. Indian scouts came upon a work party of eight in a field and killed four, captured three. A boy escaped. From the fort Colonel Butler sent out scouts and awaited their return.

Inside the two-acre palisade of Forty Fort—so called because it had been built by forty of the Connecticut settlers—Colonel Zebulon Butler, regular officer of the Connecticut line detached for service in defense of Wyoming, called for such men as were available to his command. At last the valley was alive to its danger. In through the gates, which were about eighty feet from the

123

river, had trudged six companies averaging about forty men apiece. One of these was made up of recently enlisted regulars of the Continental Army. The others were independent companies which had made quick marches from Upper and Lower Wilkes-Barre, Plymouth, Kingston and Hanover. The fort held, besides these, most of the rest of the population of Kingston—old men, women, children, civil officers, and of all these some seventy males chose to bear arms in the battle.

Fifteen-year-old Daniel Washburn had come up from Shawnee the night before and was standing guard on the north corner the sunny morning of July third when the squealing of a fife drew his attention to two men in green uniform marching through the shadowy woods nearby. The man stepping beside the fifer carried the flag of the enemy and, as it developed, a message from Colonel John Butler demanding surrender. At once Zebulon Butler held a council, wrote a refusal and sent the fifer and flag-bearer marching back with it.

The Yankee colonel then continued the conference of his captains. Should they defend the fort or attack the enemy? He was for defense, but Indian-hating Lazarus Stewart, who had led the wild Paxtang Boys and now commanded the Hanover Company, was not. Stewart made out a good case. The fort was not provisioned for a siege, and a surrender would soon be inevitable. While they were cooped up inside, the Indians would burn cabins and crops, steal cattle, murder women and children. The logical course was to try to drive off the enemy at once. The final decision was to attack.

In the early afternoon Zebulon Butler spoke to the more than three hundred men who were to sally from the fort. He told them to stand firm, and if they withstood the first shock the Indians would lose their spirit and begin to retire. Pails of rum were passed around, and everyone who wished to drank from them. Then, four abreast, the little army marched from the fort. A new bridegroom dashed back for a last kiss from his bride. A bewigged oldster, marching with his grandsons, turned his silver knee buckles over to the women of his family for fear the Indians might take them from his body. Inside the walls "the Reformadoes"—a few white-haired and weak old men—and the women and children heard the tramp of marching feet grow dim as the companies marched upriver. From the south then suddenly came the clatter of hooves, and a moment later anxious male voices were calling at the gate. Three young officers and a middle-aged Negro private (Gershom Prince), from a detachment of Continental troops fifty miles away, had ridden their lathered mounts all night to help defend their families and homes. They were exhausted and hungry. Quickly the anxious women served them food, and they were gone—all to their deaths before sundown.

The enemy forces had dined well that midday. Knowing their strength, they had no doubt of the outcome of their expedition and were gaily celebrating. The Yankees might have taken them by surprise at their feasting had not a hostile Indian seen a Wyoming advance scout and fired at him. This forewarned John Butler's forces who were already in position when Zebulon Butler's army marched into the river meadow beside Fort Wintermoot. The Yankees entered the battlefield single file and at order wheeled right to face the enemy. The Tory Rangers and Royal Greens, each with their quota of Indian allies,

125

were drawn up on a line from the river fort to a thicket-filled marsh in which the greater part of the Indians lay concealed. Zebulon Butler had told his men to fire, advance a step and load, then fire again. It was about four in the afternoon when their first volley raised sharp echoes above the river. Though the green-uniformed troops tried to take cover among the sparse shrub oaks and yellow pine in the meadow, Yankee bullets brought many of them down and the rest—frightened by the inexorable rhythmic advance—began slowly to give way. The Indians on the field were apparently divided into six units, for during the first half-hour of combat a sudden concerted war cry from one of these would bring in rapid succession five answering cries. So the battle developed a strange antiphony—Fire-Step-Load-Fire—and the separate wild yells of the six Indian bands.

Now, as the Yankees advanced and the Tories gave way, the great force of Indians hidden in the swamp, already behind the valley militia on the left of the line, suddenly struck. Howling fiercely they poured a devastating fire into the backs of their foes. Colonel Dennison, commanding the left, at once ordered the end company to wheel to face this new threat. Seeing this maneuver as an apparent withdrawal the Indians dashed from the marsh—a screaming horde of painted wildmen with upraised tomahawks. A few of the left company turned and ran—then all. The remaining companies, outflanked and hopeless, strove desperately to keep their positions. Zebulon Butler galloped over from the right urging them to make a stand, but the Indians by this time had raced between them and the fort and their only recourse was to flee across the flats through fields of high-growing grain

126

to the water. Down a wide funnel of death the Yankees raced to the Susquehanna. The Indians, yelping, closed in on them, viciously striking tomahawks into the skulls of running men, impaling their bodies on their sharp spears, kneeling to scalp dying victims. The butchery was appalling. The Tories, long embittered and stirred to blood-thirsty fury by the savagery about them, joined the orgy of killing. The captains of all six of the Yankee companies—still trying to rally their panic-stricken men—sank to their deaths, beaten down by many assailants.

Fugitives hid in the water under overhanging bushes growing along the riverbank, but relentless Indians found and killed them with tomahawks and spears. In the middle of the river stood the wooded, vine-hung island of Monocksy, and the settlers who could swim made for it in a frantic attempt to escape the man hunters. Those who first arrived crossed the island and escaped to the far shore, but Monocksy soon held more of pursuers than pursued. No written history of that bloody sunset hour would be necessary for generations to come—so deeply was it bitten into the minds of surviving settlers of the Susquehanna. With a kind of stricken wonder at mankind, the river folk still tell how Giles Slocum, hidden among the bushes, witnessed the meeting of the Pensil brothers—Tory John and Whig Henry. Henry, having thrown his gun away to swim the river, came out of hiding in a clump of willows to kneel at the feet of his brother and ask for mercy. As John was reloading his piece, Henry said:

"I will go with you and serve you as long as I live, if you will spare my life. You won't kill your brother, will you?"

"As soon as look at you," said John, and shot Henry down, dispatched him with his tomahawk and scalped him.

"What have you done? Have you killed your own brother?" said a Tory who came upon John completing his gruesome deed.

"Yes," said John, "for a damned rebel."

"I have a great mind to serve you the same way," said his horrified companion, but soon he and the murderer walked away.

Sixteen prisoners who had given themselves up to the Indians were marched a short distance upriver and seated in a circle about a big boulder since known as "Bloody Rock." Two strong savages held each as Esther Montour, "queen" of an Indian town of about seventy houses on the river flats near Tioga, began a fateful ceremony. Large, straight and regal, this woman, whose grandfather had probably been French and whose physical appearance seemed more French than Indian, had been a friend to the white settlers of the Susquehanna until, on the day the Tories landed at Exeter, one of her sons had been killed by the invaded Yankees. Since that moment she had thought only of reprisal. Waving her tomahawk, chanting a vengeance song, she circled the rock in a running dance and as she ended each round sank the blade of her weapon into the skull of a prisoner. Three chose not to await their turn. William Buck, a tow-haired boy, wriggled away and ran, but pursuing Indians caught him, drove a tomahawk into his head and threw his body back into the circle. Joseph Elliott and Lebbens Hammond, by sheer strength, broke away at the same moment from those who held them. Elliott ran into a field of rye taller

128

than his head and laced with many paths. In this labyrinth he deceived those who chased him long enough to reach the river. Swimming under water as much as possible he reached midstream before, as he came up for air, a bullet pierced his shoulder. On the far bank he stuffed part of his wet shirt into his wound and kept on to the Wilkes-Barre fort. Hammond raced for the woods and there, arming himself with a heavy pine knot, turned about to face two pursuers. He never knew for sure whether they lost sight of him or pretended that they did, but they halted and went back to the rock. Hammond spent the night furtively edging through the blackness of the woods toward Forty Fort which he reached in the morning.

Zebulon Butler and fifteen regulars, all that had returned to the fort, slipped out of the gates during the night and made their way downriver to the Wilkes-Barre fort. He and Colonel Dennison had decided that this was the only common-sense course. Surrender was inevitable and the less able-bodied soldiers captured the better. The escaping sixteen could hear, as they stealthily moved toward safety, the cries of their comrades of the day before dying from torture. Men who had fought beside the captives lay under the bushes on the east bank and saw across the moonlit river naked white men driven by the spears of Indians in ever-decreasing circles around the leaping flames. They sickened as they heard screaming and groaning, and they were glad that at that distance they could recognize no one. At last came silence. In the six hours since the beginning of the battle more than half of the men of Wyoming's defending army had been killed. None of their bereaved families dared search for their bodies in the clear white moonlight. Women who had waited in their cabins downriver gave up hope of seeing their husbands again, placed the children on rafts or in canoes, took a last look at their river farms and shoved off into the current where an occasional lifeless body, bobbing and twisting, bore them company.

With daylight came the expected messengers from John Butler. The Yankees must surrender, said the Tory, and the men must swear never again to bear arms against the British. The fort must be destroyed and all supplies belonging to the rebel army must be confiscated. He pledged he would use his utmost influence to protect the settlers' private property and insure their personal safety. Though this wording proved the Tory's lack of confidence in his control of the Indians, Colonel Dennison considered the terms as reasonable as he could expect and acquiesced. He ordered no one to leave and the gates to be unbarred. In the confusion that followed, the "Dutchman Fitzjerl," who had been one of the nine old men left to guard the fort, slipped away with a number of the women who placed no trust in John Butler's guarantees, and they set off downriver in canoes. As they embarked in frantic haste they saw the Indian army parading downriver to enter the stockade.

To the brisk rhythms of fifes and drums, John Butler marched his Tories six abreast into Forty Fort. He wore his white plumed hat (his battle cover had been a black handkerchief) and his bright-green dress uniform. At a table near the center of the fort he seated himself beside Colonel Dennison to oversee the occupation. Through the opposite gate, eyes flashing, Chief Gi-en-gwah-toh (He-Who-Goes-In-Smoke), who had planned the strategy of the battle, stepped proudly at the head of his painted warriors, and the despairing Yankees looked on the torturers and murderers of their fighting men. Behind him, with the scalps of her fourteen victims dangling in a long string from her hand, the bells on her pantalettes a-jingle beneath her knee-length blue skirt, strutted the tall, erect Queen Esther, her son's death avenged.

"Well, Colonel Den-i-sen," she jeered, "you made me promise to bring more Indians here; see [waving her hand] I bring all these."

Said Tory Butler, incensed, "That woman should be seen, not heard."

But she was not silenced. "I was never so tired in my life as I was yesterday, killing so many damned Yankees."

The Indians were no sooner inside the walls than control of them ceased. Though they respected the order to spare the lives of the conquered, they broke ranks in a wild scramble for personal properties. Inside and outside the fort they ranged, pilfering blankets, kettles, food, horses and cattle. Threatening the prisoners with their bloodstained tomahawks, they took from them any clothing that pleased them. Queen Esther, who had entered like a savage fury, was soon indulging her inherent French love of fashion by acquiring a new wardrobe and a collection of millinery. That afternoon she rode from the fort astride a stolen horse on which she had placed a stolen sidesaddle hind end forward. Beneath a stolen scarlet riding cloak her stalwart figure bulged with as many stolen dresses as she could get on, and on her head seven bonnets, placed one upon another, made a grotesque tower of finery.

Vainly Colonel Dennison reminded John Butler of his

131

promises and demanded that he order the Indians to stop their thievery.

"I tell you what, sir," said the portly Tory officer, nervously, "I can do nothing with them. I can do nothing with them."

Two hours after the Indians had entered the fort they distributed to the prisoners vermillion paint, with instructions that they should daub their faces with it so all Indians would recognize that they had been made captive and would not harm them. Colonel Butler then informed the Yankees that they must leave the valley within five days.

As the forlorn groups of bereaved women, children, and old men plodded up the slopes of the mountains to the east they looked down on harvest crops and cabins aflame. Still dazed by grief and fright, they dared not make campfires at night for fear of the raging wildmen. On the mountain trails young women birthed their children without aid of doctor or midwife and trudged on toward the Hudson and their old homes beyond it in Connecticut. Mothers stayed awake all night to protect their sleeping children from myriads of mosquitoes, by waving pine branches above them.

Those who had set out downriver found other hardships. About ten miles below the Forty Fort lay the rockstrewn Nanticoke rapids, where many craft piled up or ran aground. Male fugitives worked feverishly here to set the boats once more moving downstream. Some, being Yankees, charged for their services, and those who received them, being of the same breed, expected to pay and did so. The North Branch grew crowded as settlers below Wyoming joined the flight. By the time the flotilla reached Harris's Ferry and Paxtang, the number of flee-ing settlers was so vast that it engulfed the town. Never-theless the inhabitants of the Scotch-Presbyterian com-munity welcomed all these desperate people, fed and housed them, comforted them as best they could.

Word of the advance of the Tories and their murderous Iroquois allies had spread to the West Branch, and the people of the Buffalo and White Deer valleys were in a panic-stricken flight that has been ever since known as "The Big Runaway." Nine days after the battle, Harris's Ferry was jammed with fugitives who had left almost everything to the invaders' torches. Observers reported two hundred wagons on the road coming down, and "the banks of the Susquehanna from Middletown to the Blue mountain were entirely clad with the inhabitants of Northumberland County who had moved off, as well as many in the river in boats, canoes, and on rafts." William Maclay, who claimed ownership of many acres of the land which the Wyoming settlers had occupied as their own, wrote from Paxtang:

> I left Sunbury and almost my whole property on Wednesday last (July 8th). . . . I never in my life saw such scenes of dis-tress. The river and the roads leading down it were covered with men, women, and children flying for their lives. North-umberland County is broken up. . . . The whole county broke loose. Something in the way of charity ought to be done for the many miserable objects that crowd the banks of this river, es-pecially those who fled from Wyoming. You know I did not use to love them, but I now pity their distress.

Robert Covenhoven who, with a young miller's appren-tice, had made a heroic ride up Bald Eagle Mountain and along the Indian-infested West Branch ridges as far as Pine Creek, to tell the settlers of their danger, wrote the most colorful report of the Big Runaway:

> I took my own family safely to Sunbury and came back in a keel-boat to secure my furniture. Just as I rounded a point above Derrstown, now Lewisburg, I met the whole convoy from all the forts above. . . . Boats, canoes, hog-troughs, rafts, hastily made of dry sticks . . . were crowded with women, children, and plunder. There were several hundred people in all. Whenever any obstruction occurred at any shoal or ripple, the women would leap out into the water and put their shoulders to the boat or raft, and launch it again into deep water. The men of the settlement came down in single file, on each side of the river, to guard the women and children.

So the vast, disorderly rush continued. Somehow the women guided their incredibly varied craft, laden with chairs, tables, spinning wheels, bedsteads, kettles, cows and sheep, downstream while their men waded the shallows, swam the creeks, scrambled—guns in hand and ready—up and down the high and wooded bluffs. So close was the pursuit that a settler who had launched his family on the boat and then returned to get his horse was shot down as he rode to the shore. Another, a young woman fleeing from an Indian, was seen to jump down the riverbank and fall. The Indian, grabbing her hair, hacked the scalp from her head and ran, leaving a victim who was to live, though bald, for some seventy years thereafter.

The news of the Wyoming slaughter had in a few days caused a recession of the frontier for many miles. The towns of Sunbury and Northumberland were now the farthest north outposts against the Indians and Tories,

134

and only a few of the braver settlers had had the courage to remain there, "though doubtful," as Colonel Samuel Hunter, commander of the local militia, put it, "whether tomorrow's sun shall rise on them freemen, captives, or in eternity!"

11

Rehearsal for Vengeance

🌿 *Follow well in order, get your weapons ready.*

—WALT WHITMAN

Thomas Hartley was thirty-one years old, a colonel of the Eleventh Regiment of the Pennsylvania Line, when he was named Commandant of the Northern Frontiers and ordered to the Susquehanna. He had served under Anthony Wayne in helping to cover General Benedict Arnold's retreat from Canada and he shared the country's admiration of "Mad Anthony."

When he arrived at Sunbury a month after the battle at Wyoming and the Big Runaway, he was in a reluctant and disappointed mood. Born of prosperous parents in Berks County, educated at a Reading school, an attorney of the Pennsylvania bar, he would have preferred service with Wayne against British troops who accepted, at least in principle, the laws of warfare, instead of the treacherous, cruel, and unpredictable wild men. "Fate ordained," he wrote his former commander, "that I was to go to make war on the savages of America instead of on Britain."

Aware at last of the defenseless plight of the frontier, the Supreme Executive Council of Pennsylvania had with

136

optimistic assurance ordered over a thousand troops to assemble on the West Branch under Hartley's command. Aside from two detachments of his own regiment, these included a hundred men recruited at Wyoming, four hundred from Lancaster County, a hundred and fifty from Berks, three hundred from Northumberland. While some of his men were building Fort Muncy upriver on the West Branch, the colonel reported from Sunbury to the Council the condition of the community as he had found it:

> Four-fifths of the inhabitants fled with such effects as they could carry from this country. Many of the men are returning but . . . I fear few of the women will return again to their former habitation. A most extraordinary panic seems to have struck the people.
>
> The Wyoming settlement is almost totally destroyed. The most of the surviving inhabitants have fled to Connecticut, or are now removing as paupers to that State.

A month later the impatient colonel was still at Sunbury. The fort at Muncy was nearly completed, but the troops which the Council had promised were slow in assembling. Northumberland County had been unable to furnish but a small fraction of the three hundred troops the Council had promised because, "distracted and distressed" and with many of its inhabitants not yet returned from their flight, it "could afford but few men" to perform "the services wanted by an unhappy and intimidated frontier." Lancaster County had also fallen far short. Indians, rich with loot and grown bold through their successes, had made two effective raids. Young James Brady, courageous member of a famous Indian-fighting family, had been scalped in one of these and had died days later. The woods were full of painted warriors and reports of

137

them were coming downriver daily. When soldiers had tried to attack them they had taken to their heels, and Hartley reported, "The Barbarians have frequently appeared in open ground and do fairly outrun the most of white men. . . . I have wrote to the Board of War to send an officer and 12 horses here; I hope they will comply."

Gradually the promised number of his possible command dwindled. The thousand became seven hundred, then four hundred. From Philadelphia the Council wrote, "The ideas which Congress entertain of fortifications in the interior part of the country will not admit of any expense in erecting them. . . . We are sorry to inform you that we, at present, see no probability of our being able to procure the cannon which you mention in any reasonable time." Nevertheless, as the precious summer weeks moved on the young Colonel remained bold of purpose. On August twenty-second he wrote to Zebulon Butler, then commanding a small garrison at Wilkes-Barre, "My firm intention is to act offensively against the enemy adjoining these frontiers. I go to Muncy tomorrow and am collecting a clever body of men there."

Still discouragements piled up. Ill-health delayed him. The men of his regiment, ordered from Northampton County, arrived at Wilkes-Barre after an incredibly difficult march and from Sunbury he sent another urgent plea to the Council: "I am told their clothes are all torn by the woods; they are in utmost want of hunting shirts and woolen over-alls or leggings. I hope 200 of each will be sent up immediately."

Despite the obstacles an impetus for the expedition was building. Though the recruits ordered by the council were not reporting, the men of Wyoming and its vicinity realized that, though the goal of the expedition had been kept secret, it would soon be on its way against the Indians. That was enough for them. "I am informed," wrote Hartley to the Council, "many of our people have the highest inclining to go against some of the Indian towns that they may avenge the murder of fathers, brothers, and friends, besides serving their country." Bitter, hard men who knew the ways of the Indian and had no fear of him had taken the trails toward the West Branch forts.

By mid-September the colonel could wait no longer. He ordered all troops available for the expedition to Muncy. On the eighteenth they arrived—and the four hundred on whom he had counted had shrunk to half that number. A hundred and thirty of these had come from Wyoming. Hartley allowed only two days for equipping, rationing and instructing his command. In the blackness before the cloud-covered dawn of the twenty-first, he led his men from the gateway of the small new fort into the woods and along Bonsell's Run to the ravine of Lycoming Creek. Weighed down with their long-barreled "Queene Anne" muskets, forty rounds of cartridges, overcoats, blankets, and cooked rations for four days, the two hundred scrambled over boulders, pushed through tough webs of vine, slipped and slid on steep slopes for eighteen miles before their hardy commander ordered them to make camp and await the pack horses, slowly laboring under two boxes of ammunition apiece and enough rations to last the expedition for an additional eight days.

Because of the delay in starting, the September equinoctial storms had come to the Susquehanna country. "In our route we met with great rains," Hartley later reported, ". . . prodigious swamps, mountains, defiles and rocks im-

139

peded our march. . . . We waded or swam the river Lycoming upwards of 20 times." He compared these hardships with those of Hannibal crossing the Alps and of
Benedict Arnold ascending the Kennebec. Many fellow
Pennsylvanians had given him vivid descriptions of the
latter when he had joined them on the retreat from Canada.

In drenching rains the two hundred doggedly fought
their way up the rock-strewn, log-blocked gorge. Again
and again currents of the flooded stream threatened to
carry them under but, clinging to each other, they somehow made foothold and handhold, cut away the entan-
gling underbrush, waded the treacherous marshes, and
inched forward. Aware that only their leaders knew their
secret destination but certain that, whatever their path,
it led against their enemies, they slept in soggy blankets,
ate water-soaked rations, went without fires lest smoke
reveal their whereabouts. It was a muscle-straining, bone-
tiring, skin-scraping job, a job done in silence, all breath
spent on movement alone. Only their eyes—meeting—
told their feelings as the hours dragged on.

"In lonely woods and groves we found the haunts and
lurking places of the savage murderers who had desolated
our frontier. We saw the huts where they had dressed and
dried the scalps of the helpless women and children who
had fell in their hands."

They had covered eighteen miles the first day, only ten
on the second, but they were approaching high ridges
where the stream, nearer to its source, was smaller and
less powerful. On the twenty-third they advanced eleven
miles and on the twenty-fourth, fourteen. They had
reached the valley of the Towanda Creek and encamped

140

on a high, dry hilltop. The cooked rations were gone now. The morning of the twenty-fifth the cooks went to work on the provisions carried by the pack horses and the remainder of the troops rested. In the afternoon Hartley ordered them on toward the North Branch of the Susquehanna. This was enemy country and he sent a score of scouts ahead and flankers out on either side to guard the main body against attack or ambush. Progress in this formation was careful and slow.

The troops had hardly begun their march the next morning before the advance guard saw a party of nineteen Indians coming toward them. They fired at once. The leader of the enemy band, an important chief, fell and the marksman who had shot him took his scalp. The rest of the Indians fled. Following at a rapid pace they came upon a campsite where obviously more than seventy savages had slept the night before. On the sudden warning of their fleeing comrades they had run away, leaving many evidences of panic-stricken flight.

Hartley urged his men into double time. His march was no longer secret. It would be fruitless unless he struck the Indian towns at once. Down Sugar Creek the two hundred raced, forsook its rocky bed and made for the Susquehanna and the cabins at Sheshequin.

There they had the luck to surprise and capture fifteen prisoners who told them news of the expedition had been spread by a turncoat named Van Alstyne who had deserted the troops at Wyoming and hastened north. Darkness had settled when they reached the empty round-roofed huts of Queen Esther's Town, but the commander kept his exhausted men moving. The seventeen horsemen were already loping on ahead, the advance guard was

141

jogging only a short distance behind them, and Hartley's crisp orders to follow were not to be denied. Almost in a stupor, their legs moving mechanically, the main body splashed across the shallow ford of the Chemung and, muskets ready, crept into Tioga (now Athens). The town was empty. There was no need to conceal their fires now. Quick-kindled flames disclosed that an enemy troop had just dashed away leaving many effects, but the raiders, after covering twenty-two miles, could think of nothing but sleep. Only the knowledge of desperate danger kept the pickets awake through the night.

In the morning (that of September twenty-seventh) another prisoner was taken, and from all information then available Hartley was able to analyze his situation. The force which had fled Tioga at his approach had been composed of three hundred green-uniformed Tories under Major Walter Butler (son of Colonel John Butler). They had fled to Chemung, only twelve miles away, "the receptacle of all villainous Indians and Tories from the different tribes and states." His horsemen had pursued them three miles north to Shawnee but, upon his failing to come up to them, had returned. He had reason to believe that more than five hundred troops at Chemung were planning action against him. He had only one day's supply of cooked rations. If he were to push on, or to stay where he was, his whole force would certainly be destroyed. Indeed it might be annihilated before he could retreat. To the chagrin of the enemy, he had by his lightning tactics routed an enemy force half again as large as his own, liberated a number of their prisoners and recaptured much of the cattle and property taken at the time of the Wyoming battle. Only courage and bluff had saved them thus far from de-

142

struction. He was convinced that they were now so well advanced into enemy country that they would have to fight their way home.

Accordingly, Colonel Hartley ordered his command up at daybreak on the twenty-eighth. They crossed the Susquehanna at once and took the old Warrior-path down the east side of the river. Besides their arms and blankets, their impedimenta included fifty head of cattle, the Wyoming plunder they had recaptured, and their pack horses. Knowing that an unencumbered force of Tories and Indians would overtake them before they could reach the safety of the forts to the south, Hartley hurried them on in the effort to stretch out the line of the pursuers. Cooked rations gave out, flour gave out, whiskey gave out, daylight was gone, and still they marched. One hour before midnight they arrived at the flats of Wyalusing, footsore and utterly fatigued.

Hartley knew that he would be overtaken the next day and would not allow his men to enter combat weak from lack of food. "On the morning of the 29th we were obliged to stay until eleven o'clock to kill and cooke Beef. This necessary stop gave the Enemy Leisure to approach." It took another hour to organize the little army to move with a maximum of safety. Hartley was a realistic officer and not without a sense of humor. He was aware that his troops were very tired—also that soldiers are not inclined to walk if they can ride. "Seventy of our men, from real or pretended Lameness, went into the canoes; others rode on the Pack Horses, we had not more than 120 Rank & File to fall in line of March." He sent an officer and fifteen men in advance with eight of the horsemen. Following this guard were the pack horses and the cattle.

143

The main body, divided into three small companies, marched next and a group of thirty with the remaining horsemen formed the rear guard. The steepness and roughness of the terrain greatly obstructed the use of flankers.

After two miles of level going the troops were slowed by a mile-long mountain slope. They had just reached the summit of this long climb when a sharp volley aimed at the advance guard let them know that the Indians had not only caught up with them, but had raced ahead and were now between them and their downriver base. The fire was at once returned and the Indians almost at once gave way. Hartley, suspecting a scheme to lure his men into ambush, ordered them not to follow. A half hour later and a mile farther along, the Indians attacked the advance guard again and in greater force. Holding the center with his own Pennsylvanians, Hartley ordered the two companies behind to deploy in the effort to flank the enemy. Again the savages fled only a few moments before the men on the river had beached their canoes and charged up the slope. Again Hartley warned against pursuit. This attack, he surmised, was like the other—"only amusement."

The real strategy of the Indians became apparent at two o'clock when they suddenly attacked the rear of the retreating column with their full force of two hundred picked warriors. The thirty of the rear guard were immediately driven back on the main body. Hartley, again holding the center, ordered his men up a ridge just ahead and they gained its crest "almost unnoted by the Barbarians." They were immediately followed to that eminence by the third company while the second company joined the rear guard in opposing the attack. At the same time a small

144

force was sent by the left flank around the enemy in order, at an advantageous time, to attack from the rear.

The Indians became then the victims of the very sort of strategy they had previously attempted. When the opposing rear guard retreated they impetuously advanced. One of Hartley's men who knew their language later translated their chief's encouraging shout: "My brave warriors, we drive them; be bold and strong, the day is ours." He had not reckoned, however, with the elements which would turn the tide. Once more the men from the canoes, disregarding their "real or pretended lameness," rushed to the point where the fighting was hottest. The moment of decision had come. They raised a wild war whoop and Hartley's men answered from above. At the same time, setting up a fearful yelling, the little band that had circled to the left around the enemy attacked their rear. Suddenly the Indians found themselves apparently surrounded by a force advancing on all sides. They held out for a few minutes—then discovered an unoccupied pass and dashed through it in frantic, pell-mell retreat, leaving ten dead on the ground.

Colonel Hartley's report of this happy conclusion of the fighting was unadorned, realistic, soldierlike:

> We had 4 killed and 10 wounded. They received such a Beating as prevented them from giving us any further trouble during our March to Wyoming, which is more than 50 miles from the place of Action. . . .

He praised his officers, mentioned his seventeen cavalrymen who were very active until the horses were fatigued, hailed the marksmanship and knowledge of Indian fighting of the New Englanders engaged.

145

The men of my Regiment were armed with Muskets & Bayonets. They were no great marksmen and were awkward at wood Fighting. The Bullet and three Swan Shot in each Piece made up in some measure for want of skill. . . . We performed a circuit of nearly 300 miles in about two weeks; we brought off near 50 head of cattle and 28 canoes besides many other articles.

He had, moreover, recovered sixteen captives and burned four Indian towns—Tioga, Sheshequin, Queen Esther's and Wyalusing. And he had made a raid that would be listed in American military history as a classic.

12

The Big March

❧ *The nests are destroyed, but the*
birds are still on the wing.

—MAJOR JEREMIAH FOGG

❧ REMEMBER WYOMING!

Americans, scholars and amateur historians alike, still debate the motives that brought about General John Sullivan's big march from Wyoming to the banks of the Genesee and return. Blessed with hindsight, a well-justified admiration of the great Washington, and a desire to please patriotic readers, some analysts of the Revolution argue that the commander-in-chief had in mind more far-reaching effects than he ever stated. Basing their arguments on deduction and conjecture, they say Washington wished by conquest to make secure the new nation's title to the western lands and thereby to guarantee the nation's post-Revolution expansion toward the Mississippi.

At least some of the immediate causes for Washington's decision to order about a third of his whole army on an expedition against the hostile tribes of the Iroquois Confederacy are clear. The Wyoming Massacre, while not a defeat from an objective military standpoint, had horrified all supporters of the Revolutionary cause. Delays in retaliation had created a highly disapproving public opinion.

Since more than a third of the population of powerful New York State were of Tory persuasion, the inability of the Continental forces to protect the lives and property of their own families and other sympathetic civilians living along the Susquehanna proved a strong argument on the tongues of the loyalists. Since the victims of the Wyoming attack were, in their own convictions and those of the state whence they came, citizens of Connecticut, much of New England was aroused to indignant criticism. Even the Pennsylvanians, who had been eager to drive the Yankees out of the Susquehanna valley by force and if necessary at the cost of lives, had been so shocked by the massacre that they demanded retributive action. The raid of Hartley's two hundred, perfect exploit though it was, had ended in a precipitate retreat from larger enemy forces. The attitude of the Wyoming population had not been improved when they saw the properties recaptured by Hartley sold at auction for the benefit of the soldiery and realized that in order to regain them those who had owned them must outbid others who desired them.

George Clinton, Governor of New York, had stated the people's motives for demanding an expedition against the Indians very logically in a letter to General Washington written from Poughkeepsie in October, 1778, a little over three months after Wyoming's fatal July third:

> I find it impossible to secure the Frontier Settlements ag't the Depredations of the Enemy by the utmost exertions I am able to make with the Militia. I am led to fear that unless some effectual Check can be given to their Opperations, exclusive of the Distresses which they bring on Individuals, who more immediately suffer by them, they will sensibly affect the public as the last settlements they have destroyed usually afforded greater supplies of Grain than any of equal Extent in this State.

148

Less than a month after this was written the massacre at Cherry Valley, New York, emphasized the importance of Clinton's argument. In that disaster the enemy was reported to have destroyed the crops in the fertile countryside, "burnt all buildings in the settlement, killed a great number of inhabitants, men, women and children, carryed off many prisoners . . . collected all the cattle, horses, and sheep they could and drove off."

The Continental Congress, which had in June voted an expedition and appropriated nearly a million dollars to finance it only to find that their action was too late to save Wyoming, decided in August, when little had been accomplished, that the project should be "for the present laid aside."

Nevertheless General Washington continued through the fall and early winter months to plan an invasion of the Tory-and-Indian country by way of the Susquehanna. In mid-December he had ordered Brigadier General Hand to command a division of the expeditionary forces officered by Polish Pulaski, French Armand, German Burchardt and Pennsylvania's Colonel Thomas Hartley. At the beginning of March, 1779, after he had decided to entrust the execution of the entire operation to Major General Gates and so wrote that officer stating: "The objects of this expedition will be effectually to chastise and intimidate the hostile nations, to countenance and encourage the friendly ones, and to relieve our frontiers from the depredations to which they would otherwise be exposed." The existence of what has been known as the "Conway Cabal" has been questioned by modern historians, but there is no doubt of the asperities, the jealousies, the petulancies expressed by general officers of the Continentals toward their commander-in-chief. Washington had been so sure of the negative content of the reply he would receive that he enclosed a letter of similar import which, in case of Gates's refusal, was to be forwarded to General John Sullivan. He could hardly have expected, however, Gates's surly answer beginning: "Last night I had the honor of your Excellency's letter. The man who undertakes Indian service should enjoy youth and strength; requisites I do not possess. It therefore grieves me that your Excellency should offer me the only command to which I am entirely unequal."

Sullivan, able and courageous brigadier general, dutifully accepted Washington's offer and was informed that General James Clinton—brother of Governor George Clinton of New York—had been ordered to assemble at Canajoharie in the Mohawk valley an army which he should hold in readiness to march either west to take Niagara, the chief British stronghold of the Iroquois country, or south to join the army moving up the Susquehanna. General Clinton would be under General Sullivan's command, said Washington, and apparently fearing a lack of harmony between the two officers he emphasized over and over again in his communications the necessity for co-operation between them. Sullivan set out for Easton, Pennsylvania, to make the initial arrangements for the project and immediately met difficulties in assembling both troops and supplies. Delay followed delay. The failures of the commissary and Sullivan's insistence on a force he considered large enough to accomplish his mission postponed the beginning of the march until most of the summer had passed. Washington had in mind a swift, economical, decisive thrust—as much like Hartley's in 1778 as could be accomplished with a large force. He wrote Sullivan it was "essential that your operation should be as rapid and that the expedition should be performed in as little time as will be consistent with its success and efficacy. And here I cannot forbear repeating my former caution that your troops may move as light and as little encumbered as possible."

When these instructions seemed disregarded and Clinton's preparations at Canajoharie seemed too elaborate, Washington rebuked Sullivan, emphasizing his belief that Clinton might endanger his force if he were to march "encumbered with useless supplies and has his defense weakened by the attention he must pay to convoy and the length of his line. . . . I had not a doubt of its being fully understood, and took it for granted when he was placed under your orders that he would have been instructed accordingly."

Smarting under this expression of disapproval, and still unable to get the expedition under way, Sullivan made an appeal to Congress which in its implications was so critical of Washington that the commander-in-chief felt the necessity of answering it. This he did in mid-August— while the expedition was on the march—with a masterful letter to the President of the Congress in which he logically disposed of Sullivan's expostulations:

> I am sorry to find in the appeal which General Sullivan has made to Congress that he has misstated several particulars of importance and that in providing for his own justification in case of misfortune he has left the matter upon such a footing as to place me in a delicate situation.

Washington then with patience not unmixed with exasperation quoted Sullivan's statement "that the plan for carrying on the expedition was not agreeable to his mind, nor were the number of men for it sufficient in his opinion to insure success" and showed the unreason and impracticality of Sullivan's proposal "to have two bodies each superior to the whole force of the enemy to operate both on the Mohawk River and by way of the Susquehanna." Aware of the adverse criticism already launched at him for sending nearly a third of his available troops against the Indians, he continued: "The force actually detached left the Army so weak that I am persuaded every officer of reflection in it, who knew our true circumstances, was uneasy for the consequences; and if a larger force had gone, we should have been absolutely at the discretion of the enemy. . . ."

While generously agreeing that his subordinate (motivated by his own lack of materials and provisions) was right in ordering Clinton to obtain adequate supplies, Washington scorned Sullivan's attitude that men engaged in transport of supplies, herding cattle, cooking and other noncombatant duties could not be regarded as fighting troops. Finally he expressed his doubt of the truth of Sullivan's claim that "one third of his men are without a shirt to their back." Stating that he had taken every step in his power to afford a competent supply, Washington added significantly: "I have the greatest reason to believe that the troops with him had more than a proportion to the general wants and supplies of the Army."

It came as a welcome surprise, then, to Washington, the Congress, the majority of revolutionary patriots, even to its commander, that the Sullivan Expedition, conceived in response to a public demand for vengeful reprisal, and born in unbecoming bickering among high officers, was a singular success. Though harassed on its outer edges by

152

occasional Indian scalpings, it met with no important opposition. Its one engagement, entitled the Battle of Newton, cost the lives of but four of its men in the brief time before the Indians, terrified by artillery fire, broke and fled toward Niagara. Its major tragedy was the destruction in the Genesee valley of a thirty-man scouting party under Lieutenant Thomas Boyd. About half of this advance group was killed by Indian fire, and the remainder either escaped or lost their lives by scalping and torture after they had surrendered. Boyd himself and his sergeant, Michael Parker, were unspeakably mangled while still living by the desperate savages who knew all too well what horrible results the burning of their homes and crops would produce in the coming winter.

Had General Sullivan decided to move west to conquer Fort Niagara, as Washington had suggested, the military consequence of his invasion of enemy country might have been of major importance. Since he chose rather to return to the forts on the Susquehanna after destroying the orchards, crops, and prosperous towns of the fertile Genesee country, the strategic value of his raid has ever since been a matter of controversy. Some historians claim that it "broke the backbone of the Iroquois Confederacy," destroyed the morale of the hostile Indians, discouraged the British effort to hold their western outposts.

Against these arguments others point out that many of the Indians, and particularly the Onandagas and Mohawks, had been neutral until enraged against the Continentals by this "total warfare" raid which resulted in the deaths through slow starvation of many women and children. They add that instead of ending Indian raids in the Susquehanna country, the expedition inspired further and

153

more savage atrocities in the following year. Whatever the resolution of this debate, there can be little doubt that the narrative of the Big March offers more to scholars of the social history of the nation than it does to those of its military annals. Described in the diaries of many officers and a few of the rank and file, the Sullivan Expedition proved one of the most important influences in the development of the Susquehanna valley and gives contemporary readers by significant though minor details a considerable understanding of the life of Continentals-on-the-march in 1779.

On April third the Providence *Gazette* reported that General Sullivan, who had been in command of troops in Rhode Island, had departed to begin performing the duties of his new assignment:

> He was accompanied out of town by the Honorable Brigadier-Generals Glover and Varnum, a number of Officers from each Corps of the Army in this State and many respectable inhabitants, attended by a band of Music and under a discharge of Thirteen Cannon. The Company attended him to the town of Johnston, where, after partaking of an elegant Dinner that had been provided on the Occasion, he took a most affectionate leave of them and pursued his journey.

This social-military amenity was the first of a series fashioned in a pattern adopted on many gay occasions before, during, and after the Big March.

While Washington fumed at the delay of the start of the expedition and Sullivan fretted because promised supplies had not arrived, the regiments of Colonels Cortlandt (the second New York) and Spencer were busy building an artillery road over the steep wooded ridges that separate the Delaware from the Susquehanna. Late in May, Cortlandt reported to Governor George Clinton from "Great Swamp Wilderness, of the Shades of Death" that he was within twenty-five miles of Wyoming, that General Hand was already there, and that Colonel Proctor's regiment of artillery was awaiting at Easton (with General Maxwell's "Jersie Brigade" and General Sullivan) the moment when the road would be completed.

By the end of the first week of June, though the laborious effort was handicapped and sometimes stopped for days by heavy rains and by lack of provisions, many troop units were on the march for Wyoming. From the daily journals of many of these soldiers much of their life can be reviewed. They were fascinated by the Moravian settlements along the way and described in detail the unique religious services. They were awed by the big swamp, "a horrid, rough, gloomy country," and especially by its last vale called the Shades of Death "which is a dark and dismal place," "a gloomy grove of Cypress, Hemlock, Pine, Spruce, etc.," "where there was not a house nor fense nothing but Rocks and Mountains and a Grate part of it was as Dark as after Sun down when it was noon Day . . . for the timber the Swamp [was] so thick you could not see 10 foot."

Stepping to fife and drum through this ominous twilight, late in April a detachment of two hundred had nearly reached the sunlit landscape beyond when those in advance thought they saw a deer. Eager for venison a number of them, including Captain J. Davis and Lieutenant William Jones, ran forward thinking to capture the animal. There was a volley from unseen Indians and six of the hunters, including these officers, were slain and scalped before help could reach them. Davis and Jones were both members of the Ancient Order of Masons, and their deaths have since been memorialized in many fraternal ceremonies. When a major force marched through the Shades of Death on the rough, newly completed road two months later, General Sullivan and Colonel Proctor (both Masons) saw to it that Proctor's brass band slowed its quickstep to the melancholy strains of a tune often used at funerals—*Roslyn Castle*—as they passed the two wooden boards (one of them said to be stained by Davis' blood) which marked the graves of the ambushed officers. The next day the troops arrived at the Susquehanna and their twenty-eight-year-old chaplain, William Rogers, wrote in his journal, "Being St. John's Day a number of Free-Masons met at Colonel Proctor's marquee; at his request (though not of the fraternity myself) read for them the Rev. Dr. Smith's excellent sermon on Masonry." This was the first of a series of Masonic rituals which were to continue throughout the ensuing months.

Arriving troops welcomed the vista of regiments encamped in bush huts on the banks of the river, "an exceeding fine pretty river, and opposite the town in midsummer five or six fathom of water, as clear as it can be." It was literally crowded with fish. Those privates were now appeased who had grumbled over their rattlesnake rations in the Shades of Death where officers had so enjoyed a mess of trout that they had entitled the spot "Chowder Camp."

The last days of June were hot and sultry, punctuated by smart showers of rain. The waiting regiments settled into a routine that soon became monotonous. An athletic and enthusiastic young surgeon, Dr. Ebenezer Elmer, spent the twenty-eighth "as usual in the duties of my Station," but reported "a dance on the green" beside the river in the evening. The next day he wrote, "34 boats arrived at this place from Sunbury with Flour, beef and military stores. This was very fortunate as there was not one day's provision in the Stores after all their great Spunk in furnishing the army with provision for this campaign."

July first gave relief from ennui when all troops were paraded for the execution of two Tories found guilty of "enticing Soldiers of the American Army to desert." Three chaplains, Samuel Kirkland, Hunter, and William Rogers, succeeded in persuading General Sullivan to promise, with the proviso that they would keep his agreement secret, to pardon the more deserving of the unhappy pair after the execution of his companion. The parsons walked with the prisoners to the gallows about which stood hundreds of civilian inhabitants and the regiments in column under arms. Sergeant Thomas Roberts, of the fifth New Jersey Regiment, a former shoemaker, wrote the most succinct and detailed though not the most literate report of the event:

> Theare was Tow men Condemned for to Bee hung. Tha was Drove to the Galles with theare halters Round theare necks. One was hung and the other Repreived which Shocked him so he almost Fanted A way.

Officers and men spent the long hot month awaiting supplies and re-enforcements and amusing themselves as best they could. They visited the scene of the battle of Wyoming and found grisly relics. Major James Norris of the third New Hampshire Regiment wrote:

> We saw more or less of bones scattered on the ground for near two miles, and several Sculls brought in at different times

that had been Scalped and inhumanly mangled with the Hatchet. A Captain's Commission with 17 Continental Dollars was found in the pocket of the Skeleton of a man, who had laid above ground 12 months. Our guide showed us where 73 bodies had been buried in one hole.

The story of the fratricidal slaying of Henry Pensil by his Tory brother, John, and the report of Queen Esther's slaying of fourteen with her tomahawk had become favorite folk tales among the troops and were recorded in variant forms in many soldier-journals.

On July third, the first anniversary of the massacre, the social Dr. Elmer recorded that most of the subalterns of his regiment "met at the Colonel's Marquee to take a drink." After several toasts had had time to take effect "being Saturday night they agreed to drink Sweethearts and Wives on Honor," and the doctor mischievously listed the young ladies so honored. Thus the names of Abby Wheeler, Minney Baldwin, Phebe Atwood, his own favorite —Mrs. Jelph—and a half-dozen more girls became a part of military history. The jolly occasion was a far cry from the panting flight, the shrieks for mercy, the tortures by fire of the awful afternoon and evening just one year before.

The fourth came on Sunday, and young William Rogers wrote proudly into his journal the conclusion of his sermon "to the brigade and regiment of artillery":

> Hark! what voice is that which I hear? It is the voice of encouragement; permit me for your animation to repeat it distinctly: 'Our fathers trusted and the Lord did deliver them . . . they trusted in him and were not confounded.'

Secular recognition of Independence Day was set for Monday and it was elaborately celebrated, especially by

General Poor who entertained no less than eighty-seven officers including General Hand and his retinue at an elaborate dinner in a diningroom consisting of "a large booth, about eighty feet in length, with a marquee pitched at each end." The hills lining the river gave back loud echoes as the whole party "graced the feast with a number of good songs." The usual number of toasts—one for each of the thirteen warring colonies—left all in high good humor. Aside from the customary drinks—to Washington, the King and Queen of France, fallen heroes—were two less usual. Number 10 was "Civilization or death to all American savages"—and number 12—"May this New World be the last Asylum for freedom and the Arts."

While the whole day, as Captain Daniel Livermore reported, "was spent in civil mirth and jollity," young Lieutenant John Hardenburgh was sent out with a party to hunt game and returned disconsolate at sunset with nothing to show for it. Evidently not as sociable as his brother officers, he later wrote: "During our stay at Wyoming we had nothing to do but to keep guard and disciplining our troops." Another discouraging note on the same day was recorded by Chaplain Rogers: "An Express arrived from Sunbury announcing the destruction of nine persons out of twelve by the savages at Munsey, as they were working in a field."

The next day, despite an afternoon storm of "thunder, hail, rain and wind" which exhibited hailstones "as large as hens' Eggs," Colonel Proctor entertained a number of officers and "a truly merry career was the consequence."

There was time for fishing and for games of shinny and ball in the next few days before another major social engagement, that of July thirteenth, when Colonel Zebulon

159

Butler and Captain Simon Spalding, both residents of the region, brought to the encampment under the chaperonage of their wives "½ doz. Young Ladys from Wyoming with whom we pass an agreeable afternoon." The girl guests shuddered as Colonel Butler showed them "a death Mall, or war Mallet that the Indians left by a Man they had knocked in the head."

Shinny had become an almost daily exercise among the officers by the middle of the month. Dr. Elmer, Lieutenant Samuel Shute and General Hand were enthusiastic players, and General Sullivan attended the games and "was much pleased with our activity in the performance." Sam Shute, and other young officers equally indefatigable, were also playing "fives"—a game similar to modern handball—nearly every day and using up their excess energy with wild "buck dances." After one of these he reported "colonel De Hart, General Hand and myself slept together in the open air, but with a canteen of spirits at our head."

"Disciplining of the troops," however, had resulted in discontent and boredom among the rank and file. An order of late June which forbade going swimming in the river except before troop beating (assembly) in the mornings of Tuesdays, Thursdays, and Saturdays, proved so unpopular that it was generally disregarded until, being "determined to prevent a practice so dangerous to the health of the troops" headquarters issued another order threatening any soldier who disobeyed it with twenty lashes "instantly inflicted." Apparently after this the crime of going swimming was ignored for there are no records that the sentinels appointed to guard the two most popular swimming holes ever reported a violator of the rule.

Among the German regiments, many men became desperately homesick for their families and their farms down-river. On the fourteenth of the month, thirty-three of their number calmly asserted that their time of enlistment had elapsed and set out for their homes, marching to the rhythms set by a fifer and a drummer. A detail of fifty was sent after them and they were soon returned to camp where a court-martial sentenced five of the ringleaders to be shot and others to run the gantlet through the entire command. Sorrowfully, the chaplains visited the doomed men each day to prepare them for their deaths. They found the deserters so miserable and penitent that their reports to headquarters influenced General Sullivan to re-prieve the lot on the understanding that under similar circumstances he would never again show mercy.

Just before this happy event, on Saturday the twenty-fourth, considerably more than a hundred boats appeared on the Susquehanna bearing long-awaited supplies. Wrote Chaplain Rogers: "On the river they appeared beautiful as they approached the village in proper divisions. Those with field pieces on board discharged several rounds for joy which in the surrounding woods produced a pleasing echo. Sergeant Roberts wrote: ". . . theare was 26 Rounds of Cannon fiered, 13 from the Boates and 13 from the Camp. Theas Boates had four 3-pounders and one howet that three Burns for thear Securety on the River." Four days later eighty loaded wagons and a large number of pack horses arrived from Easton, and all knew that the great expedition was ready to start. The last week of the long boring encampment was relieved by two heartening events.

On Monday Dr. Elmer reported: "All hands dined at the Colonel's today and after dinner we took a hearty game of

Bandy Wicket" (apparently the farewell game of shinny)
and on Thursday, the twenty-ninth, there were Masonic
ceremonies attendant upon the re-interring of Captain
Davis and Lieutenant Jones, "the afternoon very rainy,
otherwise the appearance would have been tolerably
grand, as they all marched in order with the band of
music playing." Chaplain Rogers noted "the brotherhood
met at five o'clock and marching by the General's marquee, had the pleasure of his company; Colonels Proctor's
and Hubley's regiments, with drums, fifes and the band
of music accompanied them. Reaching the graves an exceedingly heavy shower of rain prevented the delivery of
a discourse designed for the occasion; however a short
prayer was made, the bodies were interred in Masonic
form and three volleys of small arms fired."

❦ ON THE VENGEANCE ROAD

On Saturday, the last day of July, at noon, Colonel
Proctor's artillery let go with a salute to Wyoming, a farewell to the "elegant and delightful" valley between the
mountain ridges, to the "pitiful widows and orphans who,
by the vile hands of the savages, have not only been deprived some of tender husbands, some of indulgent
parents, and others of affectionate friends and acquaintances, besides robbed and plundered of all their furniture
and clothing," to the green bush huts of the corps men,
the marquees of the officers, the swimming holes and the
shinny fields. The salute "was returned to the mutual
satisfaction of all present."

The brass band, already aboard some of the hundred
and twenty river boats, blared a march as the long columns began their rhythmic stepping northward. General

Hand's Brigade of Light Troops was almost a mile in front, then came the commands of Generals Maxwell and Poor, then the twelve hundred pack horses and the eight hundred head of cattle, moving raggedly and slowly to the shouts and curses of the herdsmen, and at the end Colonel Ogden's regiment, the rear guard. General Sullivan's caution and meticulous attention to detail was now to be rewarded. With scouting units on either flank as well as in the advance and rear of his column, with his ten cannon and two howitzers on the big Marietta-built bateaux in mid-channel (protected by marchers on each bank), he moved ten miles upriver and encamped at sundown. One of the boats sank, another was damaged, the whole fleet was delayed by shallows and swift water, the land, soggy with two weeks of intermittent rain, offered a heavy, sticky marching surface, but the big unwieldy force reached the banks of Lackawanna Creek in good spirits.

At once the journalkeepers burst into lyric praises of the Susquehanna valley. The New Hampshire, New Jersey, New York troops had never seen such landscape—such trees, such promise of fertility, and the pens of the journalkeepers scratched it all down diligently. Occasional glimpses of the flowing waters through the trees and underbrush inspired constant tributes. Even Sergeant Roberts overcame his lack of education in language to remark "the Land is the best that Ever I see—Timmothy as high as my head . . . the Warter is but poor, the Wild turkes very plenty the young ones yelping through te Woods as if it was inhabited Ever So thick."

The twelve-day march covering the hundred miles from Wyoming to Tioga did more to establish the reputation of the Susquehanna among Americans than any event in the winding river's history. The mountains at the narrows were so close that the flowing water looked dark and brown below. The paths along their sides were so steep and rocky that the troops scrambled along them in single file. They lost horses and cows that frequently fell from the rocky heights, and great quantities of baggage were spilled (later collected with infinite pains and long delay).

The weather was mostly hot and steamy during daylight and added to the fatigue of the long up-and-down slopes. With nightfall usually came fogs and sudden rains. Each hour showed new wonders of nature, and the marchers gazed on them with an almost childish wonder. They admired the spring-fed waterfalls that sent foam-whitened waters plunging down high cliffs with a constant roar "uttering forth a beautiful echo." They groaned that orders allowed no shooting at deer and turkey they saw along the way until they discovered the hilarious sport of trying to catch them alive by hand. Hazelnuts were ripening in the woods "in amazing quantities." In the swamps and along the river bottomlands the tall black walnut trees were sometimes four feet through—"the stateliest I ever saw." The men enjoyed the taste of the little "Indian apples" growing on bushes only two feet high.

Chaplain Rogers wrote on August fourth: "Towards evening our fisherman Hansell returned from his flanking manoeuvre and introduced himself with a good string of fish, on which having refreshed ourselves we retired soldier like to our hard beds and devoted the night to invigorating sleep." Despite the damp hot weather, the hardships endured by those poling the boats up the shallow stream, the steep rocky trails infested with big blacksnakes and

164

dangerous whirring rattlers, the army was having a good time.

The buttonwoods amazed them with their thickness, and one measured twenty-one feet around. Other tremendous trees were the rock maples, the pines (white, pitch, and yellow), the ash, myrtle, elm, beech and hickory. Beside the water, wide meadows of English grass, "the greenest and Richest carpet that Nature ever spread," and of blue-grass and clover were interrupted here and there by "a root called Sweet Sicily, of a similar taste with anise-seed."

Major James Norris wrote of the "green hills as far as the eye could reach rising like the seats of an Amphi-theatre and the distance of the prospect gave the River and the boats the beautiful Resemblance of Miniature painting."

After passing the ruins of the old Moravian town at Wyalusing which, in happier times, was "occupied by Indians and white people" until the Indians were forced to move west, the army reached Standing Stone Bottom Sunday, August eighth. Two men had died of fatigue. A drummer of Colonel Proctor's Artillery had fallen off one of the boats and drowned. Sergeant Martin Johnson, notorious for his hard drinking but "having a great Spirit," continued to march until "overcome with heat and fatigue." Dr. Elmer wrote: ". . . having his vitals decayed by Spirituous Liquors readily accounts for his sudden death."

General Sullivan had become increasingly ill on the march and here left the meadow camp for the comfort of Colonel Proctor's "flag-ship," *The Adventure*. The troops observed the slanting monolithic marker rising in the swirling current with speculative interest. A sunset gun,

165

aimed by the caprice of a proud artilleryman, proved his marksmanship. The ball chipped off a corner above the water and by misfortune permanently erased Indian marks that might have been of value to future archaeologists. Parson Rogers went for a walk, ate some wild gooseberries, "exactly similar to the tame kind," plucked some wild pinks, saw a wild tulip and also plenty of crabapples.

Plodding on in intense heat through "wild grass and wild beans higher than a man's head," the army climbed Break-Neck Hill on a very narrow path "with scarcely room for man and horse to walk in." Here, according to Chaplain Rogers, "in case of a mis-step nothing seemingly could preserve from instant death as the fall must be at least one hundred and eighty feet perpendicular down rocks into the river." That night the camp was on the beautiful plain of Sheshequin. Rain gave the army rest the next day, except for a large detail sent ahead to explore the entrance to Tioga. The boats, far behind, were enabled to catch up, bringing with them delayed provisions.

Early on August eleventh, the whole army marched for Tioga, crossing the river to the west bank on a ford newly discovered by general officers on the previous day's reconnoitering. Proctor's men fired a few cannon into the woods ahead to rid them of possible enemy forces and then the troops, taking off their overalls and tying them about their necks, hanging their cartouche boxes on their bayonets, waded across in platoons "each soldier grasping the hand of his comrade next to him for support."

General Hand, "in order to animate his brigade," quit his horse "and waded with cheerfulness" at their head. Sergeant Roberts reported heroic action: "Several men wold Bin Drounded if the horsemen had not helped

166

them. Colonel Barber had like to Bin Drounded and his
hors by Riding after A man Down the Falls—the Warter
about up to our arms and the Stream as Strong as a Mill-
tail."

Refreshed by their bath, the army (having lost not a
single man) marched on through a rich bottom which the
literary Major Norris described as "covered with strong
and stately Timber which shut out the Sun and shed a
cool agreeable twilight" until suddenly they were thread-
ing an open sun-drenched plain where once "that Easter
Queen of the Seneca Tribe dwelt in Retirement and Sullen
majesty." Colonel Hartley and some of the participants of
his raid of the previous year looked once more on the ruins
of the palace they had burned—still surrounded with
"fruit trees of various kinds." On the site of the homes of
the Indians "whether through principle of Avarice or
Curiosity, our Soldiers dug up several of their graves and
found a good many laughable relics, as a pipe, Tomahawks, and Beads, etc."

A few miles farther the marching army in order of battle crossed the Tioga River and began its highhearted advance on the green, tall-grass levels into Tioga. Chaplain
Rogers was so inspired by the sight that he called it
"grand beyond description" and then could not forbear to
describe it. "Drums were beating, fifes playing, colors flying. Getting to the mouth of the Tioga, we found it in
width one hundred and forty-two yards, and the water
much deeper than had been imagined. Verdant plains in
our rear, the flowing Susquehanna on our right, Ourselves
in the Tioga or Cayuga stream, with a fine neck of land
in our front and mountains surrounding the whole afforded
pleasant reflections though separated from friends and in

an enemy's country. Surely a soil like this is worth contending for. . . ."

Already, as the army had begun its work of burning Indian towns and laying waste their harvests, doubts of the justice of the expedition were assailing the minds of the more thoughtful soldiers. Dr. Jabez Campfield on the same day that the young parson was moved to his patriotic outburst wrote in his journal: "I very heartily wish these rusticks may be reduced to reason by the approach of this army without their suffering the extremes of war; there is something so cruel in destroying the habitations of any people (however mean they may be, being their all) that I might say the prospect hurts my feelings."

The next day a young lieutenant reported: "We set fire to all the buildings in the town, about twenty, then marched across the river and destroyed three or four fields of corn, cutting and throwing it in heaps, the corn being then in the milk."

A lightning raid on Chemung, calculated to surprise this Indian town at sunrise, resulted in an all-night march and the bad luck, on Friday the thirteenth, of finding the town evacuated, though fires were still burning and an Indian dog still slept. The journalists exclaimed over the beauty of the town, its more than fifty houses "built chiefly with split and hewn timber" on the bank of the river in a "most beautiful, fertile and extensive plain."

"About sunrise," wrote Major Norris, "the General gave orders for the town to be illuminated—and accordingly we had a glorious Bonfire of upwards of 30 buildings at once: a melancholy and desperate Spectacle to the Savages many of whom must have beheld it from a Neighboring Hill." It was hardly surprising, therefore, that the distant spectators ambushed a detachment of General Hand's troops sent in pursuit of them and killed a commissioned officer and six men besides wounding Captain Carberry (cavalry hero of Hartley's campaign the year before) and ten others. In this engagement the army suffered its greatest losses along the Susquehanna.

General Sullivan ordered fortifications built along a two-hundred-yard line between the Susquehanna and the Tioga (now the Chemung) rivers some distance above their junction, waiting meanwhile for the arrival of General James Clinton's army, then on its way downstream from Otsego Lake.

❦ RIDING THE FRESH

Clinton's forces, encamped at the source of the Susquehanna, had also had a long wait. Gathered at Schenectady they had marched along the Mohawk to Canajoharie. More than two hundred of the boats they planned to use in their descent of the Susquehanna had already been built on the banks of the Mohawk. The troops loaded these and their three months' supplies on hundreds of big horse-drawn wagons and soon the air above the roads south was dense with dust as the whole expedition rattled the twenty miles from Canajoharie to the north end of Otsego Lake. Late in June, fanned out in a wide, heavily laden flotilla, the boats carried all troops and supplies to the south end of the lake where the Susquehanna begins. Tradition has it that James Clinton was nonplussed when he realized that the river was not navigable at this point, but was saved embarrassment by a young frontiersman, anonymous folk hero, who suggested damming the outlet until the water was so high in the lake that when released the "fresh" would sweep all the boats downstream.

For a whole month, while the waters gathered against the dam, Clinton's army of about eighteen hundred lived much the same life as did Sullivan's troops at Wyoming. On July fourth the entire brigade paraded the bank of the lake and fired a salvo in honor of the country's natal day. The whole American army had adopted the French name for such salutes—*feu de joie*—but in their daily journals there were about as many different spellings of the term as there were journalists. A Lieutenant van Hovenburg with Clinton's forces called it a "fudie joy." Baptist Chaplain John Gano preached a sermon from Exodus XII,14: "This day shall be unto you for a memorial . . . throughout your generations"; and the hearty, gay French officer, Colonel Rignier, helped make it more memorable by an evening grog party for officers in his wide lake-shore Bowery. According to Lieutenant Erkuries Beattie, "We sat on the ground in a large circle and closed the day with a number of toasts suitable and a great deal of mirth for two or three hours." Three days later Colonel Gansevoort's officers gave a similar affair at another bower and on the morrow a journal entry reads: "The officers drew each one more keg of rum."

The waiting was monotonous and hot. It seemed to Clinton and his men that Sullivan, far to the south, would never be ready to order them to ride the Susquehanna to their rendezvous. They fished and hunted and drank. Drills and target practice were part of every day's routine. Parading for the cruel lashing of violators of regulations (once for the execution of a deserter) occasionally interrupted the dull procession of days. A trifling incident made Colonel

170

Rignier the most popular man in camp. Drilling a company of colored Continentals who wore wool hats, the brims and lower halves of the crown being black and the upper portion much lighter, he saw a soldier through lack of attention fail to execute a command.

"Halloo," shouted the Frenchman, "you black son-of-a-bitch wid a white face—why you no mind you beezness?"

This admonition so convulsed the rest of the Negro company that they were helpless with giggles and the colonel, realizing their predicament, ordered them to halt and ground their muskets.

"Now," he said, "laugh your pelly full all," and himself joined in the prolonged and boisterous explosion that followed.

The water in the lake had risen noticeably and the army was wild with impatience. Rumors of immediate departure spread. At last Chaplain John Gano persuaded General Clinton to allow him on Sunday, August eighth, to announce as the text of his sermon Acts XX, 7. "And upon the first day of the week," read Gano "when the disciples came together to break bread, Paul preached unto them, ready to depart on the morrow."

The excitement caused by this obvious hint, seemingly made official by the presence of their commander, took such hold on the troops that they heard little more of the sermon which, by fortunate design, did not last, like Paul's, until midnight. Indeed by that time the more than two hundred boats moored on the lake side of the dam had been moved to the river side and, the dam having been razed, were straining at their moorings as the massed waters rolled south in depth sufficient to make the shallow Susquehanna navigable. By dawn the heavily laden craft

171

were being released, each with a three-man crew to pilot it down the long winding stream. The sudden rise in the river level, advancing downstream like a tidal bore, is said to have terrified the Indians who had been planning to oppose the Continentals. They assumed, according to some accounts, that the white men had used supernatural powers to raise the water and were disheartened that such powerful gods had enlisted against the British. Meanwhile logs and rocks that had been out of water the day before had now been "imersed" and were impeding the jubilant, shouting boatmen. Their craft winged up on the banks, whirled about and proceeded stern first, crashed into shallows that stove sudden holes in their bottoms. Nevertheless at the end of the first day the majority of them had floated more than thirty miles, while the troops marching along the banks had covered only sixteen.

Now that Clinton was on the way, General Sullivan sent a strong detachment of about nine hundred men north to meet him and to bolster him against an expected Indian attack. While Sullivan's army waited for Clinton at Tioga, Chaplain Rogers got the opportunity on the hot morning of August eighteenth to preach "in the Masonic form" the funeral sermon prepared for the reinterring on July twenty-ninth of the bodies of Captain Davis and Lieutenant Jones. No rain forced a repostponement and the brethren of Military Lodge Number 19 of the "honorable and ancient Society of Freemen . . . attended on this occasion in proper form and the whole was conducted with propriety and harmony." Generals Sullivan and Maxwell with their official families were there and the Eleventh Pennsylvania Regiment of which Davis had been an officer paraded for the solemn fraternal ceremonies. Immediately thereafter young Parson Rogers preached another sermon over the corpse of Philip Helter, formerly a Philadelphia biscuit-baker, who had been slain and scalped while searching for some strayed horses. "The day being sultry," wrote the chaplain into his diary, "was, after so much preaching, a good deal overcome." Since his text for the Masonic discourse had been the first clause of the seventh verse of the seventh chapter of Job—"Remember that my life is but wind"—this entry gave his words an unintended significance that has since amused the irreverent.

The meeting of General Poor's advance troops and Clinton's army was successfully accomplished at a spot ever since called Union. As soon as "Mutual congratulations and complements" had been exchanged, the united forces marched downriver to the beautiful Indian town of Oswego which "was made a burnfire to Grace our Meating." Though delayed by rain, the combined unit marched into Sullivan's camp at eleven o'clock on the Sunday morning of August twenty-second and there was general rejoicing. The army waiting at Tioga cheered as they heard from upriver the echoes as "Clintin fiered six pieces when he got Wathin one Mile of our Camp."

When Clinton's 208 boats, moving over the water in a close formation, reached the camp, Colonel Proctor's cannon replied with "seven pieces of Cannon For Joy of our armey's" while the encamped brigades were paraded under arms and the welcome was made more impressive by "a Band of Musick which played Beautiful as we passed them by." A shower cooled the afternoon as the officers and men of Clinton's army visited their friends in the encamped regiments. General Sullivan entertained all field

173

officers at dinner and afternoon entertainment was provided for rank and file when a "Drum mager" convicted of stealing from the rum rations was sentenced to march through his regiment wearing his coat inside out and his canteen around his neck. Two privates who had been accomplices in the crime were compelled to strip and run through their brigade with "Every Man a Whip Corporal."

❦ THE SCYTHE OF DEATH

> Battles are not measured by their
> death-roll but by their results.
> —GENERAL W. T. SHERMAN (1879)

It was noon of August twenty-sixth before the entire expedition had been organized and was ready to begin the destructive march which was its major purpose. It was impossible to continue to move the artillery by boats, and dragging the guns at once became the major hardship of the campaign. Though sometimes more than two hundred men tugged at the ropes, the big guns jolted along slowly and often balked the most strenuous efforts to move them. "A universal cry against the artillery," wrote Major Jeremiah Fogg on August twenty-seventh, while Sergeant Moses Fellowes proudly boasted "Such Cursing, Cutting and Diging, overseting Wagons, Cannon and Pack Horses into the river etc. is not to Be Seen Every Day."

There were recompenses, however. Major John Burrowes reported on the same day a march of only six miles ending on a flat "where corn grows such as cannot be equalled in Jersey. The field contains about 100 acres, beans, cucumbers, Simblens [a kind of squash], watermelons and pumpkins in such quantities . . . would be almost incredible to a civilized people. We sat up until

174

between one and two o'clock feasting on these rarities."
The athletic Lieutenant Samuel Shute sat up late enough,
according to his own count, to make something of a record.
"I myself ate 10 ears [of corn], one quart of beans, and 7
squashes." Major Fogg's breakfast menu the next morning
was so worthy of note that he recorded it. "This morning
we had a dainty repast on the fruits of the savages. Our
friends at home cannot be happier amid their variety of
superfluities than we were while sitting at a dish of tea,
toast, corn, squash, smoked tongue, etc." After the battle
of Newtown two days later, when General Sullivan called
upon his troops to go on half rations of meat and flour,
the unanimous favorable response was partially dictated
by overstuffed stomachs and the realization that the major
problem of the next few weeks would not be that of getting enough to eat but that of doing away with tremendous crops now ripe, tasty, and ready for harvest.

The battle of Newtown (near present-day Elmira) developed when scouts reported a detachment of the enemy
entrenched on rising ground behind pine-log breastworks
masked by green shrubs. Since this force had been waiting for eight hot days, the camouflage had withered and
was easily detected. General Sullivan ordered his riflemen to keep up a diversionary fire on these fortifications
while he disposed the rest of his men in such ways as
to outflank the opposing troops. Outnumbered by more
than three to one, the Indians and Tories put up a considerable show of resistance. The journals emphasize the
wild yelling of the Indians and their making numerous
sorties from their lines in the apparent effort to provoke
their foes into making a frontal attack.

As soon as Proctor's artillery had been brought forward

and had begun its cannonading, however, the enthusiasm of the tribal warriors waned. Encouraged by their remarkable chieftain, Joseph Brant (a courageous man of education and cultural attainments), they withstood the shelling for about a half hour before they ran away in terror. They and their Tory allies succeeded in killing only three of Sullivan's men in the entire engagement which lasted from about three to five o'clock in the afternoon. All of these were New Hampshire men in General Poor's command. About forty (most of these also Yankees) were wounded in charging up a hill where, for a short time, the enemy attempted to make a second stand. A few died later of the effects of their injuries. The Continentals proved their courage and their ability to obey orders with precision while under fire, and their officers were very proud of them. The losses of the enemy were larger, since eleven dead were afterwards found on the field and, after Indian custom, a considerable number were probably carried off in the retreat.

General Sullivan's appeal to the army to "live on half a Pound of Beef and half a Pound of Flower Pr. Day for the future as long as it might be found Necessary" was made at the right psychological moment. On the day after the battle, his troops, jubilant with easy victory, unanimously granted the request and added three enthusiastic cheers. On that same day many of the men exulted to see the heavier cannon being shipped downriver in the flotilla that carried the wounded. Two officers were even happier when Lieutenant William Barton at the request of his superior officer Daniel Pratt, major in the First New Jersey Regiment, sent out a "small party to look for some of the dead Indians." It took a half day of searching, but toward "noon they found them and skinned two of them from their hips down for foot legs; one pair for the Major the other for myself."

The expedition was now leaving the neighborhood of the Susquehanna for the Finger Lake country northwest of Newtown. For almost a month, sometimes as a unit, sometimes in separate detachments, the troops busied themselves destroying the prosperous villages, orchards, storehouses, gardens of the Iroquois. They were surprised that many of the Indians lived in well-built, glass-windowed houses, faring better in the fertile valley of the Genesee than did many a white farmer along the Mohawk. So extensive were their fields, so lavish their crops that the work of destruction became a colossal bore. The soldiers threw millions of ears of corn into the rivers, devastated by fire thousands of acres of growing foodstuffs, cut down or girdled countless apple and peach trees in the widespread orchards, slaughtered pigs and cattle. The slim silver lakes, lined with orchards and vines, were charred to the water's edges. The long houses—sacred to the religious faiths of the Iroquois—were heaps of sodden ashes. "I should not think it an affront to the Divine will," wrote Major Jeremiah Fogg, "to lay some effectual plan either to civilize or totally extirpate the race."

❧ "AND HE MARCHED THEM DOWN AGAIN"

I had rather be the advocate of the
Indian before a just tribunal than of the white man.
—GENERAL A. S. DIVEN (1879)

At Niagara the British and their disheartened allies grimly awaited the attack they believed sure to come. For reasons never to be quite understood, Sullivan, having marched to the Genesee, turned about and marched back again. Despite the horrible nightmarish discovery of the incredibly tortured and mangled bodies of Lieutenant Thomas Boyd and Sergeant Michael Parker who had been captured and fiendishly executed, the army was in high spirits when it once more, late in September, neared the Susquehanna. A small garrison sent with provisions up the Tioga to Fort Reed, near Newtown, welcomed the marchers as soon as they came in sight with a thirteen-gun salute and they answered in kind. The full meat ration was restored and every officer and soldier was rewarded with "one Jill of Whiskey."

The sight of the familiar brown ripples of the Susquehanna brought realization to the sun-tanned weary troops that with mission accomplished they would soon be resting and accordingly set off a sequence of wild and antic revels. The saturnine and realistic Major Fogg reported September twenty-fifth in his journal with Yankee economy: "A Feu de Joie for Spain's declaring war with England." From more articulate officers the true story of that happy Saturday is revealed in more detail. Soon after the good news from Spain arrived, Sullivan ordered the entire army to parade at five o'clock. At the same time, he presented the officers of each brigade with "one of the best oxen there was and 5 gallons of spirits." Thirteen round of cannon began the demonstration. "Then," wrote Lieutenant Barton, "began a running fire of muskets from the right through the whole." This was not performed "to the General's liking" and he requested all to reload and be prepared for a repetition of the salute. Having ordered not a man to fire until he should come opposite him he "put his horse off at full speed and rode from right to left with whip and spur,

178

men all firing according to orders, which made it very grand."

"It went like a hallelujah!" said the general.

The army gave three resounding cheers, one for the United States, one for Congress, and one for the King of Spain before dismissal. Many of the officers, each bringing his own bread, knife and plate, assembled for supper soon thereafter at a large bower which was illuminated with thirteen pine-knot fires and thirteen candles burning. The guests sat on the ground with General Hand at the head, Colonel Proctor at the foot, and devoured vast quantities of roast bullock and "a great plenty of liquor." The thirteen toasts proposed by General Hand between the program contributions of his brigade's massed fifes and drums went much as expected, except for the twelfth (offered in compliment to General Sullivan), "May the kingdom of Ireland Merit a stripe in the American standard" and the last, "May the enemies of America be metamorphosed into pack horses, and sent on a western expedition against the Indians." As might be expected the rest of the evening was spent with the greatest sociability and mirth and soon throughout the whole camp there were spontaneous outbursts of "Buck and Indian dances." Lieutenant Beatty's first entry in his journal for Sunday morning read: "Did not feel very well this morning after my frolick but was ordered on detachment but it rained a little which prevented our going."

On Thursday, the last day of September, the jubilant columns "with Musick playing and Colours flying" marched proudly into Fort Sullivan, and again there was exchange of cannon salutes, the issuing of whiskey for the officers, rum for the men. The garrison offered another elegant feast to all general and field officers, and, to add a distinctive elegance hitherto unachieved, Colonel Proctor's brass band and all the drums and fifes "played in concert the whole time." After the dinner and a "pouring out pretty free of libations of Bacchus," the event was concluded with an Indian dance directed by an Oneida chief and led off by General Hand. New elements had now been added. The dancers had powdered their heads with flour and daubed their faces with paint, and with their previous practice were able to give a much better account of themselves than previously.

Two days later, on October second, General Sullivan gave a dinner, "an elegant entertainment" to which all general and field officers were invited. This time the "young sachem of the Oneida" led off his native dances, followed by several other Indians and the highly stimulated officers. The Oneida produced his own rhythms by clashing together a rattle, a knife, and a pipe and singing in his own language the whole time. At the end of each dance the whole party joined together in producing an ear-splitting Indian war whoop.

As these gay farewell affairs were being held, the minds of a few of the more reflective officers were concerned with other subjects. Lieutenant Colonel Hubley was moved to write sentimentally on the departure by river boat of "our cow which we had along with us the whole expedition and to whom we are under infinite obligations for the great quantity of milk she afforded us which rendered our situation very comfortable, and was no small addition to our half-allowance."

Major Fogg's contemplations were less whimsical. Making a succinct review of the whole enterprise, on September thirtieth he commented in his journal on the frustrating delays of early summer but added "a march of three hundred miles was performed, a battle was fought, and a whole country desolated in thirty days . . . the special hand and smiles of Providence being so apparently manifested that he who views the scene with indifference is worse than an infidel. . . . Not a single gun was fired for eighty miles on our march out or an Indian seen on our return . . . nor has there been an hour's rain since the thirtieth day of August." Aware that there might be some discomfiting inquiries on the success of the expedition, he wrote an uneasily ironic last paragraph: "The question will naturally arise, what have you to show for your exploits? Where are your prisoners? To which I reply that the rags and emaciated bodies of our soldiers must speak for our fatigue, and when the Querist will point out a mode to tame a partridge, or the expediency of hunting wild turkeys with light horse, I will show them our prisoners. The nests are destroyed, but the birds are still on the wing."

The units of Sullivan's Army had all been redistributed before the heavy snows had begun to fall and the Indians camping at Niagara under the protection of the British had begun to feel the full effect of the campaign. The winter proved so severe that little hunting was possible. Scurvy killed many of them, and the warriors, watching their wives and children die from want of food, vowed renewal of their ferocious raids as soon as the weather abated. When spring came, the war whoop once more sounded in the Susquehanna settlements.

To this day many of the people of the Susquehanna valley and the Finger Lake country, particularly those of the older families resident in America during the Revolution, regard Sullivan's Big March with discomfort. Much of the unfavorable comment has come down through the years from the mouths of the marchers themselves. The peace-loving Quakers of Pennsylvania never approved it. The God-fearing Yankees, answering savage cruelty with savage cruelty, tried hard to agree with Major Fogg that the Indian must be civilized or totally destroyed, but their consciences were troubled. It did not seem Christian to them to avenge atrocities with atrocities. There were efforts to prove the expedition magnificently heroic. The Congress expressed its gratitude for a thorough and efficient accomplishment and there was much praise for the sure handling of the big force which returned with a loss of less than fifty men. A hundred years later there were many celebrations along the path the army had taken and at each one there were long and grandiloquent speeches.

Near the site of the Battle of Newtown on August 29, 1879, however, one speaker dared to criticize Sullivan for not following Washington's wishes and attacking Niagara, for making prisoners of Mohawks who had been "neutral in war, peacable as neighbors," for rousing the Iroquois to return with "the torch and the scalping knife in quick and terrible retribution . . . in 1779-'80-'81-'82. General William Tecumseh Sherman, leader of another famous march of devastation, addressed the same audience with remarks not as well remembered as his famous "War is hell." Said he, "When all things ought to be peaceful, war comes and purifies the atmosphere . . . we are all better for it. Wherever men raise up their hands to oppose this great advancing tide of civilization, they must be swept aside peaceably if possible, forcibly if we must."

Another Civil War hero at the same celebration, General H. W. Slocum, caused embarrassed concern by stating, "But I say to you that Sherman's army never committed the atrocities that were committed by General Sullivan's."

The nearly five thousand men who made the Big March, however, remembered little of its difficulties. Their ragged shoes and torn uniforms were soon replaced, their tired bodies soon refreshed. They remembered most the massive black walnut trees, the sun-flecked waters, the rich loam of the river bottoms. They remembered the Indian orchards with boughs bending under the weight of ripening fruit, the neat gardens strewn with golden pumpkins and reddening beets, the cornstalks rising to heights far above a man's head. As an advertisement of prize real estate, the Big March reached its greatest success. Many a Yankee soldier made an inner resolve to forsake the rocky barrens of New England for these lush lands. Some later fulfilled this promise they had made to themselves. Here and there along the river, descendants still work the land chosen by the marching men.

13

Pennymite War III

ELISHA AND THE PENNYMITES

Veterans of the two Connecticut companies furnished by the Yankees of Wyoming to Washington's army discovered, when they returned to their Susquehanna homes, that they were still in a war. The British had been defeated, but not the Pennymites. The downriver counties were more bitter than ever over what they regarded as unjustifiable invasion, and ardent patriots who had fought against Cornwallis were now so incensed by differences over Susquehanna land that they sought to dispossess by force and, if necessary, to kill their former comrades.

A federal commission containing delegates from both of the warring states was appointed by the Continental Congress in 1782. It met at Trenton, New Jersey, and reached the decision that Connecticut had no jurisdiction over residents of disputed lands but that they might hold acres they occupied until conflicting claims had been settled. This seems reasonable to the Yankees who were bone-weary of the long quarrel. Many were content to become citizens of Pennsylvania in hope of recognition of their claims.

But the Pennymites assumed their own interpretation

184

of the decision. They announced that it had abrogated all rights of the Connecticut immigrants and at once organized still another expedition to evict them from their homes. Raid and counterraid followed. At the time when the young Republic's most able men were exerting every effort toward a harmonious union of the states, forces from two of the former colonies chose to continue a civil war that began nearly thirty years before.

A new leader, Colonel John Franklin, had come to Wyoming from Connecticut, and he was as ready as the Pennymites to set aside the Trenton Decision. Gathering about him those who felt, as he did, that no Pennsylvanian could be trusted and that the only salvation of the Yankees lay in their establishing an independent government, he and his adherents stoutly fought off the enraged enemy.

Elisha Harding, when he was an old man, set down some vivid reminiscences. He told of the fatal July third of 1788, when he was a boy of fifteen, and he also described the violence of life along the Susquehanna six years later when Connecticut and Pennsylvania wrangled over possession of the Wyoming valley.

In the spring before he was twenty-one, Elisha Harding, riding toward Wyoming, discovered that an armed body of Pennymites had invaded the valley and turned helpless families out of their homes. Among these had been aged folk and "widows whose husbands had fallen by the Savage with there helpless children." At point of bayonet, these miserable people had been compelled to set out through the cold wilderness for the Delaware River sixty miles away.

Elisha asked to be allowed to stay a few days before leaving and was peremptorily told that he must go at once, "which went down heavy." On his way he hitched his horse to a wagon that somehow carried four families, and he walked beside it all the way to Orange County, New York.

He had threatened the wielders of the Pennymite bayonets with vengeance, and without delay he set out on the return trail. Approaching the Susquehanna, he found two-score fellow Yankees living the life of outlaws at a place called "The Coalbeds" back of Wilkes-Barre and planning an attack on the men who had evicted them. They raided some of the outlying farms and collected about twenty Pennymites whom they delivered to the jail at Sunbury, lodging charges of riot against them. They were enraged to find that their prisoners had been freed immediately and were back at the places of their capture by the time that they had themselves returned.

Persevering, the Yankees moved across the Susquehanna from The Coalbeds to four log houses in Kingston. A small group of Pennymites ordered them out, but a surprise sally captured the Pennymites and they were "well singed with an iron gunrod." This success gave courage to the Connecticut men, and they marched up and down the river evicting Pennymites, "doing unto them as they did unto us," and forcing them to seek refuge in the fort at Wilkes-Barre or to make the dreadful journey out of the valley through dripping swamps and the dismal jungle of the "Shades of Death."

Warned of a Pennymite expedition of reprisal, Elisha and his companions set out to ambush it. "We found them Jus at the Rising of the Sun. Some were in a house and some setting under a tree playing cards. We out of compliment gave them a Shot and wounded two of those under the tree. The Rest fled, leaving their hats."

Now, Colonel John Armstrong, the officer who had a few years ago written the "Newburgh proposals" which General Washington had so justly scorned, was sent by the Pennsylvania government with a regiment of militia to put a stop to the civil conflict. To the Yankees he "pledged his honour and that of the State," that if they would lay down their arms no advantage would be taken of them and they would be detained no longer than an hour. No sooner had they given up their guns than the colonel proved himself consistently ignoble. They were his prisoners and he marched them "with the tune of yankey doodle" into the fort where they were "confined in a Close room without aught to Eat for about 48 hours."

On the eighth of August, 1784, Elisha's twenty-first birthday, he and his companions were given food.

> . . . some poor old widows brought some Dried venison, and gave us to Eat. Our hands being tied it was put into our hands behind us, and placing ourselves in a ring Each with his meat in his hand and the one behind Eat out of the hands of the one before him forming a very Grotesque appearance. These were times that tried mens souls.

After Elisha's birthday feast, he and the other prisoners were taken out and roped together "like a train of oxen." Then they were told they were to be marched sixty miles to the Easton jail. If an attempt were made to free them, said the Pennymites, they would shoot the prisoners first before fighting off the would-be rescuers. Elisha wrote later: ". . . poor fools, ther was nothing to fall on them Except the wild beasts which would dispise their Com-

187

pany." He and his companions, all tied together, bore the hardships of their long march as best they could. At the end, he wrote, they were "lodged in a miserable, filthy, lowsey prison," and held there "until the next Spring, fed on bread and water of affliction." Each prisoner was allowed only a pound of this mixture per day except on Fridays when old Michael Hart, "who by Jewish Custom was taught to feed the poor," made it his custom to send "two young women with two wooden vessels filled with beef soup with beef and bread." When he was aged, himself, Elisha recorded this generosity and wrote of the long since deceased giver: "I hope he is Received to rest."

On a Friday evening in the spring, Elisha and his prisonmates staged a loud pretended quarrel. The jailer chided them and offered a glass of whiskey for them "to drink friend." They received it with thanks and requested a loaf of bread to eat with their drink. This was too big to pass through the bars, and as the jailer opened the gate to pass it through, Edward Inman, a giant of a man, knocked him down and he was immediately trampled upon by liberty-bent captives. Seizing billets of wood from a pile beside the oven, the Yankees beat down the outer door of the prison and rushed into the open. An old woman had shrieked an alarm and already a group of the citizens of Easton awaited them. Wielding their billets as clubs, the fugitives tried to beat their way to freedom, but the Pennymites hurled heavy stones which knocked down and injured several. Re-enforcements from the upper part of Easton arrived, and the Yankees found themselves attacked both from behind and before. Eleven of them, however, succeeded in escaping the town. Without shoes or moccasins, they set out to return over the sixty-mile

188

trail to the Susquehanna. Four days later, their feet bloody and sore, they were back at their rendezvous in the Wyoming woods.

Finding out that a reward of twenty-five pounds per head had been advertised for their capture, they joined with ten other Yankees in a midnight raid on the Pennymite fort where they set fire to the officers' barracks before they were driven off. Hardly had they returned to their quarters than Colonel John Armstrong and his men were upon them, swiftly surrounding the house where they were sitting down to dinner. Rushing to bar the doors, the twenty-one Yankees peered out of the windows at a hundred and fifty besiegers. Undaunted, they poured out such a galling fire that the Pennymites soon carried off "three horse loads of wounded," and shortly thereafter began their retreat through moonlit woods to the fort.

> The officer of the fort party, [wrote Elisha] had raised a large Peace of buckwheat over agains the fort and had imployed Soldiers to thresh it. We discovered them at work and found that they had a goodly heap and . . . we gathered all the Carriages and teams we Could get and in the morning by daylight we had it loaded. . . .

The Pennymites fired their fort cannon against them but missed, and the Yankees were soon out of range. A soldier in the fort shouted after them in grim humor: "Don't you damned Yankees want some molasses to eat with your buckwheat?"

Soon the Pennymites under cover of night left the fort, and the Yankees laid it low. The Third Pennymite War was near its end. It was ordered that the Connecticut men be reinstated on their farms. Wrote Elisha, "A man will do anything rather than be trodden on."

❧ ETHAN ALLEN AND THE WILD YANKEES

Sensing the lack of a ruthless, swashbuckling leader like Lazarus Stewart, who had died at Wyoming fighting off a circle of vengeful Indians, John Franklin had made Ethan Allen, captor of Ticonderoga, an offer of prestige and land so tempting that the Vermonter roared down from the north to hurl defiance at Pennsylvania. Waving his feathered hat, Ethan cursed the Pennymites so mightily that along the Susquehanna for generations an accepted folk definition of a brave man used to be: "He was not afraid of bears—he had heard Ethan Allen swear."

John Franklin was soon plotting with this plumed opportunist a new state along the upper river. Secession from Pennsylvania and Connecticut alike, was the cry. The conspiracy was looked upon with disfavor, however, by the more conservative Yankees. Zebulon Butler, grown old in the wars, had now turned conservative and peace-loving. He would be satisfied with Pennsylvania's governing if the Yankees might hold their lands. While Franklin's radicals were aligning themselves against such a surrender, cruel raiding between the opposed Pennymites and Connecticut men continued.

The new-state men had been dubbed "Wild Yankees" by their opponents who now included some of the most illustrious Connecticut settlers. Ethan Allen was out of patience with the latter. He had expected unanimity of purpose when he arrived and loudly blustered that, having made a state out of Vermont, he would now make another of north Pennsylvania. Give him a hundred Green Mountain Boys and two hundred riflemen, he shouted, and Pennsylvania could never stop him! Deflated by the sur-

190

prising and stubborn objections of some of his fellow New Englanders, he now swallowed his pride and went home.

❦ THE ARREST OF JOHN FRANKLIN

As John Franklin walked near the Susquehanna Ferry at Wilkes-Barre on an autumn afternoon, he was set upon without warning by four deputies who had been commissioned to arrest him and bring him to Philadelphia to be tried on a charge of treason. Franklin, courageous and powerful, fought so fiercely that the four had a difficult time. Most of his male supporters in the town were sowing grain in the outlying fields, and the only opposition was offered by a Quaker housewife who, gun in hand, made a vain attempt at rescue. Even after his arms had been tied, John Franklin kept on fighting. His captors placed him astride a horse but he threw himself to the street, and repeated the action as often as they returned him to the saddle.

The posse forced their frantic prisoner up the river bank and along Wilkes-Barre's Main Street to the house of Colonel Timothy Pickering, a veteran soldier and diplomat of the days of the Revolution. The colonel had recently been appointed by the Pennsylvania Assembly a member of a board of commissioners which should pass upon conflicting claims for land in the area and eventually bring about an end to the land wars. Though the deputies' horses had been stabled in his barn, Pickering had not thought to participate in the arrest. He later wrote an account of his actions:

> The four gentlemen seized him—two of their horses were in my stable, which were sent to them; but soon my servant returned on one of them with a message from the gentlemen that the

191

people were assembling in numbers, and requested me to come with what men were near me to prevent a rescue. I took loaded pistols in my hands, and went with another servant to their aid. Just as I met them, Franklin threw himself off his horse and renewed his struggle with them. His hair was disheveled and face bloody with preceding efforts. I told the gentlemen they would never carry him off unless his feet were tied under the horse's belly. I sent for a cord. The gentlemen remounted him, and my servant tied his feet. Then one taking his bridle, another following behind, and the others riding one on each side, they whipped up his horse and were soon beyond the reach of his friends. Thus subdued by six, he was hurried with painful speed to the jail in Philadelphia.

❧ THE PLEASANT KIDNAPING
OF COLONEL PICKERING

The temper of the assembling Wilkes-Barre citizens was so aroused by John Franklin's arrest that, to save himself from violence, Colonel Pickering was obliged to race into a neighboring wood, ill-clad and with only a few biscuits for food. Rioting in the town grew so furious that loyal neighbors sent word to him not to return. He therefore set out over cold and lonely mountain roads toward Philadelphia. An exhausted fugitive, he arrived at that city, then the national capital, to find that while he had been striving to bring peace to warring factions of Pennsylvania and Connecticut, the Federal Constitution binding these two and eleven more into a national whole had been evolved by delegates from all the states and now awaited general confirmation.

During Pickering's enforced absence from Wilkes-Barre the people of the town, including some of those most determined to avenge his treatment of Franklin, nevertheless elected him delegate to a state convention to consider ratification of the new constitution. Apparently believing himself once more safe from molestation, the colonel returned to his home on the Susquehanna in January, 1788, and spent the rest of the winter there without untoward incident. He was amazed, therefore, on a night of late June while he was sleeping with a small child in his arms, to be awakened by the gruff order to get up. Sensing that there were many about him in the darkness, he rose and began to dress. When his wife, who had slipped into the kitchen, returned with a torch its flickering revealed a mob of armed men who had blacked their faces and covered their heads with handkerchiefs. They bound the colonel with ropes, urged him to bring along his heavy surtout for protection from the cold, and set out up the river. On the way, one of the band told their captive that if he would sign an order of release for John Franklin he would at once be allowed to return to his home. Pickering refused.

The colonel soon realized by the respectful and courteous treatment he received, that these Wild Yankees did not intend to kill him. They offered him whiskey, presented him with a broiled steak from a deer they had killed, ordered one of their number to carry him pick-a-back across the Susquehanna lest he get wet. They took careful precautions against his escape, however, fettering him with a chain which, when the party slept, they either stapled to a tree or wound around the leg of one of his guards. The band frequently changed its hiding place, camping in sequestered wooded valleys, building leaf-covered booths for shelter against thunderstorms and spring rains. Captors and captive became friendly and the days passed as enjoyably as if all were on a hunting and

fishing party. The colonel, while still refusing to intercede for Franklin, offered to use his influence to obtain pardons for his companions for his illegal capture and detention. To this all were agreed, and with mutual expressions of good will they parted. The colonel went to his home none the worse for his experience.

❧ THE YANKEE-PENNSYLVANIANS

As the decade of the 1780's drew to a close, strong feeling still existed between the Pennymites and the Yankees. Conservative judgments like those of Pickering and Butler were gradually prevailing, but no one could be sure that armed outbreaks were over, even though the Pennsylvania Assembly adopted a conciliatory measure, the Confirming Law which established beyond question the proprietary rights of all Yankees who had settled on the banks of the Susquehanna before the Trenton Decision of 1783. There were many die-hards among the anti-Connecticut Pennsylvanians, however. Even as late as 1795, when the Assembly passed the Intrusion Law barring further settlement of the river lands except under title derived from Pennsylvania, there was "Wild Yankee" outcry, and hearty and bold in the taverns of Wyoming rose the song:

> *A cruel law is made, boys,*
> *Which much our place and wealth destroys.*
> *A cruel law is made, boys,*
> *To frighten and distress us*
> *But if we firm together join*
> *Supported by a power Divine*
> *Our Yankee cause shall not decline*
> *Nor shall it long oppress us.*

As the echoes died away in the valley, the contentious, hard-bitten Yankees resumed their characteristic practice of making the best of things and began to become thoroughly stateminded and patriotic citizens of Pennsylvania.

14

The Nest of the Eagle

On Tuesday, August 25, 1789, William Maclay speaking before the high crimson-canopied President's chair in the Senate chamber of the renovated Federal Hall of New York City, presented to his fellows the names of some recommended sites for a permanent seat of Government. As he read them—"ten miles square including the borough of Lancaster; Wright's Ferry on the Susquehanna; York Town, west of the Susquehanna; Harrisburg, on the Susquehanna; Reading, on the Schuylkill, and Germantown, in the neighborhood of Philadelphia," some of the senators seated in a wide semicircle lighted by windows curtained in crimson damask gazed upward at the gold sun and thirteen gold stars blazing from the center of the otherwise plain ceiling and sighed. It had been a hot and disputatious summer. Disagreements on Alexander Hamilton's bill providing for the federal government's assumption of the debts of the states, on Negro slavery, on taxation had frayed tempers. There had been threats of secession. The designation of a capital city, many had hoped, could be put over to a later meeting of the congress.

As long before as 1783 that body had voted to construct a "Federal town" on the banks of the Delaware near the falls. Southern members had protested and another vote favored the building of two such towns—one near the falls of the Delaware and another near the falls of the Potomac. A third consideration effected the adoption of a site near Lamberton on the Delaware and an ambitious plan for a public building to house the meetings of the Congress, elaborate office structures for each of the executive departments, mansions for the President and each of the members of his cabinet and a cluster of residences which would be reared for their delegates by the separate states each vying with the rest in the effort to achieve consummate elegance.

Now the whole business must be repeated. Regional jealousies would flare again. Yankee and Quaker and Southerner, Federalist and Antifederalist would shout their rhetoric through the hot days as August dragged into September. The Senate adjourned in unhappy mood.

Two days later the matter was introduced into the House of Representatives. There in the thirty-six-foot high octagonal room with the light pouring down upon him from the big windows, sixteen feet above the floor, Mr. Thomas Scott of Pennsylvania rose before fifty of the delegates who were seated in a curved double row before the raised chair of the Speaker and addressed that gentleman, Frederick Augustus Muhlenburg of Philadelphia. In accordance with notice previously given, he said, he moved the following:

> That a permanent residence ought to be fixed for the general government of the United States at some convenient place, as near the center of wealth, population, and extent of territory as may be consistent with convenience to the navigation of the Atlantic ocean and having due regard to the particular situation of the western country.

At once Thomas Hartley was on his feet asking his fellow Pennsylvanian for recognition. The gentlemen who lived near New York, he said, and by this he included men of the New England states, might perhaps be satisfied if this resolution were not discussed for years to come, but justice to the union at large and to the inhabitants of this city in particular required that it should be soon settled since a palace for the President must be erected and this and other projects essential to a national capital would put the country to great expense.

In the discussion that followed Mr. Samuel Livermore of New York awaited the opportune moment for the introduction of an informal and humorous note which he hoped would modify the intensity of those who were for immediate removal and perhaps restore them to a *laissez-faire* state of mind. Then with genial irony he said that he did not understand that any of the gentlemen of the Congress was uneasy in his present New York surroundings. He for one had heard no complaints from them. Moreover, New Yorkers seemed equally satisfied with the Congressional visitors. They had not told the members of the Congress that they were tired of them or asked them to move. "Many parts of the country appear extremely anxious to have Congress with them," he said and carefully avoided naming that part uppermost in most minds, the banks of the Susquehanna, as he listed them. "There is Trenton, Germantown, Carlisle, Lancaster, Yorktown and Reading have sent us abundance of petitions setting forth their various advantages," he said. "We wish the inhabitants may enjoy the benefits of them, and if they are pleasantly situated and have plenty of fish we are very glad to hear it; and if it should ever suit Congress to remove to any of them"—he paused to give emphasis to his weighty conclusion—"why Congress will enjoy the benefit of them also."

Despite this teasing the Pennsylvanians pressed ahead and finally succeeded in passing a resolution setting further discussion for the Thursday of the following week, September third. On that date they were ready. Benjamin Goodhue let a very important cat out of the bag early, however, when he said in conciliatory manner, "The Eastern members with the members from New York have agreed to fix a place on National principles without a regard to their own convenience and have turned their minds to the banks of the Susquehanna. . . ."

Before the Southerners, who held strong views on the subject of the Potomac, could give adequate expression to their resentment of the deal made by the Eastern states and of the hypocrisy of their pretense at compromise, they were listening to Thomas Hartley as he enthusiastically supported Goodhue's idea and added to it the final cap of its structure.

"I consider this as the middle ground between two extremes. It will suit the inhabitants to the north better than the Potomac could and the inhabitants to the south better than the Delaware would . . . Respecting its communication with the Western Territory, no doubt that the Susquehanna will facilitate that object with considerable ease and great advantage; and as to its convenience to the navigation of the Atlantic Ocean, the distance is nothing more than to afford safety from any hostile attempt, while it affords a short and easy communication with navigable rivers and large commercial towns. . . . I think it would be better to come to the point at once and fix the precise

201

spot, if we could. . . . I mention Wright's Ferry on the Susquehanna."

Now the whole scheme of the Eastern delegates was out. The Southerners raged that the coalition of New England and New York was planning a virtual dictatorship over the rest of the country. If they could choose the nation's capital they could also determine its policies. To gain time and be further informed on the purposes of the East, Thomas Lee of Virginia rose to ask how the banks of the Susquehanna provided the advantages they were all agreed upon as requisite. Did the connection with the West actually exist? How did the river communicate with the navigation of the Atlantic? What of the salubrity of the air, the fertility of the soil?

Mr. Hartley had expected these questions. Modestly he wished that some other gentleman would answer them, someone who could describe the Susquehanna in more beautiful language than he could command, but since no such gentleman had volunteered he must do his best. Because he had already mentioned Wright's Ferry, he would argue for that as the specific and proper spot.

"Now, Wright's Ferry lies on the east bank of the Susquehanna about thirty-five miles from navigable water; and, from a few miles above, is navigable to the source of the river at Lake Otsego in the upper part of the State of New York. The Tioga branch is navigable a very considerable distance up, and is but a few miles from the Genesee which empties into Lake Ontario. The Juniata is navigable and nearly connects with the Kisskemanetas and that with the Ohio. The West branch connects with the Allegheny establishing communication with the distant parts even of Kentucky."

The valley of the Susquehanna in the neighborhood of Wright's Ferry, he went on, was as thickly populated as any part of North America. As to the quality of the soil, it was inferior to none in the world and, though that was saying a good deal, it was no more than he believed a fact. And if his hearers "were disposed to pay attention to a dish of fish" he could assure them their table "might be furnished with fine and good from the waters of the Susquehanna. . . ."

But the Southern champions of a site on the Potomac were obdurate and bitterly articulate. They said Pennsylvanians had not told the truth when they said Wright's Ferry was near the geographical center of the settled areas; it was much nearer to Portland, Maine, than to Savannah, Georgia. South Carolina protested that Pennsylvania Quakers "were continually dogging Southern members with their schemes for emancipation" of Negro slaves. The climate of the Susquehanna valley was too cold for health and comfort, almost as bad as that of New England which would soon be deserted by sensible men who would prefer going south of the Potomac where land was rich and food came easy to scrabbling for a meager living on rocky barrens.

To such arguments Theodore Sedgwick of Massachusetts replied in a cold fury: "It is the opinion of all the Eastern States that the climate of the Potomac is not only unhealthy but destructive to northern constitutions. . . . Vast numbers of eastern adventurers have gone to the Southern States and all have found their graves there; they have met destruction as soon as they arrive. . . ."

Now Delaware in the person of its pompously poetic delegate, Mr. Vinny, threw in her lot with the South.

"I am yet to learn whether Congress are to tickle the trout on the stream of the Codonus," he declaimed, "to build their sumptuous palaces on the banks of the Potomac, or to admire commerce with her expanded wings on the waters of the Delaware. I am in favor of the Potomac."

As for the Susquehanna's vaunted connections with the West, it seemed that he did not regard these as unmixed blessings.

"I look on the Western Territory in an awful and striking point of view. To that region the unpolished sons of earth are flowing from all quarters."

Again a Pennsylvanian took the floor to give the assembly opportunity to contemplate a posterity in which the capital of the United States would be Peach Bottom on the Susquehanna, and still another extolled the virtues of Harrisburg on the ever more navigable stream. At this point Fisher Ames of Massachusetts thirty years old and next-to-youngest present rose with the manner of a man prepared to deliver a master effort. Though privately he had said he was disgusted with the "despicable grog-shop contest, whether the taverns in New York or Philadelphia shall get the custom of Congress" he was mindful of the fact that a speech both logical and at the same time conciliatory might at this moment bring him the distinction of having won the gratitude of a nation by effecting the placement of its capital where it should be. Therefore he addressed his elders, now so heated that they had abandoned logic for intrasectional malice, with that precise admixture of flattery and moderation which had won him recognition as a sound young man and consequent election as a delegate.

With a casual disregard of the Susquehanna's stony shallows he made the round statement that the eastern branch of the stream "is navigable to the head of Lake Otsego" and documented it then and there with a bit of history. "A detachment of General Sullivan's troops came in boats from the lake quite down the river." (He did not mention the damming of the stream at its source or the long wait for enough water to float the shallow-draft barges.)

The Potomac, said Fisher Ames, is exposed to invasion from the sea and from the mountains; "contrast this with the Susquehanna . . . the country is perfectly safe from both dangers." In haste, then, as he saw some of his hearers stirring angrily, he appealed for "moderation and good sense of gentlemen who possess public spirit and private honor," saying, "I rely upon the calm review which they will make of my observations a week hence, when the fervor of this debate has subsided. I appeal to their candor at that time, to decide whether, in point of centrality, accessibility, protection to the Union, salubrity and safety from insurrection and invasion, there is not solid reason for establishing the seat of government on the Susquehanna." Further to appease the Southern delegates he went on to make concessions with which many of his fellow Yankees would disagree. "I will not say that the Potomac is insalubrious; but it is well known that northern constitutions are impaired by moving to a more southern latitude. The air may be healthful, but the change is found to be pernicious to them."

Now he was ready for the peroration which would conclude his masterpiece. There was a foreshadowing of the great Webster in it.

"The preservation of the Union is the worthiest object of a patriot's wishes. The world has doubted our success. I feel a consolation in the opinion that the measure I am contending for will best contribute to that end. An American Legislation may seek true glory by such measures as will tend to secure the Union, to preserve peace, and to diffuse the blessings of science, liberty and good government over a greater extent of country, and in a higher degree than the world ever enjoyed them. Surely this will interest the pride of every honest heart. It is the religion of politics."

Fisher Ames had done his best for the Susquehanna and seemingly he had won. The opposition protested bitterly as it foresaw defeat on the ultimate vote. Thomas Lee denounced the Northern delegates for attempting to sacrifice the South on the altar of their own greed. James Madison, who had previously said that the Virginia Convention would not have had such strong objections to parts of the federal Constitution, had it been able to foresee the calm and objective reasoning of the First Congress, now voiced hot resentment, saying that if a prophet had been able to picture to the convention the events of this day "I as firmly believe Virginia would not at this moment have been part of the Union."

At once the Yankees angrily rebuked Virginia. It was the Southerners who had demanded an immediate vote on this question, they said. Now that they saw they would be outvoted by the coalition of New York, Pennsylvania and New England they were squalling for more time and whining that they had been unjustly treated. Said Wadsworth of Connecticut, if the seat of Government went to the Potomac the whole of New England would consider the Union dissolved. Three days of such ill-tempered bickering ended in a vote on a resolution that a commission be appointed to select a suitable spot on the banks of the Susquehanna, purchase enough lands to accommodate the seat of government, and construct the buildings in which it would be housed. There were twenty-eight votes in the affirmative, twenty-one in the negative and the advocates of Wright's Ferry were wild with delight. Already in their joyous minds they could see, reflected in the Susquehanna, a shimmering vision of stately buildings separated by wide avenues.

Their dream was short, terminated by practical politics. Alexander Hamilton needed more votes in order to pass his Assumption Bill and was willing to buy them with votes for the permanent residence of the Congress. As soon as he had let this be known traders eager, for a price, to change their minds in favor of the national government's assuming the debts of the separate states, made their attitudes clear to him. Pennsylvanian Robert Morris wrote Hamilton in June of 1790 that on the next morning he would be strolling early on the Battery and if the Secretary of the Treasury had ideas in mind that might prove of mutual benefit, perhaps he might choose to stroll with him. When they parted, Morris had agreed to suggest to the Pennsylvania delegates that for one vote in the Senate and five in the House favorable to Assumption, they could be assured of having the permanent capital within the borders of their state. Hamilton waited for an answer—but being impatient he did not wait long. Instead, he adopted Morris's morning-walk technique but with another companion, the new Secretary of State, Thomas Jefferson of Virginia. The result of this Broadway stroll was a gathering at Jefferson's house on that street, a dinner to which, as William Maclay later pointed out, supporters of a Susquehanna site for the capital were not invited. Though the Pennsylvanians soon thereafter gave a dinner at which both Hamilton and Jefferson were honored guests, a deal had been made. Washington would be the capital of the United States. Symbol of the nation, the great American eagle whose shadow had rested momentarily on Wright's Ferry, Harrisburg, Peach Bottom, river towns of the Susquehanna, spread his wings and sailed south to hover above the Potomac.

15

Pantisocracy

*❧ Yet will I love to follow the
sweet dream where Susquehannah
pours his untamed stream.*

—SAMUEL TAYLOR COLERIDGE

Best remembered of all plans for idyllic living on the banks of the Susquehanna is a fancy that lived for a few months in the minds of three English poets. One, a not widely known Quaker, Robert Lovell, died soon after the idea had been launched from the teeming minds of the others—Samuel Taylor Coleridge, then twenty-two, and Robert Southey, twenty. These two had met in 1794 and at once had felt closely bound by a sharing of disillusion. Each had watched the hopeful fires of the French revolution become ashes under a pelting rain of injustices.

"I look around the world and everywhere find the same spectacle—the strong tyrannizing over the weak, man and beast. . . . There is no place for virtue," said Southey.

As early as November of 1793 he had been speculating on a possible "place for virtue." He wrote to a friend: "If this world did but contain ten thousand people of both sexes visionary as myself, how delightfully would we re-people Greece and turn out the Moslem," and he remembered that "it was the favorite intention" of Cowley

209

(Abraham Cowley, English poet) "to retire with books to a cottage in America, and seek that happiness in solitude which he could not find in society."

A month later Southey had definitely decided on America: "Now if you are in a mood for a reverie, fancy only me in America; imagine my ground uncultivated since the creation. . . . After a hard day's toil, see me sleep upon rushes, and, in very bad weather, take out my casette and write to you, for you shall positively write to me in America."

In the following June Coleridge, for military ineptitudes recently discharged from the Light Dragoons of the British army, met Southey and mourned with him over the state of the world.

The melancholy of the two was suddenly lightened, however, by a message from a mutual friend who had done what they both longed to do—find a wild, faraway spot, uncontaminated by human faults, where nature would provide such beauty and demand such simplicity of living, that man could not help but be both happy and good.

Joseph Priestley, Dissenter minister turned scientist, living in the Pennsylvania town of Northumberland where the bright waters of the West and North Branches of the Susquehanna meet, said Come. At once their brains were fevered with thinking on a life which Coleridge envisioned as "trying the experiment of perfectability on the banks of the Susquehanna."

Though years afterwards he said, smiling at the memory, that they chose the site because of the "pretty and metrical" sound of the name, Coleridge proved the more practical-minded during the scheme's development (as

Professor John Livingston Lowes stated in his *The Road to Xanadu*). Early in September of 1794 he had met an articulate and "most intelligent" young man "lately come from America to sell land," who had rhapsodized over the Susquehanna for its "excessive beauty" and reported it secure from hostile Indians. The poet had been so enchanted by the glib salesman's talk that he had visited with him "every night" for a while. Coleridge reported him as saying "that we shall buy the land a great deal cheaper when we arrive in America than we could do in England" and adding the persuasive question "or why am I over here?" Moreover, Coleridge added, the young man said two thousand pounds would do to start the enterprise and "twelve men may *easily* clear 300 acres in four or five months . . . for 600 dollars a thousand acres may be cleared and houses built on them. . . . Every possible assistance will be given us; we may get credit for the land for ten years or more." Most extravagant of the real estate agent's arguments may well have been one composed in the fervor of the moment because his listeners would most like to hear it. Coleridge reported it triumphantly and italicized its major word—"literary characters make *money* there." This boast, capping all other arguments, sent the poet into an ecstasy of anticipation. "My God! how tumultuous are the movements of my heart. Since I quitted this room what and how important events have been evolved. America! Southey! Miss Fricker! Pantisocracy! Oh, I shall have a scheme of it!"

Mundane affairs were not, however, the main subject of talk among the poets. More important to them was the structure of the ideal society they would create. Coleridge, tireless inventor of new words, had a name for it—Pan-

211

tisocracy—and his mind was so full of the idea that he constantly talked of the book he would write about it, as if it were already accomplished. He added another new word, Aspheterism, representing an idea which both poets considered a concomitant of Pantisocracy. Southey wrote his brother in September of 1794 that "Coleridge was with us (at Nether Stone) nearly five weeks. . . . We preached Pantisocracy and Aspheterism everywhere. These, Tom, are two new words, the first signifying the equal government of all, the other the generalization of individual property."

It was with the practical application of these two ideas in mind that they planned their experiment. It would begin with twelve young couples, each person to have an equal share in the administration of the whole. Somewhat similar in plan to that later literary Utopia, Brook Farm, Pantisocracy would require its men to plow and sow and reap in the three hours a day considered necessary for making an adequate living, while the women would attend to the housekeeping, cooking, and other domestic duties. The community as a whole would own all products and determine their distribution. Such a program, they were sure, would give all members sufficient time for their reading, writing and contemplative discussion of philosophic truths, thus bringing to them willy-nilly in their river paradise the virtue and happiness which their native goodness and intelligence must create.

The Pantisocracy would be a selective community of course, excluding much of the conventional civilized world as then constituted. In the hash of playful whimsy and serious thought which frequently characterized his informal writings Coleridge suggested, in a letter to a friend, the restrictions he favored:

"I call even my Cat Sister in the Fraternity of universal Nature. Owls I respect and Jack Asses I love: for Aldermen and Hogs, Bishops and Royston Crows I have not particular partiality; they are my cousins, however, at least by Courtesy. But Kings, Wolves, Tygers, Generals, Ministers, and Hyaenas, I renounce them all—or if they *must* be my Kinsmen, it shall be in the 50th Remove—May the Almighty Pantisocratizer of Souls pantisocratize the Earth, and bless you and S. T. Coleridge."

When they came to a specific choice of the twelve couples who would occupy land said by Coleridge to be "at a convenient distance from Cooper's Town on the banks of the Susquehanna," the three poets naturally started with themselves. Fortunately, at least so it seemed to them, all wives or fiancées were sisters. Had their plans materialized, scholars of literature might today be speculating on those issues which developed between the three Fricker girls and their three poets, family loyalty versus those qualities that bind creative artists together. The facts have best been told by Arthur Herman Wilson, Professor of English at Susquehanna University, who reports: "Pantisocracy did not have any effect upon the Susquehanna, but it did seem to have an effect elsewhere, that is, in the Fricker family, because it brought husbands to all three girls, Mary, Edith and Sara. However, Robert Lovell died young; Coleridge deserted his wife; and so Southey was the one man in the world who felt the full weight of Pantisocracy because he was left to support all three of the Fricker girls for the rest of his life."

The poets' plan had one other effect. It inspired Coleridge's *Monody on the Death of Chatterton,* verses mourning the suicide in 1770 of the seventeen-year-old poet, Thomas Chatterton. Though the Susquehanna was to Coleridge only a mirage created by his fancy, and though without justification he happily assumed that Chatterton would have joined with him and his fellow poets in their venture, the poem transmits with truth the romantic dream which the lovely name created on the minds of sensitive men in troubled Europe:

> *O'er the ocean swell*
> *Sublime of hope I seek the cottaged dell*
> *Where virtue calm with careless step may stray;*
> *And, dancing to the moonlight roundelay,*
> *The withered passions weave an holy spell!*
> *O Chatterton! that thou wert yet alive!*
> *Sure thou would'st spread the canvas to the gale,*
> *And love, with us, the tinkling team to drive*
> *O'er peaceful freedom's undivided dale;*
> *And we, at sober eve, would round thee throng,*
> *Hanging, enraptured, on thy stately song!*
> *And greet with smiles the young-eyed poesy*
> *All deftly mask'd as hoar antiquity*
> *Alas, vain phantasies! the fleeting brood*
> *Of woe self-solaced in her dreamy mood!*
> *Yet will I love to follow the sweet dream*
> *Where Susquehannah pours his untamed stream;*
> *And on some hill, whose forest-frowning side*
> *Waves o'er the murmurs of his calmer tide,*
> *Will raise a solemn cenotaph to thee,*
> *Sweet harper of time-shrouded minstrelsy!*
> *And there, soothed sadly by the dirgeful wind*
> *Muse on the sore ills I had left behind.*

The three poets never raised their cenotaph to the dead boy. Perhaps on the banks of a quiet meander of the Susquehanna men who love English verse will some day raise such a monument and dedicate it to dreams that do not come true. On three of its four sides will be the names of Lovell, Coleridge and Southey, and on the fourth that of the genius whose ending of his earthly dreaming inspired the monody envisioning a never-seen poet on the banks of a never-seen river.

16

A Settlement for the Friends of Liberty

🌿 *They constantly try to escape*
From the darkness outside and within
By dreaming of systems so perfect
that no one will need to be good.

—T. S. ELIOT

In 1774 at an elaborate dinner given by the chemist Lavoisier at his Paris home, the guest of honor—Joseph Priestley—rose to address the most distinguished scientists of France. He was a little English minister just entering middle age, and his talk was labored because of a speech defect—but what he had to say, his hearers recognized to be of vital importance. Known to them as a friend and protegé of the greatly respected and versatile American, Benjamin Franklin, they did not hesitate to accept his announcement that his recent experiments had proved the existence of "dephlogisticated air"—a substance later called oxygen.

In Birmingham, England, almost twenty years afterwards, as he sat at home playing backgammon with his wife he received sudden warning that a mob was almost at his door, raging against him. The Priestleys escaped with their lives but the mob, incensed by the preacher's previous espousal of the cause of the French Revolution-

216

ists and by his urging—in defiance of the Church of England—a return to the simple faith of the earliest Christians, roared through his house, pillaging and destroying. Crying "Church and King," they gathered his thirty thousand books, his laboratory equipment, his diaries and journals, and his furniture into a great pile and burned it all to ashes. From behind a near hedge the preacher-scientist saw in one direction the flames of his chapel, in another those of his books and the records of his experiments.

The fugitive was soon writing from London a letter to his persecutors, the "Inhabitants of Birmingham." In it he summarized the vast damage unjustly "done to one who never did, or imagined, you any harm," and calmly went on to a more fundamental issue: ". . . recourse to violence is only a proof you have nothing better to produce. Should you destroy myself, as well as my house, library and apparatus, ten more persons of equal or superior spirit and ability would rise up; and, believe me, the Church of England, which you now think you are supporting, has received a greater blow by this conduct of yours than I and all my friends have ever aimed at it."

His chapel razed by fire, his scientific essays, "the result of the laborious study of many years and which I shall never be able to recompose," also given by the incendiaries to the flames, Priestley set about finding a place in the world where the spirit of free inquiry would not be opposed by ignorant prejudice. His hopes for France had been shattered, and regretfully he wrote, "The conduct of the French has been such as their best friends cannot approve." He therefore encouraged his son, William, and his son-in-law—Thomas Cooper, lawyer and scientist—to journey to the United States of America, where they

217

hoped to establish "a large settlement for the friends of liberty in general near the head of the Susquehanna in Pennsylvania." The sense of their report was soon expressed in a book, *Some Information Respecting America,* Collected by Thomas Cooper, Late of Manchester. Of the physical aspects of the waiting valley, Cooper had written:

> On leaving Hamburg, the mountain scenery begins, and continues for 60 miles to Sunbury; all this is a succession of mountain and valley; the former covered to the very top with trees and shrubs; white, black and chestnut oak, pines, beech, hiccory, &c. —The valleys intersected by large streams rolling at the foot of the mountains, and breaking out here and there amid the forest which covers their banks. Here and there (at every three or four miles, for instance, on the average) log-houses, mills, and plantations, give relief to the grand, uncultivated mass of forest. . . .

> . . . you look down upon the Susquehanna, about three or four miles off; a river about half a mile broad, running at the foot of bold and steep mountains, through a valley, not much above three miles broad in that part, rich, beautiful and variegated. . . . you catch the town of Sunbury, and on the opposite side of the river, about two miles farther, Northumberland. These are towns of about two or three hundred houses each, delightfully situated near the Susquehanna. The houses are partly built of logs, and partly of frame-work, one or two stories high, sashed and glazed, some of them painted on the outside, all of them neat without, and clean within; comfortable and commodious.

> The noble masses of wood and mountain, the Susquehanna sometimes rolling through rich valleys, and sometimes washing the base of stupendous rocks, almost everywhere taking the form of a lake, and interspersed with numerous islands, well wooded, of all forms, and stretching out in a variety of directions; these combined with the brightness of the atmosphere; the distinctness of distant outlines, and the clear wholesome cold of the season; the

sky undeformed by wintry clouds, and free from the foggy vapor I had been accustomed to execrate in the old country, made this journey one of the pleasantest I had ever experienced.

As for the American political atmosphere in the valley during the early years of the republic, citizens of today will read Cooper's description of it with interest: "There is little fault to find with the government of America either in principle or practice: we have very few taxes to pay, and those of acknowledged necessity are moderate in amount; we have no animosities about religion: it is a subject about which no questions are asked; we have few respecting political men or political measures; the present irritation in men's minds in Great Britain, and the discordant state of society on political accounts is not known there. The government is the government *of* the people and *for* the people." (The italics were Cooper's.)

In the year of the book's publication, 1794, Joseph Priestley, aged sixty-one, arrived in Philadelphia ready again to begin his career—this time in a settlement on the Susquehanna where men might live in peace and seek truth without fear.

The French *émigré* colony at Azilum on the North Branch of the Susquehanna was already in operation, but his old friend Lavoisier, at whose dinner he had talked of oxygen, would not be there. His life had that year been ended by the guillotine.

Priestley was surprised by the warmth of his welcome to America. The great men of the nation were delighted that so distinguished a thinker had cast his lot with the new and free republic. Scholars sought his company and learned societies of the seaboard cities paid him honor. The University of Pennsylvania offered him a lectureship in chemistry but with modesty and truth he refused it, saying, "For though I have made discoveries in some branches of chemistry, I never gave much attention to the common routine of it and know but little of its common processes."

With the purpose of a settlement of "friends of liberty," still in mind, he made his way to the "forks of the Susquehanna" to await its realization. The proposal was soon abandoned, but not before he had so fallen in love with Northumberland that he decided to make the town his home. On the banks of the North Branch and near its confluence with the West, he built of kiln-dried lumber the spacious, well-proportioned Georgian Colonial mansion still centering a panorama of flowing water and towering hills so moving that it once drew from him the tribute: "I do not think there can be in any part of the world a situation more beautiful than this."

Here, far from the intemperate violence of street mobs,

with his family beside him—including his brilliant and congenial son-in-law—he resumed his career as scientist and philosopher. In his quiet laboratory he made empirical experiments which brought upon him the criticism that his work lacked logical pattern. But from his failures and successes came results that added to the world's knowledge of chemistry. He analyzed the atmosphere of the valley and reported with some disappointment that it did not differ greatly from that of the country that had driven him into this happy exile. He made intelligent efforts to discover the physical qualities of light and to explain its actions. Most important of his chemical activities was his forcing steam over heated charcoal—an experiment which resulted in the discovery of carbon monoxide.

Priestley's mind would not have allowed him to confine his speculations to chemistry, had he so desired. Revolt against the grim teachings of Calvinism had found expression in America through the quick growth of Unitarian theology and the philosophy of Transcendentalism, and among rebels he usually found himself a happy warrior. He founded the first Unitarian Church of Philadelphia but, preferring life in his river home to a return to the ministry, refused an offer to be its pastor. He was a crusader against the African slave trade, when to advocate Abolitionism was to court bitter denunciations. He campaigned for returning Palestine to the Jews long before Zionism became an issue. He so heartily believed in the America described in the book of his son-in-law that he declared himself for teaching emigrants our national ideals, and in 1801—when Tsar Alexander came to the Russian throne—he urged President Jefferson to have a description of the Constitution of the United States sent to him in the hope that he would give his people the benefit of a liberal and democratic regime. In his correspondence with Jefferson, who was then planning the University of Virginia, he discussed his educational theories and plans for a university at Northumberland, which reached actuality to the extent of an academy, later abandoned.

As important to the nation as Priestley's scientific discoveries was his expression in matters political of a liberal attitude which was echoed and emphasized by his son-in-law. If their friends Southey and Coleridge could not bring about the realization of a "Pantisocracy" on the Susquehanna, if their former church associates in England would not or could not join them in establishing a Utopia of Dissenters on its banks, then they in their house beside its waters would be a "settlement for the friends of liberty" that would make itself felt throughout the republic.

Thomas Cooper came to the forks of the Susquehanna in 1793, the same year that *émigré* Du Petit-Thouars, of about the same age, came to Azilum. Both young men—one a French aristocrat and devotee of Rousseau, the other a liberal English lawyer who had been elected a member of the National Assembly of France by the Birmingham Philosophical Society—had high hopes of living in colonies so ideally administered that the early nineteenth century would become a "golden age" along the river. The Frenchman was a poet and soldier. The Englishman, also a courageous man of action (as proved by his drawing his sword on Robespierre in a Paris street and vainly calling on him to defend himself), was at heart an advocate, an argumentative, fiery champion of democracy. With his own phrase "government *of* the people and *for* the people" in mind, he set about seeing to it that the national government lived up to the liberal ideals set by its founders. As might have been expected, he was an ardent Antifederalist, and Vice-President Jefferson, then in his early fifties, looked upon him as among the most valued of the younger supporters of Republicanism. Wrote Jefferson: "Cooper is acknowledged by every enlightened man who knows him, to be the greatest man in America, in the powers of mind and in acquired information, and that without a single exception."

This opinion was not shared by President John Adams and other Federalist leaders, who felt that sympathy with the ideals of the French Revolution was equivalent to sedition. Democracy they looked upon with horror as an alien philosophy imported direct from Paris. They heartily approved the stern measures taken by the English Parliament to suppress such subversion and planned similar legislation. In the summer of 1798, the Alien Enemies Act was passed by the Congress and signed by the President. Among other strict provisions aimed at natives of foreign nations then resident, it gave that executive in time of war—then deemed inevitable between America and France—the power to deport without trial and at his own discretion all aliens he considered dangerous to the nation's peace and security. Antifederalists against whom the Act was directed included the two English fugitives, Joseph Priestley and Thomas Cooper, whom the Federal press accused—with other foreign-born Republicans—of being "wandering vagabonds who had trampled under foot the laws, the government, the sovereignty of the United States." To make sure that no native democrat who dared to express his derogatory opinions of the President might do so with impunity, the Federalists then passed the Sedition Act which, among other like provisions, made punishable by imprisonment and fine the writing, publication or speaking of statements denouncing the motives of Federal officials.

Obviously these laws were carefully tailored to fit the more ardent supporters of Jefferson and especially the two English-born residents of the beautiful mansion on the Susquehanna. Indeed, the Federalist Secretary of State, Timothy Pickering, looked upon Joseph Priestley, who had not become an American citizen, as eminently qualified to be the first deportee under the Alien Act. President John Adams, possibly feeling that prosecution of a frail, small, absent-minded scientist who had done much for humanity might not be regarded with favor even in his own party, denied Pickering the pleasure of seeking his banishment—saying that the intended victim was "weak as water." Not foreseeing the consequence of the discovery of nuclear fission a century and a half later, he added that Priestley's power to convert people to his own subversive convictions was "not an Atom in the World."

The chemist's son-in-law—Adams went on to say—was quite another kettle of fish. Thomas Cooper—contentious, bull-necked, florid, aggressive—had been the criminal who had diverted Priestley from the ways of truth and honesty.

Though Pickering felt frustrated by his discovery that Cooper had become a citizen of the United States at Sunbury in 1795 and was therefore not deportable under the Alien Act, a detailed perusal of his writings gave ample proof that he could be indicted as the author of an article

224

considered as violating the Sedition Act. In June, 1799, he had published in the Northumberland *Gazette*, of which he was editor, an *Address to the People of Northampton County* in which he gave his readers to understand that the President of their country was an ambitious monarchist who hoped, by using a standing army, to enforce the Sedition Law, and by its aid become a national dictator. John Adams, he continued, at the time he had entered into the office of the presidency, "was hardly in the infancy of political mistake." Added years had but made him a past master in the field. Though this denunciation, republished and distributed by Priestley as a political broadside, so stirred the President's resentment that he declared, "I have no doubt it is a libel against the whole Government and as such ought to be prosecuted," Cooper fearlessly continued his attack on the Sedition Law and its advocates.

Irish-born William Duane had been summoned before the Senate for inquiry after he had claimed that a junta of seventeen Federalist Senators determined the laws of the nation. Cooper had been asked to attend the inquiry as one of the counsel for the accused, but when the Senate announced that it would listen to no proof of the truth of Duane's charges he refused and published his reason: "I will not degrade myself by submitting to appear before the Senate with their *gag in my mouth.*"

Two weeks later Cooper was indicted for committing a libel against the President of the United States in violation of the Sedition Law, and within a month he was confined in a Philadelphia jail. His trial began in April of 1800 and was marked by extraordinary partiality on the part of the presiding officer, Associate Justice Samuel

Chase of the Federal Supreme Court. The accused made a gallant fight against the prejudiced decisions of this Federalist judge, against the Sedition Law itself, and against its interpretation. He claimed he had acted not for personal reasons nor out of malice but from the highest motive—love for his country—which transcended party considerations. He asked the right questions: "Is it a crime to doubt the capacity of the President? Have we advanced so far on the road to despotism in this republican country that we dare not say our President is mistaken?" In his own defense he made a three-and-a-half-hour speech, so impassioned that he nearly fainted and was given a long respite by Justice Chase who seemed to feel at this juncture that he could afford to be magnanimous. There was nothing magnanimous about his charge to the jury, however, and the jury agreed with him so thoroughly that they brought in their verdict of "guilty" just twenty minutes after they had begun their deliberations.

Cooper was sentenced to spend four months in prison and to pay a fine of four hundred dollars, and he complied in full. The Federalist enemies of freedom of expression had won a battle. They won others, too, against other Republicans who dared defy the Alien and Sedition Acts, but each victory proved a weakening of the defenses of these laws. Public opinion was changing, and much of the change was due to a song Cooper wrote in his cell, realizing that logic has summonable allies.

The Bill of Rights had been endangered by men who under pretense of patriotism had acted from political motives. Cooper in prison was a greater argument against

226

the Sedition Law than all his speeches and tracts against it. It was doomed. The two "friends of liberty," in their one-house settlement beside the Susquehanna, had done much to establish the pattern of American freedom. The guarantees of the first five Constitutional Amendments were more than liberal phrases—they formed a realistic, unsinking foundation for a way of life.

Thomas Cooper was to do one more inestimable service for his fellow citizens in the Susquehanna valley. As soon as he was released from prison he was appointed by the Governor of Pennsylvania to a commission for compromising the conflicting claims of Yankees and Pennsylvanians which had caused the "Pennamite" wars. Elected chairman by this commission he accomplished much of its work with great energy and such fairness that he won the confidence of those most concerned. Later he became a judge, presiding first at Sunbury in 1806, but his extremely severe conduct of his court caused his impeachment and removal. He left the Susquehanna and, turning to college teaching, figured in various disputes— many of them caused by his unorthodox religious views and leading to his successive resignations.

He was eighty-one in 1840 when he died in South Carolina where, for many years, he had been a disputatious and aggressive figure—a free-thinking man, a free-trade man, a nullification man, a States' rights man. He had outlived his companion in the "friends of liberty" settlement by more than three and a half decades. Priestley's grave is at Northumberland where, after peaceful years of experiment, backgammon, whist and talk with friends and admirers who made pilgrimages from far and near to his fine house, he died in 1804. The house still stands and is a Priestley museum, well-kept and beautiful. Cooper, uncompromising and consistent, fearless lover of truth and mankind, lies far from the flowing waters beside which, shoulder to shoulder with his great father-in-law, he fought for government *of* and *for* the people.

17

La Rivière Lointaine

🌿 *I will meet you in America by some river.*

—MADAME DE STAËL (1794)

When Aristide Aubert du Petit-Thouars first disembarked at Azilum, leaves from the sugar maples and shagbark hickories on Rummerfield Mountain were tumbling in erratic flight, scarlet and gold, to the brown ripples of the Susquehanna. On the next to the last day of October, 1793, the short, slim French naval officer trudged up the west bank leading a band of Philadelphia workmen whose labor he was to supervise. Already spades and hammers were sounding the prelude to the building of a town. Roofs must be completed, chimneys and fireplaces erected before the first snows.

Though the young sailor was penniless and distrait, the dramatic quality of the place could not fail to excite a man of sensitivity. A semicircle of land (looking now much as it looked then) had been given seeming geometric exactness by the line of the river. It lay flat and green under the almost vertical face of a wooded cliff that shadowed the water at its eastern edge. The curving stream separated mountain and plain and created a tryptich offering tortuous Gothic wilderness, shining waters,

229

lush disciplined farms—all framed into a unified composition by the encircling horizon.

The employment of du Petit-Thouars had marked a happy turn in a career darkened by frustrations and disappointments. Born in 1760, near Saumur in Bon Moi, a many-gabled chateau beside the winding Loire, he came naturally by the eighteenth-century passion for simple living in rural surroundings. In his boyhood he had read *Robinson Crusoe,* and it had made on him a lasting and deep impression. At the College of La Flèche he was confined in a cell for an experimental effort to live as did Defoe's hero. Released, he took unannounced leave to seek a Paris military-school preparation for a life ordered on Crusoe's adventurous pattern.

Shipwreck and lonely island still in mind, he chose to follow the sea and, when France recognized the American colonies, became an officer of their navy. In four years of naval engagements "in the American seas," he became a captain and, while on shore leave, lost the use of his left hand—seriously maimed in a hunting accident.

In the French navy, after the end of the Revolution, he again satisfied his yearnings for romantic adventure in primitive lands by sailing in 1792 to search for the French explorer, La Pérouse, last heard from on Australia's east coast four years before. Rumors that he was living a Crusoe existence on a South Sea island so excited du Petit-Thouars that he spent all his own funds to fit out his expedition and, having obtained audience with Louis XVI, personally persuaded his king to give financial support.

Months later du Petit-Thouars's ship—the *Diligent*—was skirting the coast of Brazil in an almost helpless condition. An epidemic fever that had killed a third of the crew still raged among them, and the desperate captain put in for medical aid at the volcanic island of Fernando de Noronha, off the east tip of South America. All aboard were immediately arrested as French revolutionists, and though the young captain protested the error he was sent to Lisbon under guard and clapped in prison. On his release, in August of 1793, he set out for America.

Philadelphia was teeming with refugees from the red terror of the French revolution and the black terror of slave insurrection on the island of San Domingo when he disembarked. Nearly seven hundred had arrived from the latter country during the year, and more who had escaped the Paris guillotine were arriving each day.

Among the loyal fraternity of French veterans of the American Revolution then living in Philadelphia was Louis-Marie de Noailles—brother-in-law of the Marquis de Lafayette. At Yorktown General Washington had given him command of the construction of the breastworks and had also appointed him one of the French officers to arrange the details of the surrender of Cornwallis. Aristide du Petit-Thouars had known him in those exciting times and, having heard of his presence in the city, sought him out. De Noailles told him of the plans for a French city on the Susquehanna and introduced him to the wealthy and powerful Antoine Omer Talon, former Chief Justice of the Criminal Court of France, and once head of the secret service of Louis XVI. Both of these city planners recognized that a naval officer accustomed to command would be useful to the project and soon, having recruited a number of American carpenters, they sent them upriver with du Petit-Thouars at their head.

The new overseer immediately, and with great enthusiasm, went to work. The idea of erecting for his
countrymen a river city in the interior wilderness of
America—two hundred miles upstream from Philadelphia
—was wholly satisfying to his nature. The surface of the
big half-moon of land outlined by the river had been
cleared by previous American settlers. De Noailles and
Talon had bought it on the recommendation of a French
lawyer, Charles Boulogne, an expert in the purchasing
of American lands, and an American authority on real
estate, Major Adam Hoops, who had been an officer of
General Sullivan's forces as they marched up the
Susquehanna. He remembered the spot with admiration and guided Boulogne to it. The main purpose now
was to supplant with suitable buildings the cabins of the
former owners.

A partial plan for the city had been drawn by the self-
taught French engraver, St. Memin (entitled "Designs
for Public Buildings for a Proposed French Settlement
on the Susquehanna"), which may still be seen at the Cor-
coran Art Gallery in Washington, but, if it was used, the
resultant town was far from an exact compliance. Probably the actual plan developed on the location and was
made meticulously and with accuracy by French surveyors, under the direction of Talon and Boulogne. On three
hundred acres of the flat fertile land, in the exact paral-
lelogram formed by its streets, the city lay with its long
side crossing the arc of the Susquehanna from water to
water. Behind it rose wooded, rocky hills. Before it lay
the rippling current and, beyond that, the steep sides of
Rummerfield and Rock Mountains and Lime Hill. The
main street—an avenue a hundred feet wide—led from the

river wharf to a market square covering two acres at the center of town. Eight other streets, sixty-six feet wide and running parallel to the center avenue, were intersected by five running across them. This pattern resulted in the outlining of four hundred and thirteen lots, each of about a half acre.

Aristide du Petit-Thouars attacked his job with enthusiasm and confidence. Accustomed to the leadership of men and sufficiently competent in the English language (through his experiences in the American Revolution) to make his wishes clear, he was soon "the Admiral," and "Petty-toy," to the workers under him. The little man with only one good hand was an indefatigable worker, an ardent but always just supervisor. A lover of people, he inspired their love in return.

One of the first houses which he labored to complete was a matter both of mystery and wonder to his workers and to all Americans in the countryside. Always carefully referred to in their records as *"La Grande Maison,"* the ever-loyal French refugees nevertheless made it an ill-kept secret that they were building the remarkable dwelling—said to be the largest log residence ever built in America—as a new-world palace, a safe haven for those unhappy captives across the water, Louis XVI and Marie Antoinette. News of the guillotining of their king in January of 1793 only made them the firmer in their purpose of rescuing his widow with her children, and the big house was soon openly referred to as "the Queen's house." Although du Petit-Thouars's labors on it did not begin until after Marie Antoinette also had been beheaded, news of that event did not reach the city beside the Susquehanna until her spacious log refuge was nearly complete.

The big house, standing near the upriver end of the town, was eighty-four feet long and sixty feet deep. Two stories and an attic high, its hewn log walls were interrupted by many wooden-shuttered windows—eight in each story on the long side. Four brick chimneys rose above its sloping shingled roof, providing for sixteen fireplaces, eight on each level. A wide hall ran the full length of each floor. On the river side of the second story, four rooms of equal size looked out upon the water and the mountain beyond. The space covered on this floor by the two middle rooms was occupied on the first floor by one great drawing room, about forty feet long and twenty-five deep. At each end double doors opened on the hall and flights of stairs rising to the floor above. A tremendous fireplace with a mantel as high as a man was centered in one end wall, a smaller one in the other. In the center of the river side double doors—their upper panels fitted with small panes of glass—gave entrance to the center of the room, and further glimpses from the interior of flowing water and towering crags. Behind the big house an even bigger barn, three hundred feet long by fifty deep, gave shelter to the newly purchased elegant carriages and spirited horses which—the settler-conspirators dreamed—would one day convey the Queen and her children about the Susquehanna valley roads.

Smaller houses of similar, somewhat austere design continued through winter and spring to rise on the streets of Azilum, as the eager naval officer and his crew of landsmen worked with unflagging zeal. Rafts continually floated oxen, lumber, and other heavy supplies downriver from Tioga Point. Big dugout canoes, pirogues, brought food and lighter articles. But the major interest of Talon, now

234

living in *La Grande Maison* with du Petit-Thouars as occupant of one of its rooms, was in arrivals from the south. Before the first day of summer the little city was beginning to come alive as the weary travelers of the long, hard trail from Philadelphia finally reached its end. Some rode all the way to the ferry on the east bank and were floated across—their eyes ablaze at the sight of this wilderness home. Others, having ridden to Wilkes-Barre, came on the big, flat-bottomed Durham boats that brought their supplies, their household belongings, and themselves to the Azilum wharf. Candles began to flicker behind the small square panes of the windows, voices to echo from the water and re-echo between the hills lining the valley. A piano arrived and there was music in the big drawing room. With characteristic resilience, the families of the French loyalists, who had read with delight the teachings of Jean Jacques Rousseau, now returned to them and relied upon them. The qualities of birth and breeding, they knew, could not be conquered by adverse circumstances. A new world lay before them, offering the "return to nature" Rousseau had recommended. There could be no failure in it for men of their stamp. They would cultivate their fields, grow their grapes, win honey from the bees, draw sugar sap from the maples. Meanwhile, philosophy would be their solace and their guide to the joyful serenity that only simple living in a wild and beautiful country could create. Happily they sowed their flax, planted their gardens, tended the nurseries that would furnish their blossoming orchards, ordered blooded cattle and sheep to be set to grazing on the lush river flats, prophesied that the waters flowing by their doors would one day be made navigable all the way from their source to Baltimore and that then Azilum would be a great and prosperous inland port.

Meantime Aristide du Petit-Thouars looked upon each new arrival with fascinated interest. Himself a product of a rural province and of naval experience that had required absence from his native country, he knew few of the aristocratic families now seeking, after terrifying escapes from the guillotine or the raging slaves of San Domingo, idyllic peace beside a faraway river. A sort of gallery of vignettes, based on his observations of these people, was developing within his mind.

As the work of constructing what the *émigrés* looked upon as only the first group of houses, numbering about thirty, neared its end, the managers presented him as a reward for his services three hundred acres a few miles away on the Loyalsock Creek, tributary to the Susquehanna.

His first reaction was of intense delight. At last he could be a latter-day Robinson Crusoe, living by his own ingenuity from the land, building his home from materials of the region, delighting in a life based on the familiar principles of Rousseau. But his journal, kept meticulously through most of the following months, shows Aristide to have been a very troubled and uncertain man. He had a great love for his family—and especially for his young twin sisters to whom he wrote devotedly, hoping (in vain as it later proved) that his letters would reach them in France. As the news from Paris arrived at Azilum, each message mounting horror on horror, he was ever more tortured. A fear, moreover, of disillusion with this enchanting new land of freedom entered his mind. In June of 1794 he wrote his sister Félicité that his writing to her had been interrupted by a long journey to Philadelphia to find out, if possible, whether letters from her might have gone astray—"three hundred miles afoot in a pouring rain through mire of swamp in a land that in spite of its newness has little consideration for those who have not a good horse between their legs." And he added, "I have erased many contradictions within myself without as yet being sure of anything. My situation has caused me to go much further into the depths of the human heart and I have become much sadder from finding there so little greatness."

In his more hopeful moods, the Admiral was obsessed by two conflicting purposes. The failure of his expedition in search of La Pérouse haunted him and he wished to make up for it by starting north along the Susquehanna "with the goal of learning the customs of the savages or of beginning again my voyage with the only resources which nature has furnished me: my arms, legs and head. . . . I am losing all hope. I am on the point of giving up the fruits of my labor and plunging into the vast forests inhabited by wild men, either returning the victim of their cruelty, perhaps of hunger and fatigue, or emerging where Cook ended his explorations."

Nearly every traveler from Philadelphia in the summer months of 1794 brought Azilum tragic tidings from turbulent Paris. Most stricken of all the Azilum *émigrés* was the great and good de Noailles who had planned the refugee city and dreamed that it would one day shelter those he loved most. The lives of five of his family were ended by the falling knife of the guillotine: his wife Louise (sister to Madame de Lafayette) with her mother and grandmother (duchesses de Noailles and d'Ayen), his father

237

(the Maréchal de Mouchy) and his mother, Marie Antoinette's first lady in waiting, playfully dubbed by her mistress "Madame Etiquette." Small wonder that the little hopeful settlement was racked by the sobs of the bereaved, that few of its inhabitants slept through the warm nights, that the little Admiral felt a terrible premonition, though it was never realized. Fortunately unaware that his sister, Perpetué, had been arrested and was in prison at Lyons, he wrote to Félicité:

> Great God, with what horror I learn the list of those guillotined! My sisters, my poor sisters! What with yearning and drying up in my impatience, I have become almost stupid. I smoke mechanically. I chatter sillily. . . . I have given up for the moment my trip to the northwest. I am going to occupy myself only with preparing a retreat for you. In working as I did last spring I will the more easily overcome my disorganization. You will find me doubtless less original, with less of those shortcomings forgivable up to thirty years of age, but which must give place to a better-considered life program, a more useful result. How many, I say it with regret, more favored by fortune, perhaps more enterprising, work for posterity. May their names one day enflame the burning soul of youth. Oh my sister, you are not here to console me and it is more than a year since you and the others should have known me to be here. I have not received a word from you. . . .

Five days later he wrote sister Félicité of his pleasure in rereading *The Vicar of Wakefield,* and on the following day, September first, despite the previous week's resolution to devote himself only to erecting for her "the shack I shall certainly build this winter," he announced:

> Your knight errant will then leave; taking with him only *Ossian* and this diary. He will come back as soon as he has seen

238

the children of nature and envied their lot providing, however, it may be shared with you and Couronne [his brother]. He will come back and build the cabin which must one day receive you. It will be away from the distracting river and there one must live as a hermit.

A month later the explorer had returned from Canandaigua and the lovely lake-and-stream country of the Genesee, and somewhat conscience-stricken decided to begin at once on raising the cabin by the Loyalsock: "For a thousand reasons I have decided on this place rather than on the shore of beautiful Lake Seneca." By November twenty-fifth the little log house, twelve feet square had been covered "except the opening for the chimney," and before the week was over the chimney was up and he had the pleasure of entertaining two friends overnight in his completed home. Returning to Azilum early in December he found his countrymen excitedly studying the public journals. The news of the death of Robespierre brought from him a wild emotional outburst, not uninfluenced by the reading of his precious *Songs of Ossian* by James Macpherson, whose singing English prose he tried to emulate in his native tongue.

> Oh my Country! When will your convulsions that tear me so cease? When will the blade stop? What *sang froid* remains in the midst of this drunken destructiveness? What sad laurels can one gather when they are dyed with the blood of the virtuous Elizabeth [sister of Louis XVI] ? . . . I cannot, my dear friends, escape the frightening presentiments that assail me in the midst of the sweet task of preparing a refuge for you. My sisters, my parents, my friends, what has happened to you?

Almost as he asked the despairing question it was answered. A cousin, refugee from San Domingo, brought

him news of his sisters and soon after came a letter from
Félicité assuring him of their safety. At once he was in an
ecstasy of affection and anticipation.

> Believe me, my dear Félicité, one will nowhere find a family
> like mine that I had thought lost forever. . . . On my trip to
> Philadelphia a big beautiful girl named Barclay caused me to re-
> discover some of the emotions of my youth but . . . I preferred
> to say goodbye and work for you alone. . . . How beautiful will
> be the spring! How much more beautiful the day when you will
> come, bringing life to this sad continent! . . . I spent a day at
> the cabin where I cut down a birch in front of the door. There
> remains enough shade, don't worry, but will you come? This is
> what I ask myself every quarter-hour of the day. This morning,
> lacking the two pretty hands that worked for me in happier days,
> I patched my old clothes. My mind turns on projects of voyages
> but be calm, I will not lose sight of my maisonette.

The winter was long and hard, producing "the devil's
weather," but the settler was happy. His road was covered with three feet of snow, the little streams gurgling
into the Susquehanna were imprisoned under "a triple
wall of ice that the horses refuse to cross," the sky seemed
always cloudy. Sometimes he relieved his loneliness by
staying with a French neighbor, Dandelot, cutting wood,
washing dishes and "filling at the same time the noble position of cook and that of the workman who hollows out
the troughs for collecting maple sugar." Each week end
he trudged through the winter woods the twenty miles
to Azilum. There was warmth and wine, the companionship of witty men, the charm of lovely women beautifully
dressed, but always he returned to his "sweet solitude."
And as the winter began to wear toward its end the hope
of a family reunion and his pride in his log dwelling restored his faith in the America which had disappointed
240

him. "I believe that the pleasure of ownership which I thought would never be acceptable to my philosophy has made my sadness disappear. . . . I shall not change my plan to stay here . . . to get as much done as I can to offer you a modest resource but certain and sufficient for souls imbued with some philosophy. This country seems to me to have been prepared at the hands of Providence to put a stop to the effects of the despair of Europe which sees no hopeful future. It frees England of the dissensions of the moment, it offers a refuge to the French because the hardships of nature here are almost overcome."

A letter of wild anguish from his brother-in-law in Paris, Nicolas Bergasse, confirmed Aristide's views on Europe and strengthened his belief in the country where he had built his cabin home. Wrote Bergasse:

> They have done their worst to me. They killed one of my brothers, destroyed my fortune, reduced to ashes my natal town, burned my manuscripts. I barely escaped torture. . . . My respects to the Indians whom I have always thought more civilized than our miserable scholars, philosophers, men of letters. The devil has been unchained from the depths of hell, and now we have metaphysics—that is to say, a very subtle art of tightening all the fibres of the brain, of drying up all the affections of the heart. Your good savages know nothing of all this. May they always be ignorant of our pretended principles of society and believe for several more centuries in sorcerers, who seem to me in all ways superior to philosophers.

This reflection of the pessimism of thoughtful Europeans, caused by the outrages of the French revolution, gave lonely Aristide a sense of comfort. His conscience had been greatly disturbed that, having failed in his efforts

241

as an explorer, he had been comparatively secure while friends in his native land had undergone the ultimate in human suffering. Now he felt that his industry beside the Susquehanna had not been wasted. His constructive labors had been not only material but mental. He had built a log shelter and a philosophical refuge as well. The faraway river was both flowing water and a symbol of a way of life. April had come and wildflowers were showing vivid colors above the thinning carpet of the snow. With a friend he journeyed by pirogue down the Loyalsock and on by Susquehanna water to Azilum. They left their boat on the east bank, and made their way "back across the rocks that bristle in the river." The little city was buzzing with the disturbing news that Robert Morris, the American financier who had arranged for their purchase of the land on which they lived, was now bankrupt. The troubles of the world were closing in on the town, but not on Aristide. April was in his blood and, having returned to his cabin, he set himself down at the tabouret of his own proud manufacture and wrote his sister (and through her Bergasse and the rest of the family) a letter that in style stemmed from the wild poetry of Ossian's ancient Ireland, passed through Macpherson's rhetorical adaptations and ended in rhapsodical French.

Refuge dedicated to my sister, never will luxury embellish you; never will your furnishings excite the envy of poverty, but at least our brothers will find there, if they wish to come, a shelter against the rigors of a harsh climate. . . . Happily each day I acquire more the habit of working. I am almost tempted to regret the brief time needful to write—though it is raining—for it is for you I prepare this humble retreat where the apple trees will bear their fruit, the apple trees from which comes the benefi-

242

cent cider that makes you feel so good. Also we will collect the sugar of the sugar maple where the weeping willow hangs its floating hair on the winding stream and where we will pass an old age more tranquil than our youth. Meanwhile we live on the banks of a river which love of the country, its richness of art, profusion of nature, and above all, the anticipation of our family reunion, renders so precious.

The life of Azilum had taken its pattern by the time warm days came to that river in 1795, and du Petit-Thouars could be proud of the part he had played in establishing it. The Admiral was by now a character—a well-loved original in the society of the town. His weekend visits were welcomed, and his relatings of incidents revealing his impetuous temperament, his pride, his generosity, became the favorite anecdotes of affectionate friends. Since he had arrived without money and was unable to buy new raiment, one of the most popular of these reported his meeting in the forest, on his way from his cabin to Azilum, a miserable, frightened fugitive from an Indian raid in Canada, bare to the waist and shivering. At once Aristide took off his only shirt and transferred it to the back of another wearer. Then, buttoning his coat tightly about him to conceal his nakedness beneath, he went on to the dinner party that awaited him in *La Grande Maison.*

The sixteen fireplaces at the residence of M. Talon had warmed it to a coziness. As the evening advanced, beads of perspiration formed on the forehead of the tightly buttoned guest and rolled down his cheeks like great tears. His companions chided him, asked him why he must be so formal, why did he weep, what had he hidden beneath his outer garment, was it the legendary fox gnawing at

243

the vitals of a true Spartan—but he was mute. Only the later arrival and report of the grateful new owner of his shirt gave answer that the jacket covered a nude torso and a generous heart.

Knowing that he was very poor and that his pride would not let him receive gifts, conspiring friends made secret, anonymous additions to his wardrobe at times when he could not observe their actions. No one dared suggest lending him a horse when, on setting out with mounted companions for western New York, he announced that he vastly preferred walking and merrily made the journey on foot. All openly admired his swinging of the ax, however, as he was building his cabin, and the valley woodsmen were still proudly identifying the ax-marks as one-armed strokes a generation after he had left the Susquehanna.

His last spring in the lovely valley was a happy one. Since he had been recommended to the colony by the noble de Noailles, of unquestionable social eminence and so skillful a dancer that Marie Antoinette often chose him as her partner, the little Admiral despite his poverty was welcomed by the French high society of Azilum. In the long drawing room of *La Grande Maison* there were concerts and card parties and amateur dramatics. The *émigrés* dressed as formally and elegantly in the log house as ever at the Tuileries, and in the intermissions on warm evenings they strolled outdoors by the moonlit waters. On a wooded mid-river island just opposite *La Grande Maison* they had built a dancing pavilion, and black slaves rowed them there after dinner to bow and turn and glide to the music of a slave orchestra before being returned to the oak-shadowed wharf as light from the east

244

paled the stars. There were tea parties on flat Table Rock which crowned a high hill behind the town and picnic expeditions to the top of a high ridge where Prospect Rock offered to their ecstatic gaze a vast panorama of spring-green woods, brown new-plowed fields, and the winding silver Susquehanna. In the town itself little shops, whose wares had been chosen with a taste more chic than that of American storekeepers, lured trade away from the nearby town of Troy. A log tavern offered food and drink so appetizing as hardly to be found elsewhere in the nation.

As for the individuals who made up this society, the little Admiral's emotions varied. For some time he distrusted the portly, handsome Monsieur Talon with whom he had lived in *La Grande Maison* when he first came to Azilum. Talon—manager of the colony at a salary of $3,000 a year—was of his own age, yet he shared none of his enthusiasm for the new democratic period of return to natural and simple living. Aristide rhapsodized over his little cabin in the woods. Talon dreamed of a pretentious and elaborate mansion—the center of a country seat of thousands of rolling acres beside the rolling river. There, with his steward Bartholomew Laporte, he would live a life befitting a French *émigré* of high position.

The faithful Laporte, often victim of his employer's imperious whims, had been a prosperous wine merchant in the city of Cadiz until banished by the Spanish government. On the water front at Marseille, where he sought passage to America, he had come upon a furtive companion who turned out to be Talon in desperate flight from the revolutionists who had discovered in the famous iron chest of Louis XVI letters that would doom him, if captured, to the guillotine. Since he was hated more than most monarchists because he had been chief of the King's secret police, agents of the new government were searching every outbound vessel in the effort to apprehend him. Ever resourceful, Laporte stuffed the big man into a wine cask, had it carried aboard a merchantman bound for England and, stowing it in the hold, covered it over with charcoal. Though the ship was searched from stem to stern no agent came upon the fugitive, and he was soon in England whence he immediately sailed for America—taking his rescuer with him as his confidential agent. Aristide suspected that, despite the support of his friend de Noailles, he had not the good will of either Talon or Laporte, and it was not until August of 1794 that he reported in a letter to sister Félicité: "M. Talon has convinced me of his good faith in wanting to help me."

Among Aristide's early intimates at Azilum were newlyweds—the Marquis de Blâcons and his lady, the former Mademoiselle Félicité de Maulde. In Blâcons, once a member of the French constituent assembly, he found a true friend and confidant—one who listened sympathetically to his reminiscences of his beloved family and discussed with him his plans for future explorations. As for Madame Blâcons, the young bachelor had a prospective benedict's characteristic interest in the bride of a friend—a curiosity which she amply repaid.

She had been the daughter of a prosperous planter in San Domingo when the slave insurrection had begun. Since her father was desperately ill with yellow fever at the time, and unable to take action, she had placed herself at the head of a little band of faithful slaves and marched with them into battle against the relentless and barbarous rebels. Though at first successful in protecting her father and her plantation home, she had soon realized that defeat and a horrible death would be inevitable if she stayed on. So with her suffering father on a litter carried by his loving blacks she again led the way—fighting a passage through a tangled jungle infested with a blood-crazed enemy. At the seacoast, she had the good fortune to find a ship bound for America. Her father died almost immediately, when a pirate ship attacked. The corsairs, having fought their way aboard, robbed the girl of all the money and portable treasures with which she had hoped to make a new beginning in the United States. She arrived in Philadelphia a penniless, exiled orphan, almost prostrated by her terrible ordeals, but with her courage unflagging, her beauty and wit undimmed. There she at one attracted the sympathy and admiration, later the love, of the distinguished Marquis de Blâcons. Affianced, the young couple made the arduous journey up the Susquehanna to Azilum, where their fellow *émigrés* celebrated the town's first wedding with an elaborate and merry *fête*. Soon afterward husband and wife were operating a haberdashery shop. In Philadelphia, on one occasion, Aristide met Blâcons and later reported that "his wife is extremely impatient. She loves him greatly; her charming letters, which he showed me, make it evident. Hers is indeed the eloquence of sentiment."

Others of Azilum's approximately two hundred residents had lived through melodramatic experiences as exciting as any imagined by authors of historical romances. In the security of the firelit drawing room of *La Grande Maison* descriptions of hairbreadth escapes must

247

more than once have found breathless audiences. There was the story of Charles Homet, who had served his King and Queen as a member of the household staff at Versailles. He had fled to the shores of the Bay of Biscay where friends tried their best to hide him until he could obtain passage on an America-bound ship. At last he found one and secretly placed his personal belongings aboard. Then, fearing a search of the vessel by agents of the revolution, he went ashore to spend the last night before sailing in his hiding place. In the morning, to his horror, friends informed him that the agents now knew where he had lodged and he could see that during the night—possibly to avoid a search—the ship's captain had raised his anchor and dropped five miles down the bay. Aware that he might at the very moment be in the sight of his pursuers he raced down the wharf and dove into the water. Hours later other fleeing *émigrés* watched from the ship's deck the head of a swimmer bobbing on the waves as he slowly neared his goal. Eager hands dragged him aboard and among those who saw the exhausted young man lifted over the rail was an old acquaintance of the days when life was a happy idyll at Versailles—pretty young Maria Theresa Schillinger, native of Strasbourg, and until recently a maid in waiting to Marie Antoinette. They were in love by the time they reached America, and after they were married at Bordentown, New Jersey, they went to Azilum. It is said that Talon and de Noailles had planned to build, eight miles outside of the town, a secret hiding place for the Queen—to be used in case vengeful revolutionists followed her to America—and that Homet was assigned the duty of erecting it. Whatever the reason may have been, Homet built a big house at the designated spot. Lombardy poplars still mark the site. Bricks from the huge chimneys and a dagger—both found where once the house stood—are now exhibits in the Tioga Point Museum at Athens.

That spring Aristide had the opportunity, loved by most veterans of the American Revolution, of trading reminiscences with a group of his fellow countrymen who, when most of them were hardly twenty, had seen service against the British before Cornwallis's surrender. Logically the most congenial of these was Captain Dennis Cottineau who had many memories of John Paul Jones, the most thrilling being that of the action in which, as commander of the *Pallas,* he aided his American ally's *Bonhomme Richard* toward victory over the British *Serapis.*

Among others of Aristide's comrades in arms who could spend an evening at Azilum remembering the War of Independence were Captain Beaulieu, who served in the Legion of Pulaski; Captain Montullé of the French cavalry; and three heroes of Yorktown—Baron de Cadignan, Autichamp, and Blanchard—all praised for their service by General Rochambeau.

The little Admiral gave casual attention, or none at all, to these men in his detailed letters to sister Félicité. He wrote of his constant companion, young Morés, who had been a member of the secular clergy and once owned a priory in France before joining in the search for La Perouse; of his nearest neighbor, Daudelot, who helped him build his cabin; of La Neuville (whom he met on a journey to Washington), "who is gay, knows people, drinks, hunts and lacks none of the qualities that make a *bon vivant,*" and he added the revealing sentence: "You know that for better or worse I have always needed friends of this type."

Most of all, as befitted a young unmarried Frenchman, Aristide was engrossed in the women around him. There was Madame d'Autremont, fifty-year-old widow whose husband's life had ended at the guillotine. She lived formally and changed her costume several times a day. Aristide thought "she has the most charming face I have seen for her age." One day in spring he drove her herd of cows along a woodland and, telling of it later, "that's a far cry from leading a squadron of thirty ships with which I had hoped to overthrow the maritime power of England."

Another widow, Madame Sibert, much richer, younger, and comelier than Madame d'Autremont, lived in one of the most attractive dwellings at Azilum—"a log house 30 x 18 covered with nailed shingles. The kitchen and dining room were separate, after the custom of San Domingo, and connected to the main building by piazzas. A paling fence enclosed the yard and the garden, in which a latticed summerhouse stood by a bubbling brook whose waters were shadowed by Lombardy poplars and weeping willows." Such a setting could easily lead to romance on an April night but Aristide, while tempted, did not succumb:

> This evening I had a *tête-à-tête* with a pretty woman, Madame Siber, but they are far from me—the ideas held in France on the gestures a man should not fail to make in the presence of loveliness when he has a chance. . . . The lady, though rich in comparison with the rest of her fugitive compatriots, is stingy with her negroes and workmen. In other words, my reserve did not cost me too much. . . . It was a long time ago, good friends,

that you taught me never to separate moral beauty from physical beauty.

Most disturbing of all was a charming *jeune fille,* and Aristide's attitude toward her in the late summer of 1794, as indicated in his letters, would seem to indicate both the strength of his attraction to her and a fear—based on unhappy experiences elsewhere—of her winning his affections.

> Mademoiselle Marin is beautiful, giddy and vain of the conquest she has made of him who plays the star part here [Talon]. In contrast, Madame de Noailles [who played piano accompaniments for *la Marin's* songs and was the wife of a cousin of the colony's founder] is a woman more tender than coquettish—she prefers finding a being who would satisfy her sensitivity rather than her desire to flirt. She is well made, dresses with taste, has pretty teeth and an attractive pallor. Hers are charms worth while.

Ten days later the enchanting Marin had made inroads on his peace of mind:

> Yesterday I found Mademoiselle Marin much too pretty. She has the most beautiful figure one could imagine. Her features are perfect. She sings ravishingly. Her mind lacks neither vivacity nor sensitivity—but she is a spoiled child who does not understand the true pride allotted women and who, in her present circumstances, has not yet exactly appraised herself. What love would be needed to tie up all one's life with such a woman!

There were moments thereafter when Aristide felt almost capable of furnishing the charming singer with this great love. After his long week-end walks through the winter woods from the cold loneliness of his cabin to the warm congeniality in the drawing room of *La Grande*

251

Maison, were exquisite dinners prepared by cooks Julie and Wallois in the separate kitchen-house and served with meticulous formality in the big drawing room, the good French wines and the heartwarming brandy, the slim and exquisite girl singing beside the piano, while the smiling, "well-made" Madame de Noailles played for her, made a vision hardly to be resisted. "I am tempted to prolong my last trip. After I left I felt a sort of tenderness for Mademoiselle Marin, but it was only a very pale reflection of what I formerly felt for so many pretty women; when I had returned I found that I was recovered."

The Duc de la Rochefoucauld-Liancourt, on his way to Niagara Falls, wandered into Azilum on a spring day of 1795 with a young friend (Guillemard), a servant and his dog—Cartouche. He stayed some weeks, long enough to write into his journal a detailed description to which American historians owe much that they know of the French town. Aristide set out for one of his weekly visits there but met halfway four of his Azilum friends who were guiding the Duke to his cabin. He returned with them and all spent a happy and busy day working in the garden. Said Liancourt of Aristide in his journal: "He lives free and happy, without property, yet without want. . . . His sociable, mild, yet truly original temper and character are set off by a noble simplicity of manner"— and so good was the impression these qualities made that he was invited to accompany the little expedition to Niagara.

Since once more he must walk, the little Admiral left Azilum alone in the twilight of June first. The others, mounted, would overtake him soon after they resumed their travels on the next day. Lights were coming on in the nearly half-a-hundred houses, some of which he had built, and reflections twinkled on the Susquehanna as he took the north trail lying beside it. In the shadow of the wharf rode barges which had carried cargoes of maple sugar, flax, grain, potash and tar downriver to Wilkes-Barre and would do so again. Some of these products would finally reach Philadelphia and be exchanged for imports from France. The city had made a good beginning, and he could contemplate with serenity the journal he wished to write from the notes he would take on his way to Niagara. He was walking out of the story of the Susquehanna, for there is not much to be added about the little Admiral and his well-loved stream. The two years he had spent beside it had been an enchanted interlude in the life of a man of action. He did not know, as he trudged into the dark woods, that in three years' time he would be off the coast of Egypt in command of the old French ship *Tonnant*—slowly sinking under the pounding of Admiral Lord Nelson's cannon. A leg shattered in the engagement had been amputated in his quarters below—but he had ordered his men to carry him back to the bridge from which he courteously refused British offers of generous terms if he would surrender. At Aboukir—when he was thirty-eight years old—the sea closed over him and his colors, which he had ordered nailed to the mast.

Old friends in the French town on the Susquehanna had scant time left for remembering the little Admiral and mourning their loss. The piano still tinkled in the long salon under the expert and beautiful fingers of Madame de Noailles, and six weeks after Aristide's death Mademoiselle Marin was singing Mozart, Gluck, Scarlatti for a new French visitor—le comte Colbert de Maulevrier, traveler and water-colorist who was making a nostalgic return to the scenes of his activities during the American Revolution. Yet the colony itself was shrinking: Talon had gone to Europe and would not return; Boulogne had drowned in the Loyalsock not far from the empty cabin the little Admiral had built for his twin sisters; Aristide's best friends among the *émigrés*—the Marquis de Blâcons and his courageous loving wife—had been permitted to return to France. To them, at about the time of Aboukir, had been born a daughter, whom they named Oneida d'Armand de la Forest—in memory of their happy life in the Indian-inhabited wilds where flowed the Susquehanna.

Disagreements over real estate, following the bankruptcy and death of Robert Morris, and the almost overwhelming difficulty of making a living in a town which they realized would never be the prosperous inland port they had hoped for harassed the settlers. They were growing older and *nostalgie* began to replace their dreams of an idyllic new life à la Rousseau beside the river whose murmurous shallows—once musical—now reminded them only that it might never be navigable for water commerce.

Four years after the death of Aristide du Petit-Thouars a French postrider galloped into the main street of Azilum waving his hat and shouting in a hysteria of joy. He bore news that Napoleon—now Consul of rehabilitated France—would look with favor on petitions of deserving *émigrés* to return to France. The *émigrés* crowded about the rider in the big square, embraced each other, leaped about, laughed and wept. Bonfires burned along the river front and there was feasting and dancing in the log houses and in *La Grande Maison*. Azilum had re-

254

ceived a fatal wound. In the years that immediately followed, the little town's inhabitants left it—some for return to France, others, several of whom had married into American families, for homes more prosperously situated. De Noailles died as bravely as Petit-Thouars, from a wound sustained in a naval battle with the British. Blâcons committed suicide in France after gambling losses. *Émigré* John Brevost was said to have been the last to leave the lonely streets of Azilum—after his advertisement of a school for teaching French to young Americans—published in the Wilkes-Barre *Gazette*—got scant results. He took with him his black slave boy, born at the town in 1793 and christened Azilum Peters. Then came the slow march of decay.

In Saumur on the winding Loire stands a spirited statue of Aristide du Petit-Thouars, depicting him in the last defiant moment of his life and commemorating his death.

In the river region below Athens there is almost nothing except the State of Pennsylvania historical markers to tell those who pass of the enchantment held within the half-moon bend where stood—a century and a half ago— the log-house village of the French nobles and their companions. High on the mountain on the opposite side of the river the Susquehanna Trail highway widens to give travelers opportunity to leave their vehicles and to look through a telescope far down to the fertile acres surrounding the Hagerman farmhouse. This contains some timber taken from the French homes and shows some French influence, having been built by Laporte descendants in 1839. Not far from it is the site of the Queen's house. To reach the site of Aristide's square cabin the

interested traveler will find on a road map of Pennsylvania
Dushore—a careless Americanization of du Petit-Thouars.
Through the twisted name this hamlet remembers the
brave little man with one hand who lived and worked
here, and believed with all his heart that America had
been destined by God to become the hope of the world.

18

Peace to the River Folk

🌣 *Peace is a nursing mother to the land.*
—HESIOD (700 B.C.)

As the settlers beside the winding Susquehanna began to feel secure in the tenure of their lands toward the end of the eighteenth century, the long period of violence came gradually to an end. On the West Branch the pioneers who had claimed wild acres without charter from either Pennsylvania or Connecticut began to exult in the realization that squatter rights would be recognized. The "Fair Play Men," as they called their vigilantelike protective organization, saw that they might now safely disband and allow Pennsylvania courts of justice to take over the administration of law and order.

Shaggy bison which had wandered the West Branch valleys had by the end of the century been killed or had migrated westward. Honeybees, sure harbingers of the coming of the white man but ever, according to local belief, an exact fifty miles ahead of him in the forest, now hived in hollow trees along the Ohio whence they would soon dart west to keep their distance from "those restless spirits who fancy that the land is over-crowded when the population exceeds one to every ten square miles."

Now that armed conflict between humans was no longer

257

probable the only enemies left in the valley were the wild beasts and the weather. Sometimes the latter conspired with the river itself for, while the Pennymite Wars were still flaring, the Yankees had been devastated in the summer of 1786 by a flood so irresistible that heavy pumpkins came tumbling downstream like great orange cannonballs and had much the same effect when houses or men stood in their way. Wolves threatened the domestic animals, but the winters were sometimes so cold that whole packs of them froze to death. Rattlesnakes were a dangerous summer chorus that "sang in the barns and made music in the hayfields."

The ways of peace brought other and less ominous melodies to the land. The pianos and flutes transported by the well-to-do and cultured French found unaccustomed companions among the fifes and drums of the Yankees, the zithers and fiddles of the gypsies, and occasional jew's-harps which the Indians had hailed at first hearing as their favorite instruments. Choruses of trombones announced the deaths of Moravian brethren and stirred brassy echoes along the wooded slopes beside the water.

The settlers of the long valley had become an increasingly heterogeneous lot. Members of German religious sects and tarmakers who had left the Palatine states for the banks of the Hudson only to migrate south were now river neighbors. The quiet Mennonites, dressed in black and gray, had first arrived in the late seventeenth century. A sect influenced by Anabaptists, they were, like the Quakers, pacifists who believed in humility and scorned the luxuries and vanities of worldly life. Their creed contained many tenets later adopted by the Mormon Church. Indeed, when Joseph Smith came from Western New York to the north-Pennsylvania banks of the Susquehanna to complete his translation of the golden pages of the Book of Mormon (found within Palmyra's sacred hill of Cumorah) and to contemplate the founding of the Church of Jesus Christ of the Latter Day Saints, he may have been influenced by German and Swiss sects along the river. Either from divine revelation or from his own judgment, he seems to have affirmed such practices as the election of unpaid preachers, baptism of the dead, condemnation of infant baptism, polygamy (an early Anabaptist belief already abandoned by the Mennonites), healing of the sick by anointing them with oil, prolific propagation of children, self-sufficiency as a "peculiar people," and avoidance of all public benefits stemming from state or national governments.

The Amish, followers of a Swiss preacher, Jacob Amman, who prevailed on a number of followers to leave the Mennonite Church before emigrating to America in mid-century, had settled the fertile acres that now line the river in Lancaster County. Their long-haired bearded men, wearing broad-brim low-crown hats and "barn-door" side-opening pants, and their women in black bonnets, aprons and shawls which, once doffed, unveiled dresses as green as the river willows in April, as red as the apple-laden boughs of their orchards in the fall, as blue as the summer delphiniums in their dooryards, made the clean-shaven Mennonite men in their somber suits and their wives in black and gray seem by contrast an artistically stimulating background.

The Amish were no less strict in religious instruction than the Mennonites, however, nor were the other German sects of the "Pennsylvania Dutch" (a term early adopted in America when all Germans were known as "Dutch") who had sought religious freedom in Pennsylvania—the Moravians, the Dunkards (sometimes called "The Brethren"), the Schwenkfelders and others, all of whom had at least occasional representatives along the Susquehanna.

From the distinguished families of French nobility that had founded Azilum, a considerable number stayed on in America even after Napoleon had encouraged them to return to their native land. A much larger group augmented the French population of the valley when many Huguenot refugees arrived. More adaptable and assimilable than the Germans, they soon found themselves speaking the language of the Dutch, marrying into Dutch families and gradually becoming identified as Pennsylvania Dutchmen.

Gypsy wagons began rolling beside the river soon after 1750, and the *Zigeuner,* as the German settlers called them, contributed not only to the kaleidoscopic mélange of colors in the valley but offered freer, less moralistic ideas of living than those of the religionists. By the end of the century the number of gypsies following new patterns beside the curving meanders of the Susquehanna was sufficient to have a considerable influence on the over-all population and an effect not often taken into consideration by historians of Pennsylvania.

Mutual distaste for England's highhanded attitude toward their interests had drawn the Susquehanna's widely variant groups into a regional unit that felt the stirrings of a national spirit. As early as 1780 William Maclay, writing from Sunbury, declared, "There is a love of country that really has weight. This is a strange divided quarter. Whig, Tory, Pennymite, Dutch, Irish, and English influence are strangely blended. I must confess that I begin to be national, too, and most sincerely believe every public interest in America will be safer in the hands of Americans than with any others."

The abortive "Whiskey Rebellion" served further to bind together the river settlements. Their fertile acres produced such heavy crops of grain that moving them by wagon eastward across the mountains to the Philadelphia market proved well-nigh impossible. They had no sooner solved this problem by concentrating their grains into easily transportable spirituous liquors than a heavy federal excise was levied upon such products. This the farmers of western Pennsylvania regarded as discriminatory against settlers living farthest from the market, and many of them took up arms against the national government. Adopting the old symbol of revolt against tyranny, the liberty pole, they raised many a nail-studded pine shaft

261

from which fluttered a banner of "Persian red" bearing the word "Liberty."

A detachment of army regulars was sent to destroy a pole set up just beyond Lewisburg but, forewarned, the residents of the region took it down and hid it, leaving the soldiers such relief from frustration as they could get by raiding a nearby tavern, drinking its entire supply of the commodity that was causing all the difficulty, and departing with the word that the landlord might charge the reckoning to the government.

A pole raised at Northumberland was the center of a street riot during which Mrs. Bernard Hubley ran to offer the friends of the government her ax, but was intercepted by her sister, Mrs. Jacob Welker, who was worsted in the ensuing struggle. The pole came down!

Among the rioters against the tax were many veterans of the Revolution. In one group arrested by the disproportionately large body of national troops ordered into Pennsylvania to suppress the rebellion were several of these old warriors, and it is related that their protests against being marched through the streets of Philadelphia with placards reading "Whiskey Rebel" hung about their necks so moved President Washington that he pardoned a number of them after they had been tried and convicted and had served but twenty days of their sentences.

19

Hearth-Fire Talk

🌶 *It's always seemed to me that*
legends and yarns and folk-tales
are as much a part of the real history
of a country as proclamations
and provisos and constitutional amendments.

— STEPHEN VINCENT BENÉT (1941)

The river was a winding thread stitching together communities as variegated as their patchwork quilts—Log Cabin, Tree of Paradise, Turkey Tracks, Forty Times Around the World. The wild, group miscellany of far-spread national origins began to share mutual joys. Journals of the period list names that show the melding of peoples of many traditions. The diary of the gay bachelor-teacher, Flavel Roan, who seems from his entries never to have missed a social occasion in Buffalo Valley (on the West Branch just above its juncture with the North), is liberally salted with records of hustling matches, quilting bees, barn raisings, singing school concerts, bear baitings, rope dances, militia "training days" and "kicking frolics," all made the more merry with generous supplies of "cider oil," "cider royal," and rye whiskey.

Sometimes the singing got a little out of hand, Flavel reported, as when "the ladies would not sing because

263

Tommy raised an old tune, 'Isle of Wight.' " A "tromping frolic at Uncle Clark's," he says, was attended by numerous of the valley beaux, and he intimates the magnetic quality of the girls with the hint that "where the carcase is, thither will the eagles gather together." He found an evangelistic camp meeting equally enjoyable. After drinking "wine at Calhoun's" he attended one beside the river and it aroused poetic sentiments: "The moon shining through the trees, the fire, candles in the camp, the large quiet crowd of people made the scene romantic and solemn"; but all ended in "great carrying on at camp. Criswell's boys got happy." Another pair of coupled entries read: "October 27. Five doctors tapping Davy Reasoner. October 27. D.R. died."

The tales of the river folk had altered in character by 1800. For a century they had been narratives of narrow escapes, horrible massacres, feats of physical prowess. Now, as life was less tortured by fear, fireside tales were less hair-raising and frequently humorous. Not that Indian stories disappeared. The legend of George Rote, a lame man, but so "great on a halloo" that once, by exercising his gift, he routed a whole Indian raiding party, was still enjoyed in Buffalo Valley.

Many popular stories were of captured whites who found such delight in the woodland tribal villages that they would not return to friends and relatives when they were free to do so. There was the narrative of David Emrick's widow and her daughter who, soon after being captured, married the Indians who killed their husbands. Years later they rode back "decorated with all the tinsel of Indian dress" to obtain their portions of the slain men's estate and to try to influence Northumberland females to join them in a woodland existence they regarded as idyllic.

Another convert to Indian living was young Tom Lee, captured in a savage raid in 1780. Years later his brother persuaded his captors to return him to Tioga Point. Tom was so completely a "white Indian" by then that it was necessary for the tribesmen to bind him before placing him in a canoe to travel to Wilkes-Barre. As soon as he was released, he made a desperate dash for freedom and a return to his forest home. Recaptured, he was hostile to the whites about him for a long time before, surrounded by playing white children, he finally showed some curiosity about their games. Eventually his homesickness for Indian ways wore off, and he resigned himself to life among his white relatives. Out of this story the Pennsylvania writer, Conrad Richter, fashioned a novel, *Light in the Forest.*

❧ THE MASTER OF THE SEVEN ISLANDS

The uneventful daily routines of peaceful living, as they always do, focused popular attention on the eccentrics of the river communities. As the tales of war and massacre lost their savor, the legends of odd and individualistic citizens made happier telling. Around Sunbury and Selinsgrove the story of English Jimmy Silverwood found eager hearers. Jimmy claimed a group of small islands in the river opposite the large Isle of Que and, thereafter, in lordly fashion always referred to himself as "Master of the Seven Islands." Since even his letters to friends and relatives in England bore this sounding appellation, his reputation soon took on an international character far in excess of his actual status. The population on the banks of the river was growing, however, and he and his sons earned a reasonably good living, for in the spring the waters about the Seven Islands teemed with shad which, even when sold at six dollars a hundred, brought him profits. These he quickly spent in showy ways that aggrandized his standing as an affluent and aristocratic landholder.

❦ A MESSENGER FROM JEHOVAH

A more mentally disturbed young man from near Northumberland made himself a protagonist of an oft-told tale by bursting into the chamber of the Pennsylvania House of Representatives meeting at Lancaster. There "well dressed" and speaking in a "loud, clear, and distinct voice" he addressed the legislators: "Mr. Speaker, I am charged by the Lord God with a message to this house, to direct them forthwith to pass a law for the removal of the seat of government from Lancaster to the top of Blue Hill."

The recommended lofty location had its virtues, offering as it still does, a most exciting view of both branches of the Susquehanna close to their intersection at Sunbury, but the unsympathetic doorkeeper and the sergeant-at-arms seized upon the deranged youth and were trying to eject him when he suddenly upended both and strode from the chamber leaving them prone on the floor. Soon thereafter he was galloping toward his river home more than a hundred miles away. Tellers of the story claimed he rode without stop at breakneck speed and that his horse dropped dead on arrival.

🌸 THE WOMAN-HATER OF BLUE HILL

The site the strange youth had praised was fated to have further distinction in the folk history of the river. Something more than three decades later a Philadelphia-born misogynist named John Mason chose the summit of Blue Hill as his ultimate refuge from a world which contained women. There he built a two-story octagonal tower that leaned, some say thirty-five degrees—some eighteen—from the perpendicular. A visitor, if he had the temerity to look down from its dizzy height, might see the confluence of the Susquehanna branches and the towns of Northumberland and Sunbury. Inside the tower's second story, the eight walls were lined with shelves that held hundreds of rare old books. There John Mason swung his hammock and read, secure in the knowledge that no woman would invade his precariously tilted stronghold. Sometimes in winter when the river was frozen over, he would strap his skates to his feet and, umbrella always in hand, set off in vast swooping strokes for Harrisburg where he would arrive, folks said admiringly, in only half a day. People on the streets of Williamsport also became familiar with the gaunt figure of the old bachelor. One summer morning, on a farm near that town, he died. His body was transferred on a friend's sled in the middle of the next winter to the high peak where he had lived. The "Hermit of Blue Hill" was buried beneath the bare branches of a wide-spread chestnut tree standing a few feet behind the tower which slanted over the brink of the tall precipice.

❦ THE NAKED GIRL AND ALL THE SAMARITANS

Most amazing and popular of all of the turn-of-the-century tales about strange characters was that of Esther MacDowell. It began startlingly enough on a brisk October morning in 1803 when Martin Reese, an elderly German settler, opened the front door of his cabin near the West Branch town of Jersey Shore and saw, standing against a tree in his yard, a naked girl whose mouth had been stopped by a cruel gag and whose hands were tied behind her back. When she had been unbound and led to the old man's fire, she was so cold she could hardly speak but she finally said that she had been riding from her father's home in Montreal to visit an uncle in Kentucky. A young man named Benjamin Connett, who had been employed as a guard to accompany her, had on the evening before robbed her at pistol point of all the gold her fond parent had given her for the trip, then stripped, gagged and bound her. After he had left her to die of hunger or from the attacks of wild beasts, she had struggled all night to loosen her bonds and had finally been able to walk to the spot where Martin Reese had found her.

The response of the citizens of Jersey Shore to this pitiful tale was prompt and hearty. At once Preacher Grier had taken Esther MacDowell into his family and made an appeal to the community to come to her aid. While the womenfolk vied with each other in satisfying her material needs, the men formed a posse and started in pursuit of the villainous Connett. Broadsides describing him and his crime were printed and distributed among the Susquehanna communities, but he and the two horses seemed completely to have disappeared.

Esther's shy demeanor, her obvious anguish at having been so shamed in a community of strangers, her quiet manner, her simplicity and air of refinement won the hearts of the kindly housewives, while her beauty, sincerity, and modesty drew from susceptible husbands and bachelors expensive gifts, including silk dresses, such as they had never lavished on a female before. For weeks Esther was the most beloved inhabitant of Jersey Shore. The townspeople wrote to her father in Montreal, assuring him that his daughter was safe and that her every want was satisfied. She became a fêted celebrity, and many strangers rode miles from up and downriver to see her at the Reverend Mr. Grier's home and brought her gifts they considered worthy of her delicate charm and irreproachable character.

One of these curious travelers, a Mr. Hutchinson of the town of Milton came to nearby Duffies' Tavern, that he might visit the lovely Canadian and was considerably surprised by her diffidence. At length, he interpreted it as a desire to avoid him. This so piqued him that he studied the averted face closely and suddenly announced, "You are the young man who worked for me in Milton as a journey-man tailor." He was so sure of his statement that others nearby became suspicious of Esther. The discovery of a bundle of men's clothes hidden in a hollow log near Martin Reese's cabin added to the evidence against her, and at last she confessed that she had masqueraded as a male tailor in Milton and that, being of an adventurous turn of mind, she had invented the hoax which she

269

had, until the arrival of Mr. Hutchinson, performed with rare artistry. Oldsters who told the story, amid gales of laughter, said Esther abandoned Jersey Shore in a westerly direction and years later was reported to have married and to be living as a prominent and admired matron in a western town.

❧ THE SUSCEPTIBLE BUT MURDEROUS PREACHER

Since men of the professions were looked upon as outstanding and deserving of privileges at the beginning of the new century, such of them as deviated from the norm of strictly respectable behavior attracted so much attention as to become the central figures of tales told oft and again and losing no whit in each recital. Because of their calling, ministers who behaved unconventionally or worse often became the protagonists of lurid narratives. One of these which got the new century off to a flying start concerned the actions of one who signed himself with many a flourish of elegant penmanship the "Reverend Cyriacus Spangenberg, V.D.M." This man had arrived in America with hireling Hessian troops during the Revolution. Some time thereafter he had come under the influence of Philip J. Michael, described by one narrator of the story as a "frivolous preacher," and was ordained by him. His first call was to preach in the German Reformed Church at Selinsgrove. Here he exhibited such charm and articulate persuasion that he won the heart of a girl of the town. A day was set for their wedding and it would have taken place had not suspicious persons come upon and read a letter addressed to Spangenberg and signed by his wife, then living in Europe. Driven from Selins-

270

grove by an indignant congregation, he moved to Berlin, now in Somerset County, Pennsylvania, and once more took up the duties of pastor. He was soon in characteristic difficulties. At a special winter meeting called for a vote of the church members on his retention, he sat in the raised altar with his chief accuser, Elder Jacob Glassmore. As the latter was advocating the minister's discharge, Spangenberg leaped upon him and drove a dirk into his heart. The congregation sat frozen in horror as this real-life melodrama profaned the sacred altar in their presence, but in a moment the sight of their Elder dead in a pool of blood stirred them to seize his murderer. The pastor was tried in April and found guilty. Efforts were made by some of his followers who still believed in him to have his sentence commuted, but they proved vain. At Bedford, Pennsylvania, on the tenth of October, 1795, the hangman's rope ended the life of the elegantly educated Reverend Cyriacus Spangenberg, V.D.M. A hundred years later his story still chilled the blood of listeners about Susquehanna firesides.

❦ WHAT DAN DOUDLE SAID TO THE ALMIGHTY

Slighter and more frequent as religious intensity lessened here and there along the river were ironic anecdotes of falling from grace such as old Dan Doudle's remark to his Maker on the notable winter night when he was converted to the power of prayer by Mother Grove, an elderly Methodist. Eager to try the effectiveness of petition to the Almighty, Dan returned home in such solemnity that members of his family suspected its cause and listened outside his bedroom, peeping through a crack in the door. Old Dan undressed as usual, taking off all his clothes before removing his hat, then knelt by the bed. "O Lord God," said Dan in a loud voice and then paused to consider what he should say next. Then his words came clear and distinct. "It's too damn cold to pray here," said Dan to Jehovah and he hopped under the blankets.

❧ THE LETTER OF THE LAW

The establishment of legal procedures and formal justice on the Susquehanna lands brought with it many incidents that delighted the minds of the people. Judges who insisted on enforcing all the customs of the English courts sometimes found themselves opposed by frontiersmen who refused to be disciplined and who sometimes outwitted the learned and bewigged occupants of the high bench.

Of all the river justices, English-born Oxford-educated Thomas Cooper of Northumberland was most severe in his insistence on decorum. When Jack Glover, a notorious addict of spirituous liquors, entered the courthouse in his usual stimulated condition, the judge summoned him to the bar and, peering down at him through his monocle, said, "Ah, Jack, is that you, and drunk again? The court fines you one dollar and sentences you to be imprisoned for twenty-four hours."

"Please your honor," said Jack with considerable alcoholic emotion, "it goes hard to be punished twice for the same offense."

"But you are drunk again today," said the Justice severely.

"Not again, but still," said Jack. "I haven't sobered up since you last sentenced me."

"Get about your business," said Thomas Cooper, always a stickler for the letter of the law.

❦ RESPECT FOR THE COURT

At Clearfield on the West Branch courts of law were so new and infrequent that settlers were sometimes unaware that they were expected to show proper respect. When Justice James Burnside held his first court there, spectators pushed their way in among the attorneys standing before him. On hearing the name of a man indicted for an offense, the judge said loudly, "Is Pennington in the court?"

"Jedge," said a bystander, "you better call out the whole damn grist of Penningtons!"

"You are in contempt of court," said Burnside severely and with loud emphasis. "Your conduct, moreover, is such that you are liable to a fine for creating a disturbance."

"Hesh up, Jedge," said the bystander, "you're making a damn sight more disturbance than I did."

❦ "MY LEARNED OPPONENT"

Another incident of the courts became so popular that it may more than once have been emulated. The story goes that a young and learned prosecuting attorney in describing his case against the defendant displayed his brilliance and extensive education by quoting extensively from the Latin. When the wily old Indian fighter defending the accused made his summing up, he snowed his opponent

273

under with passage after passage of pure Mohawk. Other folk tell a parallel to this one as having happened in the national House of Representatives and claim that it was George Kremer, Susquehanna politician, who countered the highfalutin Greek and Latin of his associates with a speech larded by pertinent references in "Pennsylvania Dutch."

❦ THE GIRL BANDIT AND THE MORAVIAN GOVERNOR

Lawbreakers who chose to disregard the advent of enforced order were also at the beginning of the nineteenth century fertile sources of popular and picaresque tales. As is usual in such narratives, the folk have added so much of imaginative material to the facts that separation of the two ingredients has become well-nigh impossible. The most talked of outlaw of the period was a pretty and fascinating woman named Ann Carson. When a young girl she had married a middle-aged, Scottish-born ship's officer, hard-drinking John Carson, who had seen active service as a captain in the United States Navy. Shortly after the first decade of the century Carson obtained command of the ship *Ganges* and set out on a commercial voyage to China. He was gone for several years, and his wife who had expected an early return was finally convinced that he had died. A dashing United States officer, Lieutenant Richard Smith of the Twenty-Third United States Infantry, had rented an apartment in her home and probably had more than a little to do with strengthening this belief. Ann's enthusiasm for Smith may not have been wholly due to a passion encouraged by proximity, however, since the personable fellow was nephew and

274

heir of one of the comparatively few American millionaires of the time, Daniel Clark of New Orleans.

The appearance of long-absent John Carson in the autumn of 1815 was a severe shock to the infatuated young couple. Ann had no welcome for her captain, but she was eventually persuaded by her parents and their friends to receive him as her husband and to dismiss her romantic lover. But her problems were not so easily solved, since the handsome soldier still exerted a resistless power over her. On a mid-January day he strode into her home and in the presence of her parents, ordered the captain to leave.

"Shall I go, Ann?" said the husband.

"No," said Ann, and as she spoke Lieutenant Smith drew his pistol and shot John Carson down.

Now that the captain was dead, Ann devoted her every effort to saving the life of her lover. She brought very strong influence to bear on Pennsylvania's Moravian governor, John Snyder, but that upright and pious man was convinced that in all conscience he could do nothing to save the life of the hotheaded murderer.

With typical ruthlessness then the wild and lawless girl planned to save the convicted man through violence. Few realized that a criminal underworld already existed in Pennsylvania; even fewer knew that Ann Carson was one of its most powerful members. She must hasten if her beloved lieutenant was to be saved from the gallows, and like one possessed she followed out a diabolic plan. Among the practiced criminals she knew, were a pair but recently released from a penitentiary, Lige Brown and Henry Way. With them she concocted a scheme to kidnap the governor's youngest son and by threatening to take his life force the father to sign a pardon for Lieutenant Smith.

At once the three started on horses from Philadelphia and followed the Susquehanna road north toward Governor Snyder's home in Selinsgrove. When they reached Lancaster, Hank Way could not resist a seemingly easy opportunity to rob a rural drover. The countryman gave him a hard fight, however, and so injured him that he was easily captured and jailed. Ann and Lige galloped out of Lancaster only a few lengths ahead of officers of the law. The two, still confident, rode through Harrisburg that day, unaware that Governor Snyder, informed of their purpose by a near relative of the doomed lieutenant, had dashed down to the capital from his home in Selinsgrove. His officers allowed the guilty pair to ride through the city and ten miles farther upriver to Armstrong's Tavern at Hunter's Fall. There, stimulated by the drinks they had ordered after their long ride, they opened their saddlebags displaying the pistols with which they intended to carry out their crime.

"You are well-armed," said the barkeep.

"If I had one of these pistols in my hand and Governor Snyder in the other," said Lige Brown, "the question of Smith's pardon would soon be settled."

In the conversation that followed, Ann and Lige asked the age of the boy they intended to abduct, the exact location of the governor's home in Selinsgrove, the condition of the upriver road. As they talked, boasting that Richard Smith would never be executed, a Harrisburg constable with a party of deputies was galloping toward them. The criminals had hardly gone to bed before the posse was hammering at their door and they were in custody.

The penitentiary doors soon closed again upon Lige and Henry, and almost immediately thereafter Lieutenant Richard Smith was hanged. The great fortune to which he was heir ultimately became the subject of one of America's most famous and long-drawn-out lawsuits as his cousin, the Creole-Irish Myra Clark Gaines, sought to establish herself as the legitimate daughter of her father, Daniel Clark.

As for the lieutenant's violent champion, the feeling that the lovely Ann had broken the law only because of uncontrollable love for her hanged Richard so moved the general opinion that she might have been spared a prison term had it not been discovered that she had made an impression of her cell-key on a cake of soap and tried to smuggle it to confederates outside, concealed in a pile of dainty lingerie ostensibly to be delivered to a washwoman.

Later released, she became an adept counterfeiter who, clothed in the garb of a modest Quakeress, successfully passed a considerable amount of imitation currency. For this she was finally arrested, convicted, and sentenced. She died in prison in April of 1824, nobly attending other prisoners who had been stricken by typhus.

❦ HANGING DAY

The York State upriver communities were equally excited and articulate in the early days of the century about a famous "Hanging Day" at Cooperstown. The little village at the river's headwaters swelled to twenty times its size on July 19, 1805, when Stephen Arnold, a learned and formerly respected citizen, was to be hanged for whipping to her death a little girl who was his ward. The ceremonies included a parade of a brass band, military companies, distinguished citizens, and the condemned man, chained and seated on his coffin. The gallows, erected on the river flats just below the outlet of Otsego Lake, shadowed the bank where General Clinton's boats had awaited the flood waters (released from the dam above) which would speed them toward union with the northbound fleet of General Sullivan.

The arrival at the jail of a tired horseman on a foam-streaked mare early in the morning of that hot day had not been interpreted as of significance by the eager crowd of visitors nor the even more eager merchants and peddlers of the town who were doing an unprecedented business. The ceremonies following the parade to the riverbank proved most impressive—the sermon by an imported divine, the speeches by prominent citizens, the moving last words of the condemned man. Even the death of an aged lady who, given a prized seat on the gallows platform, rocked herself off that eminence and broke her neck, did not mar the atmosphere of general satisfaction. But when the sheriff, after placing the noose about the prisoner's neck, apologetically stated that the morning's rider had brought a reprieve from the governor and that the day's program must end here, the vast audience shouted that they had been cheated and accused the Cooperstown authorities of bad faith. Vainly these gentlemen explained that they had not wished, on the very day of the event, to disappoint their visitors and so had decided to give them all the joys of a Hanging Day except the spectacle of an actual hanging. Their hearers cursed them roundly for double-dealing and might have resorted to violence, had not the sheriff hastily revived the fainting prisoner and ordered the band to play a jaunty quickstep as it escorted him back to jail.

❧ THE HEROIC DESERTER

Just ten years later and shortly before the end of the War of 1812, a Yankee-born resident of Wilkes-Barre, the Honorable Charles Miner, editor and journalist, wrote a ballad which not only set the whole population of the Susquehanna singing, but captured the sentimental minds of the people of the nation. It was published in hundreds of newspapers, pasted in countless scrapbooks, sung to its sorrowful church-tune by choirs, choruses and singing schools throughout the land. Even today it continues to turn up printed on fading yellowed paper in old trunks, crowded into the flyleaves of well-worn hymnals, laboriously copied into personal notebooks. Like many another verse narrative, *The Ballad of James Bird* was based on a true incident. Young Bird had enlisted, as the song says, "in the Kingston Volunteers" at Kingston in the river-bordered county of Luzerne. He had been wounded while fighting under Oliver Hazard Perry at the battle of Lake Erie. Later he got into trouble and deserted. When he was doomed to death for this crime, strenuous efforts were made to get his sentence commuted to imprisonment because of his previous brave conduct. One authority who has studied the facts of the case states that "the President refused to extend clemency to Bird on the ground that 'having deserted from his post while in charge of a guard, in time of war, he must therefore suffer as an example to others.' "

Whatever the facts were, the song overwhelmed thousands with its heavy and lugubrious sentimentality and achieved popularity that resulted in the weeping of at least two generations of Americans. The people of the Susquehanna valley, where its hero was born and lived his short life, sang it slowly again and again with tears streaming down their faces.

THE BALLAD OF JAMES BIRD

Sons of freedom, listen to me,
And ye daughters, too give ear,
You a sad and mournful story
As was ever told, shall hear.

Hull, you know, his troops surrendered,
And defenceless left the west;
Then our forces quick assembled,
The invaders to resist.

Amongst the troops that marched to war,
Were the Kingston volunteers;
Captain Thomas them commanded,
To protect our west frontiers.

Tender were the scenes of parting,
Mothers wrung their hands and cried,
Maidens wept their swains in secret,
Fathers strove their tears to hide.

There is one among the number,
Tall and graceful is his mien,
Firm his step, his look undaunted,
Scarce a nobler youth was seen.

One sweet kiss he snatched from Mary,
Craved his mother's prayer, and more,

Pressed his father's hand, and left them
For Lake Erie's distant shore.

Mary tried to say "Farewell, James,"
Waved her hand, but nothing spoke,
"Good-bye, Bird, may Heaven preserve you,"
From the rest at parting broke.

Soon they came where noble Perry
Had assembled all his fleet;
Then the gallant Bird enlisted,
Hoping soon the foe to meet.

Where is Bird? The battle rages;
Is he in the strife or no?
Now the cannon roars tremendous;
Dare he meet the hostile foe?

Aye! behold him! see him, Perry!
In the selfsame ship they fight;
Though his messmates fall around him
Nothing can his soul affright.

But behold! a ball has struck him;
See the crimson current flow;
"Leave the deck!" exclaimed brave Perry;
"No!" cried Bird, "I will not go."

"Here on deck I took my station,
Here will Bird his cutlass ply;
I'll stand by you, gallant captain,
Till we conquer or we die."

Still he fought, though faint and bleeding,
Till our stars and stripes waved o'er us,
Victory having crowned our efforts,
All triumphant o'er our foes.

And did Bird receive a pension?
Was he to his friends restored?
No; nor even to his bosom
Clasped the maid his heart adored.

The Susquehanna

But there came most dismal tidings
From Lake Erie's distant shore;
Better far if Bird had perished
Midst the battle's awful roar.

"Dearest parents," said the letter,
"This will bring sad news to you;
Do not mourn your first beloved,
Though this brings his last adieu.

"I must suffer for deserting
From the brig NIAGARA;
Read this letter, brothers, sisters,
'Tis the last you'll hear from me."

Sad and gloomy was the morning
Bird was ordered out to die;
Where's the breast not dead to pity
But for him would heave a sigh?

Lo! he fought so brave at Erie
Freely bled and nobly dared;
Let his courage plead for mercy,
Let his precious life be spared.

See him march and bear his fetters;
Hark! they clank upon the ear;
But his step is firm and manly,
For his heart ne'er harbored fear.

See him kneel upon his coffin,
Sure his death can do no good;
Spare him! spare! O God, they shoot him!
Oh! his bosom streams with blood.

Farewell, Bird; farewell forever;
Friends and home he'll see no more;
But his mangled corpse lies buried
On Lake Erie's distant shore.

🌷 HANGING DAY II

The Hanging Day set for the execution of Levi Kelley thirteen years later than the publication of this ballad, December 28, 1827, proved that Cooperstown had profited by its 1805 rehearsal. Though rain poured down through most of the day a great crowd again assembled. An enormous scaffolding had been erected from which the spectators might watch. Before Kelley, a well-to-do landowner who had killed one of his tenants in a jealous rage, ascended the steps to the gallows, however, the improvised grandstand suddenly crashed to the ground killing some of its occupants and injuring many. The prisoner, who had been brought to the hanging grounds lying on a bed which had been placed on his sleigh and was drawn by his widely known team of handsome black horses, seemed more concerned over the fate of those who had come to see him hanged than over the hanging itself. Indeed this event, when it took place, seemed somewhat anticlimactic since it resulted in his practically instantaneous death. Once more tongues wagged. So great was the folk interest that a local versifier, Isaac Squire, wrote a ballad which was soon sung throughout the whole upper-Susquehanna region. Among many other execrable stanzas were these:

> *"Your time is set, O do remember*
> *The twenty-eighth of December*
> *Between the hours of twelve and three*
> *Be launched into eternity."* . . .
>
> *Though wet and rainy was the day*
> *The people thronged from every way*

> *With anxious thought each came to see*
> *The unhappy fate of poor Kelley.* . . .
> *Before they bid this scene adieu*
> *An awful sight appeared in view,*
> *See hundreds with the scaffold fall!*
> *And some to rise no more at all.*
>
> *Till the great day when all shall rise*
> *To their great joy or sad surprise*
> *And hear their sentence "Doomed to Hell"*
> *Or "With the saints in glory dwell."* . . .
>
> *The cry was heard once and again*
> *That "Hundreds now we fear are slain!"*
> *But God in this distressing hour*
> *Revives again each withering flower.*
>
> *Poor Kelley in this trying time*
> *Was executed for his crime,*
> *He hung an awful sight to see;*
> *May this a solemn warning be.*

These were the materials the minds of the river dwell-ers, regardless of national origins, clung to as the years of the new century advanced. These they repeated again and again—and changed to suit their own creative fan-cies. Their versions told what they felt *should* have oc-curred in order to produce the most dramatic effects rather than what sometimes-erring local historians assured them to be the actual truth. From these narratives today those who interest themselves in the history of the folk fancy of a community may draw some realization of the quality of the minds of the Susquehanna valley's pioneer settlers in their first generations without war. Their yarns, ever amended in the telling by their romantic whims, symbol-ize their unconscious revolt against the humdrum of their peaceful, chore-ridden days.

20

From Arks to Ambulatory Cottages

❧ *Rivers are roads that move.*

—BLAISE PASCAL (1670)

Early in the last decade of the eighteenth century a tall, blue-eyed military-mannered gentleman became a familiar figure on the streets of Northumberland and Sunbury. He was Charles Williamson, born in Scotland and a captain of British troops whose transport, the *Marquis of Salem,* had been captured on the high seas when bound to America during the War of the Revolution. The young officer had been quartered in a Roxbury, Massachusetts, home until the struggle was over and had married Abigail, daughter of his landlord, Ebenezer Newell.

Williamson was a dashing figure. A long blue cloak accentuated his lean erect body and floated out behind him when, leaping lightly to saddle, he galloped his spirited horse along the river roads. His interest in the Susquehanna, however, was only tangential. He had been employed by an English association, headed by William Pultney, to promote the sale and development of thousands of acres in the Genesee River country which had recently been acquired by Robert Morris, American land speculator, from the holders of the Phelps-Gorham Purchase in western New York. A progressive real estate agent,

285

even by modern standards, Charles Williamson advertised and firmly believed that the products of the fabulously fertile Genesee lands could be shipped by way of Conhocton, the Tioga and the Susquehanna to Chesapeake Bay, whence they could find market at Baltimore. He let it be known that with the development he contemplated at the headwaters of its tributaries, the Susquehanna would become the passageway of an inland commercial empire that would overshadow any other business enterprise on the continent. Soon he had Ben Patterson, the most able woodsman of the region, leading a band of surveyors on the project of pushing a road from a point near Williamsport, where the Loyalsock Creek met the river, north and west toward the Genesee.

It was Williamson's dream that upon the rich loam of the Genesee bottoms men of wealth and position from New Jersey, Maryland and Virginia would build big houses and establish themselves as the aristocrat-owners of vast estates. For attracting such desirable settlers his plans, all of which he eventually put into effect, included great fairs, widely advertised races between horses renowned for their speed, elaborate receptions and balls, and the presentation of theatrical entertainment by imported professional companies in a soon-to-be-built theater.

He and his employers agreed that in order to accomplish such an ambitious program, it would be necessary to obtain from Europe a sturdy, dependable yeomanry which would provide loyal servants for the landed gentry. An agent of the British Association had soon discovered a man who seemed fitted to recruit such a group, a German named William Berczy, an art dealer, who talked himself into the job and guaranteed its successful outcome. Once hired, Berczy made no effort to enlist the healthy, hard-working peasants he had promised. He went to the metropolitan seaport, Hamburg, and persuaded about two hundred ne'er-do-wells, hangers-on, and idlers to join his expedition to the banks of the Genesee, which he described in glowing terms. Among the party were indigent opera singers, acrobats, and ragged wastrels. They made a colorful sorry parade when they had finally come up the Susquehanna to Northumberland. Utterly unaccustomed to frontier living, or, for that matter, to any existence outside of city streets, they began to rebel as soon as blisters formed on hands that had never before held axes. As they disappeared into the western wilderness, the Susquehanna communities said good riddance and laughed.

Nevertheless, thanks to the driving energy of Charles Williamson, the first of the big freight boats which the settlers dubbed "arks" was built on the Conhocton near Bath, New York, capital of Williamson's real estate project. It had been constructed upside down on the banks of the little river. Turning it over was an operation requiring the strength of many men—for it was about seventy-five feet long and sixteen wide. Though pointed at each end to make navigation less difficult, it was awkward and hard to steer. Thirty-foot pine sweeps, which were operated from sternposts three feet high, were used both to advance the vessel downstream and to give it direction.

In 1800, when this shallow-sided, boxlike freighter laden with Genesee country grain and lumber reached the junction of the Susquehanna's West and North Branches, the people of Northumberland and Sunbury were amazed

287

and delighted. Here was proof that their river was navigable and could deliver the products of the fast-developing northwestern lands all the way to the big market of Baltimore. Susquehanna rafts and arks were soon countless. Despite many a pile-up on hidden rocks and many a sinking in swift water, the number continued to grow until, except for the winter months and the droughts of midsummer, the water was dotted with craft bound for the Chesapeake. In 1823, George Lightner of Port Deposit proudly published the *Susquehanna Register of Arks, Rafts, etc., etc. Arriving at Port Deposit in the year 1822.* Among the 142 vessels, he listed Captain Longfellow's *Susquehannah Nancy,* Captain Folly's *Sailor's Delight,* Captain Fardwell's *Hearts of Oak,* Captain Allen's *Fair American,* Captain Phillips's *Sea Flower* and Captain Biddle's *Who'd-a-thought-it.* When a fleet of these and their kind was on the river, the conch shells used as boat horns sometimes blew up an almost intolerable cacophony.

Though it is generally believed in Pennsylvania that the Indians were aware of the burning properties of "stone coal" which was uncovered by the current of the river from time to time, the realization that Susquehanna coal was valuable and even salable as fuel came slowly to the settlers. It was 1769 before any contemporary record shows that anthracite was in use in the forges of blacksmiths. Then the Connecticut Yankee, Obadiah Gore, and his brother were using it in their smithy in the Wyoming area. Wyoming coal was shipped downriver to Harrisburg and thence carted by wagon to the armory at Carlisle each year of the Revolution.

Judge Jesse Fell, who supplemented his salary as an associate justice of the county court at Luzerne by turning his residence into a tavern, had one day, in 1808, the idea that if air could be introduced under coal it might prove a satisfactory substitute for wood. He therefore constructed a cradle of green hickory withes, filled it with small fragments of coal, placed it in the large fireplace of his barroom and lit a wood fire under it. Before the wooden grate was consumed he had proved that coal would burn freely under such circumstances. An iron grate was at once built into the fireplace, and it proved such a successful heater of the exteriors of visitors who were warming their "innards," that patronage substantially increased.

The Gores and other blacksmiths were soon doing a thriving business in the manufacture of grates for home use. Spring had come by that time, and enterprising Abijah and John Smith filled two arks with coal and set out downriver for Columbia. The inhabitants of that town proved so incredulous, however, that the traders were forced to dump their cargo on the riverbank and go home without selling any of it. Undaunted, they filled their arks again and in the following year they came back to Columbia with an iron grate. Having advertised their intentions, they then publicly proved that coal is an acceptable fuel by burning a grate full before a crowd of fascinated citizens. Columbia was won over, the coal was sold, and the profits in mining and distributing coal were so demonstrated that the great Susquehanna coal-business had been set on its way.

Never abandoning their dream that the Susquehanna would prove a navigable waterway from source to mouth, the river populace excitedly advocated canals which would bypass stretches where rapids and shallows prohĭbited the passage of ships of shallow draft. The success of commercial steamboats on the Hudson, following hard upon the initial voyage of Robert Fulton's *Clermont* which had been sponsored by the influential Livingston family, stirred the Pennsylvanians to emulation. While they were making plans, a group of Baltimoreans built a steamboat of twenty-two-inch draft which they dubbed *The Susquehanna* and had her towed up the rocky, shoal-obstructed stream to Port Deposit. From there she was transferred to the Maryland Canal which provided smooth passage for ten miles above the town. A band of sweating laborers tugged her by hand the next ten miles against a swift current that sped through such tortuous curves that the men on the ropes were exhausted. She never reached Columbia and the scheme was abandoned.

The first steamboat to make an extended voyage over the shallow and treacherous river was the *Codorus*, launched at York Haven in April, 1826. During the high water of spring she delighted and amazed the people of the upriver counties by steaming up the West Branch to Williamsport, thence down to Northumberland and up the North Branch and its tributary, the Chemung, to Elmira. But the water was falling as summer came on. Delay followed delay as the *Codorus* haltingly puffed back to Tioga Point and then against the current to Binghamton. The fact that she was actually going places stirred the valley folk to a frenzy. They would connect their river by canal with the western waterways, they prophesied. The commerce of the interior would crowd their channel, enrich their ports. The Erie Canal, the Hudson River and Manhattan would languish as western trade adopted the first available southern avenue. Baltimore would soon outrank New York as a seaport. The blossoming hills about Towanda resounded with the noises of celebration when, on May 11, 1826, the people heard the steamboat was coming.

"As she appeared round the bend," reported the *Bradford Settler*, "she was hailed by the firing of a *feu de joie*, and the ringing of bells. The banks were at once lined by hundreds." The captain was honored by a public dinner at which local orators made florid speeches. His reply was an appeal for pitch-pine knots to keep his fires blazing.

All of the excited eloquence of the distinguished speakers failed, however, to deepen the channel. Though the *Codorus,* sixty feet long and with a nine-foot beam, drew only eight inches of water, she had been away from her home port four months when she completed her journey from Binghamton to York Haven where her captain, still a realist, baldly stated that her voyage had proved the impracticality of steamboat travel on the Susquehanna.

There were other failures before those whose minds were fixed on the river's being a future highway of commerce were outnumbered by their neighbors. A Baltimore boat, the *Susquehanna and Baltimore,* eighty feet long and capable of carrying a hundred people, was launched at about the same time as the *Codorus.* As she reached the Nescopec Rapids, all but a score of her more prominent passengers were invited to walk the shore and watch her battle with the tumbling waters. As they did so, they were horrified to see the boiling current stop the laboring boat and drive her back on a rock with such force that her boiler burst, killing a number of dignitaries.

New York State now took a hand in the long struggle

291

against unnavigable waters. In the mid-1830's, the elegant poet and essayist, Nathaniel Parker Willis, having happily retired from the bustle of New York City to his country villa near Owego, was invited to ride a comparatively new steamboat (again bearing the name *Susquehanna*) on a voyage downriver where her owners hoped to sell her. She had a draft of eighteen inches, and, in addition to her side paddles, boasted a huge stern wheel "which," wrote Willis, "playing on the slack water of the boat would drive her up Niagara if she would but hold together." She had been built, he said, in emulation of salmon and shad which could ascend a fall of twenty feet in the river through "the propulsive energy of their tails."

Setting out on the crest of a freshet, the *Susquehanna* made remarkable time, for the "dams were deep under water and the water was as smooth as the Hudson."

> Navigating the Susquehannah [wrote the poet] is very much like dancing "the cheat." You are always making straight up to a mountain with no apparent possibility of escaping contact, and it is an even chance up to the last moment which side of it you are to *chassez* with the current. Meantime, the sun seems capering about to all points of the compass, the shadows falling in every possible direction, the north, south, east, and west, changing places with the familiarity of a masquerade. The blindness of the river's course is increased by the innumerable small islands in its bosom whose tall elms and close-set willows meet half-way those from either shore; and the current very often dividing above them, it takes an old voyager to choose between the shaded alleys. . . .

Later critics, historians and philosophers have been inclined to dismiss Willis as unimportant because affected refinement and elegant decoration characterized both his dress and his prose style. Occasionally, however, and par-

292

ticularly in his *Letters from Under a Bridge,* which he wrote at Glenmary, his Owego retreat, nature and the life around him moved him to honest observation and sincere feeling. On his voyage downriver on the steamboat, he saw the river much as Mark Twain was later to see the Mississippi. He saw the great arks, built upstream with a sound of shouts and hammering, come down with their "singing and saucy crews," saw the curving river "put their steersmanship to the test," saw the "bulky monsters shining with new boards, whirling around in the swift eddies, and, when caught by the current again, gliding off among the trees like a singing and swearing phantom of an unfinished barn."

He stood at the prow of the packet selecting in his mind the most perfect sites for "white villas" where the river had anticipated the landscape gardener by creating natural lawns and terraces, where clumps of ancient trees with broad shadows awaited the home builder. The stream was thronged with rafts and arks whose crews were amazed to see the steamer gliding swiftly down the high current. The steersman of a shingle raft gaped as the side-and-stern-wheeler sped past—and then shouted at Willis "Wal! You're going a good hickory, mister!"

The *Susquehanna* slid smoothly by the Falls of Wyalusing ("most musical of Indian names") and the high foaming cascade of Buttermilk Falls. Dusk settled soon after, and the boat, still two hours from its destination at Wyoming, was moored in one of the many pools formed by natural promontories extending into the water. That evening some of the passengers who had long been rivermen swapped tales of the trickery and skill of the Susquehanna traders. One said that while he lay sleeping in the

293

penthouse of his grain-filled ark, which he had tied up in a quiet eddy, another arkmaster had surreptitiously cut his moorings, and his vessel had fetched up high and dry on an island a few miles downstream. He was further distressed when morning broke and he watched his laughing rival oaring his way down the stream.

His anger was then so great that he seized shovel and pick and dug a canal into the slimy channel of which he was able to launch his craft. Running without mooring for the next twenty-four hours, he sneaked by the trickster who had betrayed him and was on the dock with his cargo already sold when that culprit arrived.

As Willis listened to the tale he looked on the darkly flowing current. "It was a still, starlight night, and the river was laced with the long reflections of the raft-fires, while the softened songs of the men over their evening carouse, came to us along the smooth water with the effect of far better music."

No one has written more effectively and with more truth of the upper Susquehanna than Willis. "There is a charm to me in an in-navigable river which brought me to the Susquehanna. . . . I love haunts where I neither see a steamboat nor expect a city. What is the Hudson but a great highroad?"

Willis truly loved the Susquehanna, as all his writings about it from Glenmary show, and, when forced by financial difficulties to leave his rural retreat, he did so with a heartbroken reluctance. He had a poet's dream for the river, not quite as impractical as that of the businessman who still prophesied that its waters would bring argosies laden with the treasures of the west. He was dismayed by the swift progress of money-making media of transportation. When a railroad commissioner assured him that in five years' time he would "devour the way" between Glenmary and New York in seven hours, and a canal engineer in the same morning said that in three years he would be able to take a steam packet from his cottage to tidewater, he was as unpleasantly amazed as "the toads disentombed by the blasting of the rocks . . . they, poor hermits, fancying themselves safe from the troubles of existence till doomsday, and I as sure that my cottage was at a safe removal from the turmoil of city propinquity."

He saw his Owego not as a profitable busy river port, but as a mecca of the traveler in search of beauty—"all the way by the most lovely river-courses in the world."

Most startling to the Willis reader of today whose eyes are accustomed to luxurious "trailers" that crowd our highway, may well be his prophecy of a "tenement on wheels" which shall be furnished with a "convenience for wheeling off the track whenever there is occasion to loiter." It would be, he suggests, "considerably longer than the accommodations of single gentlemen at hotels, with a small kitchen and such a cook as pleases the genius of republics," and he asks, "What could be more delightful or more easy than to furnish this ambulatory cottage with light furniture from your stationary home, cram it with books, and such little refinements as you most miss abroad, and, purchasing provisions by the way, travel *under your own roof* from one end of the country to the other."

When the popularity of this invention came to its full bloom, the enthusiastic Owegan foresaw, "We shall take our fashions from New Orleans and I do not despair of seeing a café on the Susquehannah, with a French *dame de compton,* marble tables and the Picayune newspaper. If my project of traveling cottages should succeed, I shall offer the skirt of my Omega to such of my New Orleans friends as would like to pasture a cow during the summer, and when they and the orioles migrate in the autumn, why, we will up cottage and be off to the south, too."

The suggestion of the French café is herewith offered to enterprising Owegans who might well place it, balconies and all, on their too-often-deplored "backs" that rise sheer in faded colors from the rippling Susquehanna's edge. No populated spot along the whole river is more beautiful than that where, crossing the Owego bridge in "ambulatory cottage" or afoot, the traveler sees the rear walls of old buildings lining the water and lending it their time-gentled hues.

21

The Fishing Creek Confederacy

Late in June, 1863, Jubal Early, "Old Jubilee" to his gray-clad troopers, rode out of York, Pennsylvania, the richer by $28,000 and a thousand pairs of shoes. He was bound for the Wrightsville bridge across the Susquehanna. General R. S. Ewell, he knew, would soon be making a frontal attack on Harrisburg, and when the frightened city was making its defense, he was to swoop down on it from the rear. The road was jammed with the wagons of panic-sticken refugees fleeing the Confederate advance, and the troopers could not travel at their usual pace. When they loped into Wrightsville, a lift of smoke down by the river gave them unwelcome news. The defenders of Columbia had burned the bridge. Old Jubilee took one look and galloped north to meet Ewell.

While the Harrisburg militia drilled desperately in the streets, many carrying scythes and old fowling pieces, the two Confederate units joined and moved against the city. Their advance scouts were only three miles from its outskirts when riders from General Lee delivered orders to turn about and make for the main army at Petersburg. Reluctantly they left a position farther north than any Confederate advance would reach. Gettysburg was a few

297

hours ahead of them. The Susquehanna had seen the last of Southern invaders.

Had Early reached Harrisburg, he would have found enthusiastic support from many of the inhabitants of adjacent reaches of the Susquehanna. Republicans and pro-war men encountered strong opposition to the armed struggle after the national conscription law of March 3, 1863. Most of the "Plain People" and all of the Quakers were strongly pacifist and had for years held that the differences between North and South could be settled by discussion and arbitration. The terrific losses suffered at nearby Antietam had increased the bitter feeling against war, and news of the Draft Riots in New York had made many Pennsylvanians realize that they were not alone in their objections to the conflict. Hundreds of the men of the Susquehanna valley had joined a secret society organized in the South, "The Knights of the Golden Circle," which met to denounce, sometimes to plot action, against the Union cause.

Antagonism toward the Lincoln administration was especially bitter in Columbia and Snyder Counties where hills slope steeply upward from the winding river. In this region an army officer attempting to enforce the draft was killed by a gunshot, another wounded. The effort of a Union sergeant to arrest a deserter at the funeral of his sister resulted in a wild gun battle in a hill-town church and the wounding of both men. Another church service was interrupted by "Copperheads" (the popular title for sympathizers with the Southern cause) who informed the minister that if he was a Democrat he might continue his sermon, but if he was an abolitionist they would hang him.

298

The preacher chose a surprising alternative, diving through a window to safety.

By August of 1864, tension was so great that frightening rumors were circulating. One, given general credence, was that above the headwaters of Fishing Creek which rises high on North Mountain and flows a short tumbling course into the Susquehanna, Confederate sympathizers, possibly with the aid of a detachment of the Confederate Army, had raised an impregnable fortress. A battery of four tremendous brass cannon, so the story went, had either been smuggled down from Canada or spirited through the Union lines and dragged, with almost incredible effort, up the precipitous rock walls of the mountain into positions that commanded all possible approaches. Visions of these invincible bastions rising far within the Federal lines in a state predominantly favoring the Union had given loyal citizens sleepless nights. Urgent appeals had been sent down the Susquehanna. The safety of Pennsylvania, they said, possibly of the Union itself, was in danger.

Then, on the warm Saturday evening of August 13, 1864, the inhabitants of the river town of Bloomsbury, county seat of Columbia County, heard the creak of saddle leather, the clop of hooves, the tread of marching men, as a detachment of eight mounted troopers and forty infantrymen moved with two cannon into the Agricultural Fair Grounds and there bivouacked. As they did so, runners raced through the hills warning all Democrats that Union troops had come, bidding them meet in John Rantz's big barn in Benton township on the morrow. By Sunday afternoon a huge crowd had gathered there, and many were armed. Some urged resisting the soldiers if they marched farther into the hills, but the majority decided to wait and to commit themselves to battle only if their homes were molested.

On Tuesday morning two hundred and fifty more soldiers from downriver paraded into the Fair Grounds. At their head rode Major General Darius M. Couch, commander of the Department of the Susquehanna. At once, after conferring with leading citizens, he tried to lessen the insurgent forces in the high stronghold above by offering amnesty to all draft dodgers and deserters in Columbia County who would report to him before noon on Saturday. There, for the next few days, he awaited reenforcements. These were already on the way. The Sunbury *Gazette* of August twentieth reported:

> Led on by the prompting of a most desperate set of political villains, a number of the citizens of the neighboring county of Columbia have organized and armed themselves to resist the national authorities, and from what we can learn a state of war really exists in that county.
>
> The authorities have taken prompt measures to put down the Columbia county rebels. The safety of the people required this. On last Saturday a cavalry company of about one hundred and fifty men, with two cannons, passed through this place on the way to the scene of the disturbance, and on Monday some three hundred infantry proceeded in the same direction.

The expedition numbered five hundred soldiers when it set out to attack the position on North Mountain's summit. Marching to the music of fife and drum, they left the Fair Grounds on the hot Sunday morning of August twenty-first. They were accompanied for some miles by a swarm of approving citizens in buggies and wagons. The
300

first night's bivouac was at Stucker's Bottom and the second at Appleman's Bottom. By this time hundreds of the families living along hill-walled Fishing Creek were streaming down the slopes to see the bluecoats. Many of them brought gifts of food to the invaders who were surprised to find themselves so cordially received in the heart of what they had been told was enemy country. As the week went on with no further troop movements, the curiosity and the tension of the population increased. Then, on Sunday the twenty-eighth, General George Cadwallader and about five hundred men encamped beside the Susquehanna at Bloomsburg. On the next day they marched to join their comrades at Appleman's Bottom. The army besieging the mountain fastness of the Fishing Creek Confederates now numbered a thousand, and the people of the region realized that its commanders planned decisive action.

On the night of the thirtieth it came. A number of squads were assembled in the darkness, given instructions, and sent out along the mountain roads. Moving swiftly and silently, they surrounded the homes of persons suspected of holding opinions unfavorable to the national administration. Men who had been watching the troops parade that very day now heard the quick knock on the door, the words of the order of arrest, the desolate farewells of their wives and children. In the Benton Church where the squads converged, an army lieutenant colonel reviewed the prisoners, listened to the advice of their Republican neighbors, and selected forty-four to be marched eighteen miles to Bloomsburg. There they were forced aboard a downriver train bound for Fort Mifflin on the Delaware River six miles below Philadelphia.

The expeditionary force had now weakened its opposition as much as possible. There was left only the capture of the Confederate fort. General Cadwallader ordered his men to break camp and marched them to the foot of North Mountain. There they pitched their tents expecting to hear at any moment the firing of the cannon high above them. A correspondent of the Philadelphia *Inquirer* sent in a dispatch which was published on September sixth:

> On Friday we once more took up our line of march and are now in the mountains. Our camp is located in a valley on the east branch of Fishing Creek. Mountains are all around us. The valley is barely wide enough for our camp, the mountains on each side rising almost perpendicularly for over seven hundred feet. Of course, I am not aware of the information possessed at headquarters: but from all that I can learn, the insurgents are encamped in a gorge in the mountains where they have intrenchments mounting two field pieces. They are said to be from three to five hundred strong and from their location, it will be extremely difficult to approach them with sufficient numbers to overcome their very strong position. It is the prayer of every soldier in the command that they remain and give us fight. We hardly have hopes of this from the cowardly course they have pursued up to this time. Still they are hemmed in, and may be brought to bay.
>
> The "Army of Fishing Creek" commanded by General Cadwallader in person, is spoiling for a fight and is praying that the insurgents will give them an opportunity of achieving something worthy of their mighty powers and the labors and expense of a thousand men.

At about the time these brave words appeared in print, Cadwallader's bugles blew the advance. The general had divided his men into three columns which, spreading fanwise over the steep slope, scrambled over boulders, slid

302

on treacherous gravel, pulled themselves upward by grasping the huckleberry bushes. Briers tore their shirts, sharp rocks cut their boots, the early September sun beat down on their sweat-streaked faces. Somewhere above them, they had been told, their traitorous countrymen waited, with their cannon primed, their rifles ready. The renegades would fight to the death and give no quarter, for if they were captured they would be hanged. Somewhere along the next rise, the attackers would see the steep rock walls and the grim barrels pointing down.

Lying flat on the steep inclines, the bluecoats inched along to more level areas where a man might grasp his gun, stumble to his feet, and race ten yards to the welcome shadow of a thorn tree. The columns moved slowly. If one was delayed by difficult terrain, the other waited. When the slowed column caught up, all three set out once more, doggedly.

It seemed to the soldiers that they had been climbing for hours when excitement in the voices of their officers told them they were nearing the summit. They looked ahead and saw only a few yards above them, the mountaintop standing against blue sky. Yelling they ran for it.

They stood breathless on a small plateau. On the uneven ground lay bits of newspaper, a discarded sandwich, a berry basket, evidences of a recent picnic. The air was still. The moonshine fortress of the Fishing Creek Confederacy had fallen.

Down at Bloomsburg on the Susquehanna the next day General George Cadwallader, embarrassed and disgusted, pronounced the whole "Copperhead Rebellion" a farce. It was a lie woven out of whole cloth and it was a matter of the past—except for forty-four men deprived of their civil rights and confined in a dirty, unsanitary prison because of their ideas. Most of these were at various times released. A few were tried. Seven were convicted. Of these, one paid his fine, one was pardoned by President Lincoln, five by President Johnson.

22

The Detective and the Molly Maguires

No one ever commits murder with a golden dagger.

—HINDU PROVERB

The bespectacled detective in the witness box was slim, wiry, of medium height. He wore a neat, black suit and his sandy-red hair was close-trimmed and carefully combed. His gray eyes showed no emotion nor did his clear voice as he spoke, without emphasis, in a recognizably Irish brogue.

The room was crowded and had been for an hour before the judge had taken his seat on the bench. Important professional men, mostly lawyers and clergymen, had come early to the square Bloomsburg courthouse above which Mount Spectator raised a snowy head, below which, at the town's edge, rolled the ice-dappled Susquehanna. There, in the last week of February, 1877, three men of the order called "Molly Maguires"—Patrick Hester, Patrick Tully, and Peter McHugh—were on trial for the murder nine years before of mining superintendent Alexander Rea whose bullet-riddled body had been found on a lonely wagon road near Centralia in Columbia County.

The defendants stared at the witness in mingled consternation and despair. This had not been their mood when, soon after the crime had been committed, their accomplice, Tom Donahue, was being tried by this same court. Then Pat Hester, patiently waiting in the Blooms-burg jail for Tom's certain acquittal and the equally certain dismissal of all other indictments, had been over-heard to say of the circumstances that he and his friends now faced, "He is killed and it's no use crying about it, but . . . we are all right. I can at any time get four to five thousand that will swear we were not there at the time."

Now, those thousands who would have perjured them-selves to establish an alibi could no longer be summoned. For months in the courts of Pennsylvania's anthracite re-gions the clipped, almost professorial words of this wit-ness had frightened them into silence.

The defendants had known that this man would appear against them. He had already testified against others like them, and some of those others had already been hanged. Yet when he said that he was thirty-one years old, that he was a detective in the employ of the Allan Pinkerton Detective Agency, Chicago office, that his name was James McParlan, that for about two years he had lived as Jim McKenna, secretary of a chapter of the Molly Maguires, they looked on him incredulously. They had known Jim McKenna for those two years—a carelessly clad, loud-mouthed, boasting roisterer with tumbled red hair and bleary eyes, a drunken tavern brawler, flirter of fighting cocks, bearded and moustachioed dancer of Irish jigs and bawler of sentimental Irish ballads, "the best Molly of us all."

That often-used appellation hurt. Five months after the October of 1873 when this vagabond began his stumbling rounds of the cheap saloons of the coal districts, he had been initiated into the Molly Maguires, the murderous tribe of lawless Irishmen which had since the early 1860's dominated the mine regions by a policy of compliance or death. Their crimes had been so outrageous and so open that they had been disowned by the society from which they sprang—the respectable Ancient Order of Hibernians—denounced by the Roman Catholic clergy, and condemned to extinction by Franklin B. Gowan, American-

born citizen of Irish parentage, who had worked his way up to be president of the Pennsylvania Coal and Iron Company. It had been Gowan who had visited Allan Pinkerton with the purpose of persuading him to send to the coal country a detective who would be able through joining the Mollies to run down the murderers of scores of faithful employees of the mining companies.

If it was hard for the three Mollies on trial at Bloomsburg to believe that this coldly objective, reserved witness was so great an actor that for two years he had been the Jim McKenna they knew, it was even more difficult for

307

those leaders of the organization who had not yet, as a result of his testimony, been hanged. They had been his intimates. When, at the age of twenty-nine, he had come among them, a fellow malcontent cursing the bosses, the forced trading at company stores, the miserable wages, they had welcomed him. When he intimated that the police of Buffalo, New York, were on the hunt for him because he had killed a man there, they were impressed. When he proudly displayed crisp new bills which he said could hardly be distinguished from those made by the United States Treasury and added that putting these counterfeits into circulation, "shovin' the queer" he called it, was his favorite occupation, they were unanimous in the opinion that he could be useful to them.

And so, on April 14, 1874, he went through the initiation ceremony, learned secret words and signs, swore horrendous oaths of loyalty till death and became one of the Molly Maguires. After that, because he seemed to have more education than most of his brothers in the order, he became secretary of the chapter. He sat in the councils of the "bodymasters" (as the chapter heads were called) and their fellow conspirators. He was present when they sent out "coffin notices"—threats of death illustrated by crude drawings of the recipient as a corpse in a pine box surrounded by grisly skulls and crossbones. He always drank a great deal at the beginnings of these meetings and usually seemed too drunk to be consulted when discussion turned on the actual murders of policemen, foremen, superintendents, owners, even of such German, Polish or Welsh miners as had offended one or another of their all-Irish membership.

Indeed, after one experience that ended in failure, it

was agreed by the shrewd planners of these crimes that Jim McKenna was too given to drink to be appointed to one of the "committees" of younger men who were called upon to perform "clean jobs"—executions so deft that no clues to the identity of the murderers could be found. He was one of the Mollies ordered to burn the railroad bridge over the river at Catawissa and, thanks to his advice, the job was thoroughly bungled; and during the "long strike" (from December 1874 to June 1875) he was one of the leaders of a march on a colliery still operating. With a mob of Mollies, he faced the twenty-five leveled Winchester rifles of the company police under command of Captain R. J. Linden whom he knew to be a fellow detective of the Pinkerton Agency. It was again at McKenna's advice that the mob decided not to risk the certain losses they would suffer if they decided to charge.

For two years, in constant danger of detection and death, Jim McKenna was one of the bodymasters' most trusted lieutenants. Not a man accustomed to excessive drinking, he forced himself into what seemed to be a drunken stupor night after night, but never into such a condition that he could not listen and remember. He heard the leaders arrange that the murders they had decided upon be committed by young Mollies imported from distant towns who could not be recognized by possible witnesses. He heard the plans for guiding the killers, once a job was done, through wild wooded valleys to secret hiding places. He heard the artful scheming to have prominent local Mollies conspicuously present in public places at the exact time of the killings. And with all these things stored in his mind, he left his companions, staggered back to his rented room, pulled down the window shades, hung his coat on the doorknob so that it covered the keyhole, and wrote down what he had heard. Pinkerton officers and mineowners were receiving from him almost daily reports, methodical, accurate, detailed, on every criminal activity of the Molly Maguires as they tried to dominate the mine districts through a campaign of terror.

The society had succeeded better than any of its members had dreamed when its first American chapters had been organized. The original Molly Maguires had been rebels against the injustices practiced by the tyrannical landlords of Ireland. The woman for whom the society was named was a stout and ruthless widow who wore under her red petticoat a pistol strapped to each thigh. She was said to have used these weapons more than once with deadly effect on rent collectors and officers of the law, and to have planned the murders of other men slain by her associates. Her red petticoat, some Irish patriots have said, became the symbolic banner of those who plotted and fought for a free Ireland. The American chapters of Molly Maguires were a living proof that the organization had other and farther-reaching plans—plans for a lawless international organization of Irishmen who would frighten those they chose to regard as enemies into flight or kill them if they would not run. The Mollies of the anthracite regions of Pennsylvania had already murdered scores of men when James McParlan became Jim McKenna. No other similar organization in the nation's history—not the Mafia, not the Ku Klux Klan—has ever been so deadly.

But now in the courtroom of the river town of Bloomsburg, detective James McParlan was telling again a narrative that most Pennsylvanians already knew almost word for word. He had been telling it in a calm matter-of-fact manner, again and again for months. The first trials had been east of the Susquehanna in the heart of the mining country. The Molly Maguires had seemed stunned when the murderers had been sentenced to hang. They had believed that their power and influence would prevent such an outcome. James McParlan had not originally planned to appear as a witness. He had hoped that the evidence he had gathered would result in the administration of justice. But this was not to be. In May, 1876, at the trial of five Mollies for the murder of a policeman, he had spent four days on the stand, presenting the evidence himself as a careful industrious workman. By the time he arrived at Bloomsburg, he was accustomed to the armed guards who sat near him, their eyes constantly searching the crowd. He knew, too, that the danger to his life was lessening. The Mollies were on the run. Eight who had prided themselves on "clean jobs" would be hanged at Mauch Chunk at the beginning of summer. Three more, he felt sure, would be sentenced to death by the rope in the jail yard behind the Bloomsburg courthouse soon after he had completed his testimony.

And so he went on in his almost monotous way, telling how these three defendants had boasted, in what they thought to be the security of their society, the thing they had done nine years before on a lonely wagon road near Centralia. Then politely nodding to the judge, he stepped down and walked away with the men of his guard.

After these convictions, McParlan knew that there would still be the trial of Jack Kehoe, shrewdest and most dangerous of all the bodymasters. It had been Jack who

311

had finally, when the newspapers of the Susquehanna valley had begun publishing amazingly comprehensive lists of all the Molly Maguires, deduced the truth and ordered Jim McKenna shot. The Mollies who had been given that job could not believe that Jim was an informer and had disobeyed Jack's command. They were bitterly regretting their failure now.

Jack was in the Pottsville jail awaiting trial for a murder he had committed many years ago. He had shouted after his arrest, "The Old Man at Harrisburg won't go back on us," but time was passing and Governor John F. Hartranft by his silence was letting it be known he would not surrender to the pressure the Molly Maguires were exerting on him.

And after Jack was hanged, the detective knew, there would be still another trial—and a hanging, the nineteenth, at Sunbury. The river, western edge of the Mollies' domain, would see the last of it. Then James McParlan might try to recuperate from two years of heavy drinking that had well-nigh ruined his health. He had made himself the most famous detective in the United States. Allan Pinkerton would have other work for him to do.

23

Down the River

🌿 *And when I asked the name of the river*
from the brakeman, and heard that
it was called the Susquehanna,
the beauty of the name seemed to be part
and parcel of the beauty of the land. . . .
That was the name, as no other could be,
for that shining river and desirable valley.
                                    —ROBERT LOUIS STEVENSON

COOPERSTOWN

🌿 WHERE THE WATER COMES FROM

The water brims steadily over the southern edge of narrow hill-bordered Otsego Lake and seeks a lower level in a walled stream bed. It follows a man-made culvert under a road and emerges, widening, in a lawn that edges the brick walls—faded salmon pink peppered with burned black—of a big and rambling house. That the Susquehanna begins in the "back yard" of Riverbrink, as the house is called, is meaningful. The lake water here, for all its long and winding journey of five hundred and twenty miles to Chesapeake Bay, establishes a definite character.

The Hudson rising high among Adirondack peaks and long miles from any dwelling of man, has two distinctive river personalities. For half its length it is a shallow, trout-haunted stream. Then it makes a sharp turn to the south

313

and becomes the Hudson as most people think of it, lordly and majestic, a channel of ocean-going vessels, one of the greatest rivers of the world.

The Susquehanna, though more than two hundred miles longer than the Hudson, is born among men. A few yards from the lake it is not quite four feet deep, and there children swim, shadowed sometimes by the high bank across from Riverbrink. Canoes drift here and fishermen, hardly expecting a catch, idle with short lines dangling in water so clear that the fish can see them. In spring and summer, lawn and stream and high bank across meld varying shades of green, making a lush and subtly arranged background for the fading hues of the house, like a landscape by the French painter, Courbet. And, somehow, ever consistent, through other back yards and through coal towns, through deep chasms and wide flat bottoms, the Susquehanna always keeps a relationship to the men on its banks. Sometimes dangerous, sometimes friendly, it ever maintains its unique unchanging quality, minding its own business, a "character" among streams.

Otsego Lake was once made famous throughout the world under a different name—"Glimmerglass"—and the man who so named it was James Fenimore Cooper, writer of *Leatherstocking Tales*, novels of the American frontier, whose father, William Cooper, had given his surname to the town in which the river begins.

When William Cooper first came to this spot, in 1785, as he later reported in his *A Guide in the Wilderness*:

> . . . there existed not an inhabitant nor any trace of a road; I was alone three hundred miles from home without bread, meat, or food of any kind; fire and fishing tackle were my only means

of subsistence, I caught trout in the brook and roasted them on the ashes. My horse fed on the grass that grew by the edge of the waters. I laid me down to sleep in my watch coat, nothing but the melancholy Wilderness around me. In this way I explored the country, formed my plans of future settlement, and meditated upon the spot where a place of trade or a village should afterwards be established.

William Cooper was far from the first visitor to this spot in the "melancholy Wilderness," though this paragraph might not lead a reader to think so. George Croghan was one of a hundred associated partners who in 1769 obtained patents to a vast tract of land stretching from Cherry Valley on the north to the shores of Otsego. A Dublin-born trader, he came in that same year to the foot of the lake and with the aid of fellow Irishmen and some Indians raised ten buildings, cleared four fields, launched a bateau and erected a bridge across the Susquehanna. Through such beginnings Croghan might have eventually achieved a real estate empire. He had already created a "place of trade or a village" where later William Cooper dreamed one, but western lands offered even greater opportunity and he moved on to further and more ambitious land schemes on the Ohio.

Other visitors to this lonely forest spot had been soldiers. More than fifteen hundred men under General James Clinton had encamped there only six years before William Cooper, "alone, three hundred miles from home," napped where they had bivouacked. While the level of the waters against the dam they had built crept slowly upward, the army had waited there impatiently for weeks against the time when they would ride the suddenly released floodcrest downriver to join other forces moving to-

315

ward them. And General George Washington, remembering this exploit, after Yorktown and setting out to visit the scenes of war triumphs he had not witnessed, "traversed the country to the head of the eastern branch of the Susquehanna, and viewed the lake Otsego."

Croghan was a man of failures to the end of his life. William Cooper was a man of successes. A year after his visit to the "rough and hilly country of Otsego," he offered forty thousand acres of his purchase of Croghan's lands at sheriff's sale, and so great was the demand that in sixteen days all were bought and by "the poorest order of men." In making his contracts with them the landlord adopted a policy much wiser, as Louis Jones, Director of the New York State Historical Association, has pointed out, than that of his friends, the Manor Lords of the Hudson Valley, who "were selling no land but devising indentures which gave their tenants the shadow of independence but the reality of perpetual servitude. The sturdy Judge sold his land outright, as much or as little as a man wished to buy, giving them seven to ten years in which to pay off the cost." By so doing he avoided the land-rent wars which plagued the Hudson's vast estates in the 1840's.

Partly because the poverty of these settlers prohibited their clearing large areas, the first years of the community's growth were difficult: "their grain grew chiefly in the shade; their maize did not ripen, their wheat was blasted," but William Cooper would not let them fail. An aristocrat by nature, a rigid Federalist in politics, he had an overwhelming sense of *noblesse oblige.* "I erected a storehouse, and during each winter filled it with large quantities of grain, purchased in different places. . . . I procured . . . a credit for a large quantity of sugar kettles. . . . I established potash works. . . . I gave them credit for their maple sugar and potash at a price that would bear transportation."

These and other efforts turned the adverse tide. The poor among whom William Cooper had chosen to live began to prosper, and their ever-helpful landlord was idolized. In three years came the establishment of Otsego County; Cooperstown became the county seat, and William Cooper, naturally, first judge of the County Court. He had moved his family from Burlington, New Jersey, the year before (1790), and the story is that when his wife refused to budge from her chair to go into the wilds, he ordered her loaded, chair and all, into the nearest wagon.

Judge Cooper was a hearty, physically strong man of violent opinions. He was a good wrestler and once offered ʌ hundred acres to any man who could throw him, which he promptly and good-naturedly paid when, after several opponents failed, one succeeded. He also fought with his fists a hated political enemy and thereby established a lasting controversy, for witnesses of that street battle differed as to who won. Like his fellow Federalists he was an ardent supporter of the Alien and Sedition Act and, in the period when Judge Thomas Cooper of the downriver town of Northumberland was convicted of violating it, Judge William Cooper of Cooperstown at the river's source had Jedediah Peck, advocate of free speech and free schools, arrested for urging the law's repeal. One-eyed and aged, Peck was carted off to Albany in chains on a ride that did more than all his spoken words to arouse its witnesses to fiery denunciation of the doomed statute. It was doubtless the extreme bitterness of Judge Cooper's political convictions that led to his death. In Albany, after having left a hall where he had delivered a stormy political harangue, he was murdered by a never identified enemy who, sneaking up behind him, struck him a crushing blow on the head.

William Cooper's son, James Fenimore, was twenty-two when his father was slain. He had arrived in Cooperstown at the age of one, had been ten when the family moved from their frame house into the grandeur of Otsego Hall which his father had ordered constructed as more suitable to the community's first family. He saw little of it in his early youth, however, for at about the time of the removal he was sent to Albany where he prepared himself for matriculation at Yale. He entered that college at thirteen, but in his junior year was expelled for a violation of college rules. He spent two months in Otsego Hall before go-
318

ing to sea in the merchant service from which he soon transferred to the Navy. He resigned in 1811 and shortly afterward married Susan De Lancey of a widely known landholding Tory family in the Hudson Valley. For a while they lived in Westchester County, New York, but the banks of the headwaters of the Susquehanna which he had wandered during his first decade had made such a lasting impression that he could never deny their claim on him, and he returned to Cooperstown and built, not far from Otsego Hall, such a stone house as a young country squire might consider fitting.

In 1817, he moved his family back to Westchester. He did not return to the loved haunts of his boyhood for seventeen years. Then, having become one of the most widely known literary figures of the world, having done his native country high honor by his popular novels of America's early days, having lived abroad where he was the welcome associate of Europe's great, he came home to Cooperstown.

To the amazement of his fellow townsmen who felt flattered by his continued love of their beautiful lake-and-mountain landscape, one of the returned author's first acts was to forbid them their long-accustomed use of Three Mile Point as a picnic ground. They protested that they had so used it in the days of William Cooper who had never discouraged their happy gatherings on this little wooded peninsula which, jutting out into the water, provided magnificent views both up and down the lake. The crotchety son of William Cooper said that he owned the land and he would have no further picnic trespassers. The citizens of Cooperstown, feeling that long custom had established a sort of common-law right, denounced him in public print. Many of the newspapers of New York State concurred and said so. Cooper sued them all for libel and won suit after suit. These cases, while occasioned by the landowner's insistence on his property rights ended in decisions which established in the law of the United States that a man may not publicly attack the character of another without producing evidence of the truth of the charges.

But the neighbors of James Fenimore Cooper were not grateful for these benefits. They regarded his attitude toward them as arrogantly aristocratic and subversive to a democratic society. His espousal of the cause of the tyrannical Hudson River manor lords in their quarrel with their tenants in 1845 still further embittered the common people. When he died in 1851, James Fenimore Cooper, the man who had brought to the village its greatest fame, was not mourned by the descendants of the settlers who had looked upon his father as their great friend and benefactor.

The town at the headwaters of the Susquehanna, like the river itself, has run a consistent course through the generations. In 1815, another "big house," Hyde Hall, was built by George Clarke, Anglophile descendant of a lieutenant governor of the Colony of New York and it was soon evident that there would be more than one "first family" in Cooperstown. Since that time the village, blessed by great natural beauty, has become representative of a type not unusual in upstate New York in which homes like those of English "County families" give aristocratic flavor to communities not otherwise distinguishable from neighbors they regard as less fortunate.

James Fenimore Cooper as early as 1838 foresaw with

keen intuition the town's future. He prophesied "no mushroom city" but "a provincial town of importance." Its natural advantages, he felt, made it suitable for a summer resort habitable during the warm months by "those who live less for active life than for its elegance and ease." For the past hundred and fifty years Cooperstown has been this and, recently, a good deal more.

In its journey through this period the village has acquired, as have most of its American counterparts, a legendry. The American originals and eccentrics, the "characters," enjoyed their heyday in the Eastern and Southern states in the first half of the nineteenth century, and Cooperstown had its share. There was Doc Powers who won immortality and banishment (regarded as a fate the equivalent of death by most citizens) by slipping an emetic into the punch at a community frolic. A colleague of his, Dr. Gott, sent bills for his services in rhymed verse that sometimes reached surprising heights of emphasis. He traded suggested epitaphs with the town printer, Elihu Phinney, one bibulous evening with the result that they never spoke to each other again. The fiery physician enlisted in the War of 1812 and was reported missing when it ended. Some years later an American traveler in Spain, seeing on a doctor's shingle there a familiar name, took steps to identify the bearer. Dr. Gott sighed and came back to his considerable family in Cooperstown. Phinney, the printer, was also publisher of the *Phinney Almanac* which sold in hundreds of thousands, partially as a result of his weather predictions. The accuracy of these was attested by the fact that one year he predicted snow for the fourth of July and all (including Phinney, himself) were amazed on the morning of that day to see the white flakes swirling down.

Phinney loaded book wagons which he sent rolling over the state to tempt farmers and villagers into buying his publications, and after the Erie Canal had been opened he launched a fleet of book boats which sold their wares at canal towns from Albany to Buffalo.

As the town grew more prosperous and more of the big houses appeared—Lakelands, Brookwood, Apple Hill, Fenimore Farm—the vivid hues contributed by a generation of amusing nonconformists faded away, giving place to the solid, if dull, colors of Victorian conservativism. Cooperstown went through the years of America's cringing cultural deference to Europe without such serious damages as are still visible along the Hudson. When her novelist first citizen returned from his European wanderings to Otsego Hall, he added to that simple building crenelations and other Gothic defacements. These, as depicted in a contemporary painting, create a feeling of resignation to the fact that the house burned down in 1853. Edward Clark, an attorney who had married a Cooperstown girl and had later become the partner of I. M. Singer, inventor of the enormously profitable Singer Sewing Machine, built a summer home near the shore of Otsego in 1854, and in 1876 reared a castle on a little promontory. European visitors had condescendingly pointed out to Americans that they had "no sense of antiquity," and castles were one of the New World's major answers.

"Kingfisher Tower," wrote Edward Clark, "consists of a miniature castle after the style of the eleventh and twelfth centuries . . . it adds solemnity to the landscape . . . it gives a character of antiquity to the Lake. . . . The effect . . . is that of a picture from medieval times," and he recommends it to those "whose minds can rise above simple notions of utility to an appreciation of art joined to nature."

Cooperstown is today a unique, many-faceted jewel in the treasure chest of New York State. Enter it in summer (and this is advisable since its winters are strenuous) and you will realize that it is a quiet, tree-shaded, well-to-do village. Its business section is not unlike that of most of the state's communities of about the same population, except that there seems to be less ambition; there is no bustle here. It has in its past been avoided by canal and railroad. It may be reached easily only by priviate automobile. Yet it is one of the most sought-out towns in all of America.

The reason for its popularity lies not in its exquisite landscape nor in its beautiful old homes, but in the civic enterprise of Stephen C. Clark, descendant of the Edward Clark who built Kingfisher Tower. When Edward Severin Clark, bachelor elder brother of Stephen, died in 1933, he left a record of benevolent paternalism seldom equaled. The success of I. M. Singer and Company had made Edward a very rich man, and he lavished noble gifts on his loved community. He built a gymnasium and recreation center for his neighbor's children, a verandaed hotel, the O-Te-Sa-Ga, with a portico lined with tall white pillars, and he established and endowed the Mary Imogene Bassett Hospital (named after a distinguished physician and greatly admired friend) which (with further aid from the Clark family) provides for the community and rural districts of which it is the center, a medical service equaled only by the most favorably known hospitals of the nation.

When Stephen Clark succeeded to the control of the late Edward's properties, he made an effort consistent with more modern ideas of philanthropy to turn such of his brother's former properties as were suitable into assets of value not merely to the town but to the people of state and nation. This purpose has borne fruit in three astonishing museums that have brought millions of traveling Americans to this unpretentious town.

The most generally known, the most visited and, in some respects, the least valuable to the national culture of these educational institutions is the Baseball Museum. The story that the game, approximately as played today, was "invented" by Abner Doubleday in Cooperstown about 1840 has been discredited. The game known as baseball was being played under that title almost a century before Doubleday (who never claimed to be its inventor) wrote out his "scheme for playing it." Nevertheless, the nation as a whole has accepted Cooperstown as "The Home of Baseball," and tens of thousands of family-laden cars with license plates representing every state in the Union roll into the town each summer. The museum itself is a neat, architecturally uninteresting building and, to the everlasting credit of the management, it is blessed with an absence of exploitation and receives dignified promotion. While most other national shrines are approached on highways lined with one-story white shacks announcing "Frozen Custard," "Hot Dogs," etc., the motor-borne pilgrim frequently passes the baseball mecca without noticing it and is obliged finally to ask a pedestrian where it is.

The most publicized exhibit in the museum is "Baseball's Hall of Fame," several scores of plaques bearing on each bronze surface a likeness of a selected player, one of the game's "immortals." The first six of these were displayed at the grand opening of the museum on June 12, 1939, when the Postmaster General of the United States

324

appeared with seventy postal clerks and, with the politician's insouciant disregard of historical fact, sold to eager collectors 500,000 stamps recording the National Government's recognition of the date as the hundredth birthday of a game which was already about two hundred years old.

Baseball's relics impose greater demands on the viewers' imagination than do those of the historic scenes of our past. The latter through costumes, settings, properties stimulate the fancy to re-creation of dramatic moments. But the diamonds, the uniforms, the gloves, the balls, the bats, have been so nearly alike through the years of baseball's history that only the most sensitive minds may consider them evocative. The last ball pitched in a famous "no-hitter" looks identical with the first one to be pitched tomorrow. The bat that was responsible for a record number of Runs Batted In in a season is not easily distinguishable from one that a new pitcher will soon strike out with. One worn catcher's mitt looks pretty much like another. The most colorful materials in baseball history are not among the annals and old properties of the big league teams. Millions have attended the league games and more millions, though never present at them, have kept eager watch over fielding and batting averages, but the most widespread interest of the vast nation has centered on Saturday and holiday ball played by countless local "home-town" teams.

Late in the nineteenth century and early in the twentieth, traveling teams of professionals willing to meet town teams along the Susquehanna and elsewhere for not unreasonable fees were very popular. There were the Cherokee Indians who donned paint and war bonnets to leave their highly decorated private car and parade through

325

town, then danced and howled about second base before playing almost errorless ball. The Cuban Giants, whose accents were more Deep South than Spanish, were another such team, and the Susquehanna countryside for miles around used to be empty of humans on afternoons when the locals met the Bloomer Girls who played quite as well as men after the female pitcher had been replaced, at the end of the first inning, by a male substitute. The posters, private-car decorations, and properties of these itinerant teams may someday add exciting color to the Baseball Museum's nationally popular exhibit. But today, it must be confessed, little color is evident. Nevertheless, hundreds of thousands of Americans visit Cooperstown each year, hoping that by looking long at the objects there displayed they may recapture in memory the white-lined greensward, the brown of the bare base-paths, the sharp crack of a bat, the white ball in long trajectory against blue sky, the high-leaping catch and the diving "shoestring" catch, the pitch so fast the eye loses it, the swelling roar of the big crowd—all the poetry of the game.

The great figures of baseball's past, moreover, do not live in the minds of succeeding generations. Grandfathers stand reverently before the plaque of Hans Wagner, fathers before that of Lou Gehrig, young sons before a ball that Mickey Mantle hit over the fence for one of the longest of measured home runs. The older men are pathetic in their puzzlement over the boys' lack of interest in their own idols.

Unfortunately, only a small percentage of the vast number who enter the Baseball Museum to stare at the plaques leave the Hall of Fame to visit the Hall of Life Masks in Fenimore House where they may see exact plaster likenesses, sometimes the only likenesses we have, of many heroes of early American history. Made from masks which the sculptor, Browere, fashioned by applying plaster to the face of the subject, letting it dry for a while, and then removing it, these likenesses form a portrait gallery of inestimable value to the nation.

In the tremendous "cow-palace" barns which Edward Severin Clark built to house his blooded cattle, Stephen Clark established The Farmers Museum—the most comprehensive of its kind in the world. Here American families come to see the agricultural utensils that their ancestors used in other years. They may also see weavers at work making homespun, a blacksmith shoeing a horse, and other processes once matter-of-course in American life. In the level field beside the barns stands an early New York State town, constructed piecemeal of especially representative buildings that have been moved from other parts of the state to this site—a schoolhouse, a doctor's office, a general store, a lawyer's office, a tavern.

Across the road from the mammoth exhibit is Fenimore House, built by Edward Clark for his residence but occupied by him for only a year before his death. This is now also a museum, but more conventional than the other two. It contains paintings of significance to our early history, a very important American folk-art collection, an exhibit of Shaker furniture, and the Hall of Life Masks already described.

And so it is that the headwaters of the Susquehanna begin their flow in a town that is a kind of epitome of the life that has been lived along the river's banks. Not that Cooperstown is a part of the past which the visitor may by some psychic process step into. Its inhabitants do not worship the good old days. They look upon them with affection and respect and, being folk of common sense, with a gratitude for the fact that a general interest in them brings many a spending traveler into their shops and tourist homes. Being prosperous and more homogeneous than many towns on main transportation routes, Cooperstown has little difficulty in achieving a happy democratic way of life. It has its Sunday night sings when crowds of its residents sing old hymns and sentimental songs, its square dances in which young and aged violently participate. It awaits each year with particular pleasure the opening, on July fifth as a rule, of the Seminars in American Culture, sponsored by the New York State Historical Association, the headquarters of which are at Fenimore House. Then, for five days or so, all the town becomes a sort of university campus. Scholars, museum directors, librarians, teachers, historians pour into town, and some phases of American culture get a good going over from their beginnings to day after tomorrow. The discussions are held in tents, under trees, on verandas. There is a panel of experts in front of each audience, but that body frequently contains experts also and arguments wax hot. The "courses," selected usually by the Director of the Association, have had such titles as "The Frugal American Housewife" in which those enrolled engage in churning butter, baking bread in "beehive" ovens, and other hard old-fashioned ways of doing things which result in products of better quality than we get now from mass-production techniques.

In "Looking at the Landscape" all enrolled go by bus to such towns as downriver Bainbridge or Afton, and there disembark to discuss how the history of a community may be deduced from the architecture of its houses and busi-

328

ness buildings, the crops that surround it, its cemeteries, its location in the landscape, its roads and streams. A new course, title self-explanatory, has recently been added— "The Life and History of the American Parlor."

As the seminars progress, town and so-called gown become firmly enmeshed in a happy treasure hunt of the past. Laughter drifts across sunlit lawns, the inevitable concomitant of good talk. Folk singers, their guitars hung on straps over their left shoulders, amble from tree to tent to veranda, ever ready with apt music and song. Cooperstown has a good time with its profitable avocation.

❦ THE FIGHT AT THE TUNNEL

The narrow Susquehanna moves nervously into the pastures south of Cooperstown. It is less a river than a creek here and cows, mostly Holsteins, graze contentedly beside it. It searches each meadow with as many sudden turns and dashes as a young bird dog. By the time it enters busy Oneonta, the hills are gathering above it, but not until it reaches neat Victorian Bainbridge do they close in. Then the river runs deep, often in shadow, between them.

Bainbridge and Afton are towns that change little. Look at the former's decorated red-brick business buildings on Main Street and you could guess they were erected in 1870 or thereabouts even if their dates of origin were not occasionally emblazoned upon their walls. Afton obviously flowered at approximately the same time. Yet these towns, quiet and proud and wishing no other life than that they have, were once shaken by a melodrama that threatened civil violence between bands of armed men.

The first of the events that led to so startling a climax was the publication in the Binghamton *Courier* of a letter

329

dated December 31, 1844. The writer, who signed himself A. Keyes of Bainbridge, New York, said he was in favor of building a railroad between Albany and Binghamton and that he wished to bring the project to the attention of residents of towns that would naturally be stations on the completed line. Mr. Keyes's idea received scant attention. Six years later, however, the demand for adequate transportation of farm harvests to metropolitan markets and the possibility of rich profits to be derived from delivering coal from Pennsylvania's anthracite district to northern New York and New England brought action. At Oneonta on April 2, 1851, no less than two thousand citizens, representing twenty towns in the area that would be affected, met to organize the Albany and Susquehanna Railroad Company. A board of thirteen directors was chosen, and among these was one each from the river towns of Oneonta, Bainbridge, Unadilla, and Windsor.

The spring of 1852 along the upper reaches of the Susquehanna was full of talk about the new railroad and the prosperity it would bring. There were enthusiastic meetings at Cooperstown, Otego, Oneonta, Unadilla, Sidney, Bainbridge, and Harpursville, and the directors who planned them, having the good sense to recognize the influence of wives on prospective buyers of stock, invited women to be present, stating in their announcement "the Women of America have never yet been found wanting when Civilization, Progress, Morality and Religion, needed advocates."

Despite the opportunity of furthering so many good causes by investment and despite Oneonta's wildly patriotic July Fourth celebration of its pending release from rural isolation, interest in the project declined in 1853.

Many who had bought stock on installment in the fine frenzy of the first meetings defaulted on their payments or canceled their subscriptions. Nevertheless the officers of the company never wavered. They succeeded in getting a number of the river towns to buy blocks of stock, and they obtained grants in aid from the state legislature. Years went by and still they persevered. Eventually, stretch by stretch, the services of the road were offered to the public. There were happy celebrations along the Susquehanna as these sections of track were put in use. The road from Unadilla to Bainbridge was opened with appropriate ceremonies on July 10, 1867; Afton celebrated on November eleventh and Harpursville on Christmas Day of the same year.

Then there was a delay of a year as the builders fought their way through the hills between Harpursville and Binghamton. Their major triumph was the completion of a tunnel of twenty-two hundred feet. Exactly twenty-four years from the date of the letter of Bainbridge's Mr. A. Keyes the last rail was set in place—December 31, 1868. On January 12, 1869, the first excursion train left Albany, picking up notables at all stations along the way, and in Binghamton that evening, in an utterly happy and exultant mood, the completion of the whole length of the Albany and Susquehanna was celebrated with a lavish banquet, many speeches, and more toasts.

The peaceful prosperity which the officers and the patrons of the new railroad said they were anticipating at this memorable dinner was at that very time being seriously threatened. Two of the shrewdest and most unscrupulous of America's scheming railroad grabbers, Jay Gould and James Fisk, had already determined to seize control of the Albany and Susquehanna and add its facilities to those of the Erie which they had recently acquired over the futile opposition of another financial giant, Commodore Cornelius Vanderbilt.

Six months after the new road had been completed, Gould and Fisk were claiming control of it through purchase of stock owned by the towns through which it passed. President Joseph H. Ramsey fought valiantly for the company's independence but found serious defections, including that of his vice president, among his own board of directors. In the legal battle that followed, receivers to operate the road, James Fisk and Charles Courter, were appointed by Judge Joseph H. Barnard at offices in the Grand Opera House in New York on the evening of May sixth at almost exactly the same moment that Judge Rufus H. Peckham of Albany appointed a receiver favoring Ramsey and the anti-Fisk interests. When James Fisk arrived in Albany on August ninth to take control, he discovered that Judge Peckham's orders had left on the eight o'clock train and were being communicated to county sheriffs as it proceeded to Binghamton. He immediately wired Judge Barnard's order to Binghamton where it was received a few hours before the train bearing Judge Peckham's orders was scheduled to arrive. The sheriff of Broome County, acting on the orders wired by Fisk, immediately took possession of all the line's property then in Binghamton except one of the three locomotives which were in the city. This a loyal employee of the Albany and Susquehanna surreptitiously boarded and, at the auspicious moment, gave it a full head of steam. Engine and driver were soon out of Binghamton bound for the company's end of the line.

Since Gould and Fisk could command many employees of the nearby Erie at Binghamton, they were in complete dominance there. When news of this reached Albany, the Ramsey party immediately evicted from the offices of the road all supporters of their opposition and sent out an extra train carrying a hundred and fifty stalwarts enlisted in their interest. Under command of master mechanic R. C. Blackall, who was being advised by one of the com-

pany's legal councillors, this formidable group arrived in the peaceful river town of Bainbridge well on in the evening of August ninth. The train was here shunted to a siding and its occupants wakefully awaited developments. Not long before dawn, guards they had sent down the track reported the approach of a train from the south. As it puffed into the Bainbridge yard it was suddenly, by preconceived plan, derailed, and about a score of Fisk men inside were surrounded and captured.

When daylight came, emboldened by this success,

Blackall ordered his little army back into their train and moved it on downriver toward Binghamton. Through Afton, Nineveh, Harpursville, it made triumphant progress to the sound of puffing steam and clanging bell. At each stop it paused long enough to restore to their jobs those whom the Fisk group had deposed the previous day. Then it returned to the west end of the tunnel to await re-enforcements. Now the two factions were separated only by the approximate seventy-four yards of the tunnel. All day long the Fisk army grew until it numbered more than eight hundred men. Then in the evening, confident of an overwhelming victory, they sent their train through the tunnel.

The Ramsey forces had anticipated this move and they rushed to set their own train moving. The Fisk locomotive had emerged from under the hill and was careening around a curve east of the tunnel when it crashed head on into the westbound Ramsey engine. As it did so the battle was joined. The company's men attacked with bare fists, sticks and stones and, though they were greatly outnumbered, their impact was so strong that the enemy gave way. Unfamiliar with the ground and not expecting such spirited resistance, the Fisk-Gould hundreds lit out in panic-stricken flight for Binghamton.

Shouting derision, the Albany and Susquehanna army by herculean efforts placed their locomotive, which had been derailed, back on the track west of the other train. Then they raced it into the tunnel after the fleeing foe. By this time the fugitives had come out on the other side, turned about, and were awaiting their pursuers as they sped out of the blackness of the underground passage. But as the combatants faced each other in the increasing darkness and were about to start again, they heard a rhythmic sound which swelled as they listened. It came nearer and grew louder. Marching steadily, with army rifles aslant on their shoulders, obeying instantly the sharp commands of their officers, the 44th Regiment of the New York State Militia moved into position between the two enraged mobs. There would be no more disorder. Reluctantly the Ramsey men straggled back through the tunnel and, having blocked it with a freight car, withdrew to bivouac at Harpursville.

Though Fisk and Gould used all of their cleverness and their influence in the litigation that followed, they were unsuccessful in their efforts to capture the railroad. In February of 1870 the Delaware and Hudson Canal Company's offer for a perpetual lease was accepted with the stipulation that the control of the stock would remain with the original company. In 1945 the lessee, having since changed its name to The Delaware and Hudson Railroad, bought the road from its owners. It is now known as the Susquehanna Division of the Delaware and Hudson, and the tracks along the river bear the highest ratio of freight tonnage per mile of road (with the exception of certain short connecting lines) in the United States. While the passenger traffic on the Susquehanna Division is very limited, the river towns still hear with pride the roar of the crack freight train of the Delaware and Hudson, the "Rouse's Point—Wilkes-Barre Number One," on its dash with over a hundred carloads of Canadian newsprint for America's daily journals.

GREAT BEND

South from Nineveh the Susquehanna flows through Doraville and dignified and beautiful Windsor to Damascus. Deep below the height of Gulf Summit it runs sullen in half-light, but the hills are soon gentler and the water enters Pennsylvania to throw a loop about a lovely country landscape before, having bordered Hickory Grove, it reaches the town of Great Bend and sets its course for New York State once more. On its way to Binghamton it is joined by pleasant rural streams, Salt Lick and Snake Creek. The small sector of Pennsylvania it has encompassed is so picturesquely rural as to seem a fitting subject for the pictorial clichés of magazine covers and art calendars.

In summer black-and-white Holstein cattle doze beneath elm-parasols and from their shade brooks wander uncertainly toward the river. In winter the fields are white with snow, and the white farmhouses, almost invisible against them, produce an illusion of unsupported dark roofs streaked by red chimneys whence cumulous smoke pours into the sky. There is a tradition of early luxuriance of wild life here. Before hunter Abe Dubois built his tavern beside the river and began to charge travelers for ferry service, he lived in a log cabin jacketed by the pelts of bears, wolves, panthers and wildcats. Preacher Dan Buck and his brother celebrated the end of harvesting in August by summoning their respective families to a huckleberry picking at Red Rock above the river. Having filled their pails with the berries, they spent the rest of the day in killing four hundred and eleven rattlesnakes.

Even gayer than this was a "play day" to celebrate the

end of spring planting. The settlers began their holiday by building a willow-and-brush fence across a channel between the mainland and one of the larger islands. The channel on the other side was effectively blocked, at least to fish, by three boys who rode their horses back and forth, making as much disturbance in the current as possible. Many of the community's citizens gathered three miles above the fence and at a given signal entered the water, stretching a crudely woven brush net from shore to shore. Here they began to "drive the river," pushing the net ahead of them, splashing, swimming, wading and shouting. Countless shad which had been moving upriver to spawn turned about and swam away from the frolicking pioneers. Diverted by the three young horsemen into the channel blocked by the willow fence, they were soon so crowded in the improvised pen that they made wild dashes against the legs of the advancing fishermen and in frantic efforts to escape the trap leaped high in the air.

Now the entire population—men, women and children—began the hilarious sport of seizing the big creatures by hand and throwing them high on the river's bank. Exhausted at the end of the day, they found that their catch numbered eighteen hundred shad. Each boy and girl of the village received five, each woman thirty, and the men divided the vast remainder equally among themselves. Happily then the settlers trudged back to their homes through the dogwood-haunted dusk. No one need worry about going hungry for months to come. There would be salted shad in plenty along that wide curve of the Susquehanna known as Great Bend.

Two events added popular tales to the folklore of Great Bend in its early days. One was the building of the turnpike from New Milford, eight miles south of the town, to Owego. Completed in 1821 the high-angled slopes and sharp turns of this road caused many an ironic remark. "They made one mistake," said a traveler. "Back there's a level stretch where, by turning a bit to the right, they could have gone over a hill."

Said a European resident of the vicinity, "If I believed in the transmigration of souls, I should hope the soul of the surveyor of the Owego Turnpike might be given to an old horse and might be doomed to pull the stagecoach."

The second event was the arrival in the mid-1880's of the young clairvoyant and mystic, Joseph Smith of Palmyra, New York. The moody dreamer, then about nineteen, stated his belief in a divine mission for himself with such assurance that many orthodox church members in the valley of the big bend were both horrified and antagonized. A folklore about Smith grew up that still exists and is told even now with a bitterness that reflects the feelings of the neighborhood a century and a quarter ago.

❦ THE SPANISH TREASURE AND THE WHITE DOG

"The story goes that Old Joe, young Joe he was then, heard from an Indian that there was a Spanish treasure buried on Turkey Hill high up above the river. He got a rich man to pay him and his money-diggers to dig it out. Well, they dug and they dug, but couldn't find nothing. Then Joe says there's a spell on the place and they can't get the treasure less'n they kill an all-white dog and sprinkle his blood around the place. So they looked and they looked but there wasn't an all-white dog in the county. So Joe says maybe a white sheep'll do and they kilt a sheep and sprinkled the blood. Then they dug some more but they didn't uncover anything and Joe finally says whatever put the spell on the treasure was mad because they thought he couldn't tell the difference between a sheep and a dog. Then they quit."

The likelihood that this tale is of folk origin and invented in malice is heightened by the fact that it is told with a pointed conclusion intended as ridicule. It appears in substantially the same form in an old history of the county and has a particular interest to scholars of the American Indian who at once connect the fact that it begins with an Indian informant and continues with the sacrifice of a white dog, one of the best known of the rituals of the Iroquois tribes.

TRI-CITIES: BINGHAMTON, ENDICOTT, JOHNSON CITY

❦ THE VALLEY OF OPPORTUNITY

Where seven hills clustered about the joining of little Chenango and the wide-wandering Susquehanna was the place the Indians called Ochenana. They surrendered it to white ownership in 1785 at the Treaty of Fort Herkimer, and a year later a Philadelphia merchant, William Bingham, bought it, knowing that here was a likely site for a town. He wrote later to his friend Joshua Whitney, who organized a chopping bee to clear "Chenango Point" for its first cluster of cabins, that he considered the new village "for a quiet industrious people who may give reputation to the neighborhood, as well from their skill as from their orderly moral conduct." Bingham so much wanted to realize this conception that he made generous gifts of

339

land to the community, and its citizens, out of affection and gratitude, named their town Binghamton.

Some of the seven hills have been graded out of existence now, but from Mount Prospect and old "Asylum Hill" men still gaze on far-flung panoramas through which the crooked channel of the Susquehanna gleams like an arrested stroke of lightning.

Binghamton is a roomy old industrial town, dark at its center with the Victorian darkness of blackening red brick and grime-stained stone. Its river fronts sprawl along the water without symmetry or logic but with disarming picturesqueness. Its main approaches are as spokes of a wheel leading to its courthouse hub. Over streets in its early residential sections, limbs of old maples in summertime form leafy arches, and green lawns spread proudly about rambling houses built when elegance, spaciousness and decoration were valued more highly than simplicity, compactness, and functional quality.

The big residences once held a special breed of humans, described by their descendants and other respecters of what they represent as "Old Binghamton." This group laments its own fading away. They deplore the razing of any of these dated dwellings, the conversion of some of them into clubhouses and funeral parlors, the occupancy of others by newly prosperous immigrant families a generation removed from the lands whence they came. Old Binghamton recalls fondly the days of the 1880's when the town was second most productive in the country in the manufacture of that symbol of conservative prosperity—the cigar. It regards the growth of the community into a factory town of thousands who create settlements according to national origins—Polish, Russian, and Czech to the north, Italian to the east—as a regrettable whim of destiny.

Many other New York State cities have had a parallel history, and Binghamton would possibly deserve only casual notice among Susquehanna towns were it not for the growth of two newer communities, Endicott and Johnson City. The three together are known to Yorkers as the Tri-Cities and the area they occupy, generally thought of as a unit, has an influence extending beyond state and nation.

When twenty-four-year-old George F. Johnson came to Binghamton and got a job in a shoe factory in 1881, he was already a veteran of eleven years' experience in the business. Born in Massachusetts, he had left school at the age of thirteen to make boots for a salary of three dollars a week. The Susquehanna valley must have stirred his imagination for, though his progress had been slow in the first decade of his labor, he proved himself in the second to be a man of extraordinary vision and still more remarkable character. He saw, soon after his arrival in Binghamton, the advantage of constructing a business outside the crowded, busy city and persuaded his employers to erect a factory at a peaceful spot on the Susquehanna, which was eventually to be known as Johnson City. As soon as business conditions warranted the kind of investment he was about to make, Henry B. Endicott, major stockholder in the company, put Johnson in charge of reorganizing procedures and "George F.," as he was to be known for the rest of his long life, went enthusiastically to work putting into effect his new program: "Cut out the frills and give the workers an incentive to produce—put them on piecework at a decent rate."

Thus began an experiment in benevolent paternalism which was to be so overwhelmingly successful as to win

341

large profits, flattering praise and more flattering imitation. Shorter hours and higher pay brought financial returns that enabled George F., when he became head of the business, to invest large sums in providing further incentives to produce. He built and equipped three company hospitals for which he hired able staffs. He gave generous sick leaves, pensions, death benefits. All medical care at births was free, and George F. gave every mother a ten-dollar bonus and a pair of shoes for the baby. At company expense he built neat modern houses for his employees and sold them on generous terms. He instituted a system of profit sharing (50 per cent went to stockholders and 50 per cent to employees).

When Union organizers came to his plant in the aftermath of the financial disasters of 1929, George F. welcomed them and said capital and management in the United States were too prejudiced, ignorant and unimaginative to safeguard their employees or to pay them what they should have. The employees responded not only by refusing to join the unions, but by accepting two cuts in pay which left them with only 85 per cent of their former incomes. In 1940, the Congress of Industrial Organizations and the American Federation of Labor, claiming that they were obliged under Federal law (the Wagner Act) to seek an election in the Johnson plants, were given every opportunity to accomplish their purpose. Labor's representatives realized that fate had turned against them, however, in the week of the vote when George F., then eighty-two, became seriously ill with pneumonia. Workers kneeling in the churches beside the river, many of which the old man had given them, offered heartfelt prayers for his recovery. In the election each Union received more than a thousand votes, but the ballots for "no union and George F." numbered more than twelve and a half thousand. Then the prayers were answered. The old man was well again and lived awhile longer. And in 1944 the tannery workers in his company voted to organize.

George F. said that he had learned not to value money and he wanted to rid himself of the fortune he had made before he died. He tried but did not succeed. Had he done so, however, the methods he had established in his plant, as it still proves, could not fail of earning monetary rewards. His son, George W. Johnson, carried on in his father's tradition, and the factories still keep on making shoes the American public is glad to buy.

George F. had been on the Susquehanna for more than three decades before Thomas J. Watson came to the Binghamton area. Born in 1874, Watson had grown up in the picturesque upstate New York community of Painted Post. His first job, as salesman in a home-town store, brought him six dollars a week. The life of this small, country village made a lasting and deep impression on him, and men who have sometimes been puzzled by his later motivations could well trace them to the simplicity, the love of schooling, the emphasis on "horse sense," which have always been treasured qualities of rural upstate life.

Thomas Watson's post-high-school education consisted of one year at a business college in nearby Elmira. After that, impatient to begin a career, he went back to Painted Post to sell sewing machines and pianos. The first job that showed the bent of his career was selling cash registers on commission for John Henry Patterson, then president of the National Cash Register Company. He failed

343

miserably at this until he went to his sales manager who, after the fashion of the day, tried to inspire the young man with slogans similar to those Elbert Hubbard was composing and popularizing farther west in the state at East Aurora. These struck a responsive chord. "Plan your work and work your plan," "Think in Big Figures" set Watson's mind ablaze. Suddenly he became a master salesman. He had been with the company only ten years when he was sales manager himself. But when, in 1913, Patterson failed to make a sufficiently strong and uncompromising fight against a suit charging him with violation of the Anti-Trust Act, Watson moved on, disgusted.

When he came to the banks of the Susquehanna to combine three independent companies into one which he chose to call International Business Machines, Thomas Watson had no realization of the business future of the region. Indeed, Binghamton folk love an anecdote which relates that the president of the new corporation, despairing of obtaining skilled labor so far away from a big city, was planning to move his plant elsewhere when George F. Johnson had a talk with him. Don't move, they say Johnson advised Watson; if you provide sufficient incentive, skilled workmen will hear of it and seek you out.

The difference between the basic philosophies of these two men soon became evident. Johnson was a hearty man, a lover of good things to eat and drink, of loud jokes, and gay camaraderie. For the first few years of his operations on the Susquehanna, he had known every employee by name. Even after the list of workmen grew too long for him to remember them all, he had insisted that every one of them call him "George F." The atmosphere at Johnson

City was and is charged with a light-hearted good fellowship and an easy security.

But Thomas J. Watson with perceptive wisdom chose stronger incentive to fill his factories with eager workers. The slogans and mottoes which had been his inspiration had been fermenting in him to produce a heady moral ambrosia. At I B M, he declared, there are no bosses. All are members of a team advancing toward a common goal. Some are "leaders," others "assistants," and on the former lies the heavier burden, the responsibility of serving their subordinates and the aims of the company as well.

The idea of co-operative "team play," product of the intense interest of American schools and colleges in winning victories in sports, must inevitably have led to a consideration of education itself. Possibly because, in the early days of the nation, Europe despised our cultural efforts, Americans have had an insatiable interest in "self-betterment" schemes. From the age of the Lyceum through that of the Chatauqua to the current days of best-selling books on positive thinking (one of Mr. Watson's especial antipathies is "negative thinking") and attainment of peace of mind through philosophic contemplation, the citizens of the United States have offered open pockets and open minds to the prophets who can tell them how to improve themselves.

Watson's reflections led him to the genuine conviction that education and good business are so closely and inextricably bound as to form an identity in which what is good for one is good for the other, and he at once set about creating at Endicott-on-the-Susquehanna an enterprise by which both would benefit.

The visitor arriving for the first time in Endicott sometimes becomes confused as to what he is witnessing. Here lies the rolling green landscape which has been dubbed "The Valley of Opportunity." It looks like a college campus, and in some respects it is. Ivied towers, well-kept lawns, tasteful houses, well-designed and many-windowed buildings that might contain either classrooms or business-machines-that-produce-business-machines are part of a river panorama that reproduced in full color might represent on a magazine cover the American business plant at its best. As the day starts, bell notes from the carillon tower sound the great institution's spiritual "Alma Mater"—*Ever Onward*—which the I B M Glee Club, at school commencements and on other state occasions, sings soulfully:

> *There's a thrill in store for all, for we're about to toast*
> *The corporation known in every land*
> *We're here to cheer each pioneer and also proudly boast,*
> *Of that man of men, our friend and guiding hand,*
> *The name of T. J. Watson means a courage none can stem*
> *And we feel honored to be here to toast the I.B.M.*

There are two choruses that follow this lyric, each beginning "Ever Onward! Ever Onward!" The first states:

> *We're big but bigger we will be*
> *We can't fail for all can see that to serve humanity*
> *Has been our aim.*

And the second ends with a stirring crescendo:

> *So let us sing men—Sing men*
> *Once or twice then sing again*
> *For the* EVER ONWARD I B M !

If the visitor is fortunate enough to wander these acres when the revered conceiver of this combined campus, factory, and residential area is also inspecting it, he will find

346

that happy-sounding songs often rise with apparent spontaneity into the almost smokeless atmosphere and drift out over Susquehanna waters. Should the dedicated leader come upon a group of his workers stepping to a classroom under purple company banners emblazoned with their golden motto "Think," the valley will fill with echoes of the "I B M Marching Song" which states the firm's high purpose:

With T. J. Watson guiding us we lead throughout the world
For peace and trade our banners are unfurled
March on with I B M.

Or should the visitor have the luck to near a class of newly graduated college men learning to sell machines when (to quote from another hymn of the I B M songbook) "our leader fine, the greatest in the land" appears, he may listen as fresh male voices lift in chorus:

Our voices swell in admiration
Of T. J. Watson proudly sing:
He'll ever be our inspiration
To him our voices loudly ring;

The I B M Country Club (serving twelve thousand members who pay dues of one dollar a year and offering forty-one forms of indoor and outdoor recreation) has a ditty of its own in the songbook, and the visitor, looking on its rolling fairways and clipped putting greens, may possibly, on a party night when workers and their wives are sedately celebrating, hear the I B M Country Club Song:

Come on you lovers of good bowling,
Come on you swimmers one and all;
Join with the golfers and the archers,
Bring on the teams that play baseball.

347

> *Lay down your rifles and your pistols,*
> *Put up racquet and your cue;*
> *Join in the chorus as all members praise*
> *the gold and blue.*
>
> *Stand up and cheer for our fine*
> *Country Club*
> *Where recreation is the theme.*
> *We thank you, T. J. Watson,*
> *the leader of our team.*
>
> *We know the practice of good sportsmanship*
> *Will build a finer group of men.*
> *The greatest team in all the world is*
> *I B M.*

In their songs as in their thoughts, the workers for Watson express attitudes more dignified and on a higher level of conventional quality than those of the neighboring shoemakers. "I couldn't sing highfalutin songs about the Johnsons," said an employee of that family. "Why, they're as common as we are." Others have been known to jeer at the motto *Think* by shouting in tones meant to be heard by the I B M workers:

> *While you're thinkin'*
> *We're drinkin'.*

This unmannerly witticism makes pointed reference to the fact that, while there is no set regulation against drinking alcoholic liquors at I B M, the employees—almost to a man —consider the fact that Mr. Watson neither drinks nor smokes as an index of his beliefs (as indeed it is) and choose to regard his opinion as the equivalent of a rule. Like many a neighboring country farmer, it would seem,

348

Watson refuses to employ a "drinking" hired man or to keep one whose behavior might tarnish the standing of what he calls a "human asset." This has led in some instances to furtive drinking and also, according to believable report, the effort of some employees to better their own standing in the company by reporting to high authorities the giving of cocktail parties or other evidences of alcoholic divagation on the part of their fellows. The company's over-all policy on the social behavior of employees is best expressed in a sentence of Mr. Watson's, as quoted by Gerald Breckenridge in *The Saturday Evening Post* in May of 1941. In implication, not unlike Lord Nelson's message at Trafalgar—"England expects every man to do his duty"—it reads, "All company members are assumed to be representative of I B M at all times."

The influence of the leader extends considerably further into the customs and mores of Endicott and the company's other widespread projects. The most notable effect of it is in dress. All I B M men except factory workers are attired so conservatively that minor differences are not easily noticed. A stiff, white, detachable collar is the unvarying convention. Suits differ but are not conspicuous. Ties are rich of fabric but are not overgaudy of pattern or color. Said a potential customer who recently witnessed a meeting of I B M employees, "I never saw such dress-alikes outside a parade or an undertaker's."

The family is properly emphasized as a sacrosanct unit at I B M. The fitness of a wife as an unofficial but important aid to the "team" is considered in appraising a human asset's prospects for promotion. Christmas office parties which in other firms sometimes become wildly uninhibited are influenced toward decorum by wife-

349

guests and tempered, if not gentled, by the presence of the children.

These details of policy some employees regard as trivial; others, as invasion of their private rights. It cannot be doubted, however, that I B M lays great stress on its own democratic processes. A recent picture of Mr. Watson shows him pointing out that the three letters M A N appear in all the basic titles of the business—Manufacturers, General Manager, Sales Manager, Sales man, Service man, Factory manager, Factory man, Officer manager, Office man. Through his long life, moreover (he is now over eighty), he has underlined his interest in the first word of his firm's name. I B M songs and speeches and everyday conversations repeat again and again the motto "World Peace through World Trade" or its equivalent. Thomas J. Watson gives heartfelt credence to his slogan, though before World War II his efforts to persuade Hitler to accept it and abandon his war aims (an incident comparable to Ford's "peace-ship" mission in the previous war) ended in failure. American business and American culture, he believes, are an inseparable duo which can succeed where diplomats fail. Hence, I B M has sometimes bought good paintings and sent them on traveling exhibits through South America with never an accompanying sentence that could be interpreted as advertising. Eventually the firm's fine arts collection will be housed in a museum, toward the realization of which distinguished experts are now devoting full time at company expense.

As might have been expected, the United Nations received hearty support from Thomas Watson and the Tri-City area as soon as it was founded. To the man who had worked for international amity through most of his adult life—not merely because that amity sells business machines but because of a deep-seated personal conviction —the U.N. seemed one of the world's greatest conceptions, and he has done much to further it. At Endicott, speakers in its behalf make frequent appearances before the I B M Study Club. A United Nations Forum also meets regularly for spirited discussions.

When a former American soldier in Binghamton remembered at the approach of Christmas, 1947, a wartime Yuletide made happy by his welcome into an English family, his idea of inviting United Nations workers to spend their holidays in homes beside the upper Susquehanna was heartily cheered. The Tri-Cities welcomed nearly two hundred members of foreign secretariats with a self-consciousness that soon wore off. By the time of the dinner given at the I B M Country Club on December twenty-sixth, hosts and guests were fast friends. Since that beginning, Binghamton and its smaller neighbors have become the most world-conscious of upstate New York communities.

With I B M's earnest cultural programs, the presence of new Harpur College (begun as Tri-Cities College, an institution primarily for the education of veterans of World War II), the assumption of intellectual interest on the part of "Old Binghamton," it might be supposed that this area would give evidence of high cultural attainment, but this is hardly the case. Bookstores reap no golden profits from the volumes (mostly second-rate best sellers) which they sell. The paintings bought by I B M, many of high merit, draw more appreciative observers in other sections of the country. Even some of I B M's highest executives have been known to recite doggerel under the misconception

351

that it was poetry. Concerts by distinguished interpreters of the world's best music do not crowd the halls of the Valley of Opportunity.

Tri-Cities is a kindhearted community. Led by I B M, which in its remarkable human relations program has included the training and the hiring of handicapped persons (more than seven hundred of these are regular employees), the three towns are a generous trio, ever ready to help the unfortunate, to comfort the sad, companion the lonely. Its tolerance and fair dealing (except for occasional regrettable events in its political history) have won it the love of thousands of foreign born and their children. Its two newspapers are alert and more aware of the world at large than the press of many other comparable cities. Sometimes one of these publishes a column that reveals the warmth, the picturesque speech, the sly and easy humor, the intimacy which upstaters like to think is characteristic of their land. Old Binghamton then glows with a consciousness that this is more effective expression than the formal wordings of the slogan makers. They will also pit it any day against such sententious paragraphs as the great business magazine *Fortune* sometimes fulminates: "I B M is not just a company but a Cause; not just a Cause but a Conviction; not just a Conviction but a Religion of Corporate Happiness."

Such words stir in them memories of the happy shoemakers:

"One time there was a holiday and both the big companies were to get together for solemn exercises at the ball park. First came the I B M marching steady and true in their white collars and dark suits and looking noble for the occasion. Then came the shoemakers, their feet out of step

352

and the tails of their sport shirts out of their pants. One of the younger Johnsons spoke—seems to me it was Charlie. He said 'Now Tom Watson's boys marched down here with their pay for the afternoon guaranteed. Just look at 'em. The Johnsons ain't payin' anybody a nickel but ain't we havin' a whale of a time?' The shoemakers sure yelled at that one."

And of all the loved anecdotes of old George F., the one Binghamton loves best and tells oftenest, is here told by a shoemaker:

"George F. bought a high hill with woods on it. From the summit you could see miles of Susquehanna water. He made it into a picnic grounds for us and he put a sign over the gate that said 'Round Top, Private Property; Visitors Welcome.' Well, on moonlight nights those woods and the river would be mighty pretty and the young folks used to go there to do their wooing. Folks got to talking and the police finally went up there and flushed a few brace of loving couples. Some old fuddy-duddies said 'Entrance to this park has got to be restricted.' 'You're damn right,' says old George F. 'From now on Round Top's closed to the police.' If you ask me George F. did more to get this part of the Susquehanna called 'The Valley of Opportunity' than all the motto-pluggers."

Though Binghamton has added other than its two major industries, it is losing population, perhaps because swift travel by bus, train and automobile makes it possible for workers to live farther into rural districts than before. Once it had about ninety thousand inhabitants; now there are eighty thousand or less. One particular opportunity its citizens value more highly than any other—that of living longer than residents of other comparable cities. About 11

per cent of Binghamton's people live to be over sixty-five.
In New York City, less than 8 per cent live to that age and
the state average is but eight and a half. Binghamton says
it offers a good kind of living, too.

WAVERLY

Waverly lies between converging rivers, the Susquehanna and the Chemung, which meet in Pennsylvania
shortly after they have crossed the New York border.
Owego and Binghamton lie to the east on the Susquehanna. Elmira and Corning lie to the west on the Chemung.

Since the town also stands at the northern end of the
highway that follows the Susquehanna south along the
great gaps it has cut through mountain ranges, Waverly is
strategically placed. Just below it in Pennsylvania are
Athens and the prosperous railroad town of Sayre.

Waverly is a sprawling, hearty place of wide streets and
roomy houses. Many of its inhabitants work in the railroad shops at Sayre, but it somehow keeps, and seems to
want to keep, its identity as a York State rather than a
Pennsylvania town. Its citizens claim they can tell the difference when they cross the state line.

Having long been a community of importance both to
travelers and itself, Waverly has amassed a number of
amusing tales based in its own history. That most often
told is one of its oldest.

❦ HOW THE PROTESTANTS GOT RICH

Once a gang of skillful and successful counterfeiters
who carried on their illegal business in many of the big cit-

ies of the east chose a Waverly Hotel—the Christie House
—as a base for their operations. Situated within a few
yards of the New York-Pennsylvania border, this tavern
allowed of hasty departure to the latter state whenever
arrest by officials of the former seemed likely.

In order to protect his neighbors from being mulcted by
these ruffians, Waverly's Chief-of-police Haynes made a
bargain with them that he would not disturb them if they
would not pass bogus money in the vicinity. This agreement was meticulously kept until the arrival at Waverly
one day of important officers bent on taking the "Christie
Gang" into custody. Chief Haynes had no choice but to accompany these authorities as they raided the hotel and
captured a number of its "wanted" patrons.

Haynes was left in the suite of rooms occupied by the
criminals while those apprehended were taken to jail, his
superiors having ordered him to stay there and arrest
others of the counterfeiters in case they should return.

Some months later members of the false-money gang informed the chief that a vast store of true legal tender
which they had acquired by their crimes had disappeared
from its hiding place at the hotel and accused him of having taken it. The counterfeiters said they would kill him if
they obtained proof that this was true and immediately
ordered one of their number to watch his every action.
From that day to the hour of his death the criminals kept
Haynes under constant observation. They obtained detailed information on his bank deposits, his business transactions, his salary, his every expenditure. For thirty years
the vengeance-bound gang kept up their constant vigil,
and when, at the end of that time, Haynes died, they transferred it to his widow. Mrs. Haynes lived on a few more

years, always modestly and without giving any indication that she might have more money than the small amount left her by her husband. When she died, however, her will provided inexplicably large bequests to the Baptist, Episcopal and Methodist Churches.

Just outside of Waverly where the main road north reaches the crest of the eminence known as Waverly Hill there are two interesting restaurants that overlook, in the valley south of them, mystic Carantouan. The higher of these is the larger, and a folksy welcome awaits the traveler at its door. The proprietors and their assistants are not unaware that history sells food. Their place mats in the wide-spread dining room with its tremendous thermopane window giving a magnificent view of the vales of the Chemung and the Susquehanna are maps showing the route through this very country of General John Sullivan's Punitive Expedition against the Iroquois in 1779. Promotion folders describing the expedition are distributed to guests who are lured to order "crusty fried chicken and tender vegetables" with such appetite-provoking distortions of history as "hand-to-hand fighting was common and the stench of scalpings filled the air" (actually there was little fighting and scalpings were few) or with such solecisms as "although protected by breastworks the cannon fire confused the Indians." These the very personable waiters from Tuskegee Institute in Alabama could easily improve upon if they were studying to be public-relations representatives here instead of "to be dieticians, chefs or headwaiters for the country's best hotels." The soups are hot and tasty, the steaks keep on "sizzling" until devoured, the pie pastry is a dream of incredible richness, the service is elaborately courteous, the outlook awe-inspiring, the conversation of the patrons gay and loud.

But for those on whom a visit to Carantouan has worked a spell there is a quiet restaurant not so big and not so high where the service is so unobtrusive that the guest forgets that he is being served, where the steaks are hot and tender but make no noise about it, where the window is a frame for a landscape and not a panorama, and in the valley the summit of Carantouan guides the mind into revery.

OWEGO

> The faculty for myth is innate
> in the human race. . . . It is the protest of
> romance against the commonplace of life.
>
> —W. SOMERSET MAUGHAM

The ride from the immaculate modernity of the suburban towns in the Valley of Opportunity to the elderly enchantment of Owego is short, and much of it beside the swirling Susquehanna. The stream moves into the town in a broad sweeping curve, and the traveler beside it can see for a while spires rising from high and widespread trees. As he nears the high iron bridge that will take him over the rippling waters directly into the courthouse square, he will, if he be a man of sensitivity, gasp at sight of the backs of a row of old business buildings lining the river.

Modern Owegans, ambitious for their community and proud of its good name, have bitterly complained that their town, which contains many a sightly house surrounded by a big lawn, is most often presented to the eyes of strangers through depictions of these shabby crumbling rears. But time and the exhalation of river waters have muted the reds and yellows and blues of these balconied walls. They fade into each other with much the same kind of ragged variation as the walls themselves (through rickety outside stairways and the occasional loss of a brick or two) present by merging of compositional lines into a harmonious and enchanting oneness. I have never known an artist to pass this scene by. Travelers bound for towns farther west avoid other routes advertised as shorter to get one more glimpse of this canvas painted by the unwitting hands of nature and forgotten builders. The subtle hues and the irregular lines meet their own reflections rising from the clear brown waters in an unreal, "nonobjective" design, the juxtapositions of which make a surprisingly satisfying impression.

Across the bridge the road divides to encompass the courthouse square with its ornate bandstand and its dark Victorian public buildings further dimmed by the shade of trees. At the far end stands a statue of a fireman, in old-fashioned helmet and rubber coat, rescuing from flame the child he holds on one arm while he lights his way with a lantern held in his other hand. Suddenly the Susquehanna seems to have been a stream that, like the circling fire of the Nibelung saga, has long guarded a town which has lived from one century into the middle of the next in unchanging beauty. A "modern" black-and-white restaurant denies it—but the feeling is strong.

"You are to phone the Old Ladies' Home," said the friendly lady behind the desk at the roomy, high-ceilinged Ahwaga Hotel. I phoned and a cordial voice said, "We're having a tea party and we want you to come." So I came, and if ever a historian wishes easy access to the folk history of a town, I recommend that he go straight to the Old Ladies' Home (if the community is blessed with one) and pay his respects. I came to know Owego in the soft light of candles while I sipped tea and ate cakes and listened, as I never would otherwise have known it. Even the next day's chats with village historians and picturesque old-timers seemed anticlimactic after those few hours in that pleasant rambling house whose front windows look out across the wide, tree-lined street toward the Susquehanna.

While Owego has more elegant Victorian homes in well-kept condition than most comparable communities along the river, this did not interest my lady guides (some of whom had lived in them) as much as it did a few of my male informants of the next day who laid emphasis on the facts that their town was old (organized in 1791), aristocratic, and thriving, all of which may not be denied.

They said I should know that the first interesting narrative of the vicinity had to do with the famed Indian founder of the Iroquois Confederacy, Hiawatha. On the hundred-acre tear-shaped island about three miles east of the iron bridge, they said, the mystic seer and dreamer had received the revelation that had influenced even such world-important events as the framing of the Constitution of the United States. In 1950, they added, the eminent scholar of American Indian History, Professor Erl Bates of Cornell University, had spoken on Hiawatha Island and had said it was more fittingly named than most historians had hitherto believed.

❦ HIAWATHA ISLAND

The greatest of Indian psychic leaders, Hiawatha was doubtless an Oneida, said Dr. Bates. He was a gentle prophet but courageous and he spoke for peace among the most warlike of the tribes, the Mohawks. He also recog-

nized in the Onondagas the supernatural qualities which
gave them, more than any other tribe, communion with
the Great Spirit, and he named them keepers of the central
council fire.

In 1550 the noble dreamer left Onondaga in melancholy mood, paddled "down the river with the flowers on
its banks" (the Tioughnioga) and turned west on the
broad Susquehanna. As day ended he saw ahead an island black in the blaze of sunset. Here he beached his canoe and for six days he fasted, meanwhile summoning
great men of the five tribes to come to the island that they
might hear from him of the sign that would surely come.
On the seventh day, standing among the emissaries of the
tribes, he beheld on high a sacred vision. Then he drew an
arrow from his quiver and broke it easily with his hands.
Taking five others, one for each of the tribes, he bound
them together with buckskin saying, "Together ye are
men of oak; singly ye are of willow." This was the beginning (so considerable early documentary evidence
shows) of the great union which would, in future days,
serve as partial model for the union of the white men's
states.

Ahwaga meant in the Indian tongue "Swift Water" and
the name was given because the Owego Creek here tum-
bles down the high hills behind the town into the Susquehanna. The Indians loved the level triangle bordered by
the big river, the splashing creek, and the steep hills and
they built here the prosperous town which General Sullivan's punitive expedition against them destroyed in 1778.
Indian tales to this day are more popular here than in
other historic towns of New York State.

❦ THE STORY OF SA-SA-NA

Among the descendants of Mohawk refugees who had fled from this neighborhood to the Canadian community known as Mohawk Woods on the Salmon River there were in the mid-nineteenth century a brother and two sisters who were of the blood of the famous chieftain, Joseph Brant. Dedicated converts to Christianity, these three—Rok-wa-ho, Ya-go-weia, and Sa-sa-na Loft—had become educated and skillful musicians, and they came to New York State to give concerts for the benefit of a fund to be spent for publishing the Bible in Mohawk.

The young trio gave two concerts in Owego in February of 1852 and aroused so much admiration and sympathy for their cause that the distinguished jurist, Judge Charles P. Avery, invited them to be his guests in his fine house. They traveled to Deposit on the Delaware River for a concert on February seventeenth, and on the next day the two girls sat in a car of a train while their brother was purchasing tickets to the place of their next appearance. Sudden shouts and screams came from the station dining room where most of the passengers were eating dinner. They had been informed that a locomotive engineer had lost control of his freight train eight miles up the steep grade and had jumped. The train was now wildly careening down the track, its speed increasing with every second. Someone ran to warn the Indian girls. They rushed to the car door and Ya-go-weia flung herself down the steps to safety. Sa-sa-na stumbled and at that moment the runaway locomotive with heavy-laden cars behind it struck the passenger train with a terrifying crash. When Sa-sa-

363

na's body was recovered from the wreckage, it had been torn and scalded almost beyond recognition.

On hearing of the tragedy, Judge Avery was so moved that he requested the grieving brother and sister to bring the remains of Sa-sa-na to Owego for burial. The funeral services for the girl were held in St. Paul's Church, and the coffin was carried at the head of a long line of mourners to the Avery vault in the old Presbyterian churchyard on Temple Street. Schools were closed and most of Owego's children marched in the sorrowing procession. Owegans to this day remember the description of the ceremonies as told by their parents who, when youngsters, saw the black-clad tall, thin figure of the brother walking ahead of them, his straight black hair falling over his gaunt cheeks down to his shoulders.

Rok-wa-ho planned to remove the body when spring warmth came to the hard-frozen land in Mohawk Woods, but at Judge Avery's earnest request he agreed to designate as his sister's last resting place Evergreen Cemetery, which slants up a steep hill behind the town. Then the good judge set about raising the money to buy a fitting memorial shaft to mark the grave. Some of the places in which the little company had given their concerts sent contributions. The women of many Susquehanna valley towns, and particularly those of Owego, gave more.

Eventually a white marble obelisk was raised at the loftiest point of the cemetery. Seventeen feet high, it stands on a base of veined marble which rests on a subbase of blue granite. The girl's body lies buried at its foot. On one side of the shaft are inscribed these words: "In memory of Sa-sa-na Loft, Indian maiden of the Mohawk Woods, Canada West, who lost her life in the railroad disaster at Deposit, N.Y. Feb. 18, 1852, aged 21 years." Cut into the opposite side is a representation of a wild rose with broken stem. And on the side sometimes lighted by Susquehanna sunsets the words: "By birth a daughter of the forest; by adoption a child of God."

For a century, some Owegans say, a little group of Indians from the Mohawk Woods of Canada West paid annual visits to the high grave of Sa-sa-na in the time of the Wolf Moon. There they held ceremonies before leaving hothouse flowers to wither on the winter snows. They still come, according to the tell of a few who claim to know, but are not always observed. It is a steep and difficult climb to the windswept spot where the white shaft overlooks the river, a gleaming wampum belt once dropped by the Great Spirit between the hills that guard it.

❧ OWEGO'S INDIAN SHOW

Three years after Sa-sa-na was carried to the high place where she lies, another trio, two of them Mohawks, arrived in Owego with the intent of entertaining the populace. The reception, in May, 1854 of E. S. Washburn's "Indian Show" was so hearty that the showman, his wife—the Princess Ne-os-ko-le-ta (Mohawk for Prairie Flower)—and her six-foot brother Joe all decided to stay on in the valley for a while.

They stayed through the following winter, for two of Owego's most enterprising citizens had plans for them. Colonel Theron Seymour and Frank Phelps, perhaps influenced by the esteem in which Mohawks were held in their community since the railroad accident at Deposit, thought Washburn had a good idea which needed only expansion to bring all concerned handsome profits.

365

Through the early months of the new year they worked at perfecting their project—an "Indian Show" of colossal proportions. From the counties to the north they hired twelve Onondagas to give the entertainment thorough authenticity. From more populous centers they obtained the services of renowned gymnasts. They stained the latter with black-walnut juice to the color of the former and by the same method added several gifted white Owegans to their tribe of performing braves.

By spring they had made great strides toward perfection. They had shortened Mrs. Washburn's Indian name to "Wynima" which, they said, also meant "Prairie Flower" in Mohawk. Her brother had now taken the surname of his brother-in-law and was known in Owego as Joe Washburn, but his presence was so commanding that he was to be billed as "the celebrated Chief Red Jacket, the most eloquent warrior living"—though that great sachem had been in his grave for twenty-five years. The program they announced as follows:

1. Scalping
2. Rescue from Burning at the Stake
3. War Dance
4. Pocahontas Saving Captain John Smith
5. The Murder of Jane McCrea

The first performance was at Union (where the revolutionary armies of Generals Sullivan and Clinton had become one force), and it was a huge success from the gruesome scalping in the first scene to the realistic sadism of the last, where the lovely heroine, riding to wed her fiancé, was horribly dispatched by her Indian escorts.

More profits rolled in as the troupe moved downriver

into Pennsylvania—to Great Bend, to Montrose, to Pittston. Then came shocking news. The advance man who had been arranging for a booking at Wilkes-Barre came rushing back to the show to report that the descendants of the Connecticut men who had been butchered on July 4, 1778, were making ready for a massacre in which they would not be the massacred. He said they had agreed to receive the show, but he had found out privately that the items on the program aroused painful memories among them and they had begun oiling their rifles. By the end of the performance (they were saying to each other) there would be no live Indian in the troupe. Being Yankee stock, they weren't going to pay good money to see an Indian scalp a white man without seeking rewards of their own choosing. If they were arrested, they said, no jury in their part of the Susquehanna valley would regard the action they planned as a crime.

Mournfully, then, the Owegans came to the conclusion that America was not yet ready for Indian shows and forsook their enterprise.

Ever since Jim McMaster and his bound boy, Bill Taylor cleared the first ten acres of land in the township, Owego has been a thrifty town with a mind of its own. It has always had dreams of being a center of commerce. The first of these gave its citizens high hopes when they were receiving from northern counties Salina salt, lumber, wheat and plaster, to be transshipped on big Susquehanna arks to Pennsylvania and Maryland markets. The second came when the town boasted no less than six railroads leading to it or through it—the Cayuga and Susquehanna; the New York, Lake Erie and Western; the Southern Cen-

367

tral; the Geneva, Ithaca and Sayre; the Elmira Cortland and Northern; and the Delaware, Lackawanna and Western. Many Owegans still look upon their town as ideally situated for industry though others look upon the idea with horror.

The day after my rewarding visit to the Old Ladies' Home, attorney James Truman whose family has long been associated with Owego took me back among the Susquehanna hills to talk to Frank Taylor who went blind in 1913, but had known every inch of his farm so well that he could conduct its business without sight. Perhaps because the loss of one sense sharpens others Frank could remember with clarity many things about the old days:

❦ THE OLD FERRY

"Used to be ferry not so far from the iron bridge run for years by a feller named Hyatt. It was run by a rope stretched across the river. One day the rope broke and Hyatt had to quit. Old George Horton got an idee and, not tellin' anybody, set out for Jersey and got him a new rope. Then he come back and says from now on he's goin' to run the ferry and it'll be called Horton's Ferry. Hyatt sued him in the courthouse and the jedge says Hyatt can run his ferry fer a year, then Horton fer a year from then on."

❦ DAVIS'S FARM

"Lawyer Davis was a smart one. Folks around here was always suin' each other an' Davis he took his pettyfoggin' out in land, five acres at a time. One time he says 'If old man Horton had lived long enough to have another lawsuit over that ferry I'd a had that other five acres to make up an even hundred.'"

368

❧ SWART LICK

"Fellow named Swartwood was a squatter round here and he had a kind of perpetual hankering for venison. One time he and Jim Catlin and Tom Legg cut down a pine tree near a spring and made auger holes in it. They filled the holes with salt and each one built himself a platform in a tree nearby. From then on they all had plenty of venison. All they had to do was wait on their platforms till the deer come by for the salt and a drink from the spring. That place is still called Swart Lick and the pine log with the auger holes in it is still there."

❧ THE CROSS-EYED HOUND

"Swartwood had a great big cross-eyed hound named Tige. He had a voice you could hear for miles. Folks used to get together on moony nights when he was out after coon just to enjoy the music. 'Listen to that dog!' they used to say. Tige was smart, too, and the family got so they used to send him on errands. One time when Swart's father was down in the basement of the barn that hound come down the stairs with a handkerchief wrapped around his collar. The old man took it off and set out follerin' the dog. Turned out Swart had been down by the river clearin' a patch and his ax had slipped and come to near takin' off his foot. He needed help so he sent Tige after it."

❧ THE POET DANDY

His prose had a natural grace of its own.
—JAMES RUSSELL LOWELL

In the summer of 1837 the thirty-one-year-old Nathaniel Parker Willis, whom the critic Van Wyck Brooks once described as a "Scott Fitzgerald to the Saratoga Belles," was traveling about America with the English artist W. H. Bartlett collecting materials for a collaborative work to be entitled *American Scenery*. When they saw beside a bridge over Owego Creek the confluence of that dashing little stream and the Susquehanna, Willis, who prided himself on his sophistication, his acquaintanceship with the great writers of the world, his travel on "the Continent" and in England, suddenly felt that these wild acres should be his home. From his Yale College friend, George Pumpelly, member of one of the town's most distinguished families, he bought about two hundred acres and to a pleasant house thereon in the fall he brought his bride of just a year, the affectionate, lively, musical, religious Mary, daughter of the British General William Stace of Woolwich, England. There the brilliant and already famous young American writer thought to spend the rest of his days in a happy, simple but genteel "rustication."

Owego received the somewhat affected, long-haired, overdressed poet with little enthusiasm. His efforts at planting and harvesting corn and buckwheat afforded, as do the labors of most gentleman farmers to this day, many a ridiculing folk anecdote. The long blue military cloak with eagle clasp, which his father-in-law had once taken from the body of a French officer after a battle, was to his neighbors an unforgivable eccentricity of costume, and his respectful English servant William seemed somehow an insult to local democracy. Though he built a new bridge over the tree-shaded Owego, he noted that he received no thanks. Nevertheless he loved Glenmary, as he called this country home named after his beautiful blonde, blue-eyed English wife, and he loved the town. When his good

370

friend and collaborator (at a later date), Dr. T. O. Porter, accused him of having retired to the backwoods he wrote a heartfelt though good-natured riposte which gives something of the atmosphere of the Owego *haut ton* in the 1830's:

> Now consider my arms a-kimbo, if you please, while I ask you what you mean by calling Glenmary 'backwoods.' Faith, I wish it were more backwoods than it is. Here be cards to be left, sir, morning calls to be made, body-coat soirées, and ceremony. The two miles distance between me and Owego serves me for no exemption, for the village of Canewana, which is a mile nearer on the road, is equally within the latitude of silver forks; and dinners are given in both, which want no one of the belongings of Belgrave-square, save port-wine and powdered footmen. I think it is in one of Miss Austen's novels that a lady claims it to be a smart neighborhood in which she 'dines with four-and-twenty families.' If there are not more than half as many in Owego who give dinners, there are twice as many who ask to tea and give ice-cream and champaign. Then for the fashions there is as liberal a sprinkling of French bonnets in the Owego church as in any village congregation in England. As for the shops—that subject is worth a sentence in itself. When I say there is no need to go to New York for hat, boots, or coat, I mean that the Owego tradesmen (if you are capable of describing what you want) are capable of supplying you with the best and most modish of these articles. Call you that 'backwoods?' . . . Many thanks for your offer of shopping for us, but you do injustice to the 'cash stores' of Owego when you presume there is anything short of 'a hair off the great Cham's beard' which is not found in this inventory.

Willis was not exempt from the general suspicion with which all neighbors regard a writer. It was obvious that he enjoyed the company of nearby rustics and that he might make fun of them in his writings. As a matter of fact he did, but objectively and without scorn or condescension. Sitting in the shade of wide-spreading leafy limbs beside

371

his new bridge, he heard and recorded with amusement the soliloquy of a foot passenger who leaned over the railing and asked of himself, "Why don't he cut down the trees so's he can see out?" Perhaps the suggestion later caused the poet to cut down the big buttonball tree that he might see "the village spire."

Other rustics told him such immortal truths as "Streams run faster at night" and "A hog hates a straight line like pizen." One, he related, peppered him with questions:

"You ain't got no side-hill plough?"

"Yes, I have, and I'll lend it to you with pleasure."

"Wal! You're darn'd ginch. I warnt a go'n' to ask you quite yet. Writin' to your folks at hum?"

"No!"

"Makin' out a lease?"

"No!"

"How you do spin it off! You haint always work'd on a farm, have ye?" . . .

No answer.

"You haint been a minister, have ye?"

"No!"

"Wal! They talk a heap about your place. *I say, Mr. Willisy, you aint nothin' particular be you?*"

Willis learned from friendly Owegans the joys of fly-fishing for trout and of growing harvests. "There is a glory in potatoes well hoed," he wrote. "Corn—the swaying and stately maize—has a visible glory. To see the glory of turnips you must own the crop and have cattle to feed—but they *have* a glory. Peas need no paean—they are appreciated. So are not cabbages . . . beautiful as a Pompeian wine-cup and honored above roses by the lingering of the dew." Yet when well-meaning nearby farmers told him

372

the deer were browsing on his buckwheat in the hazy light of the moon he could reply only "Let them!"

So, for five happy years, marred only by sadness at the death of a little daughter, the gay, charming, eager poet lived at Glenmary. Friends from the outside world of letters and scholarship came and went. One, his brother, Richard Stovis Willis, editor, composer and poet was so charmed by his sister-in-law that he later wrote for her a musical work which, when published by the firm of Oliver Ditson in Boston, bore on its cover a lithograph of her home and the following legend: "*Glenmary Waltzes* by Rich'd S. Willis, affectionately dedicated to his sister, Mrs. N. P. Willis."

Fascinated by the life of the rough rivermen in the forests, happy in his river strolls with his dog—"a long short-legged cur of the color of spoiled mustard with most base tail and erect ears"—in love with the scenes about his home where the shoulders of the hills "by five in the summer afternoon . . . have nudged the sun and the long level road at their bases lies in deep shadow for miles along the Owego and Susquehannah," Nathaniel Parker Willis developed such a deep and abiding affection for this place that when financial and other circumstances caused him to leave it in 1842 he did so with an aching heart. Once he had written to Dr. Porter, "I beg you take a home on the Susquehannah and let us grow old in company." Now he must abandon such dreams and write farewell in *Letter to the Unknown Purchaser and Next Occupant of Glenmary.* In this he recommended to his successor a friendship with the trees, the birds, and a portly and venerable toad which had been a squatter tenant of his meadow. He reserved from the sale the grave of his little daughter "in the shady

373

depths of the glen above you," and he asked that it be watched over. "Keep it inviolate, and as much of the happiness of Glenmary as we can leave behind, stay with you for recompense."

He would soon be living at "Idlewild" on the Hudson and become in New York City so popular that Lowell called him the "topmost bright bubble on the wave of the Town," but Glenmary was always to be part of him. When his essays written for his good friend Dr. Porter were published with the title *Letters from Under a Bridge,* his readers discovered among them one of his infrequent aphorisms: "The bee and the poet must be killed before their honey is tasted."

Owego has not yet tasted to the full the honey her poet distilled. No one of Owego's former residents, not even the distinguished traveler and diplomat Raphael Pumpelly, who was an infant when Willis bought Glenmary from his family, nor the noted Washington Gladden, has written with such genuine love and such rhythmic literary grace of this colorful old Susquehanna town.

Owego was a merry village in the latter half of the nineteenth century. One of the reasons for this was that a group of French-speaking Swiss refugees arrived—all of distinguished old-world families. There were Mayers, Recordons, Roulets, Marindens, Oliviers, Darbonniers, Mattiles and a good many others. They brought fine things and, though thrifty, were a gay, fun-loving lot. Hiawatha Island became a resort that boasted a big hotel, bowling alleys, a dance pavilion, and summer houses. Two highly decorated steamboats—the *Lyman Truman* and the *Glen Mary* made excursion trips carrying hundreds of people to the island. Single-shell races became very popular and "the last one," according to Frank Taylor, "was between Charles Courtney who used to coach the Cornell crews and an Englishman named Bubear." Frank said, "The shells are still in the basement of No. 5 Fire Station right on the river. Everybody came to those races."

❦ TOM PLATT'S PANCAKE BREAKFASTS

After Nathaniel Parker Willis visited at James Fenimore Cooper's Paris house in 1832 he wrote that here the American novelist kept "the nucleus of republican sympathies in the great capital." His daily breakfast table, the poet added, was "open to all friends and comers-in (and supplied, we remember, for hour after hour with hot buckwheat cakes, which were probably eaten nowhere else on that side of the water)."

Enthusiasm for Cooper's buckwheat cakes may well have prompted Willis, when he became a fellow habitant of the banks of the Susquehanna to devote some of his acres to the buckwheat which he had not the heart to deny to browsing deer. Whatever his motivation, it cannot be denied that thousands of acres of buckwheat whitened the flats along the upper Susquehanna throughout the nineteenth century. Buckwheat pancakes for breakfast every morning were still an honored tradition among families of the region in the first decade of the twentieth century, as many residents can testify.

And oldsters can still describe with spirit the days when Owego-born Thomas C. Platt was the "Easy Boss" of York State politics and made his native town into a kind of secondary capital. Tom's invitations to his "Buckwheat Breakfasts" at the Ah-wah-ga were considered commands by many of the politically great and near great and besides, as one who attended them used to say, "They were too much fun to miss."

The most elegant of the "Buckwheat Breakfasts" was given in honor of the election of Theodore Roosevelt and Charles W. Fairbanks as President and Vice President in 1904. Crowds of curious Owegans at the railroad station watched the very elegant private cars of distinguished Republicans being shunted into sidings on the day before. That night almost all Owego strutted in a wildly garish torchlight parade, and the cheering for the Governor of the State, Benjamin B. Odell, for Chauncey M. Depew, Elihu Root and other state grandees echoed over the gleaming river. On the next morning in the dining room of the Ah-wa-ga, lavishly decorated with prize pumpkins and tall cornstalks, prodigious mounds of crisp buckwheat cakes and quarts of maple syrup disappeared as the breakfast progressed. Kate Roach, the famous Irish colleen who served the hotel's patrons, seemed to be everywhere at once. Kate, folks said, knew what everybody liked and how he wanted it cooked. Her smile was a joy to behold and a blessing on the appetite. "When she served," said an Owegan who remembered her, "everyone in the room believed she'd given him the biggest piece of pie, and when she passed a glass tumbler for her tips it would be returned to her packed with green folding money." Before she died, she owned her own home on Temple Street. She was the angel of the traveling men and the drummers. "Please have baked beans two weeks from Saturday night," they begged of her, and Kate never forgot.

❧ THE GHOST AT THE BRIDGE

No river town so filled with memories as Owego could be without its ghost, and the shrieking girl on the iron bridge should satisfy any searcher for dramatic folklore. The girl was young and beautiful, so the story goes, and was a servant for one of the most dignified and aristocratic families of the town. No one knows who betrayed her, but betrayed she was. One night she slipped from her quarters in the big house where she lived to meet her seducer and beg him to right the wrong he had done her.

As they walked across the bridge, the man threw her over the railing. She caught the floor boards with her hands and held herself suspended above the water while she screamed for aid. Ruthlessly the man stamped on her straining fingers until she was forced to let go and drop into the water. Her drowned body was found the next day, but no one has ever known the identity of her murderer. Some Owegans will tell you, however, that once in a while on a windy moonless night they have heard wild cries for help coming from the direction of the iron bridge, cries and the sound of heavy boots beating on the floor boards.

A philosophic Owegan who knew these tales of the town's past and many more expressed his reflections in a fashion similar to that of Edgar Lee Masters' *Spoon River Anthology* and had them carved as an epitaph upon a tombstone in 1935, signing his initials E.T.G.

WELL, WE HAVE GOT WHAT WAS
COMING TO US, AND HERE IN THIS
BURIAL PLOT WE LIE:—
WE FOURTEEN SKELETONS OF

The Susquehanna

GIBSONS, TINKHAMS, DRAKES
PIXLEYS AND CURTISES, THAT ONCE
WERE CLOTHED WITH FLESH AND
LIVED AND LOVED AND LAUGHED
AND DANCED AND SANG AND SUFFERED
JUST LIKE YOU, TILL THE
GOD-CREATED LIFE-TRANSMITTING SPARK
THAT HAD BEEN PASSED DOWN TO US FROM ITS BEGINNING
DIED.

    BUT WE WERE NOT ANIMALS
OR INSECTS, OR PLANTS, WHICH LIKEWISE
HAVE THEIR LIFE-TRANSMITTING SPARKS,
BUT BEINGS INTO WHOM AT OUR BIRTH
HAD BEEN BREATHED A SOUL-ENTITY
THAT CAME DIRECTLY FROM GOD.

    AND TO HIM OUR SOUL-ENTITIES
HAVE GONE TO BE DEALT WITH BY HIM
AS OUR TREATMENT OF OTHERS WHOM HE HAD CREATED
DESERVES.

    WHAT THINK YOU OF THESE BELIEFS.

ATHENS

> A small river or stream flowing by one's door has many
> attractions over a large body of water like the Hudson.
> One can make a companion of it, he can walk with or sit
> with it or lounge on its banks and feel that it is all his own.
> —JOHN BURROUGHS

Soon after the waters leave Owego in a southwest course
they curve again and move straight southward into Pennsylvania. The point of entry lies between New York's
Waverly and Pennsylvania's progressive railroad town,
378

Sayre. The placid little Chemung River rising in the hills above Corning, made famous by the Steuben Glass Company, and flowing by the old town of Elmira, home of America's first full-course women's college, now approaches the wider Susquehanna. In the triangular space between the two streams lies the mystifying mound of Carantouan, and just above their confluence stands the town of Athens, first known as Tioga Point. It bore the latter name in 1784 when the enterprising trader Matthias Hollenback made it a commercial center of importance to the settlement and development of the upper valley. It forsook its Indian appellation, Tioga (Meeting of the Waters), for its present classic title in 1831 when its inhabitants proudly proclaimed that its situation on a peninsula partly surrounded by hills gave it at least a geographic claim to be called Athens.

Athens is a distinctive town extended narrowly along the west bank of the river. Big old houses stand well back on the tree-shaded lawns of Main Street. Among them stands the Tioga Point Museum housing many relics of early Indian days, of Sullivan's March, of the downriver French settlement at Azilum. Its influence and the fact that many families have lived here for several generations have made the town conscious of its history.

"The Susquehanna," exclaimed the Misses Marian and Margaret Maurice when I broached the subject to them, "why, it flows through our back yard." On the wall of their living room hangs a painting once described by a grieving historian as "the lost John Wesley Jarvis portrait of Thomas Paine."

"When I read that I wrote him at once," said Miss Marian. "I told him it wasn't lost at all but hanging right here

379

on the wall. The next thing we knew he was at our front door."

Inherited from the sisters' esteemed ancestors, another priceless relic in the same room is a flowered porcelain churn once used in Marie Antoinette's Petit Trianon dairy in those days when she and her Court played at pursuing the virtuous simple life of the happy farmer. When I left this home I looked behind me. The Susquehanna was indeed in the back yard and moonlight was on it. Past and present seemed fused through the companionship of the river with its people.

❧ STEPHEN COLLINS FOSTER

Art begins in the irresponsible imaginations of the people.
—GEORGE MOORE

The thought brought to mind a bit of the town's history of which all Athenians are proud. Athens shares the tale with Towanda, a picturesque hill-circled river town a few miles south. To Towanda in 1839 came a young canal engineer, William Foster, Jr., informally adopted son of a relative, William Foster, who was an unsuccessful storekeeper and, on occasion, a respected public servant of the state of Pennsylvania.

William, Junior, recently bereft of a young wife, had been living in Youngstown, Ohio, where he had left his foster parents and their family when he accepted the canal job. It was prospering, and he drove his new sleigh and two-horse team back to Ohio in the winter of 1839. In mid-January of 1840, he set out from there with his thirteen-year-old brother Stephen (ninth child of his parents) on the three-hundred-mile ride to the banks of the Susquehanna. Stephen was then rather small for his age, a delicate and shy boy of olive complexion and dark hair. He had already become so interested in music and so proficient in playing a whistle and other wind instruments that his parents made the effort to discourage his giving time to it at the expense of studies they considered essential. His older brothers had ambitions for him in fields they regarded more manly. William, Junior, was debating as to whether Stephen should be encouraged to choose the Army (by way of West Point) or the Navy as a career, and Morrison, later his biographer, had given him a gun although he ardently wished for a "clarionette."

Sleighing was good on the long journey. The travelers stopped in Pittsburgh to visit with Morrison and another brother, Dunning, and when they reached Harrisburg, William, Junior, took the boy to look at the House of Representatives, to call upon the governor of the state, and to listen to a concert. These adventures in the company of his older brother, an outgoing, popular man whose company was enjoyed by all who knew him, must have been a series of delights for the little boy. Moreover, since his mother wrote William, Junior, on January twentieth, for "little particulars" about Stephen, asking, "Did he get a clarionette?" and, since he was later reported by a schoolmate as playing such an instrument, it may be with reason assumed that his hopes for this treasure had been realized.

William, Junior, had planned for Stephen to live in Towanda and attend the Towanda Academy. This he did, but records and correspondence do not make clear the dates of his attendance there. He was also a student at the older and more generally known Athens Academy which his brother came to regard as the better school. Probably because he hated separation, if only by a few miles, from his adored brother, Stephen wrote while in Towanda a pathetic letter to William, Junior, begging not to be returned to Athens where, apparently, he had already had an unhappy home experience.

> If you will let me board here (while you stay) . . . I will promise not to be seen out of doors between the hours of nine & twelve A.M., and one & four P.M. Which hours I will attribute to study, such as you please to put me into. I will also promise not to pay any attention to my music until after eight O'clock in the evening. . . . I dont see how I could have a better chance for study. & the above price [$2.00 per week for a room] is as cheap as I could live in Athens that lonesome place. . . .

Stephen's desire to live in Towanda may also have been motivated by the fact that he had found a congenial schoolmate there. A reminiscence, written many years later by William Wallace Kingsbury (first U. S. Senator from Minnesota), said:

> He was my special friend and companion; being a year older than myself and considerably larger he used to defend me in my boyhood antagonisms with belligerent schoolmates. We often played truant together . . . gathering wild strawberries . . . removed from the sound of the old academy bell.

Mr. Kingsbury goes on to tell that in happy barefooted companionship the pair frequently wandered "through Mercur's farm and down Mix's run" and waded the chattering creeks of Towanda as they hurried down to the Susquehanna. Kingsbury also reported that Stephen "was the very genius of melody" on the flute.

Apparently, it was the boy's ability with wood-wind instruments which changed Stephen Foster's appraisal of Athens as a "lonesome place." Among the friends he made in the river-girt town was a schoolmate, R. M. Welles, who met him at the Athens Academy in January of 1841. Soon afterwards Stephen was sharing his musical interests with Frances Welles, his friend's pretty cousin, member of a widely known pioneer family, and also a student at the Athens Academy. Frances was spending much time during the beginning months of the year with a suitor, Charles Stuart, who had come to Athens as an engineer working on the construction of the Erie Railroad which would shortly be competing as a transport medium with the North Branch Canal. They were soon to be married.

Through their common interest in the beauty of the river country in which their romance began and as a result of their love of music, the betrothed couple were motivated to ask their very young friend Stephen Foster to write a piece which might be played at their wedding. Stephen responded with a composition for flutes, entitled *The Tioga Waltz*. It was completed by early April, for it was played by Stephen and three of his friends at the gay wedding in the big Welles house not far from the confluence of the rivers, at the end of the first week of that month. Profiting, perhaps, by this formal rehearsal, the four flutists repeated the waltz four or five days later at an academy "exhibition" in the Athens Presbyterian Church where, despite the solemnity of the surroundings, it was roundly applauded. There is no sure copy of this first composition by the immortal songwriter. Years later, from brother Morrison's whistling of it, an effort was made to recover the melody and arrange it for its accustomed instruments. So played it gives no evidence of the qualities which made Stephen Foster one of the nation's great composers and writers of lyrics. Hearers generally agree that it is an attempt at writing a "literary piece," a musical description of Tioga—the meeting of the waters, a scene which the bridegroom a little later described as containing "all the witchery of winding stream, extended plain, and towering mountain." Elsie Murray, Athens historian, says of it: "From a hesitating start, it moves through rollicking mischief, dreamy sentiment, entreaty, exultation, to a touching close." As might be expected, it reveals none of the creative originality which was to emerge from the mind of the adult Stephen Foster.

Richard S. Willis's *The Glenmary Waltzes*, published in 1862, were also descriptive of Susquehanna scenery. Although they were the work of a trained musician, they are equally lacking in individuality. Both waltzes are of interest because both take the Susquehanna as their theme, and though they were composed two decades apart, both are revealing "period pieces." It would not be just to Stephen Foster, however, to assume that the Susquehanna inspired only his *Tioga Waltz*. Athens Academy stood, to quote an early advertisement, "on the west bank of the Susquehanna, a few yards from the channel of the river, where the water glides sweetly along in a smooth, still current. . . . Nearly opposite the building the river inbosoms a small island which with other rural prospects, meets the eye very agreeably." It would be difficult to say what words and what melodies the river, as Stephen saw it for a year and a half under moon or sun or cloud, may eventually have influenced.

❧ TOWANDA

Towanda, county-seat of Bradford County, is a lofty town on a high plateau circled by curving ranges of hills which rise here and there to steep pine-fringed summits. The river lies more than seven hundred feet below the

Main Street, and, as a result, the town offers such vistas of glittering waters below and mountain peaks in the sky as are not easily forgotten by even the casual visitor.

Against the green slopes above them gleam the white houses, many of them built in pioneer times, of some of Towanda's early families. They are symbolic of the town's sedate dignity and its interest in the past. While the business of the community is thriving, including large modern enterprises, it keeps a strong predilection for culture and a respect for its historic past. Its museum is a treasure-house of local lore and it is administered not only with meticulous scholarship, but with an imagination and humor too often lacking in the management of such enterprises.

In 1844, David Wilmot, a thirty-year-old Towanda lawyer, native of Bethany, Pennsylvania, was elected to the national Congress from a district then comprising Bradford, Susquehanna and Tioga Counties. Two years later this young attorney had so established himself in the regard of his fellows in the anti-slavery bloc of the Congress, that to him was entrusted the presentation of a proviso that would prohibit any territory acquired from Mexico at the end of the Mexican War from allowing slavery within its borders. The Wilmot Proviso, as it came to be known, was not written by Wilmot, but that ardent advocate of freedom pressed for its passage so vigorously and eloquently in the next few years that it will be forever associated with his name. Even though bitterly attacked by members of his own party, Wilmot stood firm, willing to risk his own political future rather than forsake his principles. He became one of the founders of the Republican Party in 1856, succeeded to the Senate when Cameron was appointed Secretary of War, and was eventually appointed Judge of the Court of Claims by President Lincoln. He lived to see

385

the success of the ideals for which he had so earnestly fought and he died in Towanda on March 16, 1868. Few visitors to the grave of David Wilmot in Riverside Cemetery at Towanda can fail to be moved by the modest simplicity of his marble headstone and the quotation from the famous proviso graven thereon:

"Provided, that as an expressed and fundamental condition to the acquisition of any territory from the Republic of Mexico by the United States, by virtue of any treaty that may be negotiated between them, and to the use by the Executive of the moneys herein appropriated, neither slavery nor involuntary servitude shall ever exist in any part of such territory, except for crime whereof the party shall be first duly convicted."

It is easy to understand that a man who lived high among the wild free hills that circle Towanda would have a flaming conviction that liberty is the right of all men.

TWILIGHT OF THE RACES

Wandering between two worlds, one dead
The other powerless to be born.

—MATTHEW ARNOLD

The homes of the "Pools," sometimes unpainted and tumbledown, seem to have assumed protective coloring and are hardly visible among the thorn trees and huckleberry bushes covering the hills which edge the horizon along the Susquehanna from Wyalusing north into Central New York State.

The Pools is a generic term for a wide-spread community of perhaps a dozen varying family names. These people are slim and wiry and very dark of complexion. Their

386

eyes are small, black and beady, their noses are aquiline, their teeth are white and even (at least, in youth), and their hair is straight and black. They are a healthy lot and, though frequently violent with each other, are hard to damage. The City Hospital at Sayre, Pennsylvania, is said still to keep a twenty-inch length of a chair rung which doctors removed from an intestine of a Pool who strolled in to say he had not been feeling well lately. Being remarkably prolific, moreover, some of the Pools have discovered that, by having families of twelve or more and living "on relief," they receive more income from governmental authorities than many of their taxpaying neighbors are able to earn by hard work. For this and other reasons many respected neighbors do not look upon them with the tolerant affection which they win from others by their somewhat cavalier way of life.

The Pools are a far from unique phenomenon in America. Many of the states of our Union contain isolated groups of native-born people of mixed bloods and eccentric characteristics which attract the especial attention of scholars in the field of sociology and writers of tales. The sociologists have dubbed these out-of-pattern communities "sociological islands" and often make studies of the circumstances which have led to insularity and a continuance of hereditary traits. The writers, on the other hand, usually call the separate units by their local names and, while admitting certain commonly held characteristics among them all, try to find distinctive qualities in each. There have been novels, plays and poems, therefore, about the "Red Bones" of Louisiana, the "Turks" and the "Brass Ankles" of South Carolina, the "Cajuns" of Alabama (not to be confused with the French "Cajuns" [Acadians] of the

Bayou County) the "Jackson Whites" of the New-Jersey-New York border. All of these, it may be said with assurance, are sociological islands inhabited by people in whom flows a mixture of at least three blood strains—Indian, Negro and white—and each has been provided with an origin narrative in which factual history has been enlivened by folklore. It was an easy flight of the communal fancy, for example, to suggest that the "Turks" are really descendants of the crew of a Turkish ship wrecked in the seventeenth century off the South Carolina coast. It took more creative thinking to foster the idea that the Jackson Whites are a result of a mixture of antecedents including Hessian deserters, Tuscarora Indians, Dutch frontiersmen, and prostitutes (both Jamaica Negro and English) who had been imported in days of the Revolution for the pleasure of the British troops occupying the City of New York.

The origin myth of the Pools has a quality distinctly its own, and, in its inception at least, is based in documented history. When Sir William Johnson, distinguished agent of the British Crown, wrote his will, he left to each of his eight children by his Indian consort Mary Brant (sister of the great chief, Joseph Brant) certain properties. To Elizabeth, one of the six daughters of this union, he bequeathed two large plots of land totaling in all twenty-seven hundred acres. These properties according to folk myth may have been taken into consideration by a veteran of the American Revolution, one Anthony Vanderpoel of a distinguished and aristocratic family, resident of the Hudson River town of Kinderhook, when he wooed the half-breed Elizabeth and, against the wishes of his parents, married her.

A wilder folk fancy enters the story here, and at once

388

prevails. Though Hartley's expedition had, as a matter of fact, driven Queen Esther Montour from the valley, the newlyweds were falsely reported to have joined this Indian ruler (often described as the offspring of a distinguished French officer and an Indian woman). On her "Flats," goes the poetic if wholly incorrect legend, Queen Esther had surrounded herself with many Iroquois women who, like Mary Brant, had borne to Sir William Johnson one or more of his hundred half-breed bastards. Soon after the Vanderpoel couple had entered this dream empire, a stalwart San Dominican Negro, black Peter, who had been the slave of one of the French *émigrés* at Azilum was said to have added his contribution to the kaleidoscopic character of the bloods represented there.

This, according to erroneous and highly spiced folk tell, was the beginning of the Pools. However fictional it may be, the Pools themselves are a fascinating reality in the hills that lie back from the river. There they fish and hunt with a skill said to be inherited from their Indian forebears, pick huckleberries, farm a little, and talk much.

Their talk is notable because, through generations of inbreeding, so their neighbors say, some of them have developed a physical deformity, an absence of palate which is, in many cases, hereditary. Their speech is therefore slurred, sometimes to the point of unintelligibility. Perhaps through the prevalence of this manner of talk among them even those who are not handicapped by lack of a palate also speak in the same way. To those who hear it for the first time, it seems a soft innocent sort of baby talk. Their favorite cuss word is "Teeman Tripes," not easily recognizable as the name of the Man of Nazareth, and they have difficulty in pronouncing their "y" and "j" sounds. They are not embarrassed by their speech defects. They converse easily and are much more approachable than many of the "sociological island" people in other parts of the nation. Their talk usually disproves the charges of stupidity, dishonesty, and shiftlessness often made against them by persons less clever than they. The testimony of more unprejudiced observers is that though some may be lazy, most are intelligent. Doane Pool, a friend told me, cannot read nor write and knows no formal arithmetic. Yet when loading potatoes at a quarter a bushel, he puts one small potato in his pocket each time he fills a bushel basket. At the end of the day he empties his pocket and makes little piles of four, then he knows how many dollars he should be paid.

The Pools began in a kind of historical folk tale. They continue to be the source of a whole cycle of homely communal legends. Dinner parties in Towanda, Wilkes-Barre, Athens, and Sayre are frequently graced by able raconteurs who make a specialty of telling Pool stories— to the delight of other guests. An especial subdivision of these anecdotes is a group about pious "Old Mose," most of whose adventures, even of questionable nature, were in some way connected with the church to which he had been attracted by corner concerts of the Salvation Army. Indeed, it is said to this day that when he is sober he wears a Salvation Army jacket. When about to take an alcoholic drink, however, he takes it off and folds it neatly.

At an evangelist's camp meeting, Mose was "almost persuaded" and loudly petitioned for a sign, just one sign from the Lord. As he stood dramatically waiting, practical jokers outside the tent rolled a huge pumpkin down the middle aisle. It caught Mose at the back of the knees and laid him low. He scrambled to his feet in a state of exaltation: "'At all I need, Lord, 'at all I need, but why the hell be 'oo so rough about it?"

After quarreling with his wife, Mose felt a consciousness of sin so great that he would often rush to the woodshed, throw a rope over a rafter and try to hang himself. The rafter, crumbling and rotten, could always be depended on to break and let him down unharmed. One day, however, when he swung his weight on the rope, the whole roof crashed down on him. "Come det me," he screamed, "come det me, I damn near killed myself."

At another evangelistic meeting, a handsome Pool woman "got religion" and leaped to her feet. "Glory be," she screamed, "las' night I was in de arms of de devil, tonight I'm in de arms of de Lord." Mose stepped forward. "How about tomorrow night?" he asked eagerly.

Giving his testimony at another tent meeting, Mose rose to thank the Lord for his wife's conversion. "Before she got religion she was so cross she wa'n't fit to live with," he said. "She was so unkind she wouldn't let me in her bed. Now she's seen the light, she's kind to everybody."

The Pools are proud of their reputed ancestry and are sometimes the easy prey of slick confidence men who tell them that huge fortunes that once belonged to the Vanderpoels await the rightful claimants in New York banks. All that is necessary to obtain them, they say, is twenty-five dollars to hire a lawyer to file the necessary papers. Huckleberry Conile was once so elated by this news that he not only gave over the twenty-five, but bought a Cadillac and hired a chauffeur in expectation of his riches.

The alleged connection between the lowly and too often lawless Pools and some of the highly aristocratic and distinguished families of New York has resulted in many an ironic jape. The best remembered, according to local humorists, has to do with the contretemps planned and executed by a Colonel Edward Overton who took one of the Pools to New York, attired him in a dress suit and escorted him to a "high-society" cotillion where he gravely introduced him to his "cousins," and other first families. None of the tellers of this tale seem to know what happened after that.

While the incidence of crime among the Pools has in the past been higher than that among their neighbors, this may well result from poverty, lack of privilege, and volatile temperament. They are much more engaging in personality than the majority of similar groups. Guy C. Hollen, who was for many years a Bradford County detective, spent much of his professional time in pursuing Pool malefactors, yet never lost his genuine liking for them nor his wonder at the peculiar motives that swayed them. His favorite story involving the latter began with the arrival of a Pool at his office with the offer to sell for a dollar information as to who had stolen a boat that had disappeared from its river mooring. The money having been paid, the Pool said he and his brother had stolen the boat, loaded it with purloined hides from Dayton's Harness Store, and floated their cargo down the Susquehanna to a market town. After selling the hides, they had set the boat adrift and come home. With this testimony, Hollen obtained a conviction of the brothers and was appointed to aid the sheriff in taking them to the penitentiary. On the way he asked the man who had confessed why he had done so.

"Why, Guy," said the Pool to the detective as he pointed at his brother, "that sonofabitch sold them hides for twenty-five dollars and only give me ten. Now I've got even with him."

The intelligent opinion of social workers, local justices and interested neighbors is that the Pools have improved immensely as jobs, education, and the companionship of friendly people have increased. In recent times some of their children, feeling the onus of their heritage, have changed their names, worked their way through competent schools, settled down in other regions where they are regarded as successful and entirely trustworthy citizens. A number of the Pool farmers have pridefully kept their names and are operating so efficiently and effectively that they are among the county's most able planters and dairymen.

All Pools, honest or dishonest, well-to-do or poverty-stricken have an intense, almost a fanatic, love of the hills and vales of the Susquehanna country they inhabit. They are themselves fond of repeating a story told by Detective Guy Hollen more than half a century ago. Refused enlistment in the American Army by recruiting officers in their own county many Pools, eager to fight the Spaniards in 1898, enlisted at Wilkes-Barre and Harrisburg. One found army delay intolerable at the end of the war and, deserting his company, worked his way back to the United States on an available ship. Guy Hollen arrested him two days later at his home and escorted him to Fort Slocum in New York Harbor.

After they got on the train for New York, Guy said, "Why did you come back here? You knew I'd get you if you did. Why didn't you stay away?"

The Pool looked out of the car window at green Pool Hill, gradually dimming and diminishing on the other side

393

of the river. Then he sighed and said softly, "Guy, you don't understand us folks. 'Fore God, I haint seen a huckleberry since I enlisted."

WILKES-BARRE

One of the ironies of history is that the Wyoming Valley, for the possession of which Pennymites and Yankees, both descended from English stock, fought three vigorous wars, is now occupied by a vast population of industrial workers who stem from more than fifty nations. About two-score communities occupy the valley from which Pennsylvania forces tried to drive the Connecticut men whom they regarded as invaders. Thousands of Poles, Lithuanians, Czechs, Italians, Welshmen, Germans, Croats live in boroughs bearing names reminiscent of the valley's historic past—Forty Fort, Exeter, Kingston, Warrior Run, Jenkins, Wyoming, Laurel Run.

There were Welsh families among the early settlers, and it was therefore a natural consequence that when the possibilities of the Susquehanna coal deposits were recognized, miners of experience in Wales should be among the first to begin the project of realizing them. By the middle of the nineteenth century, however, so great was the need for workers that agents were recruiting the unskilled from many European countries. As the big mines undertook the task of supplying nearly half of the anthracite coal used in the United States, the city of Wilkes-Barre changed complexion both figuratively and literally. The neat rural town created by New England Yankees in the midst of smiling, river-watered fields was soon smudged by coal dust, dotted with unsightly culm piles, defaced by mineshafts sunk in

394

treeless, barren hills. Here and there, on old streets like River and Main, are intimations of the dignity and beauty that once prevailed. They seem now to have survived an architectural massacre as devastating to houses as past Indian raids were to humans. The tenements of the mineworkers, slanting in hopelessly stained, darkly uniform rows, give no intimation that these hills were once green with trees, striped with fertile gardens. Nevertheless, Wilkes-Barre claims advantages that in the minds of many of its residents outweigh lack of beauty. The mines have made profits, and labor unions have seen to it that their members have received increasing wages through the years. Though the national groups have exhibited a natural tendency to cling together, the American melting pot, thanks to sometimes exceptional educational opportunities, bubbles steadily here. Wilkes College, in particular, has made great progress in teaching the progeny of immigrant groups, and its faculty is proud that it prepares students who can on graduation assume positions of responsibility.

The rise of the miners from extreme poverty to comparative comfort did not come about easily. They lived in squalid poverty for nearly half a century, exploited by the mine-owning moguls. In Wilkes-Barre, it has been hard for both employees and employers to realize that they share common interests. Most exciting of all the narratives of Wilkes-Barre is not to be found in records of the bloody days of the Pennymite Wars or the Indian raids, but in a report of doings in the days when Theodore Roosevelt was chief executive of the nation. It is a tale to balance that of Molly Maguires and the Pinkerton Detective, the twentieth century's answer to labor prob-

395

lems of the nineteenth. It is a chronicle of the victory of one
of those unexpected champions who appear throughout
history as if suddenly spotlighted for a moment in a dark
theater.

John Mitchell was a short, slim, dark, courteous and
reserved young man when he appeared on the banks of
the Susquehanna. He wore a stiff white collar and a long
black coat, and there was about him an atmosphere of dignity and of dedication. Born in Illinois in 1870 and soon
orphaned, he had been brought up by a strictly Presbyterian foster mother, though both of his parents had been
Irish Catholics. He became a coal-mine worker at the age
of thirteen, but some influence of his early days had made
him a tireless seeker of education, a methodical and
prodigious reader who perused book after book, always
writing on the flyleaf of each volume the monosyllabic
and significant report—"Read." Perhaps it was his long
silences, the quiet of his voice, the gentleness of his manner that made John Mitchell trusted by thousands of foreign-born new Americans whose languages he could
neither speak nor understand. Perhaps his reverent and
thoughtful attitude toward religion (he had turned to the
faith of his parents and his young bride, Kathleen
O'Rourke, after his marriage) gave breakerboys and old
miners alike the feeling that this was a hallowed man, a
leader to be followed.

He came among the anthracite miners of the Susquehanna Valley in 1900 when he was thirty. Two years before, he had been elected president of both the American
Federation of Labor and the United Mine Workers of
America. He spoke in big towns and little towns. He was
a guest in the kitchens of miners who knew not one word

he spoke—but everywhere he went he talked with calm assurance. He said that the miners must unite to win better pay and better living conditions, that there must be no further contemptuous bickerings between Welsh, Irish, Czechs, Croats, Poles, Italians and Slavs. All must be allies in a common cause. He chose men from each national group and somehow imparted to them his burning belief that only through united action could the miners gain relief from poverty and misery. These men preached his doctrine in the native languages of the widely diverse immigrants. A spirit grew among them. They caught fire from the touch of his inspiration.

When John Mitchell requested the 150,000 anthracite men to leave the mines in May of 1902, they walked out. "The time for action has arrived," he said and they believed him. There was a burst of derision from the employers. John W. Gates, Wall Street gambler "Bet-a-million" Gates, offered odds of a hundred to one that the miners would give in. George Baer, president of the Philadelphia and Reading Railroad and chief spokesman for the employers, reminded young Mitchell that religion, sentiment, academic theory were not relevant to the running of a profitable business. Mitchell smiled and waited.

A month went by. The miners planted their little back yards with vegetables. They searched the greening hills for growing edibles. They asked organized workers in other industries for aid. Little relief came and they worried. As spring wore into summer, the American public began to worry, too. Fall was approaching and cold weather. Perhaps something should be done. Said George F. Baer, "We will give no consideration to any plan of arbitration or mediation or to any interference on the part of any outside party."

Mitchell preached patience and waited. There were few outbreaks of violence, and those that took place he sternly condemned. There were parades in the coal towns along the river and Mitchell, looking like a gaunt ascetic, looked from a horse-drawn barouche upon men and women who cheered defiantly but appeared defeated. The pinch was beginning to tell on the miners. The help they had prayed for had not come, and they were desperate. Despite their pretended indifference and nonchalance, the operators were beginning to feel more than a little uncomfortable. Surprised and humiliated by the miners' tough resistance, George Baer made a statement and suddenly the workers were cheered. He had made himself ridiculous in the eyes of the nation. "The rights and interests of the laboring man," he said, "will be protected and cared for, not by labor agitators, but by the Christian men to whom God, in His infinite wisdom, has given control of the property interests of this country."

The jeers which greeted this solemn nonsense were not from the miners alone. Spurred by the nudge of passing time, the owners of furnace-heated homes throughout the nation showered the mine operators with epithets and derisive taunts. Baer met their gibes with unbending arrogance. The operators, he reiterated, would not give in and they did not feel called upon even to talk things over. Miners began leaving the valley to look for work in Philadelphia and New York. Without money they "rode the rods" of freight trains which they humorously dubbed "Johnny Mitchell Specials." "I took a side-door Pullman," they sang, "On Johnny Mitchell's train."

398

Con Carbon, a Wilkes-Barre striker whom Mitchell loved for his wit and gay shenanigans, made up a song purporting to come from the lips of a Slav striker and called it "Me Johnny Mitchell Man." There are elderly miners who to this day remember and sing the songs of their hero. Pennsylvania George Korson, whose collections of the folk songs of his state are amazingly comprehensive, recently included some of them in an anthology he edited—*Pennsylvania Songs and Legends.*

There was a nip in the air, and the people of the nation were becoming frantic. The possibility of a winter without anthracite caused a general cry for action. Pennsylvania National Guard units were marching the streets of the Susquehanna coal towns to prevent outbreaks of violence. President Roosevelt, once having recognized the situation as a national crisis, acted with characteristically swift and firm decision. When his effort to set up an arbitration board with ex-President Grover Cleveland as chairman failed, he let it be known that he was now ready to send federal troops to the area and to order the national government to assume management of the mines.

Suddenly Baer and his colleagues realized that time was the rope generously furnished by the long-enduring, ever-patient Mitchell, and with it they had fashioned the noose about their necks. Every moment that the little man had waited had served to bring to his aid an ally stronger than either contestant—American public opinion. Dazed, the operators, on October thirteenth, capitulated. A little later they found themselves where they swore they would never be, before an arbitration committee appointed by the President. They fought hard, bitterly denouncing their neat, courteous, dignified enemy. Days of stormy battle went by.

The President, who loved a fight, attended some of the sessions. Afterward he said, "There was only one man in the room who behaved like a gentleman, and that man was not I." Ever-respectful, imperturbable, reasonable, self-controlled, John Mitchell stayed on his job until he won.

The men went back to the mines, and there was coal for the winter months. On March 18, 1903, the Anthracite Strike Commission awarded to them 10 per cent increase

in wages, recognition of their union, and other advantages they had sought. Perhaps the most significant and farthest-reaching victory in the history of American labor had been achieved by this strangely quiet young man. There was rejoicing on the banks of the Susquehanna.

The workers' hero will never be forgotten in Wilkes-Barre. The miners celebrate John Mitchell Day each year on October twenty-ninth. Only a few of them know now how much of his youth and strength Mitchell sacrificed for them. In the years that followed the strike, he became a difficult, insecure hard-drinking man. One of his biographers, George R. Leighton, tells in a volume entitled *America's Growing Pains* that once at a convention of the United Mine Workers the delegates grew restless waiting in the meeting hall for their president. He was found, unconscious from drink, and when his friends tried to bring him to his senses, he shouted again and again, "I can't face them." At thirty-eight he retired and some time later went to New York to live. He died in 1919, leaving a fortune of about $250,000 which his enemies said had been obtained by corrupt acts. They would hardly dare whisper this in the valley of the Susquehanna.

Wilkes-Barre and the river towns of the anthracite region still find themselves harried by labor problems. Production in the mines has been decreasing at an alarming rate and there has been a corresponding drop in employment. In 1925, production amounted to ninety million tons. In 1953, it had dwindled to less than thirty-one million. In 1920, there were approximately 175,000 anthracite miners. In 1953, there were less than 50,000. Some experts say that only the adoption by the Federal government of a plan for a 170-mile mine-drainage tunnel from Olyphant (a few miles from Wilkes-Barre) downriver to Conowingo would reduce the cost of anthracite production enough to make the miner communities once more prosperous. At present it is necessary to pump thirty tons of water out of a mine to produce one ton of coal. This adds to the cost of anthracite about one dollar per ton. Other advisers suggest the sealing of mines, thereby reducing the need of pumping water. Union leaders and representatives of management now work earnestly on the same committees in

401

the effort to pull the region out of its slump. Wilkes-Barre, haunted by its Yankee past, animated by its thousands of inhabitants of varying ethnic origins, remains a fascinating and puzzling example of America still in the making.

BERWICK

> The axis of the earth sticks out
> visibly through the centre
> of each and every town or city.
>
> —OLIVER WENDELL HOLMES

Berwick sits high and looks higher. A painter's portrait of it would, to give the feeling of the town, be fraught with what the critics call "air." Evan Owens, a Quaker, thought it a fine place for a town of Friends back in 1786. After a group of them had settled there they named it, because it suited their nostalgic fancies, for Berwick-on-Tweed, English town on the border of Scotland.

Quaker unworldliness has not often in the history of Pennsylvania interfered with acquisitiveness, and Berwick became prosperous and has remained so. Garment mills, machine shops, a tremendous steel-car factory have brought profits that have built fine river-front homes whose backs look down from high bluffs to the river and look up on the far side to River Hill and Nescopeck Mountain. Berwick folk can also see from their side of the Susquehanna the spires of little Mifflinville which made itself famous as an American town by establishing its business buildings about a public square in which there was room for their baseball diamond.

It has been argued that industrial towns do not as a rule furnish, for the amusement of Americans generally, characters of such originality, independence, shrewdness,

402

strength and articulateness that they assume places in the folklore of their region. If so, Berwick has proved an exception and is very proud of its individuals, some still living, who have attracted more than local attention. You can hear on any corner of the town the story of Earl U. Wise who, with his mother, looked in despair at an overcrop of potatoes about to sprout, then conceived the idea of making them into potato chips which would, in turn, be saved from spoiling by being enclosed in cellophane bags. Now Earl U. Wise's potato chips in their transparent covers are famous, and there are two kinds of them—so folk say—the usual and those which are said to contain lots of red pepper to make patrons thirsty in emporiums where drinks are sold.

Berwick citizens will also tell of Abe Adams, the local bully, who once made himself so obnoxious to the town that a shrewd and physically powerful butcher suggested taking up a subscription to hire a Wilkes-Barre boxer to come to town and beat him up. Abe knocked out the boxer and dragged him into the butchershop. Incensed at the thought of the wasted money the butcher, an enormous man, started to belabor Abe, himself. Abe backed up far enough to get a running start, then with lowered head butted the butcher down and bit off his nose, a feat rendered easy by the fact that nature had equipped him with a double row of teeth.

"Berwick is a conservative town," said one of the town's most loyal adherents. "We like things the way we've had 'em. The other day I suggested to my mother that we invest in some Venetian blinds for her bedroom. She said, 'I've been around for over seventy years without livin' in a corncrib and I'm damned if I'll start now."

The Susquehanna

Start downriver from Berwick toward Bloomsburg and you'll run into tales of other celebrated characters. There was Al Abraczinskas who used to start a Model T Ford by lifting the front end off the ground with his left hand while he spun the crank with his right. Nobody will let you forget Hungry Sam Miller, either, though he's been dead for more than fifteen years. Sam put on eating shows at farmers' picnics all the way from Wilkes-Barre to Harrisburg. Hungry Sam first made a splurge in his own neck of the woods around the time of the Spanish-American War when he demonstrated that he could consume more at one sitting than any big eater anybody else had ever heard of. He was no little surprised, moreover, to discover that by so doing he would not only be fed free, but paid a substantial bonus if he would dine before an audience. For a score of years then, without self-consciousness, he devoured incredible amounts of hearty food at community get-togethers before crowds of envious and enthusiastic onlookers.

During World War I, Sam patriotically gave up his remunerative specialty in order to conserve food, but he returned to it on Armistice Day when, before a cheering crowd of happy Susquehanna farmers, he put away two whole chickens as appetizers and topped them off with a dessert of 153 waffles.

Practical jokers used to hire Sam to show up whenever the pious ladies of one of the river towns advertised a church supper with the offer of "all you can eat for 50 cents," and he was said never to have failed eating them into a deficit.

At one farmers' picnic, he ate an eighteen-pound ham;

404

at another, forty-eight ten-inch pies—the first thirty-eight in twenty-nine minutes—and, at a third, he downed a large bunch of bananas. Later, he astounded the valley by appearing at a country fair and betting hundreds of dollars that he could eat a bale of hay. He went home affluent after he had burned the hay and devoured all the ashes.

Occasionally, when business was slow, Sam would stimulate it by walking into a restaurant and ordering at his own expense a meal that would more than satisfy a dozen men. Word of this would get about town and hundreds would crowd about to watch the champion eat. When he had finished the meal, spectators would bet him considerable sums that he could not eat more. He never lost a wager. He immortalized one eating place by gobbling down 144 of its fried eggs. At another, he ate a hundred eggs raw, shells and all.

Saloonkeepers along the river fronts used to offer the gastronomic celebrity money for professional appearances and he sometimes obliged, but he confined his drinking to an occasional glass of beer, and his heart never seemed to be in his eating when it was done in a place where the sale of liquor was the major interest. The best he ever did at a bar was a mere ten loaves of bread.

Once Sam was persuaded to try his hand at beer, and he made wagers amounting to a large sum that he could drink a quarter of a barrel. He made good by regurgitating the liquid whenever he felt the necessity and replacing it. He did not get drunk but he said, "I needed a right hearty meal when I was through." This consisted, according to his later testimony, of sauerkraut, "I suppose maybe a gallon. I can't remember all my performances."

Sam died in his eightieth year. He was never troubled by indigestion—not even in his last illness.

BLOOMSBURG

Bloomsburg lies low—at the foot of Spectator Bluff which towers above the confluence of Fishing Creek and the Susquehanna. It is a neat and pleasant town made prosperous by the textile industry. It has great civic pride. Its streets are wide and scrupulously clean, and each lamp-post from early spring to late fall is decorated by a "hanging garden," something like a pendant window box in which growing plants produce colorful blossoms. Like Berwick, Bloomsburg is an old town. It was founded in 1802 and it boasts an atmosphere of independence sometimes verging on an amusing eccentricity. Its most dramatic memory is that of the days when local anti-Union sentiment brought blue-coated troops to town to crush the non-existent Fishing Creek Confederacy. On porches close to the lapping water other tales may also beguile the visitor —of Bill Hile, feather merchant, who organized the African Ostrich Farm Feather Company and his stockholders who rued the day that he did so—and of Ed Tuslin's Green Consolidated Copper Company which turned out to be a good investment long after investors had thrown away their shares.

One of Bloomsburg's most admired characters has been a professor at the town's Teachers' College who some time ago began a Wild Animal Circus by exhibiting a timber wolf, appropriately named Lobo. Further accessions increased the size and, consequently, the drawing power of his show with the result that during the summer months he employed a number of his learned colleagues, and Keller's Wild Animal Circus proved to be the only show on earth with college professor barkers. Others offered to appear as trainers in the cages, and one is said to have remarked, "It's quiet and restful after what we have to go through during the college year."

SUNBURY AND SELINSGROVE

The Indians of the Susquehanna knew, if the Council of Philadelphia did not, that with the passing of Shikellamy an epoch had ended. The strong and honest man of Shamokin was the last of his kind. There would be no other sachem who could replace him. Now, if they were to be protected from the French, it would have to be by force of arms. And so they petitioned for a Strong House at Shamokin.

In 1756, Lieutenant Colonel William Clapham was ordered to recruit a unit to be known as the Augusta Regiment and to proceed north to the meeting of the Susquehanna branches, there to build Fort Augusta. Clapham organized his regiment at Harris's Ferry and strengthened his advance by building Fort Halifax near Armstrong's Sawmill. The conscientious Irish-Presbyterian Chaplain of the expedition, the Reverend Charles Beatty, had on a previous occasion cured the American troops he served of an indifference to his ministrations by accepting appointment from his commanding officer, Colonel Benjamin Franklin, as steward of the rum rations which he passed out "only after prayers." On the way up the Susquehanna, he found no such easy remedy for his charges'

407

profanity. "If I stay in the camp, my ears are greeted with profane oaths, and if I go out to shun it, I am in danger of the enemy— What a dilemma is this!" Despite their cussing at their hardships, however, the men finished their job at Shamokin by July, 1757, and a fort with a garrison took the place of Shikellamy. Never attacked, it gave assurance of security to the settlers about it, became a refuge at the time of the "Great Runaway," served as a base for aggressive action against Indians and British in the War of the Revolution and was finally razed when success of the American armies was assured.

Meanwhile, in 1772, Governor Richard Penn had ordered that a town should be laid out at the junction of the Susquehanna branches. Much of the serene and comfortable atmosphere of Sunbury may be attributed to its founders' liberal use of space. Its streets are wide and they converge upon a central square. These business buildings and a picturesque inn offer visitors a sense of the security, solidity, and ordered practices of the town. They will remember it for its weathered brick, its widespread trees, its neat, old houses. Frequently, the inn receives distinguished Lutheran divines and learned scholars who occupy rooms there and visit nearby Susquehanna University.

The pleasant village of Selinsgrove in which the college stands grew up around the holdings of a Swiss soldier, Anthony Selin, who chose to throw in his fortunes with those of Lafayette in the days of the American Revolution. An academy founded there in 1858 as a theological seminary and named Missionary Institute was soon welcoming to Selinsgrove a sister school, Susquehanna Female College, also sponsored by American Lutherans.

408

The women's school prospered for about a decade, but was abandoned in 1873 when its remaining students were admitted to Missionary Institute. The Institute became a college with a standard four-year course in 1895 when it assumed the name of Susquehanna University. Unlike many other American colleges which though founded to inculcate the creeds of distinctly separate denominations have now become nondenominational, Susquehanna has maintained its Lutheran character in marked degree. It has held to its religious purposes and, at the same time, has made such progress in the field of education that it is highly regarded by those scholars and executives who make up the staffs of America's foremost colleges. Members of its faculty contribute important monographs to a professional journal locally published, *Susquehanna University Studies.* Students, both men and women, have upon graduation proved the worthiness of their training. Visitors to its old buildings, made of Selinsgrove brick, find the college to have unique qualities as well, not the least of which is a Lutheran pulpit predilection for flowery and emotional phrases delivered in a rhetorical manner.

WEST BRANCH

The West Branch is the wild one. The North begins in an old, long-civilized town, but if you follow the West to the splashing creeks that are its sources you will be in deep woods where you may find deer and bear and wildcat. Pennsylvania holds more wild animals than any other of the Northeastern states, and many of them drink from the waters of the West Branch and its small tributaries.

409

Virgin timber, some say, still stands along the upper reaches, but historians, who know that countless tall trunks floated down the current to the lumber markets, are doubtful. The great booms at Williamsport and Muncy floated millions of logs during the mid-years of the nineteenth century, and the enterprising merchants who bought and sold them in quantities became the lumber kings whose elegant houses rose in the frontier towns, Lock Haven and Williamsport and Muncy.

The highways wander beside the streams in this country, and most towns lie behind a screen of rocks and trees. The road along the upper West Branch is a happy revelation to travelers who seek little-known and less-frequented haunts where the world of early America lingers into the present. Here grow the same plants that John Bartram found when in 1743 he made the journey to Onondaga with map maker Lewis Evans, interpreter Conrad Weiser and the Iroquois vice-regent, Shikellamy. Here, the waters are as limpid as on the afternoon when Evans and Bartram paddled up the West Branch and diverted themselves (to use the latter's words) "with swimming water chin deep most of the breadth and so clear we might have seen a pin at the bottom." Birds of the same varieties (except for the extinct passenger pigeon) that the Scot poet and ornithologist Alexander Wilson saw in 1804, still dart among the tall trees or flash in the narrow labyrinthine clearings above the flowing water.

The brooks and creeks merge into a northeast flowing channel that traverses the grove-sprinkled counties of Cambria and Indiana and Clearfield. As the stream gathers at the end of winter, spring roarers streak the hills with their rock-blocked courses. They will be summer

410

tricklers by mid-July, but there will be enough water for a steady flow above the pebbled bottom at Cherry Tree. Chest Creek flows in at McGee's Mills, and beyond that junction Curry Run and Bell's Run. Little meanderers add their mites on the way to Clearfield, bringing waters from such diversely titled spots as Grampian, Stomach, and Rustic. The Indians gave this region a name that sounds like a hidden brook—Chinklacamoose. The current is swifter as it moves steadily northeast, and the settlements are more numerous—Bald Hill, Sandy Run, Rolling Stone—before the yellow Moshannon brings in from the south waters that skirt the environs of Grassflat, Snow-Shoe, Per Se, Sugar Camp, Panther, and Drifting. Farther along, the Sinnemahoning and the Kettle pour their waters in before the West Branch reaches Shintown.

At Renovo, the business of man interrupts the lonely beauty of the stream. Renovo has had an exciting history in the past decade. It used to be a small town dependent on the Pennsylvania Railroad shops and a tannery for its economic security. That was before Dorcie Calhoun who lived in Leidy Township, twelve miles northwest, persuaded himself and some neighbors that there was natural gas under his mother's farm. They were not surprised when the hole they hired dug became a roaring oil fountain but the nation's oilmen were dumbfounded—and envious. The town doubled in population. The tannery went into the oil business. New hotels, motels, trailer camps sprang up. A farmer mortgaged his truck to invest. Men who had bought campsites along Kettle Creek or the West Branch for as little as $100 found themselves magnates. A wife who had persuaded her husband, against

411

his better judgment, to buy the barren farm acres of one of her relatives, became overnight the family heroine. Renovo was suddenly an American boom town with a Chamber of Commerce and a Community Trade Association. Warned by the state geologist that the oil deposits might soon run out, it began to make provisions for a prosperous if boomless future. It had changed from an easy-going river town to a community-on-the-march. A shirtmaker offered to rent a factory if the town would build it. Renovo built, but at an unexpected inflation-caused deficit of $88,000. In order to save the factory, the Community Trade Association put on a Save-the-Factory drive with rummage sales, benefit card parties, a towering scoreboard, and, in the final days, a blaring sound truck to let folks know how things were going. A $1,500 bonanza from a construction company building an oil pipe line came in at the last moment and public-spirited citizens subscribed the last few hundred. Now Renovo advertises itself as a summer resort and seeks patronage from tourists who flock to Pennsylvania's Bucktail Park in which, the town does not hesitate to suggest, it is the liveliest community.

LOCK HAVEN

The West Branch reaches its northernmost point at North Bend a few miles beyond Renovo. There it turns and runs southeast through a gap in the wooded hills that rise like green dunce caps on either side of the water and, at times, throw deep shadows over the rippling surface. Past the little hamlet of Hyner, the river rolls toward Lock

Haven. There rambling Victorian mansions stand upon the banks, making a lordly façade to mask a red-brick town of factories and modest homes of industrial workers.

❦ JERRY CHURCH

Jeremiah Church came down to this place from York State in 1833 and, being a self-styled "Yankee," hoped to establish in his own interests a successful community. As a youth, Jerry had an itching foot, and his travels had taken him into West Virginia, Kentucky, Illinois, Missouri, and Canada. Fortunately for historians, he kept a lively journal. In this he recorded that he had joined a younger brother Willard, "who had come down from the State of New York into the old Keystone State to try his fortune, and was ready for anything that presented itself that he could do without capital." Willard took his brother to see the farm of old Dr. Henderson, "two hundred acres of the best kind of ground, beautifully located between two rivers, the Susquehanna and the Bald Eagle." Jerry looked on it with delight and told his brother that they "must have it in some way."

The Churches went to call on the "Old Doctor" who told them that he wanted $20,000 and "not one cent less." A little flabbergasted, they nevertheless accepted the terms and paid the owner $50 to bind the bargain. They had their bonds for the rest of the money "made by a gentleman by the name of Steel—a very honest man, considering all things." Then the old Doctor and the new owners "took a few glasses of old rye" before journeying, by stage most of the way, to the farm.

At once, with the doctor's permission, Jerry and Willard drew up a plan for a town and, calling it Lock Haven because it held two locks on the West Branch canal and a large harbor for lumber rafts, they advertised a public sale although they were not to come into full possession for some months. They succeeded in selling enough lots to be able to make a stipulated payment on their property on April first of 1844. "That was the time we were bound to meet our old friend the Dr., and I knew by the cut of his jib that he would be on the ground at the proper time."

Other payments to the Old Doctor were coming due with alarming regularity, and Jerry soon found himself embarrassed because brother Willard had "married a lady near Milton." The newlyweds moved at once to Lock Haven in company with the bride's brother, Robert Montgomery, and set themselves up in a store. "They all lived together, and too fast for their income," Jerry wrote, "so the sheriff came on them to show cause why they did not pay for their goods. They could not show any reasonable excuse, only that they had not the money, so the sheriff seized the goods and sold them for what he could get."

Then, with his brother and family gone west to Missouri, Jerry undertook to manage the town of Lock Haven himself: " . . . I had to be all the society there was at that time in the town. If there was any music to be played I had to be a full band myself."

Proudly the town manager set about making Lock Haven a county seat, a heroic labor since its first requirement was persuading the legislature to create a new county. To help present his arguments at Harrisburg, he obtained the services of a naturalized citizen, one John Moorhead, "who harped in with me—a very large portly looking man,

414

and rather the best borer in town; and by the by, a very clever man." Cleverness won its reward. Clinton County was born, Lock Haven became its capital, and Jerry made a disillusioning discovery—"the less a person has to do with law and attending courts, the more money he can have in his pocket, and the happier man will he be."

Now that he had his town underway—"seven retail stores and groceries, one drug and two candy shops, three preachers, two meeting houses, (and one 'Jerry Church')" —the said Jerry began the work of promoting his own reputation as an "original" along the West Branch.

> I had a summer seat built . . . at Lock Haven so that if I got tired I could go up and take a rest. It was formed in a cluster of black walnut trees. It was twenty-five feet from the ground, forty feet long and seven feet wide . . . bannistered, and a seat running all around, and winding stairs up one of the trees. And I must say that when I went up on to the upper seat I felt like a bird.

To give this eyrie an especial elegance, Jerry ordered it to be painted to look like marble. Since the painter was German and "did not understand English very well," his employer got more than he bargained for. Said Jerry, ruefully, "He made it what I call *Dutch marble,* all full of white and black spots."

This pocked throne won much attention, just as its builder had planned.

> The natives of that country thought it was a wonderful thing, that I should throw away my money so, to make a nice seat to sit on, and asked me why I did so. I told them that I sat far more comfortable on that seat than I did on a bag of dollars. So they gave it up. . . . However, all were willing to take a seat with me now and then.

415

Encouraged by the public amazement at his high re-treat, the town manager decided to give Lock Haven even greater glamour constructing a considerably elevated business establishment near the county courthouse.

"In order to carry out my originality, I built an office in the town, standing eight feet above the ground, on thirteen large posts, or pillars to represent our thirteen Continental States." They surrounded a fourteen-foot room "so as to form a balustrade all around it; and the roof projecting over so as to protect the building." This, Jerry, with reason, concluded "was an odd looking office, and different from any one I had seen in the country." (It seems probable that he had not heard of Shikellamy's cabin-on-stilts built at Shamokin [Sunbury] in the previous century.) "As I was no lawyer," he added bitterly, ". . . clients might look at it without any expense." To visitors whose interest in architecture led them to ask what order of building he intended this suspended one-room office to be, he gave an answer that "appeared to satisfy." He said "it was *my own* order."

Jeremiah Church left Lock Haven in 1846 and "went west." Ten years later he was reported to have "already founded two or three different towns." At that time his lofty spotted summer seat had disappeared; his office, supported by the thirteen marbleized pillars, had become a private residence. But Lock Haven, thanks to Bald Eagle Creek, the West Branch, the log boom floating in a still-water pool, the canal—and Jerry Church—had become a prosperous town. And, thanks to the interest of local historians, there is still enough of the influence of Jerry Church to be felt around Lock Haven to justify his philosophic approach to the world in which he lived:

416

I had always concluded that there was no chance for me to have any kind of a monument erected in remembrance of me, unless I should place some of my odd matters and things before the public myself, so that they could not all pass by without observing that some person had been there before.

THE LUMBER TOWNS

The woodsmen cut down the kings of the forest first—the hundred-foot-and-more white pines that would make strong masts. Lashed into rafts, guided by oarlike rudders of sometimes sixty feet, the straight long beauties drifted the slow waters, rushed down the rapids. Somehow the rafters rode them down the Susquehanna through thick water and thin, through white and dark, to the shipyards on the Chesapeake where the slim long bodies of the giant clippers waited. Soon they would be stoutly holding acres of billowing sail above the decks of the straining ocean greyhounds.

The rush of emigration to American shores early in the nineteenth century sent men to the woods for more than pine masts and spars. There were homes to be built, and maples and beech and birch would make homes. Hemlock that had been despised because it "wouldn't ketch a holt" on square-cut nails suddenly became popular when it hung tightly to newly invented wire nails. Sawmills crowded the woods, and their sharp teeth screamed through millions of logs. Into the West Branch forest marched an army of loggers, and the trees came down like tall grass before a giant scythe. All logs, stamped or branded at each end with the owner's name or an identifying mark, went into the river when it was high in springtime, and the current carried them downstream, sometimes winging hundreds up on the

417

banks again, sometimes wedging one between rocks in the shallows and then piling up against it a tremendous and wildly disordered jam which could be released only at risk of life and limb. At intervals along the stream, stopped by boomchains, the logs were diverted into still-water pools whence they could be sold.

Loggers soon drove the rafters out of business, but not without many a fight between the two factions. Life on the West Branch was made even more complicated and dangerous by the presence of bands of log rustlers who altered stamps and brands or sawed them off, then stole the lumber. These wood pirates came to be known as Algerines, named after the pirates of Algiers whom the American Navy had defeated when warring on the tribute-demanding Barbary States.

The distinctive ways of life of the raftsmen and those they chose to regard as enemies, the loggers, are well described by J. Herbert Walker in the compendium of folk materials, *Pennsylvania Songs and Legends,* written by six experts in the state's complex folklore, edited by George Korson and published by the University of Pennsylvania Press. Other states and universities might well encourage similar comprehensive surveys of folk fancy and folk history in the areas they serve. No book of this nature has yet surpassed it.

Certain spring freshets along the West Branch in the past, notably those of 1865 and 1889, were made exceedingly dangerous by the existence of the big log-covered lakes at the towns where booms had been constructed. The high waters rushed against the chain-and-log barriers with terrific force and eventually they gave way. Then the river became a vicious torrent of hurtling logs that did untold damage. In late May, 1889, the worst of these floods made the "Pumpkin Flood of 1786, which set the pioneers dodging, seem hardly worthy of notice. It broke the boom of Lock Haven, and on June first hurled a myriad of battering-rams against the walls of the Williamsport boom. This, too, collapsed and, like stampeding cattle, the big logs rushed wildly toward Chesapeake Bay. With savage force they slammed into the bridges below, forcing them off their foundations. They destroyed factories, houses, public buildings along the banks. They razed the whole town of Milton and swept on. The entire flood-fighting forces of the West Branch were marshalled against them—lumberjacks, loggers, fire and police departments, and private citizens—but all worked in vain. The result of this flood and others less disastrous has been that the people of the river towns look upon the Susquehanna with mixed emotions. On a summer day when it was a softly gurgling, well-behaved stream, I said to a banker who lived not far from the confluence of the West Branch and the North, "I find the Susquehanna a sociable and homey river—not lordly and majestic and indifferent like the Hudson, but a pleasant meandering stream that a man can live beside in friendly companionship."

My friend's face darkened.

"Then you've never seen it slipping under the cracks of your doors," he said, "rising until it has ruined your homes and places of business, racing until it endangers the lives of your children. No, I wouldn't call it a friendly river."

On the way from Lock Haven to Williamsport, a widespread elm stands close to the place where Pine Creek, having stormed down through the hills to the north, in a spectacularly deep-cut canyon, peacefully slips into the

421

West Branch. In the shade of this tree on the fourth of July, 1776, men as wild and stormy as the country they inhabited—Fair Play Boys—banded together to protect their rights to land that they had settled without official grants; pioneers who hated the British and their Indian allies, and were not overfond of neighbors even of their own Yankee sort. Belligerent and secret settlers, who would not say what place they had left for this secluded valley, they met and decided that they had had enough of British rule. Unaware that ceremonies going on in Philadelphia at that very moment would result in the formal Declaration of Independence of the thirteen rebellious colonies, these dwellers on the wooded frontier voted to let the world outside the shade of that elm know that, so far as they were concerned, they were no longer subjects of the British King.

WILLIAMSPORT

Like Lock Haven, the city of Williamsport is busy and prosperous but still nostalgic, looking back proudly on the old rich days of lumbering. The golden age of the town began in 1844 when a New Hampshire Yankee, James H. Perkins, arrived on the West Branch, saw the opportunity for tremendous profits in river-borne logs and persuaded his new neighbors to join him in petitioning the Pennsylvania Legislature for a charter to be granted to the Susquehanna Boom Company. In the spring of 1846, after the charter had been obtained, work began on a tremendous boom which stretched diagonally across the current of the river for six miles and was anchored at intervals by timber cribs filled with rocks. In a surprisingly short

422

time this barrier had filled an enormous still-water pocket with millions of logs.

Around the pocket, sawmills clustered like swarms of loud bees about a patch of clover. Walking the floating logs with practised skill, "boom rats" inspected the branded or stamped logs, chose those their employers had bought and worked them into the proper millponds. When Williamsport's thirty mills produced in one year 318,000,000 board feet, the height of the great industry had been reached, the tall forests upstream had been so ravaged that extinction was threatened, and the town was rich. Some of the homes of the lumber merchants, fabulously expensive, rambling, overdecorated ("mixed Neo-classic and early Victorian," the Works Projects Administration guidebook calls them) still stand to remind the town of the magic period. Money was so plentiful then that the town became a cultured center where the best of concerts and theatrical performances were included in the usual order of social life, and a persistent bit of folk history holds that in proportion to its population the Williamsport ladies owned more Paisley shawls, evidences of wealth and taste, than any community in the nation.

Another tradition, documented by enough evidence to make it of interest, tells of fine "furniture boats" that once a year, preceded by advance advertising, brought into the West Branch Canal from a factory at Peach Bottom near the Susquehanna's mouth elegant chests and beds and china closets of cherry, walnut and pine. Such articles, reported as purchased "off the Peach Bottom furniture-boat," are still treasured in the Williamsport region. Even more cherished are mahogany pieces said to have been removed from a fire-damaged Maryland manor house in the 1850's and shipped from Peach Bottom in a canalboat by a money-mad butler, a freed Negro slave.

The inordinate desire for easy lumber profits began to have an unfortunate effect on Williamsport about 1870. Since the Pennsylvania legislature had before that year passed a law granting workers the right to organize, and another defining a legal working day as eight hours, dissatisfaction with a twelve-hour day (from 6 A.M. to 6 P.M.) was fast growing among the mill employees. In 1871, a branch of a national organization called the Labor Reform Union was established in Williamsport and on July 1, 1872, the sawmill workers, encouraged by out-of-town labor agitators, walked off their jobs shouting, "Ten-hour day or no sawdust."

This action culminated in an exciting period of parades and "marches on the sawmills" known along the West Branch as "The Sawdust War." Bitterness between the rich and powerful millowners and their employees soon resulted in violence. In one of the first instances Harry Lentz, richly costumed and accoutred, struck a workman with his cane and the latter retaliated by knocking into the dust Harry's high silk hat. Shortly thereafter, at the request of the mayor and the county sheriff, Governor John W. Geary ordered the state militia into action. By late July, the area was under martial law. The militia camp at Williamsport's Herdic Park held three companies of Zouaves, two of Grays, four of Guards, one of Fenables, and the nearby communities of Middletown, Lebanon, Sunbury, Shamokin and Mill Hall had sent off to the Sawdust War most of their young males. Lock Haven had contributed one brigadier general.

Occupation by so overwhelming a military force had a

sobering effect on the quarreling factions at Williamsport. Only once did serious violence threaten. That was when the big and powerful Jim Washington, first sergeant of the Taylor Guards, a Negro company, led that unit in a fixed-bayonet charge against a parade of workers marching down Pine Street. Fortunately, the latter had the good judgment to retire swiftly.

The soldiers went home after a few days. Twenty-nine of the strikers and their supporters had been arrested. Tried in September, most of these received jail sentences and small fines. The organizers who had come to town to help in the fight, however, were sentenced to a year in the state penitentiary. Thanks to the intervention of Peter Herdic, a progressive and humanitarian millowner, the governor pardoned them before they had entered prison. "The Sawdust War" was over, but it had postponed fair dealing with the sawmill workers in Pennsylvania for many years.

Although caring too little for the welfare and civil rights of its own sawmill workers in the rich years preceding the Civil War, busy Williamsport was heartily, if somewhat inconsistently, interested in the fate of Negro slaves in the South. Once, to a building made of logs in 1838 and later covered with clapboard, black fugitives who had been hidden behind the barrels in the holds of canalboats and shipped from Columbia north into the West Branch were led under cover of darkness by white sympathizers. Other runaways from below the Mason-Dixon line came on foot "following the drinkin' gourd," the outline in the night sky of the Big Dipper which, by identifying the North Star for them, pointed the way to freedom. Among those made wealthy by the logs from upriver were a number of pious Quakers who counted aid to the slaves as a

425

duty rather than a crime against the law. They might not have been so successful in moving the terrified refugees on their way, however, had it not been for a Mohawk Indian, Daniel Hughes who, having been born in Canisteo, New York, knew the woodland trails of his ancestors and guided fleeing parties along the Susquehanna to Owego and on to Horseheads whence other operators of the "Underground Railroad" took them across the Canadian border. Because of these illicit activities, the wooded valley where the slaves were hid was known for many years as "Nigger Hollow." Nearly a generation ago, Williamsport chose to change the name to "Freedom Road."

LEWISBURG

To the traveler the towns along the West Branch seem notable for neat precision and ordered cleanliness. Dissenters say that this may be due to the fact that the coal towns on the North Branch make Williamsport and Lewisburg seem freshly scrubbed by contrast. Others offer the suggestion that the cities of the West Branch being nearer to wild and wooded hunting country draw from upstream a clear and healthful atmosphere. Whatever its cause, the impression is unquestionably made on anyone who visits Lewisburg for the first time. A girl student at Bucknell University, an august institution of old red-brick buildings and older shade trees, which gives Lewisburg an added dignity said: "It's impossible when you look at it, to think that the town has any of the small scandals, the petty squabbles, the jealousies and intrigues that lecturers on sociology tell us are inevitable in small-town life. It looks so rain-washed and fresh and unsophisticated."

426

Historians of Bucknell, the campus of which overlooks the Susquehanna and spreads down to the river level, tell how five Baptists yearned for a school of their denomina· tion in the West Branch valley. Since their number was too few to accomplish their purpose in a region dominated by Presbyterians, Methodists and Lutherans, they were obliged to exercise not only faith but initiative and a con·· siderable amount of planned strategy.

A well-to-do brother was prevailed upon to subsidize an experienced evangelist for a series of protracted meetings in Lewisburg. In the winter of 1843-44, Elder William Grant, guaranteed travel expenses and a hundred dollars a month, came all the way from Saratoga County, New York, to the abandoned log schoolhouse on Market Street and began to preach. At first indifferent to his sermons, the community soon found that the newcomer was a spellbinder. Each night the house was crowded by the curious who had come to watch the parade of sinners "down front" only to find themselves joining it. The number of baptisms according to the denominational requirement of immersion was phenomenal, especially, as one Baptist put it, "for a cold winter." At the end of a seven weeks' campaign, Elder William Grant had produced so many Baptists that there would soon be a new church in Lewisburg. The congregation proved so earnest in its convictions, moreover, that two years later classes in Greek and Latin were being taught in the basement of the church, and the hill acres of a nearby farm had been purchased as a campus for the great university that the Baptists knew was soon to come. It came, and now its spires rising above the tops of the shade trees are slim silhouettes against the White Deer Mountain beyond.

HARRISBURG

Come upon Harrisburg from the north if you would see
it as it should be remembered—a very gem of a provincial first city, visually so fair that few of America's state
capitals deserve comparison. Approach this town from that
point a few miles above it where the waters of the Juniata, major tributary of the Susquehanna, are ushered from
the west through copse-dotted hills into the wider stream
and you will see the first of the big homes that set the
tone of the place. It stands back on a deep lawn, and its
many windows have on an ever-changing vista of dark
waters whitened here and there on a scatter of brown
rocks. The road runs between the river and a grass-girt
row of rambling mansions, decorated with architectural
frills characteristic of the latter half of the nineteenth century; and while it would be difficult to conclude that any
one of them is beautiful, the composite brings with it im-
pressions of an over-all beauty. Here is comfort and light
and space, joy in waters, trees and hills, appreciation of the
arts of unhurried living, and a philosophic serenity that
comes with the continuance of all these through generations. The visitor's view of the river is soon interrupted by
trees that offer shadow which brightens the gleam of
waters beyond. And suddenly, up the sloping bank, above
high levels of foliage, stands the dome of the capitol building of the State of Pennsylvania.

John Harris chose well when, having moved a short distance upriver from the Indian village of Paxtang, he
raised his cabin where shallow water made crossing easy.
Here, trails of the red hunters converged. Here, too, white
traders and early pioneers might reach the western shore

428

and follow it north to the Juniata valley which would lead again westward between the mountains toward Ohio. Harris built a stockade around his home against Indian attack, but his fair dealing and genuine friendliness proved his best protection. Soon he had cleared a few acres near the rippling water. He was the first, so those who knew him said, to earth a plow in Susquehanna loam. The cabin in the stockade, the ferry barge at the dock, the ordered fields, became a setting for the life of a family of five children mothered by Esther Say Harris who had known her husband when both were young in Yorkshire, England, and had married him after she had come to Philadelphia to live in the home of her kinsman Edward Shippen, first mayor of the city.

Despite the isolation on the frontier, the Harrises were constant hosts—not only to Indians and trappers, but to distinguished guests who had the courage and curiosity to venture thus far into the wilderness. Moments of peril were rare, but the Indians sometimes became enraged at real or fancied injustices. Then Esther Harris would mount her horse and, leaving her brood behind, gallop toward Lancaster to spread the news and obtain aid. John and his Negro servant Hercules would bar the gate of the stockade, instruct the children, admit frightened neighbors, prepare their weapons for immediate use and wait.

Only once was the operator of Harris's Ferry in an apparently hopeless plight. Then Indians from the Carolinas, come north on a hunting expedition, filled themselves with rum and demanded that Harris furnish more of the same. When he refused they seized him, bound him to a mulberry tree growing beside the Susquehanna and piled dry logs about him. They were about to burn the trader alive when black Hercules, who had slipped away and crossed the river in frantic haste, raced in with a band of Indian neighbors who at once freed their white friend.

The mulberry tree lived on, according to popular tradition, until long after John Harris and the loyal Hercules were buried in its shade. There is no trace of it now, but the people of Harrisburg still honor the spot where the bodies of the two friends lie.

John Harris, Jr., was born in the stockade and grew up to be as influential and prosperous a man as his father. He realized the importance of the situation of his father's acres and, being a shrewd man and a good citizen, he undertook in 1785 to lay out the settlement about the ferry as a future county seat. To insure his interests therein, he contributed "four acres and 13 perches to be held in trust till the Legislature sees fit to use it." So great was western Pennsylvania's interest in French immigration at this time, that the county was named Dauphin (for the elder son of Louis XVI) and in 1791 Harris's Ferry was officially designated Louisburg for France's reigning monarch. This proved an aggravation too great to be borne. Only two years after Harrisburg had almost won congressional choice as capital of the United States, it was even to be denied the name of its founder. John Harris, Jr. spoke out. "You may call it Louisburg all you please," he said wryly, "but I'll not sell an inch more land except in Harrisburg." Realizing that without Harris land the county seat would be strangled out of existence, the authorities gave in, and the town became and remained Harrisburg.

The town became capital of the State of Pennsylvania in 1812, and it immediately assumed not only local leadership but national importance. In the mid-nineteenth century years, no state capital had more widespread influence. The center of the nation's population was moving westward, and the population of Pennsylvania, evermore heterogeneous, was making itself felt as an influence toward a nation of melded national stocks, English, Scotch, Irish, and German groups, each in turn threatening to assume political control of the state, gradually learned to achieve a reasonable amount of harmony while the Moravian, Simon Snyder, was for three terms Governor.

In Pennsylvania, the nation saw an admirable sample of the American "melting-pot" ideal, and in the honest education-loving religious Snyder they recognized that a political leader, though a product of a distinctively national group, might govern the state with integrity and with a desire to serve all its citizens. When, after leaving the governorship, Snyder died in 1819 at the big limestone house that he had built for himself in the leafy river town of Selinsgrove, Pennsylvanians of the bloods of many national stocks mourned him as a great fellow American.

In 1824, the idea of a heterogeneous democratic republic filled the Susquehanna valley with a wild enthusiasm. New England was solid in favoring the aristocratic John Quincy Adams for the presidency, but even the Yankee families of the Wyoming valley offered him little support. The Susquehanna counties were for Andrew Jackson. All but one of the counties in the state, at the suggestion of the Pennsylvania members of the national Congress, elected delegates to a nominating convention at Harrisburg. Cries for "Old Hickory" echoed in the streets. Delegates from the more prosperous districts wore black silk vests on which the strong facial features of the hero of New Orleans were depicted. When a vote was taken, only one

431

delegate dared to oppose the general. So strong was the popular feeling that in the next year ex-Governor Snyder's nephew George Kremer, whose constituents had advanced him from the state legislature at Harrisburg to the national House of Representatives, charged that the great Henry Clay had betrayed Jackson by selling his support to Adams in return for appointment as Secretary of State. Clay bitterly resented the charge and even suggested a duel with its author. Kremer, an eccentric and able politician who had already brought notoriety to himself and the Susquehanna by answering one of John Randolph's Latin quotations with a blast of Pennsylvania Dutch, by opposing all bills favoring education, by wearing a leopardskin overcoat, proved unable to substantiate his accusation of Clay. Deserted by even Jackson's supporters, he retired to his valley farm in 1829.

Harrisburg was a hotbed of political and economic excitement throughout the first half of the nineteenth century. Cheers for Jackson had not died down after the nominating convention of 1824 before the citizenry were entertaining a Canal Convention of delegates from fifty-six counties. Stirred by the successful completion of many sections of New York's Erie Canal, the Pennsylvanians were determined to obtain their share of the commerce of the west by diverting cargoes to the Susquehanna passage through the mountains to Chesapeake Bay and Baltimore. Canal fever brought about a noisy Fourth of July celebration two years later when, with appropriate ceremonies and much eloquent talk about a water highway connecting Susquehanna markets with the fertile western plains, ground was broken at Harrisburg for "The Pennsylvania Canal."

On July thirtieth of 1827, Harrisburg was once more invaded by delegates. This time they had been invited by the Pennsylvania Society for the Promotion of Manufacturers and the Mechanic Arts. The convention had been conceived in the interests of American sheepgrowers and woolen clothmakers and with the purpose of recommending further tariff protection for wool industries, but so many Americans were dissatisfied with currently levied duties that it became a meeting of protest against tariffs affecting many other businesses. The cotton planters of the Southern states looked upon the convention as a nefarious plot on the part of Northern manufacturers, and soon the residents of the Susquehanna towns were reading a speech that had a familiar ring to it. It was made by Judge Thomas Cooper, their former neighbor at Northumberland who had become president of the University of South Carolina, and from that state he poured out a molten flood of emphatic language:

> But I am now to learn for the first time that in the canting, cheating, cajoling slang of these monopolists, the American system is one by which the earnings of the South are to be transferred to the North; by which the many are to be sacrificed to the few; by which unequal rights, unequal burdens, unequal protection, unequal laws and unequal taxes are to be enacted and made permanent; that the farmer and the planter are to be considered inferior beings to the spinner, the bleacher and the dyer; that we of the South are to hold our plantations as the serfs of the North, subject to the orders of the master minds of Massachusetts, the lords of the spinning jenny, the peers of the loom, who have the right to tax our earnings in order to swell their riches!

Pennsylvania's capitol had seen in the five days of this convention the beginnings of a controversy which would result in such burning national issues, the "Tariff of Abom-

433

inations" and the threat of "Nullification" and disunion.

Two years later, in 1829, Harrisburg was in turmoil. The kidnaping and murder in New York State of William Morgan, a Batavia printer who had threatened to expose the rituals of the Masonic Brotherhood, had so aroused the nation that hundreds of shocked citizens had formed an Anti-Masonry party pledged to the destruction of secret fraternities. A convention of Anti-Masons had met in Harrisburg and had nominated Joseph Ritner for governor. Though their candidate lost the election, the movement against Masonry continued to grow and Ritner became governor in 1835. The investigations of Masonry that followed were so obviously in violation of the civil rights of members of the Fellowship that Ritner and his party lost popularity. In 1838, Ritner was defeated for the governorship by David R. Porter, a Democrat. The Anti-Masons were so infuriated by this that they assembled from all over Pennsylvania, planning to keep Ritner in office by force. The Democrats also crowded into the city and Ritner, fearing bloodshed, called out the Pennsylvania Militia, hoping to prevent disorder and, at the same time, to use the soldiery to maintain himself as governor. The commandant of the troops, General Robert Patterson, refused, however, to allow his men to do more than prevent disorder. Providing them with "buckshot cartridges," he awaited possible violence. Another detachment of militia soon appeared within the city, and encamped on the market square. No disorders developed and Harrisburg began to enjoy its soldier guests. Its girls had never had a better time. There were dances and dinner parties and picnics along the riverbank. Dispatches from foreign newspapers predicting that the failure of the democratic process at Harrisburg spelled doom for the United States as a nation suddenly became jokes. The Anti-Masons began to feel silly. After all, Porter had been elected by a considerable majority. Some of them left Harrisburg. Others agreed that they had lost. Ex-governor Ritner went home. Governor Porter was inaugurated. The "Buckshot War" was over.

Harrisburg's noisiest and most emotional get-together, the Whig Convention of 1839, began in December. There had been much preliminary planning to obtain the Whig presidential nomination for Henry Clay. General Winfield Scott also had his supporters. And for William Henry Harrison, the victor of Tippecanoe, a wind was rising. United in violent opposition to the nominee of the Democrats, President Martin Van Buren, the Whigs, while professing an adulation of Henry Clay, applied a giant bellows to that wind and blew it into a hurricane. When the convention was over, Harrison had been unanimously indorsed. Tyler had been nominated for the vice-presidency because, as New York State's Thurlow Weed had said, "We could get nobody else to accept." Delegates from eighteen of the twenty-two states represented had set out for Washington to visit Clay who, though bitterly disappointed, had written a generous letter of support, and to offer maudlin and teary condolences. At a dinner the day after they had arrived, prominent Whigs presented Clay with oratorical tributes dripping with sentimentality and decorated with bad puns. Since Harry could not be their candidate, they had decided upon "Harry's son" in the wonderful convention at "Harry's burg." Thus, in Harrisburg began the most colorful, slogan-filled, song-ornamented presidential campaign of the nation's history—the "Tippecanoe and

435

Tyler too," the "Log Cabin and Hard Cider" campaign that put Harrison in the White House only a few weeks before his death.

The vast movement of the pioneers westward, and the consequent growth of populations in western states, gradually lessened, in the decades preceding the Civil War, the importance of Harrisburg as a frontier capital. Since it already had a substantial German population, the town was most sympathetic toward the mid-century revolutions in central Europe. The fight of the Hungarian patriot, Kossuth, against Austrian tyranny met with heartfelt favor. When, after urging in Philadelphia the approval of resolutions recently adopted in Harrisburg, Kossuth visited the banks of the Susquehanna in 1852, the valley people went wild with delight. The city blazed with bonfires and fireworks, and tremendous crowds indulged themselves in disorders that police were unable to control. It was appropriate that Harrisburg's last popular demonstration should be its liveliest. It was saying farewell to an era and a tradition. The most important nationally of all the state capitals was soon to become a city of quiet and picturesque provinciality.

It had one lively moment during the Civil War when a rough, tough regiment of wild recruits from the West Branch floated into town on new-cut rafts, each man wearing a bucktail on his cap to signify his membership in the "Bucktail Regiment." It had a moment of panic when Lee's advance threatened to capture it in the days just before Gettysburg.

For more than a score of years afterwards the city followed an even and prosperous course. The big houses of the famous Front Street river drive appeared. The news-

436

papers ran articles on Harrisburg "Society," conservative and élite. Then, suddenly at noon on a day of blowing snow that changed to rain and back again, a fire alarm sounded. Volunteer fire fighters darted out of stores and offices, grabbed the ropes of their hose carts and began to run them north through the windy streets. They arrived at the block where they had been told the fire would be and found no evidence of it. Breathless and dripping, they looked behind them and saw smoke and flame rising above the capitol building. Hoses were finally put to work a half hour after the alarm had been sounded, but the fire had gained too much headway. By the end of the afternoon most of the capitol building was in ruins. On the next day, the legislature held its meeting in the federal courtroom of the post office building, while plans for occupation of a more suitable auditorium were being discussed. Grace Methodist Church seemed the most advisable temporary substitute, and hundreds of workmen began at once to effect such changes as were desired. In five days they had it ready, and the state legislature held its meetings there until June.

The choice of the new meeting place had an uncalculated effect, however. It enlisted the active interest of a prominent churchman, Dr. Silas C. Swallow, editor of a weekly journal called *The Pennsylvania Methodist*. The clergyman spent something over two weeks in quiet observation of the ways in which certain politicians were accustomed to meet such crises. Then on February twenty-fifth, his paper published a story of corruption in high places that horrified all honest citizens. Dr. Swallow charged that certain persons had been paid by the state for services never rendered, that others had signed re-

437

ceipts for three and four times the amounts they had received, that the contractors who had made the alterations in the Grace Church auditorium had been paid eight times what the job was worth, and that members of the Board of Public Buildings and Grounds knew of these excessive costs and were guilty, perhaps because they had been bribed, of approving them. There was considerable doubt, the irate cleric intimated, that the flames were of accidental origin, and he added that the probability of a fire had been a matter of discussion among state employees for months. At once, the embarrassed Legislature subpoenaed Dr. Swallow to testify before it, but the brave editor refused to appear except before a nonpartisan board of investigation. Charged then with criminal libel, he was convicted in the courts of Dauphin County despite a spirited and eloquent defense by his attorney, James Scarlet. An appeal to the Pennsylvania Superior Court brought about a reversal of the conviction.

The present capitol building was completed in 1906. Charges of dishonesty and graft attendant upon its building had already been launched when, in October of that year, Theodore Roosevelt, President of the United States, visited Harrisburg. He was shown the high dome, designed by architect Joseph Huston, after that of St. Peter's in Rome, the sculptures of George Gray Barnard, the mural paintings of Edwin Austin Abbey, the marble stairway in the rotunda inspired by that of the Grand Opera House in Paris. The President made a graceful speech dedicating the building of which Pennsylvania, all present agreed, might be proud.

In January, 1907, a reform governor, Edwin S. Stuart, was elected and one of his first acts was to appoint a committee to investigate the charges involving the construction of the beautiful building. Once more the state hung its head.

Despite the previous revelations of corruption, politicians and unscrupulous contractors had brazenly kept on with their dishonest conniving. Forty-eight hearings that extended over three and a half months and recorded the testimony of 159 witnesses revealed a network of corruption so fantastic that, if it had not been sordid and disgraceful, would have seemed ridiculously funny. The state was shown to have paid for furniture by the "cubic foot" including even airspace measured between the legs of tables and chairs. It bought by the pound chandeliers so loaded with lead that they weighed nearly a ton and a half apiece. It gave two million dollars for filing cases worth, at a conservative estimate, considerably less than a million.

Indictments came of the committee's report—and convictions. Prison terms were served. Citizens of Harrisburg still feel uncomfortable whenever the scandals are mentioned. One of the several reasons for this is that over thirty years after the report of the investigating committee had been received and acted upon, a significant omission came to light. Capitol guides, who do not as a rule go into detail as to the financial irregularities connected with the construction of this beautifully proportioned building which is decorated with many a symbolic representation of Justice and Religion, had for a generation called the attention of visitors to the "hand-carved oak" fixtures in the governor's reception room. To these, along with "the largest rug in the world," and paintings depicting scenes in the life of William Penn, they pointed with pride. They might still do so, had not a careless workman

439

in 1941 attempted to lean his ladder against the reception room wall and inadvertently bumped it against a section of the intricate and ornate carvings. Down it came, displaying on the floor a heart not of oak but of solid white plaster, over which a clever simulation of oak graining had been painted. *Bona fide* wood carving, it was discovered, extended from the floor up about as high as a man could reach. Above that, the flutings of plaster replaced the "hand-carved oak." An elderly Harrisburger summed up his feeling recently: "I'm still holding my breath. Who knows what they'll find next?"

Harrisburgers also feel uneasiness, not so much over these early-century crimes against the taxpaying citizenry ("There are crooks in every state," they say), but over the fact that the population of Pennsylvania, which includes great numbers of Quakers, the several sects of the "Plain People," and a very high percentage of other conscientious and honest citizens, has too often proved itself indifferent to its political duties. They believe that the exposed corruption was a result of this neglect and that their city, once politically the liveliest and most exciting of state capitals in the nation, still suffers from the effects of the unhappy events of nearly a half-century ago. Now, they say, however, strong leadership is replacing outdated "boss rule." The people are (with the exception of those sects whose religious teachings prohibit activity in politics) aware of the dangers of corruption. Their city and their state are attaining a new pride in honest and efficient administration. They recognize the fact that the river-front drive with its park and lawns and elaborate houses accentuates the dreariness and misery of poverty-stricken slums. The east-west Pennsylvania Turnpike, one of the greatest road-engineering feats of the world is at their door, promising increasing trade. They know that the nearness of the Amish, Mennonite, Moravian sects lends unique color to their streets, a distinctive quality to their cooking, a sense of quiet dignity to the smiling, fertile, prosperous landscape which surrounds them—a lure to thousands of American tourists. They are happy that the tremendous steel plants which employ many Harrisburgers and contribute much to the town's prosperity are centered in an abutting suburb to the south—Steelton— where the layman observer sees a manifold welter of wide pipes like tremendous snakes strangling a latter-day Laocoön. They often stand on the river shore to admire the green islands that rest in peaceful water below the brown rock friezes above. They idle away hours watching the steam-driven awkward barges of the fleet they call the "Susquehanna Navy." Small but heavy craft about forty feet long and twelve wide, some of these bear powerful centrifugal pumps which draw tons of coal-laden muck from the river bottom through an intake pipe, much as a vacuum cleaner sucks dust from a floor. The discharge from the pipe is poured over a series of screens which separate the coal which is then raked off the screens and loaded on flatboats towed behind. Other and more picturesque vessels of the fleet use buckets that move on an endless chain, digging from the bottom and emptying on the screen-laden decks. Both types bring to the surface coal that the Susquehanna has carried downriver on its current. It is not of a high grade, but has a value because it can be used in certain of the steel furnaces of the valley. The dredging of coal from the river by the four-foot draft barges of the fleet extends for many miles both

441

north and south of Harrisburg, but nowhere else do they draw such numbers of "river-bank admirals."

Harrisburgers remain a quiet population, so home-loving that night clubs (and symphony orchestras) find too little patronage to survive. Being citizens of a capital city, they speak of governors and senators familiarly, often by their first names, and their comments on them are personal and discerning. They love their city and they agree heartily with visitors who exclaim over the river vistas and the shade trees and the Pennsylvania Dutch food and the august beauty of the high capitol. They are inclined to protest the accuracy of the descriptions of their town to be found in the fiction of Joseph Hergesheimer, James Boyd and John O'Hara. "No other town is like it," they say. "We could never live anywhere else."

COLUMBIA

In the spring of 1774, the distinguished Philadelphian, Dr. Benjamin Rush, journeying to Carlisle, stopped for dinner at Wright's Ferry. There he was introduced by a friend to Susannah Wright, then in her eighty-eighth year. He later described her in his journal as "celebrated Above half a Century for her wit—Good Sense & valuable improvements of her mind." She said she had lived at this place sixty-two years. She had come to the Susquehanna when she was twenty-six and "there were no inhabitants of York County." Eight years before that, her Quaker father, John Wright, had received a patent for a river ferry service.

Despite the loneliness of her situation, Susannah had found her life rewarding. She had spent much time in reading, which she told Dr. Rush "was a tremendous blessing," and she said she could not live without her books. Perhaps inspired by the beauty of the river valley, she had also taken joy in writing poetry and painting landscapes. Once she had spun the silk from which a court gown was to be made for the Queen of England. She had become the good friend of the great Benjamin Franklin who admired her and envied her life at Hempfield, the name of the house her brother James had built near the ferry. "I languish for the country," he wrote her from Philadelphia, "for air and shade and leisure and converse, but fate has doomed me to be stifled and roasted and teased to death in a city."

Susannah died a year after her converse with Dr. Rush. Soon after her death, her nephew Samuel Wright began to formulate an ambitious plan for a town beside the popular ferry then constantly in use. In 1787-88, after he had divided the area into numbered lots, he sold chances on these at fifteen shillings a ticket. The renown of the lottery spread rapidly and, though there were only a hundred and sixty land prizes, the number of "adventurers," as the purchasers were called, was legion, including speculators from many parts of the country. Since there was already talk in Pennsylvania that an effort would be made at the meeting of the national Congress in 1789, to have the permanent capital of the United States placed on the Susquehanna at Wright's Ferry, and since Samuel Wright, with this possibility probably in mind, had called his town by the patriotic name, Columbia, the winners of the lots found that they had properties which had advanced in value far beyond previous appraisals.

Though the effort to make Columbia the seat of federal

government failed, the town grew and received impetus from the building of the Pennsylvania Canal. The arrival of waters in this channel was celebrated on December 17, 1830. Four years later the first train of the Columbia and Philadelphia Railroad, hauling both passengers and freight, ran between the two towns.

The original plan of the canal was to continue it south from Columbia on the east side of the river. When property owners at Columbia objected, a low double-decked roadway was constructed along the south side of the long wooden covered bridge which crossed to Wrightsville. This was used as a towpath by use of which canalboats were moved across the river. Later, a dam across the Susquehanna formed a pool in which a steam ferry towed the canalboats back and forth.

So important did Columbia become as a canal and railroad center after the Civil War that from 1880 to 1900 its population increased by one half. Now it has lost many residents who were railroad employees, but it is still a picturesque town serving as a trade center for a very fertile region in which stand sturdy farmhouses of the "Pennsylvania Dutch." Harrisburg hotels offer as tourist attractions meals which include dishes made from recipes obtained at those farmhouses; but in Columbia, even at a little roadside diner—Bill's Lunch, for instance—the influence of the food-of-the-country is so strong that a matter-of-course menu lists "Scrapple and Molasses, Dried corn and York County Apple-sauce, and Cream Cole-slaw." Many of the brick houses of the town (and most of Columbia is brick), are distinctive because the Dutch owner has painted one side red and an adjoining side purple or white.

Because some of the farm families in this region wear quaint costumes and have religious beliefs which establish ways of life to which the rest of the nation is unaccustomed, often speak the German-English dialect known as Pennsylvania Dutch, drive horses and buggies rather than automobiles, eat heavy German foods not served elsewhere, it is not to be understood that they are "backward" in agricultural methods. Most are prosperous farmers and their success may not be attributed solely to the extreme fertility of the land they cultivate. Many of the "Plain People" have degrees in agriculture from universities, and all are quick to adopt methods which they observe to have produced favorable results. Tobacco is a major and, to visitors, at least, a somewhat unexpected crop in these river counties. In recent years, the fattening of Western cattle has been an increasing business. A story goes that the Dutch farmers began buying cattle to obtain manure for fertilizing their acres, but soon discovered that by buying the animals young and thin and selling them mature and fat, they could make large profits. Lancaster has become one of America's biggest cattle markets. Texas sells her calves to Pennsylvania, and Pennsylvania later sells the same animals, fattened on Susquehanna pastures, to all Eastern beef markets.

The Susquehanna is very wide at Columbia. The highway bridge to Wrightsville is more than a mile and a quarter long, and it cost three million dollars. Many of these were spent to build walls so high on each side that neither motorist nor pedestrian can see the beauty of the river flowing below. Since the bridge connects York and Lancaster counties, there has been an effort to remind tourists who cross it of England's Wars of the Roses by

445

growing white roses on the York Side and red on the Lancaster, but some travelers regard the promotion idea as silly.

If the visitor could look above the wall and far south from the long bridge, he would realize that the river is beginning to change. It has already passed two dams—one at Harrisburg, to keep the water level high both for sanitary purposes and for water sports, and one at York Haven where the current is swift enough to supply electric power. Below Columbia it traverses the Long Level, so-called because canallers delighted in so extensive a run without locks. At its end the river drops through a narrowing channel. Conestoga Creek rolls into the surging stream near the unbending line of Safe Harbor Dam, Pequea Creek enters below. Little westbound streams have dug deep ravines that echo a mighty splashing as their waters hurry down to the sweeping Susquehanna. Shadowing bluffs and deep water color the river a darker green than any of its upstream reaches. The road is high at Pequea. Rustic cottages and a hotel let the traveler know the water is once more entering wild country where he can fish and hunt. A few minutes of riding in a steep downward direction, and he is at York Furnace close beside the water, one of the most spectacularly beautiful spots of the lower river.

Since rocky promontories jut into the stream as it narrows and increases its speed, it is necessary for those who would see as much of this highland passage as possible to travel each westbound road to its end at the river, then turn about and go back to following the main south highway until another spur leads once more toward the deep-cut channel. The Susquehanna at McCall's Ferry has narrowed to about a fifth of its width at Columbia. The water there is swift and deep. In 1815 America's great bridgebuilder, Theodore Burr, built a three-hundred-sixty-foot span above it. Though it was then regarded as one of the structural wonders of the world, it tumbled into the resistless flow of the March "fresh" of 1818. Now, as in the past, towns downriver, even those in Maryland, dread a cold winter that piles high jams of ice in the Mc-Call's Ferry narrows, for dangerous floods will surely follow.

The racing of the waters ends at the still-water lake above Holtwood Dam. There spume flies a straight white line in the air almost all the way from bank to bank. From Erb's Grove nearby comes the singing of steel teeth in wood and a yellow cloud of sawdust hangs above the sound.

MOUNT JOHNSON

❧ ISLAND OF EAGLES

When thou seest an eagle, thou seest a portion of genius; lift up thy head.
—WILLIAM BLAKE

I wish the bald eagle had not been chosen as the representative of our country; he is a bird of bad moral character . . . he is generally poor, and often very lousy.
—BENJAMIN FRANKLIN

Take a road "built after a dragging cow-chain" and, as it winds, "salad-birds" (goldfinches) will flit their up-and-down arcs before you. You are following a stream, another Fishing Creek, not the more famous one up above near Bloomsburg, and you will eventually see a sign that

447

says "Here It Is." When you reach another that says "The River," stop and look. A rambling old house, apparently an inn, bears over a side door a sign reading "Drumore P.O." Arrive in the right week of spring and trumpetlike lavender blossoms will seem to have draped a patterned print over a tree labeled "Naumesh Auna," and cleared land nearby will have disappeared under a carpet of mountain pinks. Out in the river (now wide again) you will see an island that looks like the curving tree-covered summit of a hill which water has almost submerged. A fourth sign reads: "Mt. Johnson Island, Bald Eagle Sanctuary, National Audubon Society, 1945." Dwellings of bald-eagle families have long been discoverable on this island. Some seasons eager watchers despair and report that the birds have gone but they have always come back. There have been summers when the sprawling unkempt nests have blown down, injuring the young. Brave ornithologists have often scrambled up the steep sides of the island, cameras strapped to their backs, to observe the fierce birds, but laymen do not often come here because, according to local talk, copperheads outnumber the eagles.

A 1954 midsummer report from a reliable authority on American birds estimates that there are about sixty bald eagles in the Chesapeake Bay area. One was reported flying up the Susquehanna early in the year. Pennsylvania ornithologist, Herbert H. Beck, once stated that Mt. Johnson has been a natural home for the bald eagle "since its existence as a species." The people who live along the river are proud that the big bird, symbol of the nation, still perches above the Susquehanna.

PEACH BOTTOM

> There was beauty—but I remember
> Only the smell of the evening's cool
> And one gnarled gum tree holding over
> Flame above the pool.
>
> —FREDERIC BRUSH

The waters that cover all but the top of Mt. Johnson are part of a lake caused by the river's backing up from the Conowingo Dam eight and a half miles downstream. Between the eagles' island and that barrier lies the southernmost of Pennsylvania's Susquehanna towns, Peach Bottom. To reach its sequestered circular boat basin, it is necessary once more to follow a road winding westward along the side of a ravine while a little creek sings below. Small cottages (one is named "Halcyon") dot the steep banks at irregular heights and intervals. A stone cabin has fallen apart, and some of the rocks from which it was built have spilled down the slope. Most road signs read "Narrow Bridge," preparing the traveler for a one-way crossing of one of the creek's tiny tributaries. Beyond the small boats lying inside the curving arms of the boat basin the river is a wide lake. Wooded points jut far into the southward moving water.

Called for John Kirk's peach orchard which has long since been reclaimed by the wilderness, Peach Bottom was named in 1789 as one of the Susquehanna settlements which might be made the national capital. Now it is a retreat for fishermen and those who seek the peace of seclusion in wild environment.

PORT DEPOSIT

An invisible boundary crosses the wide waters of Conowingo Lake. It is the Mason-Dixon line and the waters beyond it are Maryland waters. Little Octoraro Creek waits until it has crossed that line to empty itself—last of the tributaries—into the widening river. Only a few miles of the Susquehanna flow through Maryland, but along this short course to the big stream's mouth are many reminders of America's past. Port Deposit lies below the jagged rocks which stopped the upriver progress of Captain John Smith's barge in 1608. A two-hundred-foot cliff towers above the town which consists of the river road which is Main Street and a "dead-end" shelflike High Street slanting part of the way up the rock wall. The houses on High Street rise from foundations above the roofs of the houses and shops at the water level. From the river the upper buildings seem to have been placed, like a child's blocks, upon the buildings below. Since land traffic from downriver is funneled into Main Street along the bottom of the rock wall, the town sometimes gives the impression of great liveliness. Residents who know that once river docks here were crowded with hundreds of boats, arks and rafts bearing lumber, coal, grain, whiskey and iron from the north, often speak of their picturesque community as a "ghost town." They say that even the naval training school on the former grounds of the Tome School for boys on the plateau at the top of the bluff has not stirred the town out of its nostalgic revery.

At a fine house on Main Street, tradition says, General Lafayette was entertained when he made his renowned return visit to the United States in 1824. Its façade displays

450

a wrought-iron fencing which is worked into an exquisite sheaf-of-wheat pattern. The French hero is said to have given a reception at Port Deposit, and to it came a veteran of the Revolution with questions to ask. Did the general remember in the days of the Yorktown campaign that the boat in which he was crossing the Susquehanna ran on the rocks? And did he remember that Private Aquila Deaver carried him pick-a-back to dry land? That, said Aquila, was forty-three years ago and a man might easily forget it. The General remembered.

HAVRE DE GRACE

Otsego . . . Octoraro
Where is another stream
That starts and ends so in a dream.

—FREDERIC BRUSH

Lafayette unwittingly gave the town its name. It had been known as Susquehanna Lower Ferry, but when the gay and sentimental young officer passed through it during the Revolution, he wrote General Washington that it brought to mind the little harbor of Havre de Grace on the shores of Bretagne. After that it bore the name it bears now. Today it is a spacious town. Its streets are wide, and Victorian gables show through the trees that shade its quiet lawns. Not long ago there was a race track at the edge of the town, and during the "season" crowds bustled in to watch the horses, to bet on them, to spend their money at local hotels and restaurants. In 1929 they cheered the great Man O' War to one of his famous victories. After that race, townsfolk say, the jubilation was almost as great as when the armies of Rochambeau and

451

Washington crossed the river after their victory at York-town. Now the track has been abandoned, and industry owns the land where once the thoroughbreds galloped.

❦ THE ONE-MAN ARMY OF JOHN O'NEIL

Havre de Grace was not happy on the night of May 2, 1813. The little town of about sixty families awakened to the terrifying whistle of rockets that streaked the midnight sky with fire. Even as the inhabitants jumped from their beds, the blazing missiles set fire to Seares Tavern and bombs exploded in the streets. The people, only partially dressed, raced panic-stricken from the town.

Drums beat an alarm as a few of the Havre de Grace militia gathered in the light of burning houses. As they did so, they could see a dozen British barges filled with armed soldiers on their way toward them. Realizing that they were hopelessly outnumbered, all but eight or ten militiamen followed at top speed their fleeing fellow townsmen. One of those who remained was elderly John O'Neil. Born in the West of Ireland, he had come to America some fifteen years before. He had served in the national troops assigned to put down the Whiskey Rebellion and later in the American Navy in actions against the French. According to the American historian, Jared Sparks, who published in 1817 a report considerably prejudiced against O'Neil, "He was a sturdy vociferous Irishman" and he seemed to bear no love for the English. Trying vainly to persuade the fleeing militia to return to their posts, O'Neil worked his way down to the three-cannon battery with which he intended to defend Havre de Grace. He reported his subsequent experience laconically in a

452

letter to a friend in Baltimore written only a few days later:

> No doubt before this you have heard of my *defeat*. On the third instant we were attacked by 15 English barges at break of day. We had a small breastwork erected, with two 6- and one 9-pounder in it, and I was stationed at one of the guns. When the alarm was given I ran to the battery and found but one man there, and two or three came afterwards. After firing a few shots they retired and left me alone in the battery. The grape-shot flew very thick about me. I loaded the gun myself without anyone to serve the vent, which you know is very dangerous, and fired her, when she recoiled and ran over my thigh. I retreated down to town and found Mr. Barnes of the nail manufactory, with a musket, and fired on the barges while we had ammunition, and then retreated to the common, while I kept waving my hat to the militia who had run away, to come to our assistance, but they proved cowardly and would not come back. At the same time an English officer on horseback, followed by marines, rode up and took me with two muskets in my hand. I was carried on board the *Maidstone* frigate where I remained until released three days since.

When nearby American forces learned of O'Neil's exploit and capture, they also heard a rumor that because he was an Irishman the British planned to hang him as a traitor. An American brigadier general at once wrote to an enemy admiral that if O'Neil were hanged two British subjects would immediately be executed in reprisal. The admiral replied that O'Neil had been paroled and had departed, but he added:

> I was not informed of this man being an Irishman or he would have been detained to account to his sovereign for being in arms against the British colors.

Forty of the sixty houses were burned or otherwise damaged in the attack which lasted from early morning until sunset of a clear and sunny day. Pious citizens later made much of the fact that though many of the houses around it were leveled by the rockets and bombs, the Episcopal Church stood unharmed.

❦ THE MOST WEATHERED BOATMAN

Seldom is any good story wholly true.

—SAMUEL JOHNSON

Boats may be rented along the river front at Havre de Grace. They are most often in demand during the shad-run in April. "Shad-run begins the same time as the first dogwood blooms," says the most weathered boatman. "Seems like all them shad crowd into the head of the bay and lie there, millions of 'em, keepin' watch on the top o' Palmer's Island for the first blossom. Comes a sunrise and thar she blooms—and up the river shoots the whole mess!"

While professional fishermen continue to make their living by using shad-nets, sportsmen have found that during the run shad will rise to an adroitly cast fly. In the waters below Conowingo Dam a Parmacini Belle, they say, has won many an angler a hot fight with a pound or more lavender-and-silver buck.

Many of the tales of the fishermen of Havre de Grace center about "a good place to catch wall-eyes" called Job's Hole. Some say, "It's so deep it's got no bottom," but the guide who tells the story of the shad waiting for the dogwood bloom has another idea: "Friend o' mine is sort o' hasty an' one night on the road near Job's Hole his car stalled an' he couldn't git it started. Made him so mad he

454

got a friend to help him—they was both drinkin'—and they pushed that thing over the edge into the hole. Six months later he was to Baltimore an' he seen his car, license an' all, rollin' to a stop. So he asks the feller drivin' it howcome an' the feller says he just happened to see it lyin' in shallow water near the mouth of Chesapeake Bay and fished it out. Now that bore out the theory a lot o' folks round here have that there's a deep water underground passage mighty near the whole distance from Job's Hole to Baltimore. Yes, sir, it's my contention that a small submarine could start at Job's Hole and if the skipper knows his business he could bypass the rest of the river and most of the Bay."

JOURNEY'S END

Unpathed waters, undreamed shores.
—WILLIAM SHAKESPEARE

The Susquehanna Flats, eighty square miles at the head of the bay are the refuge of countless wild fowl. Here egrets gleam like white jewels set in the varying greens of water and of reeds. Great blue herons stalk these shallows and nest among the forests that line the marshes. In the winter months there is a crying of wild swans. Whippoorwills fill summer twilights with inexorable repetitions. The Chesapeake is a hundred and eighty miles long and its average depth is twenty to thirty feet. It might with logic be called the Susquehanna Bay since it indicates the course of the river before its banks were engulfed by the waters of the Atlantic Ocean. At the wide mouth of the river a human being is small and alone. The fresh-water stream floods into the salty bay, and a man afloat on it slowly realizes he has left the domain of man.

From here Cooperstown, with its itemized summary of the ways of folk along this watercourse, is more than the geographic measure of four hundred miles away. The Valley of Opportunity, where man-made machines calculate and remember and promise a new world, is a far cry from the vast and eternally moving loneliness.

The waters that have passed Azilum, on the faraway river of Europe's eighteenth-century dream, bring news of a promise that the French town will rise again in physical restoration because of man's everlasting hope that material objects suggesting the past may recreate things lost from the mind. The current pushing into the bay brings echoes of old wars, old industries, old crimes, old stories told before fires long since quenched by the flowing of time.

Bibliography

🌷 BOOKS

ANDREWS, CHARLES McLEAN,
The Colonial Period of American History (Vol. II).
Yale University Press. New Haven, Conn. 1934-38.

ANDREWS, CHARLES McLEAN,
Our Earliest Colonial Settlements.
New York University Press. New York, N.Y. 1933.

AURAND, MONROE A., JR.,
The Molly Maguires (Pamphlet).
The Aurand Press. Harrisburg, Pa. 1940.

BAILEY, R. P.,
Thomas Cresap: Maryland Frontiersman.
The Christopher Publishing House. Boston, Mass. 1944.

BEERS, HENRY A.,
Nathaniel Parker Willis.
Houghton Mifflin & Co. Boston, Mass. 1885.

BIRDSALL, RALPH,
The Story of Cooperstown.
Augur's Book Store. Cooperstown, N.Y. 1948.

BLACKMAN, EMILY C.,
History of Susquehanna County, Pa.
Claxton, Remsen and Haffelfinger. Philadelphia, Pa. 1873.

BOYD, JAMES,
Roll River.
Charles Scribner's Sons. New York, N.Y. 1935.

BOYD, JULIAN P.,
The Susquehanna Co.: Connecticut's Experiment in Expansion.
Yale University Press. New Haven, Conn. 1935.

BRUSH, FREDERIC,
The Alleghenians.
Blackshaw Press. New York, N.Y. 1940.

BRUSH, FREDERIC,
Walk the Long Years.
Susquehanna University Press. Selinsgrove, Pa. 1946.

BRUSH, FREDERIC,
Chosen Poems.
Susquehanna University Press. Selinsgrove, Pa. 1953.

457

Bibliography

BUMP, CHARLES W.,
*Down the Historic Susque-
hanna, a Summer's Jaunt
from Otsego to the Chesa-
peake.*
1899.

CADZOW, D. A.,
*Archeological Studies of the
Susquehannock Indians.*
Pennsylvania Historical Com-
mission, Harrisburg, Pa.
1936.

CHATHAM, JOHN H.,
*The Bald Eagle of the Susque-
hanna River.*
Altoona *Tribune*, Altoona, Pa.
1919.

CLARK, T. WOOD,
Émigrés in the Wilderness.
The Macmillan Company.
New York, N.Y. 1941.

COOK, FREDERICK, Editor.
*Journals of the Military Expe-
dition of Major General
John Sullivan against the
Six Nations of Indians in
1779.*
Contains Biographical Sketch
of Sullivan and Centennial
Address at Newtown by
David Craft. Auburn, N.Y.
1887.

COOPER, JAMES FENIMORE,
*The Chronicles of Coopers-
town (1838).*
Cooperstown, N.Y. 1929.

COWAN, HELEN I.,
Charles Williamson.
Published by the Rochester
Historical Society. Roches-
ter, N.Y. 1941.

CRAFT, DAVID,
*History of Bradford County,
Pennsylvania, with Illus-
trations and Biographical
Sketches.*
L. H. Evarts & Co. Philadel-
phia, Pa. 1878.

CRAFT, DAVID,
Wyalusing.
Towanda, Pa. 1870.

CRUIKSHANK, ERNEST, Craft Collection.
*Butler's Rangers and the Set-
tlement of Magara.*
Lundy's Lane Historical Society. Welland, Ontario.
1893.

*A Century of Progress. 1823-
1923*
Pub., Delaware and Hudson
Co. Albany. 1925.

DEVYR, THOS. AINGO,
*The Odd Book of the Nine-
teenth Century.*
Greenspoint, N.Y. 1882. (Pub.
by author).

DUNKELBERGER, GEORGE FRANK-
LIN, Prepared by
The Story of Snyder County.
Snyder County Historical So-
ciety. Selinsgrove, Pa. 1948.

EARNEST, ERNEST,

John and William Bartram.
University of Pennsylvania
Press. Philadelphia, Pa.
1940.

EASTMAN, E. R.,
The Destroyers.
American Agriculturist, Inc.
Ithaca, N.Y. 1946.

ELLIS, FRANKLIN,
*History of the Susquehanna
and Juniata Valleys.*
Evarts, Peck & Richards. Philadelphia, Pa. 1886.

FISKE, JOHN,
*Old Virginia and Her Neigh-
bors.*
Houghton Mifflin & Co. Boston and New York. 1900.

FLICK, ALEXANDER C.,
*New Sources of the Sullivan-
Clinton Campaign in 1779.*
N.Y. Historical Association
(Reprint). New York, N.Y.
1929.

FROST, JAMES ARTHURE,
*Life on the Upper Susque-
hanna 1783-1860.*
King's Crown Press. Columbia
University, New York, N.Y.
1951.

GIBBONS, PHEBE EARLE,
*'Pennsylvania Dutch' and
Other Essays.*
J. P. Lippincott & Co. Phila-
delphia, Pa. 1882.

GODCHARLES, FREDERICK A.,
Daily Stories of Pennsylvania.
Milton, Pa. 1924.

GRAY, ZENOS J., (Editor)
*Prose and Poetry of the
Susquehanna and Juniata
Rivers.*
1893.

GRIFFIS, WILLIAM ELLIOT,
*The History and Mythology of
Sullivan's Expedition.*
Report of Proceedings of July
3, 1903, of Wyoming Com-
memorative Association.
Wilkes-Barre, Pa.

GRIFFIS, WILLIAM ELLIOT,
*Wyoming the Pivot of the
Revolution.*
Report of Proceedings of
Wyoming Commemorative
Association in July, 1910.
132nd Anniversary. Wilkes-
Barre, Pa.

GRIFFIS, WILLIAM ELLIOT,
*The Rise, Glory and Fall of
the Iroquois Confederacy.*
Report of Proceedings of
Wyoming Commemorative
Association on July 3, 1914.
136th Anniversary. Wilkes-
Barre, Pa.

HALL, CLAYTON COLEMAN,
*Narratives of Early Maryland
1633-1684.*
Charles Scribner's Sons. New
York, N.Y. 1910.

459

Bibliography

HALSEY, FRANCIS W.,
  A Tour of Four Great Rivers.
  Charles Scribner's Sons. New
  York, N.Y. 1906.
HANNA, CHARLES A.,
  The Wilderness Trail.
  New York and London. 1911.
HARDING, G. M.,
  *The Sullivan Road (Easton to
  Wyoming).*
  Wyoming Valley Chapter
  D.A.R. Wilkes-Barre, Pa.
  1899.
HEVERLY, C. F.,
  *History of Sheshequin 1777-
  1902.*
  The Bradford Star Print. To-
  wanda, Pa. 1902.
HEVERLY, C. F.,
  *History and Geography of
  Bradford County, Pa., 1615-
  1924.*
  County Historical Society. To-
  wanda, Pa. 1926.
HOSTELLEY, A. E.,
  Songs of the Susquehanna.
  Philadelphia, Pa. 1901.
HOWARD, JOHN TASKER,
  *Stephen Foster: American
  Troubadour.*
  Thomas Y. Crowell Co. New
  York, N.Y. 1934.
JONES, LOUIS C.,
  Cooperstown.
  Otsego County Historical So-
  ciety. Cooperstown, N.Y.
  1949.

KLEES, FREDERICK,
  The Pennsylvania Dutch.
  The Macmillan Co. New York,
  N.Y. 1950.
KLINGEL, GILBERT C.,
  The Bay.
  Dodd, Mead & Co. New York,
  N.Y. 1951.
KORSON, GEORGE,
  Minstrels of the Mine Patch.
  University of Pennsylvania
  Press, Philadelphia, Pa.
  1938.
KORSON, GEORGE,
  *Pennsylvania Songs and Leg-
  ends.*
  University of Pennsylvania
  Press. Philadelphia, Pa.
  1949.
KRAFT, DAVID,
  History of Bradford County.
  L. H. Evarts. Philadelphia,
  Pa. 1878.
LEIGHTON, GEORGE R.,
  America's Growing Pains.
  Harper and Bros. New York
  and London. 1939.
LINN, JOHN BLAIR, Collected by
  *Annals of Buffalo Valley, Pa.
  (1755-1855).*
  Lane S. Hart. Harrisburg, Pa.
  1877.
MACMINN, EDWIN,
  *On the Frontier with Colonel
  Antes.*
  S. Chew & Sons. Camden, N.J.
  1900.

MARSHALL, JOHN A.,
American Bastille.
Evans, Stoddart & Co. Phila-
delphia, Pa. 1870.

MCMASTER, GUY H.,
*History of the Settlement of
Steuben County, New York.*
R. S. Underhill, Inc. Bath,
N.Y. 1853.

MCMASTER, JOHN BACH,
*A History of the People of the
United States, From the
Revolution to the Civil
War.*
D. Appleton-Century Co.
New York, London. 1938.

MEGINNESS, J. F.,
Otzinachson.
Henry B. Ashmead. Philadel-
phia, Pa. 1857.

MILLER, ALICE,
History of Cecil County, Md.

MILLER, JOHN C.,
Crisis in Freedom.
Atlantic Monthly Press. Little,
Brown & Co. Boston, Mass.
1951.

MILLER, JOHN C.,
*Origins of the American Revo-
lution.*
Little, Brown & Co. Boston,
Mass.

MINER, CHARLES,
History of Wyoming.
Philadelphia, Pa. 1845.

MONAGHAN, FRANK,

French Travellers in the U.S.
New York, N.Y. 1933.

MOOREHEAD, WARREN KING,
*A Report of the Susquehanna
River Expedition.*
The Andover Press. Andover,
Mass. 1938.

MORRISON, SAMUEL ELIOT and
COMMAGER, HENRY STEELE,
*The Growth of the American
Republic.*
Oxford University Press. New
York, N.Y. 1942.

MURRAY, ELSIE,
*Stephen C. Foster at Athens:
His First Composition.*
Athens, Pa. 1941.

MURRAY, ELSIE,
TE-A-O-GA
Athens, Pa. 1939.

MURRAY, ELSIE,
*Azilum French Refugee Col-
ony of 1793.*
Tioga Point Museum. Athens,
Pa. 1950.

MURRAY, L. W.,
*The Story of some Refugees
and their Azilum.*
Athens, Pa. 1903.

MURRAY, L. W.,
*A History of Old Tioga Point
and Early Athens.*
Athens, Pa. 1908.

MURRAY, L. W.,
*Notes on the Sullivan Expedi-
tion of 1779. including Col.*

461

Bibliography

Francis Barber's ORDER BOOK.
Illus.
Athens, Pa. 1929.

MURRAY, L. W.,
Aboriginal Sites in the near Te-a-oga.
American Anthropologist, V. 23—1921. Athens, Pa.

MYERS, RICHMOND E.,
The Long Crooked River.
The Christopher Publishing House. Boston, Mass. 1949.

PARDOE, H. C.,
Up the Susquehanna.
New York, N.Y. 1895.

PEARCE, STEWART,
Annals of Luzerne County.
J. P. Lippincott & Co. Philadelphia, Pa. 1866.

PERKINS, JULIA A. S.,
Early Times on the Susquehanna.
Binghamton, N.Y. 1870.

PINKERTON, ALLAN,
The Molly Maguires and Detectives.
G. W. Dillingham Co. 1877-1905.

PUMPELLY, RAPHAEL,
My Reminiscences.
Henry Holt & Co. New York. 1918.

PURDY, TRUMAN H.,
Legends of the Susquehanna and Other Poems.

J. P. Lippincott Co. Philadelphia, Pa. 1888.

ROWAN, R. W.,
The Pinkertons.
Little, Brown & Co., Boston, Mass. 1931.

SAVELLE, MAX,
Seeds of Liberty.
A. A. Knopf. New York. 1948.

SCHARF, J. THOMAS,
History of Maryland.
J. B. Piet. Baltimore, Md. 1879.

SCHARF, J. THOMAS,
History of Western Maryland.
Louis H. Evarts. Philadelphia, Pa. 1882.

SEMMES, RAPHAEL,
Captains and Mariners of Early Maryland.
Johns Hopkins Press. Baltimore, Md. 1937.

SINGMASTER, ELSIE,
Pennsylvania's Susquehanna.
J. Horace McFarland Co. Harrisburg, Pa. 1950.

STONE, WILLIAM L.,
The Poetry and History of Wyoming.
Wilkes-Barre, Pa. 1873.

STOVER, HERBERT E.,
Song of the Susquehanna.
Dodd, Mead & Co. New York. 1949.

SWEPSON, E.,
The Chesapeake Country.

462

Thomsen-Ellis. Baltimore, Md. 1924.

TONKIN, J. D.,
The Last Raft.
Harrisburg, Pa. 1940.

TURNER, O.,
History of the Pioneer Settlement of Phelps' and Grahams' Purchase and Morris' Reserve.
William Alling. Rochester, N.Y. 1852.

WALLACE, ANTHONY F. C.,
King of the Delawares: Teedyuscung, 1700-1763.
University of Pennsylvania Press. Philadelphia, Pa. 1949.

WALLACE, PAUL A. W.,
Conrad Weiser.
University of Pennsylvania Press. Philadelphia, Pa. 1945.

WARNER, CHARLES DUDLEY,
Nathaniel Parker Willis.
Houghton, Mifflin & Co. Boston, Mass. 1885.

WEYGAND, CORNELIUS,
Red Hills.

WILKINSON, J. B.,
Annals of Binghamton, and of the Country connected with it.
Binghamton, N.Y. 1872.

WILLIS, N. P.,
The Complete Works of Nathaniel Parker Willis.
J. S. Redfield. Clinton Hall. New York. 1846.

WILSTACH, P. W.,
Tidewater Maryland.
Bobbs Merrill. Indianapolis, Ind. 1931.

YAWGER, ROSE N.,
The Indian and the Pioneer.
C. W. Bardeen. Syracuse, N.Y. 1893.

❦ PERIODICALS

Bulletins of the Dept. of Internal Affairs of the Commonwealth of Pennsylvania.
Harrisburg, Pa.

Proceedings of the Northumberland County Historical Society.
Pub. by the Society.
Sunbury, Pa.

Federal Writers Project.
Guide Books to Pennsylvania, New York and Maryland.
New York. 1940.

LIGHTNER, GEORGE W.,
Susquehanna Register of Arks, Rafts, etc. etc.
Arriving at Port Deposit in the year 1822.
Baltimore, 1823.

Bibliography

Now and Then—a Quarterly Magazine of History and Biography. T. Kenneth Wood, M.D., Editor. Published by the Muncy Historical Society since 1868. Muncy, Pa.

Pennsylvania Historical Association Quarterly. A. W. Wallace, Editor.

SVITZER, JACK K.,
The Molly Maguires (Thesis) Wilkes College. 1949.

WILSON, ARTHUR HERMAN. Chairman of Editorial Board.

Susquehanna University Studies. Selinsgrove, Pa. 1948.

WILSON, ARTHUR HERMAN,
Literature Regarding the Susquehanna Valley. 1843-1943. Northumberland County Historical Proceedings and Addresses. 1946.

WREN, CHRISTOPHER,
Proceedings and Collections of the Wyoming Historical and Geological Society. Wilkes-Barre, Pa.

❦ OTHER SECONDARY SOURCES

BARTRAM, JOHN,
Observations on the Inhabitants, Climate, Soil, River Productions, Animals and Other Matters Worthy of Notice . . . in his travels from Pensilvania to Onondaga, Oswego, and the Lake Ontario in Canada, etc.
Whiston. London. 1751.

CLARK, JOHN S., L. W. Murray, Editor.
Selected Manuscripts of General John S. Clark Relating to the Aboriginal History of the Susquehanna.
1931.

COOPER, WILLIAM,
A Guide in the Wilderness. Dublin. 1810.

DE MAULEVRIER, COLBERT, G. Chinard, Editor.
Voyage Dans l'Intériéur Des États-Unis et Au Canada. 1935.

DU PETIT-THOUARS, Amiral Bergasse, Editor.
Aristide Aubert du Petit-Thouars, Heros d'Aboukir, Lettres et Documents Inedits.
Librarie Plon, Paris, 1937.

KEITH, CHARLES P.,
Chronicles of Pa. (2 Vols.) Philadelphia. 1917.

LA ROCHEFOUCAULD-LIANCOURT, FRANÇOIS ALEXANDRE FRÉDÉRIC,
Travels through the U.S. of North America, the Country of the Iroquois and Upper Canada.
London. 1799.
Library of Congress
Congressional Debates—1789.
Pennsylvania State Archives
Henry W. Shoemaker, State Archivist.
Harrisburg, Pa.
SMITH, CAPTAIN JOHN,
True Travels. Adventures and Observations. (2 Vols.)
London. 1629.

Song Book
Pub. by International Business Machine Corporation. New York.

VAIL, R. W. G., Editor.
The Revolutionary Diary of Lieut. Obadiah Gore, Jr.
New York Public Library.
New York, N.Y. 1929.

WRIGHT, ALBERT HAZEN,
The Sullivan Expedition of 1779.
Contemporary Newspaper Comment. Ithaca, N.Y. 1943.

Index

Index

481